The Screaming Wildman

*Vibrations from the
Dawn of Chicago Rock
by Carl Bonafede*

MUSIC
HISTORY

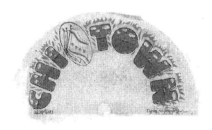

Published by Chi-Town Music History
P.O. Box 14785
Chicago, IL 60614-0785
carlbonafedecontact@gmail.com

Edited by Joel Bierig

First Printing
ISBN-13: 978-1539420965
ISBN-10: 1539420965

Dedication

For my family, friends, and the memories we created.

Acknowledgments

Right from the beginning, I have to thank my entire family. Dad, sister Nancy, brothers Jim, Louis, and Sam were always there for me, in true Sicilian fashion. I owe special thanks to Mom, who'd often run to get an upstairs neighbor to help translate phone messages so I wouldn't miss an opportunity. (I forgot to mention this in my Family chapter.)

I thank Junior Arzola, who finally convinced me this book thing was a good idea. I hope it serves as a thank you for the friendship and support of the entire cast of characters I assembled on these pages.

Bunches of people met me at my "house" (Mariano's grocery store) for interviews and snacks. I sincerely hope I remember everybody: Dwight Kalb, Cal Starr, Joe Pytel, Lori London, Joel Bierig, William Moore, Carl Giammarese (at his favorite coffee shop), Susan Rakis at Beverly Records, and Hank Zemola (at his favorite restaurant).

Ed Cody and Larry Nestor invited me to their homes. Eddie Thomas and his wife, Verlene, opened their front door several times. I paid visits to many contributors at their places of business: Paul Mally at Top Dog Disc, Jack Dreznes at Beverly Records, and Frank Milito at Orso's Restaurant. Legendary Sheldon Cooper was brave enough to let me pick him up at his front door.

I met Victor Lobello at Habetler Bowl, Dick Biondi at WLS, Ed Kelly at his office, Junior Arzola at Southport Security, Rob Matijević at Glad Cleaners, and Steve Yates at his recording studio.

Doug Gast (Cambridge), Jerry Germansen (Delights), Denny Murray (Lincoln Park Zoo), Jim Bernard (KCZQ-FM 102.3 Radio), and Phil Orsi (Little Kings and Thunderbirds) sent me a wealth of material. Time and distance limited me to phone interviews with several more of my beloved contributors. As you will see, some of them are "household" names—the rest should be!

Before I could get ink on paper, there were a lot of new and intimidating processes to get my mind around. My sincere thanks to Vicki Lockyun Tam for book production, design, indexing, editing, and overall project management. I also thank new friends Mike Wilhelm from the University of Nevada, Reno (for class picture snapshots) and Jamie Tam (for typing and transcription).

I need to thank Joel Bierig for his patience, expertise, and friendship while navigating through the entire publication project. Finally, I need to acknowledge Chicago-based editor extraordinaire Lori Crites for poring over the manuscript hours before I handed the final version to my production team.

Contents

Introduction vii
Dancing, Disruption, and Rebellion 1

My History
Little Sicily 15
Performing and Producing...29

Awe-Inspiring and Unforgettable
Eddie Thomas..43
Ed Cody...55
Sheldon Cooper 65
Ed Kelly 75
Cal Starr 81

Monster Entertainment
Mickey, Larry & the Exciters (1965-70) 89
The Cambridge Five...95
Phil Orsi 107
Ral Donner (1943-84) 115
Lori London...123

Influential Characters
Dwight Kalb...127
Industry Shapers 137
Recording Studios and Engineers..............................151

The Ultimate Social Network
Dick Biondi...157
Lucky Cordell 163
Dex Card 167
Jim Bernard...173
Beverly Records...179

Close to Home
Larry Nestor..183
The Lincoln Park Zoo (1965-70) 189
The Rail City Five...197
The Lot 203
The Ides of March 205

Closest to Home

The Delights (1961-66)..209

Jim Holvay 215

The Buckinghams (1964-present)..................................221

The Daughters of Eve..247

Safe at Home

Junior Arzola 269

Hank Zemola...279

In My Spare Time 283

The Beat Goes On ...

Lifelines 291

Lifelines Part 2...297

CASK Attractions 303

The Witching Hour...309

The Making of ... .317

Index..325

Introduction

So, it's sometime after Halloween of 2016 and you have your copy of *The Screaming Wildman* in front of you. Welcome. What took you so long? Both the book and yours truly are incomplete works. Over the years, many folks encouraged me to either write a book or warm up to the notion of having one written about me. I finally gave in and did my own.

As you may have noticed, I'm not getting any younger and neither are many of the friends I've interviewed for my book. In many ways, I'm glad I waited until now. I can safely say this book is maybe ten times better than it would have been just five years ago. I think you'll find it worth waiting for and worth every dime of the money you plunked down. Nobody plunks down money anymore, do they? Nothing worthwhile costs a dime anymore, either.

Not many folks put groups or records together the way I did. I think you'll find nobody puts a book together like I do either. It's unconventional, but entertaining. Here, I'm going to tell you what I put into it and make suggestions on what I hope you'll get out of it.

Those who know me best would probably say I am very independent and kind of a control freak. That's my way—and the only way I can proudly present this book to you. I had no idea how much work it would be or how many people I would ultimately have to trust before I could drop my book into the marketplace.

Accomplishment and Agony

It's a continued honor to know each and every one of the subjects in my book. They all have an enviable list of accomplishments, which I'll summarize for you as each friend is introduced.

As you'll see, these are not only my recollections from the years I spent in the music business. Some of my dearest and longest-lasting relationships stemmed from my non-musical obsessions. I make sure you get to know about these, too.

I wanted my book to be different from others I've seen—where someone just shares their memories. I personally interviewed nearly every living one of the folks I honor with their own chapter. Of course, that took time and a little detective work—but I think you will find it worthwhile.

In many cases, I gave them a sounding board—until they take the time to create their own literary masterpiece. Personally, I think I have the makings of a "dozen seller" here. You will notice sidebars with other comments from my contributors. No reason I couldn't make this book fun to read myself.

What's this "agony" part I mention? How do I categorize so many folks who deserve a category of their own? I completely gave up on arranging this book chronologically. There is more "chronic" than "logic" in the Screaming Wildman. But, here's my best attempt to lay it out for you …

Remember, I set up a string of interview appointments over the last couple of years. Now I have to put them in some kind of presentation order. *My History* reveals unknown facts about me. It also spills into glimpses of my "extended family," the people who taught me the ways of the music profession, and the world, while still under my parents' roof.

The *Awe-Inspiring* group that follows influenced thousands of folks (including you, whether you knew it or not) for decades. Every one is still doing their thing in their own way. Two of them are a little north of ninety years old. All in this chapter outperform me in several ways, you'll see.

The *Monster Entertainment* section lists acts that continue to impress me to this day. My *Influential Characters* category sort of says it all. There are dozens more I wish I had time to write about. My *Social Network* was built by media megastars who laid the groundwork for today's entertainment. They still thrive (and work) today. You'll most likely see them on a street, not a rocking chair.

Close to Home features gifted artists who still show me that Chicago brand of love that lasts a lifetime. *Closest to Home* reminds me why I decided to make music my lifelong calling. *Safe at Home* delves into my athletic endeavors. The *Beat Goes On …* reminds us we're just getting started.

Let me point out a few features before you start turning pages: You'll see sidebars and quotes from my contributors. I display "QR" codes and hyperlinks to give you quick access to the songs we describe. I invite you to pause and check out the YouTube® clips so you can take time to acknowledge both the groups and the fans who work to keep them vibrant and relevant.

I built a pretty comprehensive index of names, places, groups, songs and albums mentioned in the book. I also have a decent list of acknowledgments you've already seen, unless you are dying to jump into the first page. In which case, you probably didn't read this either.

I hope you enjoy yourself as much as I enjoy bringing this to you.

—The Screaming Wildman

Dancing, Disruption, and Rebellion

Hundreds of people opened their hearts, doors, and wallets on behalf of teens at the beginning of the rock-and-roll era from the mid-'50s through '60s. From the early '70s through mid-'80s, there were still scads of places young people could catch live performances at bargain prices. Musicians and singers had opportunities to prove they could command an audience.

Managers and promoters worked with studios, record companies, and radio stations to build a phenomenal music culture. In my opinion, it produced the richest (though not always profitable) assortment of entertainment and launched countless groups that were so worth recognition. Our most vivid memories are built around those soundtracks in our minds.

This book recalls many of my experiences from the time I dedicated my life and skill (such as it was) to promote groups, particularly from my hometown. Some fell ever so short of the mainstream through no fault of their own. Maybe part of the blame is mine. You'll meet a few of them here (still stunning success stories, to be sure). I wish I had the space in this book to recognize them all.

Back then, many folks thought rock-and-roll was dangerous and subversive. They were suspicious, if not frightened, by folks like me. We saw great beauty in the fusion of country, jazz, blues, soul, funk, and folk. Rock-and-roll also had a cultural (and geographic) flavor as well. The Chicago artists I honor in the following pages all know what I mean. We lived it together.

I wanted to be part of the music scene from the time I was maybe five years old. I became a musician, singer, songwriter, and producer (who even launched a couple of record labels in there somewhere). My love for music eventually shifted my focus to promoting the people who touched my soul.

I found my own unique way to get gifted artists, and the fans who eagerly supported them, together in one room. I want to do the same with my book. That's why I tracked so many of them down to help me tell my story.

I'll give you a glimpse at my methods and my passion. My nickname and reputation have served me well for nearly 60 years. I'm proud of both the things I did and the way I did them. Now, I want to entertain you the only way I know how.

I Thought You'd Never Ask …

I ran a lot of promotions and did bunches of commercials on WLS and WCFL radio, where I called myself the Screaming Wildman. When I re-released **The Good Old Days** and **St. Louie Here I Come** vinyl disc in 1967, that's how my singing credit appeared.

A Catholic priest (I can't remember HIS name, so there!) gave me the nickname when I began singing at a school dance with a group called the Gem-Tones. That didn't embarrass me—it defined me. Maybe the priest's observation was meant to somehow subdue me. Instead, it confirmed (no pun intended) that I stood out from the crowd and made authority figures shudder.

What would I do with this power? I would band together with others who were even more gifted and focused than the Screaming Wildman himself. Their stories (and more of mine) are splattered across the pages you have in front of you. You are going to love my guests and their tales as much as I do.

Radio Worked for Me, and I Worked for Radio

WJJD was *the* rock-and-roll station in the late '50s and early '60s. The only other popular station would have been WIND, though it could only be heard later in the evening, particularly outside of the Chicago area. Their signal was effectively drowned out by their 50,000-watt airwave adversary.

WIND did have an influential disc jockey named Howard Miller (who I would one day know pretty well). He previewed all of the new releases on his Sunday night broadcast. A record played on his show had a great chance to become a national hit. As I recall, Howard Miller was the first to play a Frankie Laine record. To say Howard Miller made Frankie Laine (and many others) a sought-after star was no exaggeration.

As a teenager, I began successfully promoting dances and wanted to reach a far larger audience. How would I establish a relationship with a major radio station and eventually get my commercials on the air? By advertising for them, of course. I also did the same for the record companies lined up on South Michigan Avenue (known as Record Row).

If the record company donated any discs or other free stuff, I would include them on my promotional flyer. I might have snuck in a radio station name before I actually talked to anyone there. Now I had official (sort of) sponsors for my dances and needed a memorable way to distribute everything at once. You remember the title of this chapter, don't you?

I installed a luggage rack on the roof of my '55 Oldsmobile and mounted the two giant sound columns I normally used for my PA system. I ran two speaker cables through the windows to an amplifier on the passenger's seat. I had a DC converter plugged into the cigarette lighter to power both the amp and turntable. I became a mobile disc jockey.

I would go to different schools, run a lunchtime dance, and hand out free records. School authorities didn't like the noise and confusion. Kids would rush to classroom windows when I cranked up the music. Large schools would have multiple lunch periods, so I quickly (or immediately) wore out my welcome.

Of course, that's not the last they saw of the Screaming Wildman, as I began sowing the seeds of disruption and rebellion. I have to laugh when I look back on all of that. I see some sincere imitation of both my madness and my method in the *Blues Brothers* (1980) movie.

The late John Belushi, a Chicago native from the Humboldt Park neighborhood, may have been exposed to my "urban legend" while he was growing up. I ask you, who was driving around with roof speakers to advertise an upcoming show? In 1980, it was "Jake and Elwood." A full quarter-century earlier, it would have been Chicago's first and only Screaming Wildman. You're welcome!

The Rusty Rail Days

From 1947 through 1950, I remember listening to a radio show here in Chicago (WJJD) that was aired Monday through Friday. It was a country-and-western show called Suppertime Frolic. The disc jockey was a guy named Randy Blake, who would eventually be honored by the Country Music DJ Hall of Fame in 1976. I used to listen to this show all the time. You can find out more about him at http://www.hillbilly-music.com

He kind of rubbed off on me because I was recording a lot of country-and-western groups here in Chicago from the years 1954 through 1957. Back then, "hillbilly" could be used affectionately when describing the culture and customs of hard-working and righteous folks from the south, like Elvis Presley. This period set the stage, so to speak, before I moved into the rock-and-roll scene with my own recordings, along with the production of records for dozens of other groups not long afterward.

There was a guy from the old neighborhood we called Comari Pepino. You'd have to describe his place of business as a cross between a convenience store and a fish market. As if he needed an additional gimmick, he was also a genuine organ grinder. For those of you too young to know about this type of act, or too old to remember given the age group of some of the people I hang with, he had one of these twirling type boxes that would make the music. On weekends, he would get his pet monkey and put him on top of the box and go throughout the neighborhood and collect loose change. As a prize, the monkey picked out fortunes from the hat and gave them to people who made donations.

This monkey, whose name I wish I could remember, was really remarkable because he gave me the chance to introduce myself to Comari Pepino. I came to learn that he had yet another sideline. As it turned out, he was also a recording genius. He had one of these disc-to-disc duplicating machines that would let you record things from one disc and then transfer them to another. Partly because of my fondness for Comari Pepino and his sidekick, and partly due to the impact that Randy Blake made on me, I decided to record country-and-western performers.

There was a place on the north side of Chicago called Lakeview Bowling Alley, located on the corner of Belmont and Clark streets. It had an upper floor for bowling and a lower floor for drinking. On that lower floor, the Rusty Rail featured live entertainment of singin' and strummin' from Wednesday through Sunday. Tuesday would be the rehearsal night. That was the night Comari Pepino and I would go down there and develop our recording talents and people skills.

We were pretty energetic and innovative, too. At that time, there was a very limited amount of echo on recordings. Even in a studio, nobody really knew how to create perfect echo. So we improvised. I got a Hills Brothers coffee can and I attached it to the back of a microphone with electrical tape. For many groups, this would be the very first time, and sometimes last time, that they would experience an echo effect, at least musically. At that time, many hopeful acts wrote and performed their own songs. Just like today, many would have charismatic, colorful, and talented "front" men or women. This was certainly the case with a lot of the acts we recorded.

John Dillinger Jr. and the Gas Station Gang

This group came from someplace in Indiana. I don't know if it's the eastern part or the western part. I'm sure it mattered a lot to the folks in Indiana. The infamous gangster John Dillinger Jr. was a folk hero in the Hoosier state. John Dillinger Jr., the frontman for the Cash Station Gang, was a crazy type of guy. He would come out on stage with a machine gun guitar. I don't know where he got it manufactured, but it would actually play. I never got the whole story straight, so I don't know if the rest of the band members were actually parts of his family, like cousins or brothers.

They would come out with "Lone Ranger" masks and they would be outrageously comical. Most groups took great care to distinguish themselves from the others. This was especially true when artists playing in a "hillbilly" bar wanted to create a lasting impact. That worked for me. I recorded three sides on that group. Side one was **The Banks Belong to Me**. Side two was **The Lady in Red Caused Me to be Dead**. I never forgot the band's third song. It was going to be a hit, but I don't know what ever happened. It was called **The Feds Shot Me in the Head**.

Single-Side Recordings

Some groups didn't have more than one song good enough to be recorded, or they were only in town for a single week, so we never got around to recording any more. The next four groups fall in to that category.

This group came from somewhere in Minneapolis–St. Paul, Minnesota, the best that I can remember. The name of the group was Rattle Ruder and the Rat House. The leader of the group played the organ. His name was Paul Plumber. This song called **Candy in My Toilet** seemed just right for the group.

The next group I recorded was from Des Moines, Iowa. They came into town and played for a couple of weeks at the Rusty Rail. The name of the group was That Odor and the Highway Skunks. The members came out on the stage with raccoon hats, or "Daniel Boone" hats. I remember recording a song called **Bad Smell on the Road**.

The next group I recorded was from Livingston, Illinois. Even now the population of Livingston is probably less than 1,000. This was a local group from a coal-mining town just off of I-57, called the Dots. I remember them coming to the nightclub in a fresh fruit and vegetable truck. That was how they transported their instruments. It was a gigantic group given their roots (pun intended), something like seven members including a saxophone and a trombone player. I remember recording a single side called **No Rats in My Alley**.

Billy Blade and the Bookends

This was the only polka band that I recall ending up at the Rusty Rail. They just headed straight east down Roosevelt Road from Maywood, Illinois, before the Eisenhower Expressway came to be. They were a comical group. Only part of that was intentional. The name of the song we recorded was **A Bucket of Blood in My Tub**. The group had a midget (or little person, now) named Leo, who had a wooden leg, in their act.

Satan and the Nail-Drivin' Four

I first saw this group performing on an Easter parade float. They became regulars at the Tuesday night audition-practice at the Rusty Rail. I have to say that the members were talented and amusing, with some real nice uniforms and everything else. The two sides that we recorded for Satan and the Nail-Drivin' Four (obviously written and arranged by the members) were: **Save My House From Hell on High Water** and **Save My Comforter From the Smoking Fire**. Just to add more amusement and irony to the group, the guy playing lead guitar was named John St. Peter.

Bill Tavern and the Drunken Four

I'd have to rank this group as the second best group I ever recorded. Bill Tavern and the Drunken Four came from the mountains of Kentucky, and the members were proud to act the part of stereotypical "hillbillies" as they affectionately called themselves. They created the impression they were coming out on stage with a staggering look, indicating they had serious hangovers. The group was three guys besides Bill Tavern himself, making four altogether. Apparently they were far more interested in music than math. Maybe they wanted to create the impression that the "other" guy couldn't even make it to the stage. I think the three guys were members of his family, in some capacity or another.

I remember them distinctly, because the story was that they had a still in their Bluegrass mountain backyard. Maybe it was only a story suggested by the other family members who seemed to travel with them. We could never really tell if the "staggering" was part of the act. I recorded three sides total for this group. The first was **Whiskey and Wine Bottles in my Closet**. The other two were back-to-back on one disc. They were **Pepper in My Beer** and **Bacon and Eggs in My Driveway**.

Denny Doyle and the Irish Grave Diggers

I'll never forget this next group. Denny Doyle and the Irish Grave Diggers came to the States from Ireland. If they were around today, I could make them a million dollars. They were the most hilarious guys I ever saw in my life. They commanded their audience with everything they did. Even though they only knew about 10 songs, they were very popular with club owners. While regular "club" groups took their break, Denny Doyle and the Irish Grave Diggers would do a set for about 20 minutes, or until the other groups returned to the stage.

Eventually, some club owners would charge a separate admission fee every time Denny Doyle would play because the band would get virtual standing ovations every time it came out on stage. The members would appear with black and green jumpsuits emblazoned with shamrocks. Their faces, beards, and mustaches were colored green, like a Gaelic version of KISS, clearly years ahead of their time. The psychological effect on the audience was indescribable. Everybody just went crazy with amusement and expectation. The group had makeshift instruments that I, and unsuspecting members of the audience, had never seen before.

Denny, the leader of the Irish Grave Diggers, would play the washboard, along with a wooden spoon and a cowbell. His brother, one of the geniuses of the whole group, was clearly educated in music. He had a setup that was indescribable, though I will do my best here: Four overturned wash buckets of different sizes were fastened to an elevated hollow platform. There would be a slot cut through the middle of each bucket. Each bucket would have slots cut into them at varying angles.

The "maestro" would insert a saw blade into one of the buckets and would use the bow of a cello or violin in one hand to brush the blades. His other hand would control the pitch of the sound by touching the saw blade itself. We were amazed by the different melodies that emerged during many of these songs. To produce a different pitch during the next part of the song, he would yank out the saw and dash to another bucket to repeat.

Another brother was the percussionist. He did all of the beats with a combination of wooden implements, along with conventional drummer brushes and sticks. He had a huge assortment of pots, pans, and tubs, plus a line of glassware and bells that he substituted for his drum kit. The only guy who had a conventional instrument, if you could call it that in a "hillbilly bar," was the bagpipe player, one of Denny Doyle's nephews.

I distinctly remember recording two sides: **I Got a Punchin' From Acid Indigestion** and **Bury Me With a Barrel of Whiskey**. I gathered that the band used to play at funerals in Ireland, where people would celebrate whenever somebody died. Instead of mourning, they would walk around with the coffin, while rattling beer and whiskey bottles and screaming and yelling. Their actions, and their accents, created indescribable experiences for the audience.

It was the greatest group I ever saw perform, both comically and musically, on any stage.

Mary Thompson and the Guardian Angels

While I was making my *Memorable Moments* CD, I nearly forgot about this group from Topeka, Kansas. Mary Thompson and the Guardian Angels turned out to be a cross (no pun intended) between country-and-western with a gospel spin. Mary Thompson played the organ and stood on a platform because she was only four-and-a-half-feet tall. She came out on stage with a pair of white wings strapped on her back. An iron rod extended upward a couple of feet from the leather harness that held up her wings. When she twirled her body during songs, the circular motion of that rod made it look as if she had a halo above her head. People would react as if she were a guardian angel.

Her husband was an African American man who was a full two-feet taller than Mary. He played the drums in a black devil's outfit with red horns. Altogether, this was a four-member group. With all of these acts, I wish I had someone taking pictures while I was busy recording. Rusty Rail patrons got more than their fair share of comical, visual, and musical entertainment, five nights for every week of the year. The two sides I recorded for Mary Thompson and the Guardian Angels were **I Got a Barbecue Party in Hell** and **I Got a Hangover in Heaven**.

Gone Forever

Very much to my regret, I ended up storing these recordings in the attic section of my garage. By the time I realized how a Chicago climate would disintegrate the acetate composition of the master discs and the plastic of the original tapes, none of the sounds could be salvaged. I only have the stat sheets and titles of the songs that I painstakingly recorded. I'm so disappointed that, due to my carelessness, many great groups and their original songs weren't preserved in their memory and for your entertainment. Of course, there's no possible way to re-capture those melodies or memories. Once again, I apologize to the artists for the opportunities and recognition they may have lost.

* Many of these recollections are taken from my audio CD:
   The Memorial Moments from the Great Show Groups (14:00)

The Cemetery Dance

Okay, I was always thinking as a promoter, but that is not to say all of my thoughts would be well-received. Soon, you will read about some people objecting to particular lyrics. Remember, some of my promotional tactics did not go well on, or near, campuses of local high schools. How would you react to a dance held in a cemetery? If you were a teen, this type of "underground" (pun intended) invitation would probably be appealing. That's who I was aiming to attract. I mean, what could go wrong there, particularly on Halloween?

The year was 1956. This was also the year the movies *Invasion of the Body Snatchers* and *The Werewolf* were released. Because I'm trying to be as sensitive as possible (perhaps I've become more conservative now that I'm approaching middle age), I'm not going to mention the actual location. Rest (in peace) assured, the location was a classy place, worthy of reverent recognition. Once you read the entire story, I think you'll agree that this stunt was pretty zany, even by my standards. Even so, I managed to make the event as tasteful as possible. Of course, the manager/custodian of the cemetery had several concerns when I presented my plan. Thankfully, he also had an open mind.

If I remember correctly, I had the Del Vikings booked as one of the bands for the dance. After that, I had to address the concerns of the management and the community. It was planned during daylight hours, right after school, so there would be no (illegal) trespassing. Since it was mid-afternoon, there was no chance we would interrupt any funeral services. We were not going to disrupt the grounds since there were plenty of areas where there were no graves or headstones (and that is still true). I think the City of Chicago was supposed to acquire the property and manage it as a migratory bird sanctuary and wetland. Pretty progressive mind-set. Maybe that's why I was able to get away with everything else that transpired.

The rest of the circumstances were just one serendipitous event after another. Let's start with the advertised talent. Due to a scheduling conflict (for which I may have been partly to blame), my advertised groups canceled on me. I learned there was a western show in Indiana (maybe Indianapolis) starring well-known country stars (once again, I'm going to err on the side of caution and not name them). With the clock ticking, I managed to broker a last-minute deal with a popular attraction to appear on horseback. Ask someone who was there, and he or she can fill in the blanks for you about the real story.

This promised to more than make up for the absence of the advertised talent. One problem solved, just in time to confront a new issue. I was just making this up "on the fly." Keep in mind I had just turned 16 years old. Before *Ferris Bueller* and Joel Goodsen from *Risky Business* (I had to look that up), there was Carl Buonafede (before I adopted my stage name). The plots of all three stories were set in Chicago. I think I (once again) inspired a trend.

There was growing concern from authorities (having second thoughts) that hundreds of teenagers were going to "despoil" the cemetery grounds. Those were their words, not mine. We didn't use words like "despoil" in Chicago vocational schools. The cemetery custodians didn't want anything ripped off, or trampled, for that matter. "Trampled" I understood. My customary group of security guys (moonlighting correction officers) would be on hand. I rented 42 sheets of plywood for a temporary dance floor to be set up in the deserted southwest corner of the grounds. Getting all that lumber moved, not to mention shuffling the crowd in and out, was actually far easier than I ever imagined. There seemed to be a celestial presence guiding the following circumstances (under the condition that this event must never be repeated).

Across the street from the proposed dance floor, there was a new building under construction. Iron workers were installing a welded staircase. I went over to explain my plan for the dance and asked the foreman if someone could remove about three sections of the fence for easy access. This way, we could completely avoid the main entrance of the cemetery. Without hesitation, a workman created a gaping hole to allow easy access for lumber, equipment, and hordes of teenagers. The foreman also assured me (and delivered on his promise) to have someone weld everything back into place by the end of the day. Awesome.

Another work crew delivered portable "facilities" in exchange for a few dollars of pocket change. I think they enjoyed being co-conspirators in the craziness of it all. A next-door business allowed us to run an electrical cord from their building to power the turntable and speakers. We were good to go, as long as the star of the show would make his promised appearance. As people arrived, I mentioned the advertised groups had been replaced with a surprise guest. Not only did I want the suspense to build, I needed an "out" in case my replacement entertainment was delayed. I wasn't about to let my disappointment reflect poorly on my cowboy star.

You should have heard the squeals of delight from kids who otherwise tried to appear "cool" in every other circumstance. The cowboy and his equine companion (horse, to my trade-school schoolmates) made their appearance right on time. If my guest star was surprised by the absurdity of the situation, he didn't show it. He graciously let the throngs approach with questions and autograph requests. The horse took it all in stride (pun intended), apparently used to admiring fans as well. They were scheduled to do a quick twenty minutes to kick-start the dance and be on their way. Never ones to leave adoring fans wanting, they stayed for a whopping 90 minutes. We didn't do much dancing in that time, but nobody seemed to mind, including me.

We ended the festivities on time and restored the grounds as perfectly as I ever could have expected. Sadly, or happily, depending on your perspective, this was a once-in-a-lifetime event. When you think about it, the permanent residents of the grounds already experienced their own last event of a lifetime. To my knowledge, none of them complained. I want to think they welcomed our company, however briefly. This may have been the closest they ever got to a real-life cowboy as well.

Caesar the Sicilian

Caesar was a fire-eating, sword-swallowing one-man sideshow who entertained hordes of people in Chicago for absolutely no charge. Though he didn't need a sidekick to make himself memorable, he traveled with a parrot named Comari Pepe. He was an enterprising and engaging fellow (a term that is seldom used anymore). I should tell you now he was a midget (another term that has fallen into disuse). Back then, it was only a descriptive term, and not a derogatory one. I respectfully use it here, only to describe my adventures with him. Notice I only described him physically after I mentioned his many talents.

I want to illustrate how upbeat and innovative he was. When I first saw him, he was working at a car wash. Caesar's job was to "hand dry" cars after the soaping, scrubbing, and rinsing was done. He took great pride in his job and would deftly and proudly place a bench beside the car to reach the roof. People my age will remember that there was no such thing as windshield-washer devices back then. The finishing touch on a thorough car wash would be lifting the wipers and toweling off the glass beneath. With all the strength and dexterity of a circus performer, he would heft his oversized bench so it straddled the hood of the car (without ever leaving a scratch, I might add) to finish off the job with a flourish while applause and (even better) tips rained down on him.

He was a performer. I was a promoter and performer. This was some type of celestial match I was determined to exploit. Caesar also had a trunk of props at the ready. That's how I also learned he was a sword-swallower. I visualized a road show we would roll right up to high school campuses.

"How would you like to work with me?" I asked. The rest kind of tumbled together and the act perfected itself on its own. Each of us just did our own thing, and our audience got a chance to take in the whole performance.

Distraction, disruption, and amusement are the key facets of a good performance, and we were each great on our own. As a team (including Comari Pepe, of course), we were invincible entertainers. I picked up promotional flyers for the next dance, along with free records or other prizes from DJs and record promoters. I already described my setup with a turntable and an amp on the front seat and the turntable mounted on top. With all of the precision organization of a SWAT team, we rolled up on the perimeter of the campus where Caesar and Comari Pepe immediately went to work.

On some days, we would actually do twin performances. We would set up our sideshow at Lane Tech (Addison and Western) and crank up the turntable. When kids approached, I pitched the next rock-and-roll attraction while Caesar and his colorful, winged companion never missed a cue. The kids couldn't get enough. They started asking where we were "appearing" next. I remembered heading off to a bunch of Catholic all-girls high schools like Immaculata (Irving Park near Lake Shore Drive), just as the teaching nuns were dismissing school. There was also Alvernia (just off Irving Park on Ridgeway). I seem to remember the school team nickname was the Cougars. I don't know why this stuck with me or what the significance might be now. Madonna (Belmont and Karlov) was less than 2 miles away from Alvernia. The team name was the Marauders. I had to look that one up. Their players were no shrinking violets on the gym floor, or on the dance floor either.

Imagine the horror of the good sisters as they watched their students scurry across the street, only to be swallowed up by the throng. All of their hard work and years of religious instruction were dissolving before their eyes by a Screaming Wildman blaring rock-and-roll. As if that weren't bad enough, he was accompanied by a shrieking (though harmless) bird. I'm sure the sword-swallowing and fire-breathing star of the show was far too much of a spectacle for many of the nuns to handle, given the symbolism of damnation. Oh yeah, there were all kinds of boys there, too.

You know, parrots are known to live to a very advanced age, and Comari Pepe was pretty young when Caesar and he came over from "the old country" together. He may still be fluttering around somewhere, at least in spirit.

Memorial Day Mayhem

I was always thinking as a promoter. If anyone showed up at the dances carrying my leaflet, I'd give them a discount at the door. I was also handing out a lot of promotional records (sometimes albums) I got from various local record distributors. That helped me advertise the biggest dance I ever put together, on Memorial Day 1967 at Bon Bon's Drive-In (across from the Harlem & Irving Shopping Plaza).

Don Phillips, the after-midnight DJ at WLS, helped me get the word out. The Daughters of Eve, Delights, and Buckinghams promised to thrill their fans from 7:30pm until midnight. All of my groups were "on fire" at the time, and we drew a crowd of more than 5,000 that evening. We had to turn people away. Southbound traffic virtually stood still on Harlem Avenue from the north suburbs, while northbound traffic stalled back to the Eisenhower Expressway.

Everyone who made it to the event had a fantastic time. Understandably, some folks wouldn't be able to say the same. Another factor complicated matters (but made for a better story). In 1967, Memorial Day was celebrated on May 30th, no matter where it fell on the calendar. My biggest concert (ever) was held on a Tuesday evening. That meant the peaceful town of Norridge, Illinois, would expect Wednesday to be business as usual.

The Illinois State Police headquarters was about a block or so from the shopping plaza. Around 10:30pm (while the concert was still rockin'), an extremely friendly (what else could I say?) sergeant paid me a visit. He explained how the departing traffic would make it difficult for their squad cars to return for the midnight shift change. He asked if we could wind up the event a little earlier to accommodate them.

Apparently, the safety and security in this narrow slice of Illinois would rest on the decision of one Screaming Wildman. No pressure. Fortunately, a light drizzle began just before 11pm, and the crowd began to disperse on its own. Catastrophe narrowly averted.

Even so, the city of Norridge (no wildmen or women allowed) asked I not run any more dances there, due to the tumult (how do you like that word?) caused by this one. A few short years later (1971), the Memorial Day Holiday was officially moved to the last Monday in May to permanently create a three-day holiday. I can't say my bands or I were in any way responsible for changing a national law, but I want to think we were contributing factors.

See, if you create a crazy-enough event, others will always step in to make sure it's never repeated.

Dancing Every Day of the Week

I ran dances regularly at the Vogue Ballroom (Grace and Broadway) and the Alamo Post (Chicago Avenue and Central Park), a few short blocks from Humboldt Park, a (oneday) Blues Brothers stomping ground. In 1963, I kicked off a dance series on Thanksgiving night at a place called Luigi's Banquet Hall at the intersection of Rockwell and North avenues. You're going to read about that a little later. I won't spoil it for you.

I also ran popular dances on Friday nights at the Ferrara Manor Ballroom (Central Park and North). I brought in some major talent, like Gene Pitney (when **Town Without Pity** had just broken nationally). I followed up with appearances from Jay and the Americans (well known for **Only in America**) and Jimmy Clanton (who charted with **Just a Dream**).

In 1968, I ran a dance every Wednesday night at Antoine's Ballroom (Addison and Lincoln), down the street from the WGN-TV studios. I booked a group from Portland, Oregon, called the Kingsmen, who had the very big, but controversial, hit called **Louie Louie**. Radio station managers were afraid to play that record because of the public concern that the lyrics were suggestive, even obscene. The governor of Indiana went so far as to ban the song. Even the FBI was forced to investigate, to apparently protect impressionable youth from alleged indecency.

I honestly couldn't figure out what they were saying during the song. I also wouldn't pass up an opportunity to energize rock-and-roll fans. I promised to play the 45rpm record at 33 (full volume) at my next dance so everyone could make their own judgment. We had a packed house and had to turn people away. I never get tired of saying that, and the performers never tired of seeing it. Everybody heard the lyrics they wanted to hear, I guess.

Near as I can tell, the controversy never cost the Kingsmen any fans. Jack Ely, their cleverly incoherent lead singer, passed away at 71 (on April 29, 2015).

My History

Little Sicily

When I was born (October 16, 1940), the area bounded by Division Street to the north, Chicago Avenue to the south, Orleans Street to the east, and Larrabee to the west was known as Chicago's Little Sicily. Our neighborhood produced a few people who became prominent for their entertainment or athletic endeavors. Johnny Weissmuller won three Olympic swimming gold medals in 1924 and two more in 1928, before playing Tarzan in the original movie.

Frankie Laine had a lot of hit records in the '40s and '50s but may be best known for singing the theme song for the hit TV show *Rawhide*. The recently departed Dennis Farina, who appeared in several movies, including *Saving Private Ryan* (1998), also starred in the *Law and Order* TV series and hosted the popular *Unsolved Mysteries* series on Spike (cable) TV.

This same geographic area would later be known as Cabrini-Green after the urban transformation of the area in the '50s and '60s. More on that later. Thanks in part to the legendary promoter Eddie Thomas, the Impressions (featuring future Rock & Roll Hall-of-Famers Curtis Mayfield and Jerry Butler) found international fame while living there.

Just after that, R&B artist Gene Chandler became a sensation with the release of **Duke of Earl**, which made it to #1 on Billboard's Hot 100 in 1962. There are a lot of great people who made the area, and all of Chicago, proud of them despite their humble beginnings. I'm glad I had a front-row seat for part of it and got a chance to make my own contributions at times.

As I get up in years, I'm surprised how often I think about my family. I guess I always did, but never had a reason or opportunity to tell anyone else much about them (or about me, for that matter).

My mom (Antonia Lena Buonafede) was born April 20, 1905, to Sicilian immigrants Christopher (Tony) Taruso and Anna Pettuccio. Dad (Calecero Calcedonio Buonafede) was born September 8, 1888. Both of my folks became proud United States citizens.

As you will read many times in these pages, I seldom throw anything away. While researching, I came across the death certificates for my folks. Both dad and mom got a chance to see me realize some of my dreams and share my successes (at least when it came to helping the Buckinghams achieve national recognition in 1967).

Dad suffered a heart attack on July 19, 1968, and passed at age 79. All in all, he had a good run. I think it was, in part, due to his outdoor work with the sanitation department in Chicago. Back in the day, streets were cleaned by men wielding a broom and navigating a push-cart. I guess that's where I learned the value of unselfish hard work.

Mom was also most supportive. How else can you explain my ability to get things done from my home office (before there really was such a thing)? I never missed a phone message, even though she was never really comfortable with the English language. Even someone born and raised in America would have trouble understanding people who called me. Rock-and-roll language was crazy enough.

Mom had a tough time at the very end. I didn't fare much better as I watched her painfully surrender after a bout with pancreatic cancer at age 65 in 1970. Both of my parents are now resting at St. Joseph Cemetery in River Grove, Illinois (Belmont and Cumberland).

Another thing you may have already noticed in this book is that I've pretty much given up arranging it chronologically. I've gone from my birth to bidding my parents a final farewell, though in the case of my dad, I could never have known it was going to be goodbye that day. That's both the blessing and danger of living under the same roof with your parents your whole life.

I'm still trying to understand what allowed me to do some of the things I've done (or why). Maybe if I lay out some of my experiences, you might be able to help me figure out the rest. One thing I can say for sure is that I somehow enjoyed performing. You'll see what I mean if you can get through this chapter.

OK, back to me. I started walking at the age of eight months. At least that is what my mother kept telling me. That may have been the first indication that I was often going to be ahead of the game, in whatever game I found myself. When I was four years old, I was already singing at various Italian

Mom and Dad married in 1935 at St. Philip Benizi Church

festivals, weddings, and get-togethers like the St. Joseph's Table. The master of ceremonies in the neighborhood parish was one Fr. Luigi Giambastiani, as I remember. I'm researching a lot more than I thought I would have while writing this book. For instance, St. Philip Benizi was a scholar and actually passed away during his retirement after preaching and teaching. Pretty tame, when you think about other 13th Century saints. I wouldn't have been interested in being a martyr either, just a screaming wildman.

The Neighborhood Feast was run by St. Philip Benizi Church, located at the corner of Oak Street and Cambridge Avenue. The spectacular highlight of the festivities was called Hail to the Angels. I was only around four years old when I was chosen to be one of the performers during what can only be described as part religious ceremony and part circus act.

In the local version, two ropes would be strung side-by-side from the roof of the parish convent to the roof of the building that housed a fish store (as I remember), catty-corner across the intersection. Looking back on it, I estimate that the height of the ropes where they were secured to the structures was nearly 30 feet. Leather harnesses equipped with pulleys, like the ones worn by construction workers, were attached to each angel.

Two equally proud and horrified mothers would watch their angels as they were suspended, facing one another from opposite sides, atop one of the two ropes. There would also be several men, on the two different roofs, that would pull the angels in toward each other to meet in the center of the tightrope span. Just before the angels began, the shrine of St. Mary had been ceremoniously carried by about 20 people manning long poles on all four sides. You know, kind of like Cleopatra was carried out to meet the commoners (sorry for any perceived blasphemous references). The likeness of the good saint was now resting right beneath the path of the angels.

Passers-by would kiss her statue and make donations, in hope that she would bestow a blessing. At the age of four, I knew I was more than a little bit scared. Maybe it was because people also set off fireworks as part of the ceremony. In any case, this angel made it across the entire span without any mishap. By the way, Hail to the Angels, for the Saint Mary's Italian Festival, is still held every Labor Day weekend, but now it is at Cermak Road and Harlem Avenue. Because the roofs aren't as high, the angels are now only 15 feet off the ground—compared with the 50 or 60 feet that I imagined after all of those years. Naw, it wasn't that high. Once I got older, I got a better sense of reality and altitude.

1947 - My First Communion

I'll never forget making my first Holy Communion at St. Joseph's Church (Hill and Orleans streets). Some time before, the CHA (Chicago Housing Authority) bought up a lot of property, and our old house was razed for low-income occupancy. I went to sixth grade at St. Joseph's before our family moved into a three-story house just south of the DePaul University Campus on North Seminary Street. I couldn't know it then, but our house would become the headquarters for Chi-Town Records just a few years later. I completed eighth grade at St. Vincent de Paul grammar school, at the corner of Webster and Kenmore.

Time to back up once again. Not too many people know this, because I acted like an only child most of the time. I actually had three older brothers and an older sister. I was mom's only child. My widower dad was struggling along with Jim, Louis, Sam, and Nancy when mom came into their lives. I had to wait a few years before joining them all. I've never been that patient since.

We never went for that "step" stuff when we described our relationship. We were sister and brothers who found a way to live under one roof as a family. Nancy had the other bedroom in our apartment, and the boys (actually I was the only boy, the other three were grown men) were sacked out in the living room. I found a picture of three out of my four siblings that I'm dying to share with you. When this picture was snapped, I was only six years old.

Nancy was an outstanding big sis. She and I hung out all the time. I still remember going out for ice cream on a regular basis. Women her age would have felt like they were baby-sitting, but I never felt that way when she and I were together. Those were some great years for me. I think that Nancy was the key player in all of the transitions the family encountered.

For one thing, even the grown guys pretty much stayed at home until they were ready to marry. Of course, this did make things a little cramped in our apartment. I don't even need to mention it, but I will, until Nancy was ready to start a life of her own, she also lived with her brothers. At least she got her own room in exchange for handling whatever household duties mom was too exhausted to handle.

One other thing to consider about the young men in the late '40s and early '50s staying with their parents is that it was pretty much a social issue. It was that "war that was going to end all wars" thing,

Nancy, Louis and Sam Buonafede – 1946

which was borrowed from World War I. Anyway, the moms and dads who were lucky enough to see (at least some of) their boys come home from WWII were reluctant to let them out of their sight once they returned.

The guys themselves were struggling in many ways as well. War is indeed hell on the home front and the related economy. Jobs were not as plentiful as all of the returning hoped, or were promised. The GI Bill (the marketing name was Servicemen's Readjustment Act of 1944—man, whoever wrote that should have been doing lyrics for hit songs) covered veterans' college or trade school expenses. Mainly, it was to get some needed money into the hands of returning GIs to support guys who thought they could immediately re-enter the workforce.

The bambini (you know Sicilian/Italian children) of that era knew things were pretty tense at home. Of course, we were too young to understand why. Kids who had brothers or sisters close to my age were experiencing the same thing with their uncles or older cousins. Because of this "book" thing, I'm beginning to have new appreciation and love for my family. Not only are they gone but not forgotten, they are respected much more deeply than ever. Thank you all for sheltering me from all of this stuff.

As I said, Nancy played a big part in the family transitions. Even after marrying Louis Vanno, she stuck around to take care of us all, but particularly our dad as he got up in years. Even after his passing, Nancy and her husband Louis were regular visitors, along with my niece (Bernadette) and nephew (Vincent) while they lived in Oak Park, just west of Chicago.

I didn't know how much I missed them, or more likely depended on Nancy, until her husband needed to move to Columbus, Ohio, for his work. As close as our family had become over the years, the long distance forced us apart. Nancy's Louis passed away a few short years later and Nancy herself followed in 1981.

Maybe I had no reason to feel so empty after the time and distance separated us, but I did as Sam and I flew to Columbus to attend her funeral. Sad to say, that was the last time I saw my niece, Bernadette.

Decades slip away whether or not you are having fun. Most of the time I was enjoying myself, but occasional pangs of guilt or sadness overtake us all. Writing this chapter sort of forced me to reach out to Bernadette. She recognized my voice right away, almost like she was expecting my call somehow.

My closest relative and I sort of hit it off again, if that is possible. Well, I say we made it possible. She told me that she was not a steady viewer of the David Letterman show, but was tuned in when Paul Shaffer (Letterman's musical director) shouted out to the Screaming Wildman. He recollected hearing my commercials all the way in Thunder Bay, Ontario, during his younger years. I told you all that WLS and WCFL had a long and powerful reach during the evening and nighttime hours.

My brother Jim was not the ideal draft age for WWII, so unlike my two slightly younger brothers, he didn't have to give up a day job. That was probably the only comfort and stability the family could hope for since the day of the Pearl Harbor attack, when I was only a year old.

Actually, there were other good things that mom and dad could hold onto. Brother Jim and his wife, Laura, had a little girl a couple of years before I came along. Marilyn was technically my niece, but that never needed explaining to anyone inside the family. As far as outsiders were concerned, they already knew all that we decided they should.

Actually, that situation came up a lot in many Chicago families, particularly the Catholics. It was easier for all of us to call them cousins, particularly if we shared a common last name. Like I said, who wants to know?

Jim drove for the Flash Cab Company. He also logged a lot of time on Chicago expressways working for the Illinois Department of Transportation in his later years. Even though he was no longer under our roof, he was always at Sunday dinners. His violin accompanied my accordion (or the other way around) at family get-togethers.

Back then, there was no formality tied to those weekend meals among family. We didn't call it "extended family" then either. People would just show up at the usual time (around meals, of course) and stay until whenever. Here's another thing that was different (and better) back then. Parents and kids would go their own separate ways and wouldn't see each other until it was time to leave.

There was laughter, and even fights with injuries, sometimes among the kids, too. Anything requiring stitches or setting of broken bones would seldom break up the entire party. Black eyes, bruises, and scars were worn proudly. There wasn't much time for lasting anger either (at least among us kids). It takes a true "adult" to hold a lasting grudge.

My brother Sam struck out on his own. In that era, that only meant that he was getting out of our cramped quarters. More room for me. He was still within shouting distance. That's probably where the "screaming" in Screaming Wildman started. Sam moved next door to Ed Kelly, who has his own chapter in this book. I've known Ed since I was five years old. As a park athletic coordinator, he was always dressed in a white uniform. Maybe that's were I learned that the right set of duds could make you stand out.

If you are close to my age, I want to remind you that this was an era before anyone had air conditioning. Your voice would carry through open windows. In fact, people could hear conversations, smell the food, and learn to embrace the music of their neighbors. I think that's why a guy like Ed Kelly would appeal to a number of folks, by reflecting their likes and dislikes. A politician is born.

Louis was exposed to a lot of combat during his overseas service and came back a different man. He required some additional care and was a resident for a while at an institution that we referred to as Dunning, at the intersection of Irving Park Avenue and Narragansett in the far western section of Chicago. Jim was a regular visitor and played a great part in his eventual recovery and return to a productive, though permanently wounded, society.

Over the years, I learned a lot of grown-up things about my older siblings. Everything made me appreciate the sacrifices they all made for the family. I just wish I could have had a brother or sister closer to my age to help me get through my own stuff. There were a lot of stories I never quite wrapped my head around.

A lot of family pictures required explanation. I included more in this chapter. There is something sacrilegious about throwing away pictures, so I never did. Every Sicilian household has hundreds of photos of people nobody could remember. Eventually, those who could have filled in the history or significance of the snapshot were long gone, yet dearly missed.

I do remember my mom telling me a little about her parents and what a great musician her father was. Maybe it was the respect and admiration she had for her dad that influenced me to try my hand at entertaining. I bet it also had something to do with my need to be noticed in a household full of fully established adults. Whatever the reason, music and I were forever linked from an early age.

My earliest experiences were at the only home I ever knew from the first days of reckoning. We were right across from Seward Park, at 1126 Sedgwick, until I was a teenager. I have an old news clipping from the Chicago Sun-Times of me playing marbles with my friends at the park.

I included a snapshot of my "gang" in front of Seward, with St. Philip in the background. I can't help thinking about my old friends, even though I have no idea if any are still around. Their names just spilled out of my memory as if no time had passed.

Rodrigo Ricente, Richard Martin, Phillip Marsala, and Anthony Morgan. Wherever you are, I miss you all. We might have known that we would have to go our separate ways someday. In the Lincoln Park neighborhood (closely associated with DePaul University), I began another chapter in my life story.

Aside from holding onto photos forever, there is another tradition among my people. They were never ones to sit still or be content with a single job. The easiest way for a kid my age to gain independence and respect was to start working, and keep busy while you were there. There was no downside to work. It kept moms happy and the girls interested. I was never one to stand still for long. I learned that rapid motion attracts attention. That's where the "wild" in Screaming Wildman probably came from. I was doing what came naturally.

While still in grammar school, I worked at a place called Roma Pizzeria, located at the corner of Sheffield and Webster. It was owned by the Acciardi family, also known for owning Chicago's Kiddieland amusement park. At the Roma, I waited on professors from DePaul University and other people who had long-standing social and political connections with the Acciardis. The legendary Blue Demons' basketball coach, Ray Meyer, and his long-time assistant, Frank McGrath, often ate at the Roma. So did a few future NBA basketball stars, such as former DePaul guard Emmett Bryant, who played on the Boston Celtics' 1969 NBA Championship team.

The Roma had a steady stream of customers from 7am until it closed at midnight. Neither DePaul University nor nearby DePaul Academy had adequate lunch facilities, so things stayed pretty busy. Many of the scholarship basketball players had University-issued passes, so they ate a lot of meals at the Roma. At that time, the DePaul basketball team played its home schedule at the University Auditorium and later at the new Alumni Hall (opened 1956).

Game nights were positively "electric" for the four Acciari brothers—Chuck, Bim, Lee and Geoff—during the 40 years they owned the Roma. They were the kind of guys who sat and talked with the people who came in and personally waited on a lot of customers, particularly the newcomers (whom they could spot the second they entered). In the 1940s, the Acciaris served the first big man of basketball, DePaul's legendary George Mikan, who stood 6 foot 10. Easy to notice. The Screaming Wildman had to take a back seat.

Cooley High

I continued working at the Roma through high school. I attended what was to be known as Cooley Vocational, near the corner of Division and Sedgewick, within the borders of the original Little Sicily area. When I started there, however, it was called Washburne Trade School. Back then, kids had a choice between going to college or finding a job. Well, not really.

Working-class kids were destined for the "trades" where you could make a decent enough wage to support a family, like my dad did. If I ever thought I was college material, I might have studied a little harder. No, my academic path was already pretty clear when I started as a freshman.

I considered myself somewhat of an athlete, but there really wasn't much chance to compete in Washburne, and the newly established Cooley Comets were still in their first season my senior year. I couldn't picture myself in the orange and black school colors, at least not on an athletic team. Fronting a rock-and-roll band was a different thing altogether.

In the late '50s and early '60s, the Chicago Public School system did a decent job to prepare you for a "trade." Lots of guys (and a growing number of girls) poured themselves into the educational process. Many guys (and far fewer girls) approached school as a backup plan, in case their musical dreams fell apart.

After a very short time, it was clear to me that trade careers really went to those talented or interested enough to pursue them. Once I became a real man (long before graduating high school), I came to respect all labor and made a clear choice about my future. Having no backup plan whatsoever keeps you focused and fearful. That was my personal recipe for success. I wouldn't recommend it for anyone else. Music or nothing.

I did soldier on (in a sense, since my birthday kept me out of armed conflict) through high school. My first three years, I took summer school classes, which gave me the easiest load possible when I was a Cooley senior. I did machine shop, woodshop, and print shop (where I developed my permanent hatred for keyboards while manning the linotype machine).

A couple of names and more recollections easily surfaced as a thought of my long-ago days. I found my old course books. In public-school lingo, that is where all of your grades were recorded. You only got to take them home during grading periods and had to return them for safe keeping the rest of the year.

I was painfully reminded that math was not my strong suit, and I gave up my quest for valedictorian long before the first grades hit the official books. I didn't hit the books much, as you may have guessed. We picked up our course books for the final time at graduation. Whether we wanted them to or not, every teacher had autographed them, in a way.

In public schools, there were "counselors" only for kids who had disciplinary issues. For the everyday problems of life for average students, myself included (believe it or not), you could rely on your division teacher. The term "home room" was reserved for the television version of the guy or woman who handed out advice and schedules around the lunch period.

In theory, the same person was supposed to take charge of pretty much the same group for all four years to build trust and rapport. The counseling would be a more natural by-product of familiarity. It remains a phenomenal theory to this day.

Of course, there were a few who had a great influence on me. One was Mr. Drennan, a drafting teacher in charge of my division during my senior year. Mr. Max Weinstein and Mr. Troutline were other division teachers I remembered.

I was part of the very first Cooley High graduating class. As you probably noticed, I still had my class picture around. There were 61 of us by my count. Because I had other interests, I didn't make any lasting friends during this time (at least not at school). I did pull off a rather interesting farewell at the graduation ceremony in the assembly hall, though.

In front of a packed house, I played accordion and sang **Mister Kisses in the Moonlight** and **That's Amore**, made famous by Dean Martin, among other selections. That inspiring round of applause pretty much sealed the deal for me.

Back in those days, google-ing someone would have sounded creepy. Out of curiosity, I gave it a try with the folks from the Cooley High roster. I typed in

the name of our valedictorian (Patricia Kosin) and actually found a *Chicago Tribune* article from June 14, 1959. She had noble aspirations, and I sincerely hope that she was able to live her dream, or at least do well by her standards.

Back to that graduating ceremony, with hundreds in attendance, Patricia did her thing and I did mine. We were both able to rock the house in different ways. If she ever wrote a book, I hope she included our class picture for her readers like I did in mine.

1959 – Graduation from Cooley Vocational High School

Early Musical Fame

In 1950, at the age of 10, I appeared on two different television shows. First, I was on a program called the *Morris B. Sachs Amateur Hour*. It was a one-hour talent show that aired Sunday at noon on Channel 7 in Chicago. I was the envy of other kids at school because nearly everybody wanted to be on that show.

I sang and played the accordion, then waited at home while people voted by phone or by submitting a postcard to the show. I returned to the studios the next week for the announcement of the winners. I remember finishing in third place. The experience made me realize that I was really comfortable on stage.

Keep in mind this was a live television broadcast. Actually, the trick to performing was partly being able to forget that fact. This is described as stage fright, but I think it is more accurately called microphone fright.

Many strong and confident people virtually dissolve when they see a microphone. Now that nearly everybody has a cell phone, just look around. People's faces and voices change when they are projecting their voices toward a microphone. Confident performers are relaxed. The rest are uneasy, even with something they do dozens of time a day.

More than once, I saw people freeze at the microphone during a recording session. I had studio time booked, music ready, and engineers waiting. Sometimes I had to step in myself to complete a track while a vocalist watched his big chance take flight, then disappear before his eyes.

Later in 1950, I appeared on *Curbstone Cutup*, where Ernie Simon (a popular disc jockey) broadcast live in front of the Tribune Tower on Michigan Avenue. He would stop and interview passers-by, or standers-by. The show aired live for a half-hour before Channel 9 regular weekday programming began.

Back then, the broadcast TV stations would actually "go to sleep" during the night and awaken shortly before daybreak, just like the rest of us normal people. I will never forget being interviewed by Ernie, or realizing once again how natural it seemed when standing in front of a microphone.

Nor will I forget that my dad got me down there and helped me nudge my way toward Ernie. I think it was my confident and controlled motion that got me "air time" that morning. Somehow, he could tell I wasn't going to petrify when it was my time to shine before an audience. I didn't let them down, before or since.

Born to Entertain

High School Disc Jockey and Promoter

A lot of kids had a job while they were in high school. Very few lucky kids had jobs that could become lifelong careers. Remember how I mentioned that I always had more than one job? As an eighth-grader in 1955, I started running a dance at the Swiss Hall, located at 635 Webster Avenue.

That building is gone, and you'll now find Oz Park where Webster meets Lincoln Avenue and working-class Larrabee Street turns into North Geneva Terrace. Overall, neighborhood dances were very well sponsored by local businesses who valued their community, particularly because they all lived among their customers. We would draw from 300 to 400 people every Sunday night.

By then, I was quite a familiar face because of my work at the Roma. The fact that I looked like a kid didn't seem to matter. Lots of people were willing to help me assemble the needed security force and otherwise get things set up. I was primarily in charge of promoting the dances and assembling the talent while going to high school and rehearsing my own vocal delivery.

Over the next few years, I brought in some soon-to-be-famous entertainment. Johnny and the Hurricanes, who performed **Red River Valley**; the Riverias, who performed **California Sun**; and native-Chicagoan Ral Donner, who sounded and looked like Elvis Presley. Ral has his well-deserved chapter in this book and is best known for national hits like **The Girl of My Best Friend** and **You Don't Know What You've Got (Until You Lose It)**.

Another popular theme in this book is how many more deserving Chicago acts didn't get the recognition they deserved. You'll read more about Ral and many others in other chapters.

The Gem-Tones

My professional music career began in earnest when I was only an eighth-grader, when I started singing with a group called the Gem-Tones. They were a popular local rock-and-roll band best known for instrumental numbers until I came aboard. Pete Walsh on guitar, Emil Rotondo on bass, Ken Cerretti on keyboards, and Jack Bouchelle on drums teamed with Harry Manfredini, featured on the saxophone.

We were seldom without a wedding, record hop, or high school dance gig. From there, stuff kind of happened for us fast. Of course, we had a bunch of talented musicians on board. You are going to find out just how innovative they were by the end of this chapter. The Gem-Tones were the very first Chicago band to ever appear on Philadelphia ABC TV's *Dick Clark Show*, the predecessor to the iconic *American Bandstand*. In January 1956, they performed **Hawaiian War Rock** and **Man With the Golden Arm**. They were both instrumental numbers, so you could say I had limited exposure for that performance.

During the mid- to late-1950s, there was seldom more than one television in a household (if that). NBC Channel 5 in Chicago catered to the after-grammar-school crowd at 4pm with Elmer the Elephant, hosted by John Conrad. After that, Chicago Bandstand hosted by Dave Hull aired on weekdays from 5 to 6pm. When I look back on it, there was a tremendous amount of programming devoted to the education and entertainment of kids, and we teens in particular.

I was singing with the Gem-Tones when Dave Hull decided to use us as the house band for his Sunday afternoon dances at the O'Henry (now Willowbrook) Ballroom, on West Archer Avenue. In 1957, we performed in front of a crowd of more than 2,000 at a record hop that was televised on NBC TV.

Putting this book together allowed me to reconnect with Harry Manfredini after some 55 years. He and I lived right across the street from one another for 14 or so years as we can best recollect. "So, what have you been up to for the past five-plus decades, Harry?" He's too modest, so the Screaming Wildman comes to the rescue. He created musical scores for the classically successful *Friday the 13th* Paramount Pictures series along with over 100 other films dating as far back as 1978. As I'm writing this (May 2015), he is currently in post-production on three or so films, with still more scheduled for the end of this year and into 2016.

Though he may be known by many for his work on horror flicks, he is exceptionally proud of his work on children's films. Three were awarded best children's film at the American Film Festival (*Corduroy*, *Angus Lost*, and *A Boy, a Dog, and a Frog*). Apparently, his creativity knows no bounds since he somehow found time to write a country-and-western Broadway musical titled *Play Me a Country Song*.

Much to my regret, we lost touch shortly after our collaboration on the Gem-Tones (and a brief stint as baseball teammates). He earned a Bachelor of Music degree from our neighbor, DePaul University, and then a Master of Arts degree from Western Illinois University. After completing his doctoral courses at Columbia University in New York, he was both positioned and accomplished to seize an opportunity in a dream career in film music. I'm grateful for the Harry Manfredini

(http://www.harrymanfredini.com) memories we recently shared and for our recent conversations. They let the years temporarily melt away.

Harry Manfredini—
Even from the very beginning, when you met Carl … you knew there was something special about him. You knew that somehow, someway, he was going to be successful. His personality would not be held back. When we were kids, even before the singing and playing with the band, he had an amazing personality and talent.

He would emulate baseball announcers and would record his imaginary games … and I tell you, he was great at it. As a player, he worked very hard and was one of the best at the Willie Mays patented basket catch.

His musical calling became evident from the very beginning. He would sing at the record hops and various gigs we would play … and the kids just loved him. The success was immediate. Above all of that, Carl had more to offer than just singing those crazy rock songs. His interest and his personality ingratiated him to the disc jockeys and the producers of these shows.

He learned the business end of the music and not only began to produce and promote his own records, but also found and nurtured new talent. I said earlier that this was no surprise to those who knew him: It was that evident.

That's me "fronting" the Gem-Tones at the Dave Hull Record Hop.

Performing and Producing

I still have to remind myself how much of this stuff was happening to me in the middle of my far-from-illustrious high school stint. It wasn't only me trying to make a name for myself, of course. Bear with me here—this is where my family and professional life started to intermingle. There were a lot of guys my age (or close to it) who were writing, playing, and singing in front of eager audiences.

There were so many places to play that it was only a matter of time before we started colliding, competing, and collaborating—so much so that you are going to find a number of names in this following section repeated a few times. At least a couple have their own chapters in this book.

None of us thought about it at the time, but we were actually forming our own sustainability formula. I wasn't out to corner a market as much as I was interested in helping to create one. Let me give you an example of my young mind.

While I was acting as master of ceremonies at the Swiss Hall, I still wanted to write and sing songs. Above all, I wanted to entertain the crowds. If that meant bringing in the best performers and helping them in any way I could as they inched their way to the top of the charts, so be it.

I'm proud to say that I was able to do both of those things. Most guys would have been happy with either one. This book is full of people I'm proud to know and acknowledge who took their talents to surreal levels. As the Screaming Wildman, I did what it took to get "my" folks recognized. I was there for them. I still am.

By the age of 15, I was ready to make hit records—at least I learned what actually makes a record a hit. I also developed my eye and ear (and eventually, nose) for songs that had potential. My original record was never a hit, but I did produce my first songs. I wrote and sang **Two Months out of School** and **Margie Cha-Cha**. One single disc turned out to be a wild lesson in the music business. Believe me.

I didn't play the instruments on the song, of course. That part fell to John Sills and his Rhythm Jets https://youtu.be/gK34lGoT1sE. Everyone I introduce here was (and still is) equally important to my success.

On the other side of the disc, I performed **Another Summer to Remember**, written by James (Jimmy Soul) Holvay and Gary Beisbier, released on the Impala Records label. You are going to hear more about these guys later, especially Jim Holvay (and not just from me).

You are never going to look at another record label the same way by the time you are done with this chapter. At least for the next few paragraphs, I'm going to re-define "jam session." Let's review how much collective talent and creativity we jammed into one hunk of vinyl. I included a convenient link to the record label. You'll also notice that Sue Garrett got credit for mastering the final product.

If you read the Ed Cody chapter before this one, you'll already know that she was his student. I was going to say protégé, but that is too unlike me—and way too hard to type, or spell, for that matter. The point (finally) is that we wanted to collect the best talent available and literally "stamp" a vinyl product for public consumption.

How many records and collaborators did we have? As many as humanly possible while still practicing, performing, and writing. I was promoting as well. Not bad for some girls and guys who weren't old enough to work, except in music. Unfortunately, these kids were just right for some people to exploit. I'm glad I never went that route.

Later, I wrote and sang lead on Were Wolf by the Gem-Tones. As the name suggests, it had to do with monsters – Frankenstein, Dracula, Dracula's daughter, and the Wolf Man. These were all classic books and movies, made even more popular by our song, I want to believe. Humor me. On the other side, released under the TEK (Chicago, Illinois) label, we did **Story That's True**.

There you go. Same formula, if you can call releasing songs on any label that would have us (or me). I released a slow ballad called **I'll Know Then** (once again under the Impala label). On the other side, I recorded **Baby Sittin' Blues**, written by lifelong friend Larry Nestor. The music was credited to a group called the Creations. Just a hint (and I'm not saying this happened here), sometimes guys and girls from famous groups would join studio musicians on other songs.

Sometimes they would give themselves a group name on a whim. That gives a budding superstar like myself some credibility and a great, professional sound. The studio musicians on a given record were getting paid anyway. The best among them didn't need publicity. Word of mouth from the recording studios or labels got them the gigs they deserved. More famous musicians couldn't afford to be associated with any "dogs" that would hurt their reputation, so they would just play for somewhere between union-scale wages or just for fun. This was great for guys like me.

Jim Lounsbury

Jim Lounsbury was, far and away, the most important person in my entire ca-reer. Every music fan in Chicago knew he was one of the very first to host radio, television, and live rock-and-roll programs. Aside from his Chicago prominence, he was also a nationally recognized figure. He occasionally substituted for Dick Clark on *American Bandstand* broadcasts.

He also hosted one of the last shows in the Winter Dance Party tour (Kenosha, Wisconsin, January 24) shortly before Buddy Holly, Ritchie Valens, and the Big Bopper were lost in that famous and tragic plane crash (February 1959). As I say throughout this book, you have to be someone very special to work in the Chicago market, and not all stories are happy ones.

Millions of teens and their horrified parents were introduced to the rock-and-roll phenomenon during the Jim Lounsbury Sock Hop and the Record Hop shows airing on WGN-TV and WBKB-TV (Chicago Channels 9 and 7). Folks referred to the stations only by number because there were only a handful at the time. If you asked people back then, only a few would know that Channel 7 was an ABC affiliate. WGN was just Channel 9 to us local folks.

A spot on the Jim Lounsbury show was regarded as a ticket to fame for musicians, singers, and songwriters. Some were able to take full advantage of the local (however fleeting) exposure. If you were perceptive and coach-able, however, it could turn into much more, like it did for me. I was invited to perform Were Wolf on the Lounsbury television show that aired every Saturday. The experience confirmed that I had a natural delivery that could entice an audience.

Jim was truly a multi-media force in his time. He would promote upcoming dances on his TV show and show clips of those most recent appearances. This was better than MTV (debut 1981) in my opinion because it was unscripted and personal. On-air talent of that era knew how to relate to young America by getting out among them.

There were at least a couple of reasons why Jim Lounsbury was so remark-able, beyond his obvious talent as a proven media personality. He was mature (born in 1923) and movie-idol tall and handsome. That's not the notable part. I'm saying he could serve as a leader and mentor to musicians and was trustwor-thy enough to be welcomed into households daily, just like Walter Cronkite. I wonder if they ever met.

I'm so sorry that there weren't more Record Hop clips that survived. I in-cluded a YouTube clip about his early recollections https://youtu.be/idSN8MgNewE and mention of a few folks and favorite venues. You'll see what I mean about his looks and stage presence. I think there is a clip of his record hop that fea-tures their regular beauty contest. You might be willing to check it out to see how many sponsors are still around. The commercials were actually a part of the show in those days.

Lounsbury was *the* rock-and-roll pioneer, as far as I am concerned. No artists of that era (not just Chicagoans) would have had that number of opportunities without him breaking valuable ground. Once he took us to uncharted territory, he stood back and watched proudly as hordes of eager musicians and their fans literally collided on a daily basis.

At least a couple of times in this book I mention celebrity radio. Well, think about it, celebrity radio originated on TV, with Jim Lounsbury paving the way. The most prominent example of celebrity media that I can think of would be worldwide radio icon Dick Biondi. Of course, Dick has a chapter in my book.

I think Dick would be among the first to say that he was merely carrying the rock-and-roll torch originally lit by Jim Lounsbury. In doing research for this book, I was reminded that Jim put his own book together, complete with stories and photos. Dick Biondi wrote the foreword of *Hey Look – I'm on TV*.

Could you imagine what someone like Jim Lounsbury could have done with a tool like YouTube (launched only a year before his passing in 2006)? I'm doing the very best I can to help keep the memories alive and the deserved tributes pouring in for those dear to me. That includes everyone in this book and those I may have omitted. http://www.jimlounsbury.com/

Jim, you continue to have my gratitude and admiration.

U.S.A. Records

You'll see a bunch of U.S.A. Record labels in this book. By the end of this section, I hope you'll appreciate how much respect and love I have for Jim Golden, the Chicago record distributor who founded the label. From the earliest days of rock-and-roll, the conventional and pricey methods of record production and distribution would never be able so satisfy the market.

The largest companies were having a tough time keeping up with the demand for proven and popular artists. Jim could see that a new label would serve as a springboard for groups that could never have gotten airplay any other way.

Many folks need to be reminded that establishing and maintaining these independent labels required a lot of sacrifice.

In fact, they required so much effort to keep afloat that very few people could sustain their energy much longer once the organization actually took flight. You can only attribute that to a love for the music and for the people who produced and recorded it.

The U.S.A. Record label was, and is, so important to many of the people in this book that I've included a

link to the discography (http://www.globaldogproductions.info/u/usa.html) in a few places.
I know some people are not going to get through all of my pages, so I want
to paint as accurate a picture of the way things fit together as possible.

There were a lot of loose ribbons tied around the hopes and dreams of budding artists and groups at U.S.A. Records. You can safely say one of those dreams
came true if you saw your record produced. That gave you the chance to shop it
around to radio stations and to some of the disc jockeys who appeared at dances
on their behalf.

More likely than not, groups would hope to engage people like Howard
Bedno, Jim Golden, or the Screaming Wildman to do the legwork for them
while they concentrated on the music. Once the record was produced, it was far
easier to get gigs because your vinyl "calling card" would substitute for an audition at lots of music venues. Another dream come true.

Making a little spare change would appease those parents worried that a
musician was throwing his or her life away (at least for the vast majority of musicians living with relatives). Of course, spare change wouldn't do for people with
families and spouses.

For them, when the clock stopped ticking, there wasn't an explosion. It was
more like the world just swallowed them up. Even so, the majority of the people
in that situation would not have traded the experience, or the passion it aroused,
for anything else.

Then, there is that lightning-in-a-bottle hope that your message and sound
will resonate with a crowd just rabid enough to take action. This would be an ideal
time to browse through the list in the discography (linked above). There are probably dozens of folks that could use their spot on the list as a jumping-off point
for their own book. We're all dying to know what worked, what didn't, and why.

All of them should be equally proud of their contributions to Chicago and
national music. Not all of them could carry the message themselves, but they
were an influence to those who broke into the limelight. There was very little
difference in talent between those who would be considered successful and those
considered less so. Actually, there is some sickening overlap in those types of lists.

Man (or lady), you could just start anywhere on the list and write yourself a
chapter a day. Actually, why don't you do that so I can try to stay on topic? I'll get
you started. Tobin Matthews was prominent among the earliest U.S.A. releases.

He grew up as Willy Henson in the Calumet City, Illinois, area and would
most likely credit Jim Lounsbury (among others) with getting him exposure to
the Chicagoland market. He landed coveted deals with Columbia and Warner
Brothers. Through the magic and passion of a new age, you have his songs avail-

able at your fingertips. Enjoy. Sorry I couldn't get him paid, too. The rest is history. His history, my own, and that of U.S.A. Records intersect for a fascinatingly short time.

There was a lot of lightning striking all around us. Some of us sought it out while hoping to avoid the damage associated with a direct hit. I'm going to get into specifics in individual chapters, but I wanted to give you a brief list of some artists who found their way into this book and took shelter under the U.S.A. umbrella (in nearly chronological order).

Bobby Whiteside, Baby Huey and the Baby Sitters, Phil Orsi and the Little Kings, the Buckinghams, Cambridge Five, the Screaming Wildman, the Skopes, Daughters of Eve, and Lincoln Park Zoo are all mentioned fondly in my recollections. I'm proud to say that I witnessed some of their finest moments first-hand. I think you could say Larry Nestor and I are pretty much embedded in the history of U.S.A. Records and vice versa.

A record label discography is a lot like a guest list for a wedding or (sadly and too often) a list of visitors at a funeral. For the briefest period of time, these people are gathered together for a series of events which can never be repeated. You just have to let the memories wash over you.

In 1967, I was in one studio after another with the Buckinghams, along with other talent I hoped to drag (or kick) into the spotlight. I decided to shake off a little rust myself and released Larry Nestor's **Good Old Days** and **St. Louie Here I Come** on a single U.S.A. disc. https://youtu.be/eqVZbksrr2E. This is just another example of my lifelong friendship and collaboration with Larry. We never tried to determine where one ends and the other commences.

As I said earlier, labels (like many relationships) were never destined to go on forever. All of us associated with the U.S.A. label knew that there would be a time to gather together and a time to leave. Sounds like a haunting song lyric, doesn't it? Anyway, we all had mixed feelings near the end of U.S.A. Records' run.

Among their very last releases were Greatest Moments and **Symphony of My Soul** by Lincoln Park Zoo. It makes me think maybe the label should have hung tough awhile longer. The next U.S.A. release was by John Eric and the Isosceles Popsicles. Maybe it was time to put this thing to bed after all.

Back in the heydays of U.S.A. Records, I was anticipating big things for both the Daughters of Eve and Lincoln Park Zoo. Both groups recorded **Symphony of My Soul**,

written by James Butler (Jimmy Peterson, in other places in this book – don't get me started). One version features the incredible vocal range of Tommy Murray of the Lincoln Park Zoo. https://youtu.be/6N2g89hqK9c

The Daughters of Eve's earlier release https://youtu.be/V7dFABltTh4 on U.S.A. put the signature vocal blends of Judy Johnson and Marsha Tomal on display. I wanted to give you a chance to hear them both. I imagine a reunion concert with a medley of hits from two of my favorite groups, featuring a duet by Judy and Tommy in a 10,000-seat arena. Just let me have my moment.

At the end of that fanciful performance, my co-producer Dan Belloc, Jimmy Peterson, and engineer Ron Malo join me on stage to thank everyone for their support throughout the decades. Laughter, handshakes, and hugs abound. That's just another one of those hopes I told you about from the beginning. When I allow myself to go there, I can still see it, and dream.

What Do You Want Me to Say?

I can certainly tell you that this book has been an intense labor of love from the very beginning. I can also say that it may be one of the most painful periods of my life because I had to relive so many memories, with an audience, no less. Those who lived them with me are all worth it (at least most of the time).

You won't often see me depressed. I don't let others see me then. Rest assured that it happens just like it does for everyone. I just stay too busy to let anything gnaw at me for too long.

For every setback, I have a plan to drag myself back into the reality I carved out for myself. At times, I didn't have to look any further than my music or to the careers of those I wanted to help. But what about when music was the problem? Well, I had a well-choreographed series of diversions that soon became passions. You know I didn't do anything halfway.

The Buckinghams were a passion/obsession of mine for years until they felt the need to move on. Next to bidding a last goodbye to my folks and eventually my older siblings, it was the worst time of my life. I have to say that I was more grateful than ever to be a Sicilian at that time. I could count on always being more angry or determined than ever being depressed.

For a furious and all-too-short time after the Buckinghams bailed, the Daughters of Eve took up a great deal of my time, and I loved every minute. After a whirlwind series of performances and recordings, I thought things were just taking off. Judy and Marsha were each thinking marriage and motherhood instead.

Yeah, that pretty much ripped out the heart of the Daughters of Eve—and the Screaming Wildman for that matter. OK, you got me. I was on the brink of depression, and I needed to find some substitute for my energy that had absolutely nothing to do with music. Call it burnout if you want. I was ready to throw myself into other endeavors. I didn't call myself the Screaming Wildman, but I kept his need to keep hustling. I started to compete regularly in bowling and baseball leagues.

Now I had enough diversions that could do more than keep me busy. I don't plan to mention this anyplace else than here, but I also maintained my keen eye for designer and bargain wristwatches. I made a lot of friends and deals throughout the years, even while I was navigating through the music minefields. For the first time in decades, I could completely escape from music when I felt it had abandoned me.

I even toyed with the idea of getting married and settling into a comparatively normal life with a trusted companion – Nah (at least not with the two-legged kind). She would have too many valid expectations, and I would demand unreasonable control of what used to be my own time. See why that would have never worked out?

Don't get me wrong. I craved (and still crave) female companionship. It just can't be the conventional kind that contains the entanglements that women deserve. You can call me a self-centered, obsessed perfectionist. I have always preferred to be called Screaming Wildman. That's why this book is such a miracle. It actually hit the market. Not without second-guessing every word or picture, of course.

I opted for canine companionship. This was the kind of unconditional commitment I could both accept and reciprocate. I would just have to make it a point to get dressed and go out when I needed to fulfill my daily desire to argue with somebody.

Ragin and Barebush were my lifelong companions at this point. I'm talking about their lives and not mine as you probably figured out. They are right with me as I write this. They return whenever I need them most.

The same thing can be said for my family. Here's where I remind you that I never throw anything away. Here's where I remind myself that I shouldn't spend too much time looking for anything in particular. (It's somewhere. I just have to decide how much time I'm going to spend looking for it right now.)

While writing these pages, I came across these photos and want to share the latest comfort and torture they produce.

Ragin 1980-97

Photographs and Memories

I'm not sure how much you want me to narrate this section. To make it seem like you and I are side by side, I'll just start thumbing through my stack of photos and explain why these are most important to me.

Music was in my blood as I discovered. It was also in the earliest conversations I can remember. There's something reassuring about breaking bread with folks from multiple generations. You just absorb stuff without realizing it.

Mom and Dad in 1960 –
See my pictures in the background

I learned more about my mom's parents because she kept so many of their pictures around. I think they are proud to know that they survive to this day and now are part of my book.

Grandpa / Musician Tony Taruso
(1935) – This looks like it was taken
at a funeral. Everybody's family did
stuff like that then.

Grandma and Grandpa
in their Golden Years

Mom's Parents –
Anna and Tony Taruso

I know I should have included a picture of my dear brother Jim before this. I was going to label the photo segment Gone, but not Forgotten. For a few minutes, none of them really seem gone.

Weddings produce more relatives to be sure. I didn't ever feel abandoned when my brothers left home—maybe a little by my sister's wedding. We grew kind of close in my earliest years. The brothers stayed close to "home." Nancy did for a while until her husband found work near Columbus, Ohio.

Brother Jim and Wife Laura

Sister Nancy and Husband Louis Vanno

My brother Jim was a musician, too. You might say we bonded through music more than age. Of course, I wasn't the only kid growing up with a niece older than me, but I'm not like other kids in many other ways. Maybe if my nieces were guys, it would have been different.

Like many families, we find ourselves exchanging more photographs than conversations. I apparently kept these to share with you.

1949 – Jim and I entertain my niece Marilyn at Christmas

Nancy's daughter, Bernadette, the way I still picture her after our recent conversation (2016).

My Niece Marilyn –
Still at a tender age

There's no sense lying to you. I kind of pictured myself as being famous from an early age. Let's call that "recognizable." I'm still working on that constantly. I still like to dress up, sing, and mingle, just like I did back in the '50s.

I still like to "trade" out in public. That might be due to my old-time Chicago Maxwell Street experiences. This was a lot like an Italian-Greek-Turkish bazaar. The mental toughness required to strike a bargain and get my way suited me well in the record business. Snappy clothes made me easy to find in a crowd.

Of course, I got my price for my outfits, too. Professional entertainers always dressed up before they stepped out. At age 20, my formal duds became my permanent uniform for what turned out to be forever.

My own early promo poster

Was this supposed to be a class picture or a mugshot?

Polished entertainer by age 20.

OK, by 1950 (age 10) I chose entertainer and chick magnet as my profession.

Here are my best-known posters when I was National Promotion Director for Impala Records New York - Miami - Hollywood - Las Vegas - Chicago

I adopted a different persona in the early '70s to distance myself from those grief-filled experiences when my groups and I parted company.

I started carrying a badge as a genuine hired gun for the Centennial Security Agency. I didn't say I was going to be inconspicuous, did I?

I worked in some of the toughest locations of that (or any) era, like the Cabrini-Green and Henry Horner Homes areas. I was actually a little too conspicuous there, some may have said.

The residents of those areas worked together to keep us all safe. Thankfully, I didn't encounter any but the most routine incidents.

I also started bowling in an unimaginable amount of leagues and tournaments. More on that later.

Photo-bombing a trophy presentation. I actually won a car, eat your heart out.

I started thinking of myself as the "man of many faces" while searching for a new set of friends who weren't going to ask me any questions about rock-and-roll.

I never really wanted to get away from performing in public. I sell (as in right now, present tense) my colorful and practical umbrella hats. You'll see me at numerous public events like the Bud Billiken or Chicago Pride parades. For the entire Chicago Cubs season, you'll find me trading my "wares" outside Wrigley Field during home games, when the sun shines, or sometimes when the rain falls (if it's warm enough).

I've inspired some original artwork. This piece is by the talented William Moore (who I introduce later).

I Am Who I Was

I did a little research before I used this subtitle – something I was forced to do regularly while putting this book together. You're welcome. Anyway, there are two sources for something much like this. One is God (to Moses Exodus 3:14) "I Am Who I Am." The other is Popeye (to Olive Oyl) "I Yam What I Yam."

I didn't want to get in trouble with either the folks who enforce Popeye's copyrighted material or the folks who regularly speak for God, so I made a change that reflects the thoughts of the Screaming Wildman.

The more I tried to distance myself from the music world (especially the part that I played in its early stages), the more I regretted my decision. Maybe the turning point was the re-emergence of the Buckinghams in the Jane Byrne era of Chicagofest in the early '80s.

Whatever the reason, I'm now drawn both forward and backward by the music that I love and the folks who created it. I'm starting to accept the invitations of folks who are still performing. I wasn't sure they would remember me, or admit it. They did. I finally caved into the notion of writing a book. Every day, I still regret it for a while. It's at least as much work as putting a hit song together.

Now, I take a passel of friends to see the Buckinghams, Dennis Tufano, or any number of performers who did a tour of duty with the (Turtles) Happy Together tour. If you want to get technical, I did create a book or two to accompany my CDs and also designed and published a book for my dear friends who accompanied me to the Genesee Theatre in August 2012.

It took me awhile to once again embrace those times without stressing on what might have been. My thanks to all who appreciate what I did. I'm not done yet. I see that nearly everyone who contributed to this book never stopped. Thank you all for reaching out to me and to your legions of fans.

My hand-crafted
remembrance book

Posing with my Musical "Stable"

Are We Done Yet?

Now I know why I was so reluctant to start this book. Just as I feared, it's really never done. Of course, I don't really want you to get a hold of my book and just go away. At least that's true for most of you. Every day after this book drops into the marketplace, someone is going to remind me of how much I "need" to do.

For instance, I know that my website looks as if I died at least 20 years ago. I'd like to say that my Wikipedia page has seen better days, but it hasn't. Maybe once people read my book, they'll contribute. I don't really know how these things work, so I will leave this up to both the kindness of strangers and to those who make numerous contributions of time and effort to keep me out there. I will introduce you to several as you turn the pages.

While you made your way through this chapter, you most likely noticed I intermingled my recollections of blood relatives and dear friends. That's the thought process of the Screaming Wildman. I consider every one of the characters in my book to be family.

I want you to feel comfortable and entertained while you wade in the pages you've seen tumbled together. There is something new for the folks who have known me for decades. I've given you a glimpse of my thoughts when I'm not on stage performing.

During the years I've sought the company of several women who felt the same way about me. I respect their privacy and trust they will continue to respect mine as this book trickles into circulation.

Awe-Inspiring and Unforgettable

Eddie Thomas

What would you say to a guy if you were invited into his modest trophy room and saw three platinum albums, along with another handful of golds? Couple that with another 14 golds and another platinum for 45rpm records, and you may have been as awestruck as I was. Honestly, I can't understand why he isn't in the Rock & Roll Hall of Fame. After all, some of the young people he shepherded through the competitive musical minefield attained the honor during his more than six decades in the business.

Without Eddie Thomas, young brothers Richard and Arthur Brooks, Sam Gooden, Jerry Butler, and Curtis Mayfield may still been known as the Roosters. Because he was so taken with the group's talent and saw the members' potential for creating a national impact, he suggested the Impressions. He'd be the first to admit he was learning to be a promoter as he went along. Obviously, he learned enough to take a group from Chicago's Cabrini-Green neighborhood all the way to its 1991 induction into music's highest honor.

The late Curtis Mayfield, Eddie's friend and eventual business partner, was inducted as a solo artist in 1999 (the same year as Paul McCartney and Billy Joel). Sadly, Curtis's failing health didn't allow him to attend the ceremony. He passed away right after Christmas that year. Eddie and Curtis founded Curtom Records and created a unique brand of music, melding rhythm with socially significant lyrics.

There is a British Hall of Fame group that may never have been inducted had the members not contacted Eddie Thomas to help them establish a rhythm-and-blues following. Remember those platinum records I mentioned? The Bee Gees were a prominent part of the Saturday Night Fever soundtrack album Eddie promoted. If you want to see what that platinum record (which surpassed the 40 million mark in sales) looks like, maybe you can pay him a visit, as I did.

The Impressions
Promotional Poster
Manager: Marv Stuart

I may not have been reunited with Eddie Thomas if it weren't for this book. I credit him with putting me on my career path. If it wasn't for him, there may have been no Screaming Wildman and much of the stuff you already read about (and everything that followed my "evolution") might never have happened.

He was managing the Medallionaires, who would later achieve moderate success with its original **Magic Moonlight**. In 1955, the group rehearsed near our home, within earshot of some extremely fortunate neighbors. One day, I was practicing my accordion near the window and singing something lame, even for its time, like **How Much Is That Doggie in the Window**. The humor of that was somehow lost on me then.

I was a pretty experienced entertainer for a kid not yet in high school. At least I wasn't going to be intimidated by an audience. After practice, I was shooting marbles with a couple of friends at Seward Park (Division and Orleans) right across from my house. Woodtake Anderson, the park manager at Seward, was curious enough to approach me.

"Was that you I heard playing the accordion and singing?" he asked. I may have nodded or shrugged. Anyway, he got the idea.

"I'm going to send someone over to see you," Woodtake said. A short time later, Eddie Thomas was sitting in our living room, enjoying my mom's hospitality and a cool drink, while I prepared for my audition. I must have impressed him well enough with my musical ability and showmanship. Did I have the same potential as a couple of youngsters named Jerry Butler and Curtis Mayfield? It really didn't matter. His advice was priceless.

"Drop the accordion, and focus on rock-and-roll," I heard him tell me.

I'm ashamed to say we lost touch for a full six decades. We might have never reconnected, except he and I started using the same dry cleaner. Now, in 2015, I'm sitting in his living room, after getting a customary hug from Verlene, his gracious and effervescent wife. I was laying out my recollections of our meeting and trying to thank him, once again, for his priceless guidance.

"So what have you been up to?" I almost asked. Really? After sixty years? Instead, we opened up with recollections of our first meeting. That would be me, as a man-child, and he as a dedicated community advocate. In spite of his awesome accomplishments, Eddie Thomas's infectious faith and humility made it easy to see why time flies by in his presence. He briefly chronicled the foundation of Curtom Records and how Curtis Mayfield from the Impressions would pen and record **Superfly**.

We talked about all the record labels that we worked with and compared notes on recording studios from Chicago's Record Row on South Michigan Avenue. Eddie founded and headed the Dogs of War, an organization of DJs who worked together to get promotional products and demo records into all neighborhoods and markets. That's precisely why a group like the Bee Gees sought out "the Dogs" in general and Eddie Thomas in particular. The only things that exceeded his passion for music were his faith and integrity.

By working with the Bee Gees personally, he got a chance to convey their "soul" to an energetic audience that still wanted to dance. Most of us record promoters failed to understand the immense social and economic potential of disco music. Eddie thrived during the days of "kinetic rhythm and blues." That's what I call it, now that he enlightened me during our visit. When you think about the diversity of the groups on the *Saturday Night Fever* soundtrack, it seems like a social message we've abandoned somehow. KC and the Sunshine Band, the Trammps, Kool & The Gang, Yvonne Elliman, and Tavares all stood as equals in the eyes of the God that Eddie serves and credits for his success.

Eddie fondly recalled many of the artists who gravitated toward him for a solid opinion of their talent. If warranted, he would work to make them as marketable as possible. You always got encouragement and guidance from Eddie Thomas, no matter the eventual outcome. Even established performers sought him for additional perspective. That's what Ray Charles, Barry White, Quincy Jones, Donna Summer, the Stylistics, Floaters, Independents, Manhattans, Impressions, and Van McCoy (**The Hustle**) have in common—gold or platinum recording immortality, thanks to Eddie Thomas.

He sadly recalled the story of Baby Huey and the Babysitters who gained a good deal of popularity in a short time. James Ramey, the group's charismatic and sizeable frontman, succumbed to a heart attack at the tender age of 26. The rigors and temptations of popularity claimed another victim.

Even the "ones who got away" put Eddie in a class by himself. He was working with a "family" group called the 5 Stairsteps, who eventually reached gold with **O-O-Oh Child**. At that same time, another five-member band from nearby Gary, Indiana, was looking to break into the music business. The similarities, particularly in the name, were enough to send the Jackson Five to Motown. Some

Baby Huey & The Babysitters
Promotional Poster
Curtom Records –
Personal Manager: Ted Allan

time later, the group's lead singer would knock Eddie's *Saturday Night Fever* soundtrack out of the all-time top spot in sales with his *Thriller* album. Eddie remembered Michael Jackson quite well. Maybe there is one person on the planet who didn't appear to need Eddie's guidance. On second thought, how bad would it have been to get his perspective on life and professional matters? You know what I'm sayin'?

Eddie said he never had an ego, and he credits God with his success. He truly only wants to be remembered as someone willing to help others. In addition to his awards for music, he has many others on display, of which he is equally proud. Among them, I found Congress of Racial Equality (1968) and George Foster Peabody (Broadcasting Award) for *The Rise and Fall of Vee-Jay* (1994). On March 21, 2013, the *Saturday Night Fever* album was added to the Library of Congress National Recording Registry. I think you may want to know lots more about Eddie, so I'm including this YouTube clip my long-time collaborator Joe Pytel found about the *Hitmaker*. https://youtu.be/0RiX34q93AA

Eddie continues to impress and awe me. He talked about how his personal friend Don Cornelius of *Soul Train* mentioned him (1974) in his touching introduction of the Independents on his immensely popular show. Eddie cracked open his personal laptop, found the clip, and let us watch it together. Lots of people far younger than he (myself included) fear and loathe electronic media. Apparently, Eddie uses his computer for the work he and God agreed upon. I included the *Soul Train* clip for you as well. By the way, there is a gold record on display for **Leaving Me** by the Independents. https://youtu.be/J2QME5f4Rh8

I found out Eddie also operated a limousine service for a while. He counted Quincy Jones, Stephanie Powers, Barry White, and the recently departed Ernie Banks among his clients. Even Liberace counted on him for his transportation needs (in a Rolls Royce, of course). When you think about it, his chauffeuring is a lot like his promotion work. He transported all of his stars safely to their intended destinations. What happened when they got there was out of his hands.

Just like two of the groups he helped name and support (the Impressions and Independents), Eddie Thomas is both impressive and independent. He also deserves a sincere thank you from all of us and, once again, recognition by the "Hall."

I was lucky enough to be a guest on celebrated journalist Dave Hoekstra's *Nocturnal Journal* radio program, along with founding member of the Buckinghams, Carl Giammarese. I'm going to do my best to get Eddie Thomas a spot on his show. All of us owe him that.

Another Encounter

Okay, I'm getting better about staying in touch. It has only been a couple of months or so between visits. During the last week of August 2015, we're sitting in Eddie's living room, re-visiting some earlier discussions.

We talked about my dealings with Kapp Records from New York back in "the day." I would record my groups in Chicago, but sometimes take them to Kapp and let Brooks Arthur (http://www.brooksarthur.com/) do the mixing.

Before long, Ray Buckner's **Dirty Down to the Bone** was wailing from the speakers in Eddie's trophy-laden office. I mentioned how impressed I was with the double-tracked vocal I heard. It took a little coaxing to get Eddie to admit it was his suggestion. I have an "ear" for great lyrics, too. Eddie and I both agreed "... *the only water in sight was the tears in my eyes* ..." is one powerful Buckner line. Somehow, the nastier a woman seems in a song, the better chance it has of becoming a blues hit. I noticed Ray sounds quite a bit like Brook Benton, who most folks know for his 1970 hit, **Rainy Night in Georgia**. Heartache is timeless, huh? As long as there is suffering, there will be a blues melody to make it hurt so good. Ray wrote all of the songs on the album. Alligator Records will be the distributor, if I remember correctly. I'm still promoting, every chance I get.

Eddie told me Ray asked to meet him and was very complimentary (and familiar with Eddie's accomplishments). Would Eddie be interested in hearing some of his songs? Eddie has a generous heart, but he is no "soft touch" when it comes to the entertainment business. Needless to say, he is still willing to promote music made by serious (though unproven) artists. Eddie feels distributors can still have an impact in small southern stations, even today.

Thanks to Verlene, we also learned Ray Buckner is a first cousin to Jennifer Hudson. She laughingly mentioned Eddie made a few song suggestions, and Ray returned a week later with the requested lyrics and arrangements. As you will hear (because I encourage you to seek him out), Ray is also quite a guitar player.

I changed the subject since we're constantly evaluating the likelihood that new artists can effectively break into the business. We used **Gypsy Woman** (written by Eddie's protégé, Curtis Mayfield) for an example. It hit the Top Ten on both Billboard and Cashbox (https://youtu.be/3Wd4tlX5t-Q) in 1961. The message "cut deeply" into the soul of a new, innocent (or clueless) generation. Pop troubadour Brian Highland charted (actually went gold) with a cover ten years later.

Was Highland able to enlighten his audience about the plight of misunderstood minorities? Maybe Eddie and Curtis were grateful for the opportunity to spread the message in all ways possible. I doubt Eddie would want any credit. Generous to a fault, and modest as ever.

I'm finding out so much about Eddie Thomas, the man. He inspired tens of thousands because of his music, but mostly because of his community outreach. Eddie is a humble guy, so it took a lot of persuasion to get more material for his chapter. I bet you didn't know celebrated playwright Celeste Bedford Walker and Eddie wrote a stage play called *The Eddie Thomas Story* based on his life (http://www.celestebedfordwalker.net/id1.html). Eddie Sr. had Notre Dame aspirations for his son. Young Eddie took a different path. During Scene 3, 18-year-old Eddie

 enters wearing his military uniform. There's a front-page write-up in the *Pittsburgh Courier* … Eddie Thomas Jr. … top of his class … headed for West Point Academy in New York, etc. Sometimes, the classes that you master put you in a class by yourself.

That can also be said for the company you keep. Imagine being invited to a historic one-night-only performance of *Songs in the Key of Life*. Picture yourself backstage for a photo with its creator. Eddie was kind enough to share one of his snapshots with me. He thoughtfully supplied a caption as well. To the left is Raynard Minor, Chicago-born pianist, singer-songwriter. Do you know that guy in the middle?

Raynard wrote **Rescue Me**, recorded at Chess Records and performed by Fontella Bass. I included a link to one of her "sassy and classy" live performances (https://youtu.be/QXSocE_M1G4). Coincidentally, both songwriters in

 the snapshot are without the conventional gift of sight. All three are visionary in the only ways that matter. Eddie, I treasure your friendship. Thanks for touching our souls.

I Can't Get Enough of Eddie Thomas

It was late October in 2015 and I was back at Eddie's house to stir up more memories, introduce my editor, and snap a few more pictures. Yeah, we were beginning to get serious about this book thing. After sharing hugs all around, we

Raynard Minor, Stevie Wonder, and Eddie

settled into the living room for another chat. It only takes Verlene and Eddie seconds to turn a conversation into an occasion.

I started telling Eddie that I tracked down legendary engineer Ed Cody for an interview.

"That name sounds familiar," Eddie said. Sometimes it takes a couple of reconnected friends to put together a complete memory to lay in front of a new, and probably younger, audience.

"Ed Cody bought Hall Recording Studios at 218 South Wabash from Stu Black and Bill Hall. Changed the name to StereoSonic," I mentioned to test Eddie's recollection and re-affirm my memory. Time to toss the ball to our generous host.

"Did you ever record at Universal Records, Eddie?" I asked.

"That's where we recorded **Gypsy Woman**," Eddie said. Then we started talking about our groups and how hard it was to keep them together once they've been given a taste of fame. Eddie understood how I learned to accept why the Buckinghams needed to move on. Only someone like him can relate to the hurt that could linger for fifty years, if allowed.

The Impressions were "his" group until Jerry Butler was lured away. I mentioned Butler and I went to the same (Cooley) vocational high school. I remembered he took a cooking class. I could still picture him in his white "chef" duds. Verlene told us Jerry still cooks for his mother-in-law every weekend. Public vocational education really did prepare some of us for life after all.

"So Eddie, which group did you most like working with?" I asked. Verlene gave a knowing nod well before he answered. He wasn't hesitating. He was reliving some of those fond memories right in front of us.

"Should I tell you?" he said with a smile. "The Bee Gees."

"Did they know about you somehow? Did they seek you out?" I asked.

"No, they didn't, but the guy who ran RSO Records did. Robert Stigwood was the money man for the Robert Stigwood Organisation," he said. I decided to use the funny spelling of the "O" word like they do at the London headquarters.

"Al Cory was the label representative for RSO, and he sent the Bee Gees to meet me," Eddie said.

We talked some about the Bee Gees' prominent falsetto on the *Saturday Night Fever* album. That's where Barry took the lead role from Robin Gibb, whose voice was featured on most of their early hits.

"Did the Curtis Mayfield falsetto inspire the Bee Gees?" I asked.

"It was actually Russell Thompkins Jr. from the Stylistics. It worked like a charm," Eddie said about the lead singer from his famous Philadelphia-based group.

"Why do you think that you connected so well with the Bee Gees?" I asked.

"First off, they were just incredible guys. Multi-talented. Plus, they had big hearts and were down to earth. You wouldn't believe it.

They were so nice. Andy [Gibb], the youngest one, and the first one to leave—you know, pass away—was a sweetheart. I just love them all," he said. Love has no "passed tense" in Eddie's language.

"How did you actually get to work with a group from London?" I asked, not wanting to change the subject. I could tell he didn't want to either.

"Robert Stigwood would bring them to Chicago, and we just connected. I kept a good rapport with them all the time. In my mind, I still keep the same rapport with them. Andy was only 32 when he died. They had every quality you would want. They were great-looking kids. Great family. Great mother. They could write songs. They had multi-genius talent in song writing," Eddie said. Yeah, they wrote songs for a number of famous performers, including Celine Dion, Diana Ross, and even Kenny Rogers. There were a number of brilliant moments in Eddie's career. I could tell that no task connected with promoting the Bee Gees ever felt like work to him.

Ten blocks of South Michigan Avenue between Roosevelt and Cermak roads (12th Street to 22nd Street) was known as Record Row back in the day. Actually, there were also recording studios on South Wabash, one block west. Guys like Eddie Thomas and I could "shop" a recording to several different record companies walking door to door.

Remember, that was only half the battle. In reality, it was more like one-third. Hard work and persistence could get a record produced. Getting it played was quite another thing. During our earlier visits, we briefly discussed the Dogs of War organization founded by Eddie Thomas. The members overcame pitfalls and prejudices in the musical battlefield. It was a work of inspired genius. I'll let Eddie take it away from here. You're going to get both a business and history lesson at the same time.

"The Dogs of War was a national group of guy and gal DJs in both the city and suburbs. Radio stations could play only a small percentage of the records they received. Many would promise to play a disc. It may go on the

Eddie Thomas with Platinum Plaque for Saturday Night Fever album (upper right)

air in two months, or more likely never," Eddie started. Think about how tough it was for all promoters. Ethnic and ethical barriers made it even tougher for some.

"You needed another way to get these records played. At clubs and dances throughout the country, DJs could play whatever they wanted. Really, it was the songs the crowd requested. If we could unite the DJs under one banner, you'd have a hell of an influential army. What if they all agreed to play one record?

"So now all of the 'Dog' DJs are playing a select group of songs. The kids are leaving the clubs and asking for them at the record shops. The shops are calling the distributors and requesting the records. The distributors are calling the record companies to tell them about the demand. The radio stations are getting requests from the record companies and the kids themselves. The stations had to start playing it," Eddie explained. Didn't I tell you this guy was (and still is) a genius?

"The Dogs would regularly meet to create these playlists. They were such a dynamic group and the more members we got, the better it was. The record companies began to recognize us and send us their product, just like they did to the radio stations," he continued. Once this group decided on a record, it was likely to be a hit.

"We got so big we had to hold our meeting at the McCormick Inn in Chicago. At one time, there were about 450 members. We'd say 'Dogs, here's the playlist. Take your pick.' There'd be two or three songs getting played everywhere," Eddie said. Once you got one radio station to play the song, the rest would follow suit. They would line up like dominoes. His training and discipline made Eddie Thomas a standout West Point cadet and primed him to lead the Dogs of War with military precision.

I mentioned my recent experience at Beverly Records, where proprietor Jack Dreznes found an album cover that depicted a Caucasian teenage couple, apparently enjoying Jerry Butler's music, though his photo is nowhere to be found.

"Companies did that a whole lot," Eddie said. Many of us are ready to embrace a soulful and passionate message. Others prove reluctant to welcome diverse messengers. Eddie and I are completely devoted to music. We have a lasting bond that reaches far beyond time and intolerance.

This book is about Eddie and people like him, few as they may be. Here's what I'm getting at: Eddie is too humble a guy to relate his stories to you directly, but he will talk to me. It's my job to tell you his story.

I finally got to the reason why music turned out to be his chosen "call of duty." Remember, Eddie was a Wendell Phillips high school graduate, with a military-academy appointment. Eddie's stepfather was none other than Big

Maceo Merriweather. His first record, **Worried Life Blues** (1941), would be his "signature" work. From what I gathered, he also did a mean rendition of blues standard **Sweet Home Chicago**.

"We were living at 47th Street and South Park Way," Eddie said. That was years before it became Dr. Martin Luther King Drive. I didn't really interrupt Eddie here. I just wanted to give you a little background.

"One day in 1946, Big Maceo went to get his hair cut around the corner at the Metropolitan Barber Shop and suffered a stroke. I told my mother 'I'm going to stay home, get a job, and help you.' West Point, I let it go. Some of Maceo's music kind of rubbed off on me. It took me from that point on," Eddie continued. Only he could relate a story like this without so much as a shrug. In his heart, I think he really believes that we are all capable of that type of selfless devotion to family members. The musical groups that trusted him with their livelihood got the same type of treatment.

One thing Eddie Thomas and I have had in common is our desire to get artists paid fairly. What sets him apart from anyone else I've known is how he applied all of his learning and experience to benefit our world. I don't mean just the musical world either. His military strategies organized the Dogs of War. His meager experience parking cars blossomed into a chauffeur service. His exposure to the lifestyle and challenges of musicians left an indelible mark on the lives of professional entertainers from all countries and backgrounds.

I included a brief list of Eddie's accomplishments and rewards, both musical and humanitarian. I read somewhere that Maceo was inducted into the Blues Hall of Fame in 2002. That would be nearly 50 years after his death in 1953. Seems as if our sense of timing, and of gratitude, leaves a lot to be desired.

Eddie, thanks for making my world, and that of everyone you've touched, undeniably better!

Oh, Yeah!

I forgot to tell you. Eddie was recently interviewed by Todd Mayfield, son of the legendary Curtis. If all goes as planned, expect a book about the creative genius behind (and in front of) **Superfly** by early 2017. Remember how I mentioned the need for artists to be treated fairly? Seems like Eddie and Curtis were pioneers there as well. Again, his humility gets in the way of our education.

Do your own research if you want. Here's the way I understand things. In 1960, there were less than a handful of artists in complete control of their songs. One songwriter/entrepreneur was the phenomenal Sam Cooke. His very first release, **You Send Me** https://youtu.be/pX6QlnIMqjE (on the Keen Records label), occupied the top spot on both the R&B and pop charts in 1957. This also paved the way for the creation of Sam's own publishing company and the SAR Records label by 1959.

In 1962, Ray Charles founded Tangerine Records. In 1973, he closed that label down and opened Crossover Records, where he was nearly the only artist to release any vinyl.

The third artist to extend his influence was none other than Curtis Mayfield. Until recently, I didn't realize that there was a Curtom Publishing Company as far back as 1960. Curtom Records wasn't created until 1968. The "Tom" in Curtom signified the wisdom and collaboration of Eddie Thomas.

The Staple Singers, Jerry Butler, Baby Huey, Gene Chandler, Major Lance, the Impressions, jazz and soul singer Linda Clifford, and even Eric Clapton are among the artists who released records under the Curtom label.

I even found the **Ballad of the Mad Streaker**, a novelty song by Chicago Radio DJ Larry Lujack, known locally as "Superjock," among the Curtom releases. Obviously, this label was a musical "force" in the pop, R&B, jazz, soul, and disco markets. Both the Natural Four, an R&B group from Oakland, California, and Chicago funk group Rasputin's Stash managed to find a home under the Curtom umbrella.

I hope you all get the privilege of meeting Eddie Thomas in person. Until then, rest assured that you have an advocate, confidant, and loyal supporter of whatever kind of music you call your own.

Dear Mr. Eddie Thomas:
Last year, we announced that your interview is now a permanent part of The HistoryMakers Collection at the Library of Congress.
This year, your interview has been added to The HistoryMakers Digital Archive, a unique resource which has users in 51 countries around the globe. Howard University is the first to license it for use in the classroom.

Eddie Thomas, Encapsulated

Eddie Thomas was the co-founder of Curtom Records along with partner, Curtis Mayfield. http://www.thehistorymakers.com/biography/eddie-thomas-39. The Who's Who publication board certifies that Eddie Thomas is a subject of biographical record in *Who's Who in America* – sixty-second edition.

Platinum Records

Modern Sounds In Country & Western Music – Ray Charles

Barry White's Greatest Hits – Barry White

Saturday Night Fever (Sound Track) – Bee-Gees

Gold Records

The Best of the Stylistics – Stylistics

On the Radio Greatest Hits – Donna Summer

Body Heat – Quincy Jones

And the Beat Goes On – The Whispers

Shame – Evelyn "Champagne" King

Do You Wanna Get Funky – Peter Brown

We're the New York Giants – N.Y. Giants

Platinum 45

You Are My Shining Star – The Manhattans

Gold & Platinum 45s Records Awarded

Movin – Brass Construction

Float On – Floaters

The Hustle – Van McCoy

You Make Me Feel Brand New – Stylistics

You Are Everything – Stylistics

Break Up To Make Up – Stylistics

Disco Lady – Johnnie Taylor

O-O-Oh Child – The 5 Stairsteps

Leaving Me – The Independents

Walking in the Rain – Love Unlimited

Do It Till You're Satisfied – BT Express

For Your Precious Love – Jerry Butler

Gypsy Woman – The Impressions

Ain't Understanding Mellow – Jerry Butler & Brenda Lee Eager

Special Awards

Congress of Racial Equality (1968)

Ohio State University - Artistic Relevancy (1970)

Outstanding Record Executive Legend Award (1989)

Keeper of the Sound (Contributions to the Music Industry) (1993)

George Foster Peabody (Broadcasting Award) "The Rise and Fall of Vee-Jay" (1994)

The HistoryMakers (Excellence in the Field of Music Makers) (2000)

Martin's Inter-Culture, Inc. (for Contributions to the Entertainment Industry) (2003)

Black Heritage Image Award (Legendary Producer - Thomas Productions) (2003)

National Newspaper Publishers Association (2005)

Ed Cody

While organizing this book, my thoughts kept drifting to Ed Cody, the masterful and innovative engineer for StereoSonic Recording Studios (226 S. Wabash). Most of my radio commercials and a number of Daughters of Eve tracks were recorded in his studio. He was a true audio pioneer, located in the heart of Record Row.

From the early '60s until the dawn of the 21st century, Ed welcomed hundreds of artists to his studio. Some were internationally famous. Many others were regional gospel, rock, or rhythm-and-blues hopefuls. All were treated with the respect and skill that only a true professional could offer.

I was thinking how great it would be if Ed Cody himself could help me with the details. That's where I played detective, instead of promoter. I sent a letter to his last known address. After a while, I decided to drive out to his house, just like I would have done back during the era that got me paid and made Ed famous. Actually, I still prefer to operate that way. It's a good thing that I do. Otherwise, this chapter would never have been this interesting.

Ed Cody's old address was now an empty lot. A lot of you would have given up any hope of finding him at this point. That's why there is only one Screaming Wildman. I walked across the street and knocked on a few doors. Sadly, there are so few people home nowadays. Back in "our" day, there was someone behind most doors, and most folks weren't afraid to answer them.

I approached a lady on the street (another rare occurrence) and asked what might have happened to the residents of the razed building. She said I might

Me next to Ed Cody, then Larry Nestor and Joe Pytel

try some of the homeless shelters and made some suggestions. Once again, how many of you would have given up by now? Not me, and I hope not you, from now on. I dreaded the thought of my good friend falling that hard.

"Ed Cody, yeah, he drops in once in a while," said a helpful, though weary, administrator-type woman. I bet she never thought she would be a concierge for the disadvantaged as part of her career path. I hope she won't end up being a client some day. This was truly a big break. How many patrons who walk through those doors are willing to disclose any information at all?

"If I give you my phone number, would you be sure that Ed Cody gets it?" I asked. Once again, what are the odds of getting all of these circumstances to tumble together? It would be easier than getting the Buckinghams to the number one spot on the Billboard survey! A few days after I left my number at the shelter, Ed Cody left me a voice message, and a return phone number.

You have no idea how reassuring that call was. Of course, my mind was still in overdrive. He has a phone number … maybe it's a pay phone? See how my mind works? When's the last time I saw a pay phone? I wasn't going to rest until I had some answers. Of course, I would have to answer his questions, too—like why I never visited when his building was still standing.

After one or two missed connections, Ed picked up the phone. It's really not like me to make a long story short, but I'll indulge you this once. Ed frequented the shelter to visit other folks who didn't fare too well when their homes were torn down. Ed and I reminisced and grilled each other for nearly an hour. Finally, we agreed our long-overdue reunion would be in early December 2015.

Joe Pytel deserves a lot of credit for this chapter, as well as for the entire book. He constantly reminds me of how all of this stuff fits together. For instance, one of the few guys who worked with Ed Cody as much as, or even more than I did, was a guy named Larry Nestor. Just so you know, Larry has his own chapter a little later.

"Wouldn't it be great to interview both Larry and Ed?" Joe suggested. Yeah, that would be awesome. Larry and I maintained somewhat regular contact throughout the decades. I know I should have been searching for several more throughout the years. Oh, well … Now I couldn't wait to ring Larry once again.

"I tracked down Ed Cody," I shouted at him. Only the person who answers says "hello." I took care to no longer say that I "dug Ed Cody up," as I did in my interview with Carl Giammarese of the Buckinghams.

"What do you think about coming with Joe and I to interview him?" I asked. Obviously, he was thrilled—not only about the interview, but the fact that I actually asked. Fast forward to the day of our meeting, but first …

Larry and I spent a lot of time in the area that Ed Cody now calls home. He lives at a pretty nice retirement facility in a near west suburb of Chicago. We took Grand Avenue (one of the few roads that will get you across the Des Plaines River to our destination). I was glad there were no out-of-towners in the car. They would get pretty sick of hearing about all of the buildings that used to be there.

Larry, Joe, and I found the converted-hotel high-rise easily enough. It's easily visible from the expressway. It's too bad nobody thought of putting an exit ramp there while it was still a hotel. What a rare lucky break for senior citizens. We checked in with a genuine concierge, who confirmed that Ed Cody was expecting company. We stepped aside and waited for him to amble out. During our last call, he mentioned he was looking forward to his 80th birthday on January 4, 2016. He sounded great on the phone so I assumed (correctly) he had some "amble" left.

I really didn't know exactly what shape he would be in physically. The last time I saw him was a full 45 years ago. Now, he had hippie-length hair and wore a flannel shirt. He was actually able to pull this look off. I was jealous. I always try to look spiffy in public. The rest of our group strived for comfort. After a round of handshakes, hugs, and introductions (Joe Pytel hadn't met Ed yet), he led us to the elevator, and we stepped out near the basement community area. We commandeered a table near the breakroom vending machines (our own conference table).

After doing so many of these interviews, I've developed a theory about memory. People near our age constantly admit spotty memory about recent meals or television shows. However, we can often rattle off names, dates, sights, smells, and song lyrics from experiences from decades ago. I'm not claiming to be a neurologist or psychiatrist. I'm the Screaming Wildman. Maybe record promoters of my era were like psychologists. They looked for ways to get lyrics into the heads of listeners.

Here's the theory: Short-term memory is like the junk drawer in your kitchen. It's a collection of things we feel are too valuable to throw away, but not important enough to organize.

Long-term memory is like the rest of your kitchen cabinets and drawers: You have a place for everything. While we were immersed in the activities of the music business, our passion told our brains this information was important and it would be necessary to retrieve it at a moment's notice. I bet you could cook a gourmet dinner for guests and wash the dishes after they left before you could find a paper clip in your junk drawer.

Wait until you read the stuff that tumbles out of this unscripted conversation between old friends who can pick up where they left off decades ago.

The Quintessential Engineer

First, I got a snapshot of our reunion. Ed was between Larry Nestor and me. Joe Pytel stood there at the far right. Then I got the ball rolling.

"Ed, I remember the very last time I saw you. You and I were at a flea market on Milwaukee Avenue at the double drive-in near Palwaukee Airport. You rushed away before I could get your attention," I said. Ed just chuckled. You see, flea markets were (and still are) a passion for me. To an innovative audio engineer like Ed Cody, flea markets were probably more like a pastime. That's why I remembered that day and he didn't. You know what I'm sayin'?

"How many groups do you think you recorded in your time?" I began.

"In 43 years? Maybe 500. I never kept track," Ed shot back. I reminded him the Daughters of Eve recorded there, as well as Larry Nestor, of course. I came up with a far more interesting question, and Ed took off from there.

"Which was the most popular group you ever worked with?" Out of maybe 500? It took only a second for him to answer.

"That would be the Coca-Cola commercial the Fifth Dimension did. I got a phone message from the McCann-Erickson advertising agency. Of course, I thought someone was pulling my leg. When I called back, I found out it was legitimate. Why would they come to me?" he asked us. I think he knew the answer but was too modest to say so, even now: because he was a respected and legendary engineer who could help them with their problem when none of the big-ticket "coastal" studios could.

As Ed explained it, all of the instrumental tracks for the commercial were already done. In 1969, Ed Cody just "happened" to have the necessary equipment to overdub the voices of the most electrifying quintet (perhaps of all time).

"I was the only one in Chicago who recorded 8 separate tracks on one-inch tape. They brought theirs to my studio. I could see that they were a little skeptical at first. My place didn't look anything like Universal in New York. The group was so precise and professional," Ed said. He hesitated for a short time. I could see how proud he was of his work. Apparently, a beer-and-pizza Chicago studio could effectively "mix it up" (pun intended) with a champagne-and-caviar counterpart. The commercial hit the airwaves in 1969.

"The Fifth Dimension liked my work so much they reserved a front-row table at one of their shows for me," Ed concluded. I think it was the only commercial the group ever did. Now that you know the back story, I bet you will never enjoy any commercial as much as this one. https://youtu.be/m_ecw3r8_CA.

How did Ed Cody work his way up to the pinnacle of his profession? First, let's work our way back a little bit. Hall Recording Studios was located at 226 S. Wabash and owned by Stu Black and Bill Hall, both students of Bill Putnam.

Putnam was the pioneer of recording processes still in use today. He was the founder of Universal Recording in Chicago, designed the first recording desks, and developed artificial reverb techniques.

I said *artificial* reverberation. Ed reminded us Putnam originally created the sought-after effect using the same commonplace means that produced the signature doo-wop sound for nearly all groups.

"**Peg O My Heart**" by the Harmonicats was originally recorded in the boys' bathroom at Universal. The tile walls and marble floors were a perfect echo chamber," Ed explained. Obviously, we all were interested in creating that sound. If you listened to any vintage commercials (especially mine), you'll hear what I'm talking about.

I figured this was the ideal time to ask Ed Cody how he came to take over the Hall Recording Studio and re-brand it.

"I went to Valparaiso Technical Institute, where I studied radio engineering and broadcasting. When I finished my education, I started recording in my parents' basement. My dad wasn't too pleased with the characters I was inviting into his house. He gave me the money to take over the business from Stu Black and Bill Hall," Ed stated. Afterward, Stu Black did great engineering work on recordings for the Cryan' Shames, Ides of March, the New Colony Six, Minnie Riperton, and Muddy Waters, among others. Ed Cody continues …

"When I got out of the Army, I sat in on a Frank Sinatra recording session at Western Recorders Studio in Hollywood, California. Frank was behind an old Telefunken microphone, right among the musicians. This was a single-track recording. If there were any mistakes, he would call a halt to the session and it would start from the beginning. I also got a chance to see Pearl Bailey there, before I returned to Chicago.

"I changed the name of the studio to StereoSonic and continued to upgrade my equipment to keep up with the times. I saw the recording business go from mono to stereo. Recording went to two-track, then three, and then 8-track on one-inch tape. Chess Records came up with 12-track recording on two-inch tape," Ed said.

Chess had a lot to offer recording artists at that time. It had a publishing company, recording studio, pressing plant, radio station, and distribution outlets. That's what you call the "whole ball of wax," I was blown away at the depth of Ed's recollection.

"My studio was in a high-noise area, so I had a special room-within-a-room built. That cement floor needed to be pumped and poured because there was no way to hoist wheelbarrows full of wet concrete to the upper level," Ed said. I guess you could say he inspired construction engineers as well.

In spite of Chess Records' domination, StereoSonic was a much sought-after recording studio thanks to the awesome reputation of Ed Cody.

"I specialized in blues and gospel recording. Organizations and churches would press records to make a little money. I recorded on location for Operation Breadbasket with Rev. Jesse Jackson and with Stax Records in Memphis," he continued. I forgot Ed Cody actually produced a record or two.

"I helped Wayne Worley and the Worleybirds record a song called **Red Headed Woman**. He had a house in Tennessee with a piano downstairs. I remember the house didn't have hot water. Anyway, I was right in the room with the musicians and mixing it using earphones.

"Once we created the master, I sent it to the pressing plant. I convinced the manager to throw some colored, vinyl chips into the pressing machine. Some **Red Headed Woman** records had multi-colors. The British did this very often. They would press a photo between two clear-vinyl sides. I remember some Sergeant Pepper records were done that way. Also, some from the Steve Miller Band. These designer records had a different sound. They were mostly for display," he reminded us. History, engineering, and music in one lesson: Thanks, Ed!

A Tape Behind the Vinyl

Aside from recording original pieces, Ed did a lot of restoration work. You will marvel at what he did, long before the age of computers. Check this out …

"Someone brought me one of his prized 78 records with a crack that extended through the entire grooved section. He asked if I could somehow remove the 'click' each time the phonograph needle hit it. I told him to leave it with me and I'll figure something out.

"I converted one of my machines to record at 100 inches per second. At that speed, each click on the tape was about a half-inch in length. I cued the beginning and end of each click and marked it on the quarter-inch tape.

"Next, I sliced out each segment with a razor blade and used splicing tape to mend each split. The project took about a week, but the customer was amazed and thrilled that he now had a clean recording after I duplicated the spliced version," Ed concluded.

You have to admire the ingenuity it takes to come up with a solution, given the tools available 50 years ago. Here's another restoration story for you. I swear, Ed Cody's memory and energy continue to amaze me.

"Reynolds Metals was making 'skins' for military rockets. Robotic production was managed by the old-fashioned computers resembling reel-to-reel tape recorders. A 'bad' section of the tape kept stopping production. I used my razor blade and splicing block to get them up and running," he said. Wow, Ed, it seemed the security of the nation rested on your shoulders for a while.

I got to watch Ed Cody in action and was awed by his ability to splice together a project from several reels at once. I couldn't understand how he managed to keep things straight. Radio stations had pretty strict rules when it came to the length of commercials. When they said a "spot" was supposed to be one minute, they meant one minute.

I would take my recordings to Ed Cody at StereoSonic, and he would speed them up to meet the requirements. He saved me so much time and money, you would not believe it. I could talk plenty fast because I memorized my scripts. I would rely on Ed to make them fill the slotted time exactly. I don't think he ever had to extend my recordings. Sicilians talk until their time is up and still get in a last word (or two). See?

Often, those last words repeat an advertiser's phone number. You can't just lop something off of the end of a clip; you have to have someone like Ed compress it. Remember when I talked about that "memory" thing? Here's the part of the interview where I amused Larry, Joe, and Ed with my complete rendition of the Zig-Zag Sewing Machine Company commercial. I even remembered the phone number. That's the whole idea, right? When the listeners got out of their cars after hearing my radio spot, they were supposed to remember "Randolph 6, 8600. That's Randolph 6, 8600" until they got a scratch pad and pencil.

Larry and Joe were in awe when they heard our recollections. I almost forgot there were two other guys with chapters in my book sitting here with me. I want to show the long-lasting friendship Larry and Ed developed through the years. This is a perfect way for Larry to join the conversation.

"Carl, I remember you and I sitting in Manzo's Restaurant and ordering pizza when you did that commercial for the guys," Larry said. Yeah, I'm proud of those times and the people who created them. I'm in very select company today.

Awesome Chicago Artists

Engineers and performing artists played equal parts in the production of a record. Sometimes the credits get a little confusing. On many of my Daughters of Eve records, you will see engineering credits for Ron Malo (Chess), Gary Knipper, or Ed Cody. A number of gifted songwriters had close ties with StereoSonic. The two we talked about during this "gang" interview were Jimmy Peterson (credited as James Butler on the Daughters of Eve hit **Symphony of My Soul**) and our own Larry Nestor.

"Jimmy was a little wild," Ed reminded us. From one songwriter to another, he was a bit of a mystery, too.

"Jimmy once told me he constructed a song in his head, and then wrote it out like a letter. When it hit the paper, he never made any corrections," Larry recalled. Maybe this is the first time Larry ever told anyone. It could be this "morsel" stayed tucked away until just the right time. Wherever else you read about Jimmy Peterson, you can associate this as well.

In this book, I chronicle a few "where were you when" moments. This moment dealt with the Democratic National Convention. The date was August 28, 1968. I set the stage for Ed and Larry.

I knew exactly where Ed Cody was that evening. According to Denny Murray from the Lincoln Park Zoo, his brother Tommy was recording the lead vocals on **Playgirl** (the song that Thee Prophets released—you can read the story in the Zoo chapter) at StereoSonic. I could see the spark of recognition in Ed's eyes as Larry said …

"I was working as a songwriter for One-derful! Records in the late '60s. The address was 1827-29 S. Michigan Avenue, where United Record Distributors was located. I can remember the police had jeeps with boards (topped with barbed wire) bolted on the front bumpers to push back protesters. I actually had the night off when the cops made a 'stand' at 18th Street."

For those of you unfamiliar with the Windy City, the barricade that Larry described was apparently intended to keep lower-income protesters from pushing into Grant Park a few blocks north of Record Row. There was a lot of crazy crap associated with those events. If you enter "shoot to kill / Chicago" into your search engine window, you will have your pick of articles.

We're agreed these were jumpy times. They did lead to a couple of comical stories involving Larry and Ed. I don't know how we got to this point. I'm pretty sure that these stories might have been lost, if not for our meeting.

Picture Larry on the roof of the building that housed the StereoSonic studio. He had an armload of water balloons, and someone called the police to report suspicious activity. Did you know when you throw a water balloon onto the hood of a police car, it sounds very much like a gunshot?"

Gee, Larry seemed to be at "ground zero" during a lot of mischief in the downtown area.

"Remember, Ed, I was helping you move your studio from 226 Wabash to 528 Michigan Avenue? It was a weekend, and nobody told the cops there would be someone loading a truck at the back entry," Larry said. "When we finished, one of our helpers jumped into the back for a ride over to your new place. I was following in my car, and I saw the truck ride up on the curb and nearly tip over rounding the corner at Adams and Wabash. The truck was still tilted when the cops pulled up. I'm hoping that the guy in the back doesn't tumble out right then. You remember that, Ed?"

"I was drivin'," Ed said with that same devilish glint I still remember.

Of Course, There's More

Ed didn't spend all of his time in the studio. He also had a chance to get "up close and personal" with celebrities and the public on field assignments for a number of television news crews. The experiences ranged from the awful unrest that we just talked about to things that could only be categorized as once in a lifetime.

"I worked as a sound technician during a Beatles concert. The audience was behind barriers near the stage, and several people handed me their cameras so I could snap a better picture for them," Ed said.

Ed Cody mentioned a lot of folks he's worked with in his 40-plus years in the business. There's no doubt he could still be working his magic even now.

"When the business shifted from analog to digital, I decided I wasn't going to invest in new equipment. Forty years was enough for me. I was in the business until the end of the century. The Record Dugout on West 63rd has a lot of my records," Ed said. "I did a lot of work with Phil Orsi, and I remember a song by Eddie Silvers called **Mr. Clean**. You know, like the soap. I wish I knew somebody who had a copy."

Man, we sure fit a lot of memories into that one session.

Ed talked about recording the Garrett sisters and how he helped Sue Garrett become one of the more respected sound engineers in Chicago. We wrapped up with an honorable mention for Bob and Jack Weiner at Sheldon Recording Studios on Wells Street.

Ed Cody enhanced the careers of thousands of folks during his decades of ground-breaking work. All of Chicago is grateful to you, my good friend. Here's to the old times (and many more "next" times)!

Eclectic Images

This was destined to be the only blank page in my book. I was never one to be wasteful, so I included more stuff here.

Chicago Sun-Times photo (1949) of my friends and I shooting marbles (guess where!)

I want to put as many of my childhood pictures in the book as I can.

Some of my friends at Seward Park (1949)
Anthony Morgan (top)
(left) Rodrigo Ricente, Richard Martin, Phillip Marsala
St. Joseph's Church is in the background.

Sheldon Cooper

Once again, I found myself in a position that required my dormant investigative skills. When most people reach my age, they get a little cautious when inquiring about someone older than themselves. I understandably tiptoed around when inquiring about Sheldon Cooper, the guy who started the Buckinghams' ball rolling.

Not only is he most likely the biggest name in Chicago television, but he is also a national independent programming giant. Your Google search clue should be Sheldon-Cooper-WGN. Otherwise, you'll be assaulted with an endless list of results about a character from a currently top-rated network show.

The flesh-and-blood television pioneer I'm featuring agreed to an interview for this book. (Can you believe it?) I think it's only fitting to include him in this my book. He's just another guy who deserves a book of his own. Let's hope I can give him a fitting tribute in the following paragraphs.

I found a *Chicago Tribune* article Sheldon wrote on November 10, 1968. Some readers will immediately remember that color television was a big deal then. There was a considerable investment required to beam a color signal into Chicagoland households. I could safely compare Sheldon's era to the MTV of the '60s (only better).

His vision created a phenomenon and revolutionized broadcasting. By the time he wrote that article in 1968, WGN (Channel 9) had gone from a few minutes of color broadcasting each day 12 years previously to over 5,200 hours of color programming. He describes "colorcasts" of Chicago Cubs, Blackhawks, and Bulls games, as well as Big Ten basketball and Illinois high school sporting events.

WGN and Sheldon Cooper were doing the same thing DJs were doing in the record industry. It was hard to distinguish whether color television was satisfying a market or creating one. It was a lot of both. Brilliant. Color sports programming fed the market and was responsible for the sales of thousands of color TV sets. What could justify the expense for the average household?

Children could tune in to color broadcasts of *Bozo's Circus, Ray Rayner and His Friends, Family Classics, Romper Room, Garfield Goose,* the *Flintstones,* and

Ark in the Park to start. Many of those shows featured theatrical (and educational) cartoons as well.

"We have geared our studio operations almost 100 percent to color," Sheldon stated in the article. Talk about being in the right place at the right time: With the right TV station, with Sheldon Cooper in charge, with a new studio production of his new program featuring local musical talent, what could be better? Oh, yeah, the name of the group would have to change from the Pulsations. That's never happened to anyone else before, right? (You'll see!)

Department and appliance stores would put color TVs in the window to attract customers. They would twist the dial to Channel 9 and leave it there for the whole time. Sheldon's quote reminded us of fantastic celebrity power and persuasiveness, backed by the most stunning technology of the era.

"John Drury and the News, Weatherman Harry Volkman, and sports reports by Wendell Smith. The Channel 9 news department for years has covered all local news with color film. Our Washington and Springfield news bureaus also provide 100 percent color coverage," he concluded. Actually he was just getting started.

"With the completion of the John Hancock building, Channel 9 and other stations will be moving their antennas to the top of this towering structure ... the color television we said would be coming years ago is now overwhelmingly here. Perhaps in five years from now, we will be writing about Channel 9's three-dimensional color programming," he predicted. Someone else dropped the ball on this one. Sheldon Cooper was a true visionary. Technology couldn't keep up.

Did he predict the Buckinghams' success or make it happen? It was obviously a good deal of both. I'm still blown away by how he's willing to contribute and thrilled that he is able to. Am I surprised? Not in the least. He is living proof that you can think yourself into nine decades of vitality and community building. WGN defined Chicago—and defined us (especially me). Maybe this book thing was a good idea after all.

Live and In Person ...

The one and only president of WGN agreed to a phone interview. Are you kidding? For your pleasure and amazement, he eagerly reminded me of his age. At 90, the remarkable Sheldon Cooper has the unfaltering speech of someone decades younger. Straight off, I let him know it.

I kicked off my telephone interview with my appreciation for his accomplishments, many of which I mentioned earlier here. He gave me his email address. This is a little embarrassing for me (someone with an old-school fear of computers), but such a tribute to the programming genius I have on the line.

"There's another Sheldon Cooper who everyone is talking about," he jokingly reminded me. Man, maybe that's one of the reasons he is still on top of his game. The real-life Sheldon Cooper is ready to roll.

"You probably want to go right to the Buckinghams' story," he suggested. No, I'll go wherever you lead. Good thing, because he is off like a shot.

"Right time and right place, that's what it's all about, isn't it? This was a last-minute thing. You were looking and I was looking. We put the audition together right away," he remembered. He was also ready to give us all a little background of the *All Time Hits* show and his hopes for it. I was so intent on getting exposure for the Pulsations, the rest was just a blur. Sheldon sensed that it was time to lay more of the story out there, after more than 50 years. I bet he thought I would never ask. Actually, I still forgot. He was willing to bail me out.

"We wanted to make this show like a Broadway production, with the talent to cover every type of popular song. That included the rock-and-roll Beatles," he started. Without Sheldon, it would never have started for the Buckinghams. Today, he was ready to pay tribute to the rest of the marvelous talent he assembled beforehand. Our brief mention doesn't do them justice, but here goes.

Bob Carroll (former singer with Glenn Miller and Jimmy Dorsey orchestras) was the host and singer. See, each show represented all forms of music and performing arts. This was an awesome production. The soon-to-be Buckinghams were emerging. The rest of the troupe was accomplished and well-recognized. Carroll did theatre (fancy spelling, huh?) and movies, too. He was a perfect example of professionalism (in case I wasn't enough for my guys).

Sheldon Cooper somehow knew his shows were destined to not only last a lifetime, but also be just as desirable as ever. Why else would you be able to see a color clip (https://youtu.be/UDD1AfbO9Fg) introducing his co-stars? He recognized the demand for the video before there could be any.

See why this guy is so great? He knew there would be a YouTube someday. He didn't know what it would be called, of course. He knew someone like you would want to relive the moments created by all of the artists thrown together by circumstance.

The audio on my CD made it a little hard to catch the names of the other artists. There were …

Billy Williams (earned a gold record for **I'm Gonna Sit Right Down and Write Myself a Letter**), singers **Bob Newkirk** and **Doree Crews**, the **Joe Eich Singers** (appeared on a Tony Bennett TV special and *An Evening With …*).

Bob Trendler's Band was best known as the musical backup for Chicago's famous *Bozo's Circus*. Before that, Bob was a sought-after arranger who worked with George Gershwin, Cab Calloway, and Duke Ellington in New York.

Oops, I almost forgot the **Sue Charles Dancers**.

As we now know, that 13-week series was destined to become a once-in-a-lifetime experience. I finally got a chance to ask him why.

"It was just too expensive. It was an hour-long, broadcast-live production in color. The studio was nearly booked solid with our regular programming," he said. That meant rehearsals were during rare "off" hours. Each act did a couple of numbers every week. Bob Trendler probably did the bulk of arranging. Aside from the expense, it was draining for the performers and the studio.

"It was like a regular Broadway production with costume and scene changes," he said. I could sense he loved it all. It just wasn't sustainable.

While I had Sheldon on the line, I mentioned the WGN references I already had in this chapter. He happily added a few more, including one of his rare failures.

"We thought the Chicago audience was ready for a soccer broadcast, and we set up our cameras in Soldier Field. Counting me, there were probably 10 people in the seats," he said with a chuckle. He might not have liked the overall result, but I could tell he enjoyed testing the boundaries. There were few obstacles Sheldon Cooper's WGN couldn't conquer.

"We did so much original programming at Tribune Entertainment and WGN" he continued. Sheldon had so many creative roles that it was amazing.

"We had a show called *An Evening With …* featuring artists like Count Basie, Duke Ellington, or Gary Lewis and the Playboys," he stated. Each act had the entire hour to themselves. Sheldon served as the executive producer. Oh, yeah, this show also aired in 1965, as if there wasn't enough going on at the time.

"We had the Back Porch Majority on one week. They were very popular at the time," he recalled. This folk group must have been one of Sheldon's favorites. The group was hot enough (or safe enough) at the time to entertain at Lyndon Johnson's White House in 1965.

Before the Buckinghams stood among rock-and-roll royalty, the band was handpicked to showcase a broadcasting empire headed by Sheldon Cooper. All of the other talent on that show was chosen the same way. I'm glad they got a little recognition here, too. That's the least I can do for the guy who gave us all a huge break. Finally, I asked him about more independent shows he introduced.

"Tribune Entertainment launched *At the Movies* with Gene Siskel and Roger Ebert and the *Joan Rivers Show* (awarded a Daytime Emmy). For a time, the *Phil Donahue Show* was produced at WGN," Sheldon concluded.

We could have gone on for hours about his triumphs, but I could tell we accomplished our goal. If you look around, you'll see the indelible Sheldon Cooper mark everywhere in broadcasting, and especially in Chicago and at WGN. I hope these few lines are considered an adequate thank you from us all. I'm proud I tracked him down and honored he was willing to chat. Okay, just a little more.

In 2004, Ted Okuda and Jack Mulqueen published *The Golden Age of Chicago Children's Television*. An incredible number of those shows were the work of Sheldon Cooper and the amazing family at WGN Channel 9.

At the time of Sheldon's 1968 prophetic article, he hadn't hired Bill Jackson and Dirty Dragon (one of my favorites). That wouldn't be until 1973 or so. I was watching a lot more TV during my self-imposed exile from the music business in the '70s .

Everybody Sheldon Cooper hired knew how to deliver. That's why I'm flattered he recognized enough talent in the Buckinghams to give them a shot. Actually, I'm honored we helped him realize his vision. I was just as thrilled as the band to be in the same studio that educated and entertained us all since childhood.

The *All Time Hits* show that launched the Buckinghams was considered a historic moment by many. By 1978, WGN began satellite broadcasting. The earliest dish owners and the earliest cable companies picked up the signal, and WGN became a national superstation. The Chicago Cubs gained global fans when the WGN signal went international. Okay, the Tribune Company owned both, so that had something to do with it.

WGN-TV projected a neighborhood vibe because it was actually right across the street (at least for us). As you remember, the Buckinghams spent a lot of time chillin' in front of Lane Tech on Addison Street. From there, we could cruise a couple of blocks down N. Campbell and be at its famous West Bradley Place studio.

On occasion, you could see familiar broadcast icons riding the bus to work. Are you kidding me? In 1983, WGN began branding itself as "Chicago's Very Own." We all thought of WGN as our own all along, thanks to the groundbreaking work of Sheldon Cooper.

If It's the Last Thing I'll Ever Do …

… so be it! Deadlines, production schedules, and rules in general mean nothing to the Screaming Wildman. When I see an opportunity I take advantage of it. I got this brilliant idea with my publication date looming one month away. What if I get a photo of both 90-year-old contributors to my book posing together? It's brilliant, I tell you. I made it even better by inviting Joe Pytel along.

Weeks earlier, I personally dropped off the rough draft of Sheldon's chapter. I wanted him to see that I did my homework after our earlier interview and looked up all of the other performers appearing with the Buckinghams on Sheldon's *All Time Hits* broadcasts. Now, he had a black-and-white reminder of

Billy Williams, Bob Newkirk, Doree Crews, Bob Carroll, the Joe Eich Singers, and Sue Charles Dancers. There was plenty to start a conversation rolling.

This was so much like putting a hit record together. However, Sheldon Cooper put together national broadcasts. He's also responsible for launching handfuls of careers, and propelling others on to national (if not international) fame. He's also enviably active for a man of any age. I was trying to work out the logistics and game plan for getting Sheldon Cooper and Ed Kelly together.

This turned out to be easier than I thought, because both of these guys are more adaptable and generous than the Screaming Wildman on more occasions than I'm willing to admit. I offered to chauffeur Sheldon to Ed's office and he readily agreed. He is remarkably nimble and had little problem maneuvering into the front seat of my hatchback on a drizzly Wednesday morning.

Of course, I was prepared with tape recorder rolling and ready to capture the highlights of his stream of recollections. Sheldon is a real trouper. Turns It turns out he had cataract surgery the day before our interview and a follow-up doctor's visit that very morning. He apologized for wiping away a tear or two (lest it be mistaken for his joy at seeing me). I guarantee you'll shed a few drops yourself, before this chapter is over, though.

I no more than watched my guest of honor buckle himself in and we were immersed in the interview on Sheldon's time and terms. I yield to the master.

"I just went to a Cole Porter salute at the Auditorium theater—his 125th birthday … big orchestra … deep lyrics. It was very meaningful for me. My wife loved those lyrics … I miss her every day," Sheldon began. Mary Cooper passed away the previous year (July 2015). I'm in awe of a guy so adept as weaving the present and the past together.

Let it be known, I'm still at the curb. I introduced Sheldon to Joe and mentioned how important he is to keeping me alive on the internet. Sheldon tells me about his daily use of Amazon Echo and his personal assistant *Alexa*. Guys like him are not intimidated by the technology (now or then). I think he is a little bummed that it wasn't available while he was at WGN.

Maybe Sheldon wouldn't have retired at all if the technology could have kept up with his vision. I just concentrate on remembering to shut my blinker off when I pull into traffic. I soon thrill my companions with another flawlessly-executed U-turn an head north to our appointment.

"Do you still have a license,"?" Sheldon asked (jokingly, I think).

"How old are you now, Carl?" he pressed onward. He is one of the most inquisitive guys I ever met. I bet Sheldon gives *Alexa* a workout. I see his fertile mind and active imagination turn a car ride into a chapter of broadcast history (not to mention a blueprint for project development). He wouldn't let me forget his disarming sense of humor either.

"I'm 76," I tell Sheldon, no longer used to being "schooled" by a wiser elder.

"I remember doing '76' in about ten minutes!" Sheldon counters.

We're now tooling past Wrigley Field (with my blinker finally off) and marveled at the new construction, now that the Chicago Cubs are an international brand. The corner of Clark and Addison is destined to be even more of a tourist destination and chic night spot. The old "Franksville" (featuring genuine Chicago dogs from my era) would never cut it.

I predict the Cubs will win the 2016 World Series the day before my book is destined for market. There's nothing like capitalizing on that good feeling. Sheldon, as usual, is ready with his next broadcasting lesson. He was at the helm of all WGN broadcasting, including sports, of course.

"I just went to a Cubs game a couple of weeks a go, and it was packed," Sheldon marvels. We both remember when you could make up your mind to see a game the same day and have your choice of tickets.

"On game days, I could drive right up to the door and have a couple of ballpark hot dogs while checking in on the broadcast team," Sheldon chuckled. Did Sheldon have anything to do with the Cubs becoming the blossoming franchise we now see playing out? I'll tell you—then you tell me! Follow this if you can:

Sheldon works his way up to WGN president … WGN becomes an independent station … WGN begins "colorcasts" of Cub daytime games (all there was during Sheldon's heyday), creating fans as far as the signal would reach … WGN becomes a "super station" during the infancy of cable television … all WGN programming becomes hot property (surpassing Turner Broadcasting, in my opinion) … Harry Caray turns ratings into gold (tinged with Cubbie blue).

Is Sheldon Cooper responsible? In my book (literally), he certainly is. Sheldon catches sight of the Ernie Banks and Ron Santo statues on Addison, but his focus is on the missing figure.

"Harry Caray has a statue here at Wrigley [not in our sight, on Waveland], Jack Brickhouse should be here as well," Sheldon says. I agree, he was a versatile broadcasting pioneer, a lovely guy and one-time neighbor of Sheldon in later times. Brickhouse has a statue on Michigan Ave., near the river and the Tribune Tower.

Would there be so many statues of Chicago sports figures without Sheldon Cooper and Jack Brickhouse (broadcaster of Cubs, Bears, Bulls, White Sox, as well as Chicago wrestling, soccer, and international boxing matches)?

These things are pouring from the venerated Sheldon Cooper faster than anyone could ever write or type. We're still on Addison street a couple of blocks west of Wrigley, and Sheldon is ready to transition after the mention of Harry

Creighton, the WGN sportscaster often known for tantalizingly pouring the sponsor's beer for viewers (and refusing to let it go to waste once the camera cut away). Sheldon masterfully transitions to a career propelled by the WGN springboard ...

"WGN used to do the Tavern Pale [beer] Music Contest. Do you know who the host was? Mike Wallace from *60 Minutes*," Sheldon reminded us. Yeah, Mike was a Chicago-based sports announcer turned game-show host, turned trusted television investigative journalist. He was also a pitch man for the neighborhood brewery at the time (Fullerton and Bosworth, walking distance for me).

Sheldon continues to take our interview and transform it in into an awesome educational opportunity. That's why he was named Vice President of Program Development for WGN Continental Productions Company in 1966. That would become an easier-to-remember Tribune Entertainment shortly afterward—different name, but same mission on a larger stage.

Sheldon always knew how to develop a story, so I was anxious for him to continue. The Buckinghams and I always considered ourselves lucky to work with such a classy organization, with such an awesome guy in charge of it all. Sheldon didn't merely touch and influence people, he shaped their careers in the most subtle, but powerful way.

"I would start projects, then give the producers credit," Sheldon starts.

"Do you remember the *Mystery of Al Capone's Vaults* show?" Sheldon asked. Joe and I chuckle. Sheldon pauses to allow our thoughts of Geraldo Rivera and his two-hour syndicated live show, aired in late April of 1986, trickle back on their own. We remembered they didn't find anything but a couple of bottles. That was quite a let-down, since the viewing public was expecting bodies and a boatload of cash.

"Yeah, that's how everyone reacts." Sheldon catches us laughing.

"Tribune Entertainment was the distributor," he says. What? Responsible for a loser?

"We did find something," Sheldon set the hook, and proudly related the rest of the story. He was thoroughly enjoying himself as much as Joe and I were enjoying his company.

"There was a big party planned once we signed off that night. Geraldo was a big believer in the project and certain we would find something. He was a great host and it was a great show," Sheldon said. Yeah, most of us average viewers could never relate to that much disappointment or humiliation—and had no business judging anyone.

"The next day everyone was still down. Geraldo was just crushed. When I got to the office the next day, I walked past the glass cage where those ticker-tape machines would transmit the ratings. Two sad-faced guys inside the booth waved, then came out when they saw me. 'What do you think?' one of them asked me. I said, 'Huuuuuuuge!' I actually borrowed that from a recent political figure," Sheldon laughed, before concluding.

"Actually, I smiled, and they both burst out laughing. I knew they were putting me on earlier. The ratings were phenomenal. In fact, no syndicated broadcast since has ever reached that rating nationally. It still stands as the number one show. In Chicago, only the Bears during championship runs or Michael Jordan's Bulls ever did better. What did we get out of it? The best ratings in the world!"

The "Carl" Connection

Sheldon Cooper and I had so many uncanny Addison Street connections I felt it was the perfect avenue (pun intended) for our mobile interview. We already mentioned Wrigley Field. I hosted tons of dances at Antoine's Ballroom (Lincoln and Addison). I pitched my dances at Lane Tech High School using my portable high-decibel DJ setup across the street at Addison and Western.

Nearly everyone at the WGN studios on Bradley Place spent time on Addison Street during their daily commute. Back then, many of them literally heard me before they heard *of* me. From the time Sheldon agreed to our "road trip" and finally meeting again face to face, I was trying to figure out who at WGN was responsible for the our original meeting.

I floated a name out there for Sheldon Cooper and felt a warm glow spread as he re-traced his path back to the time he last mentioned that guy. I think Carl Greyson was the reason the Buckinghams got that audition. Mr. Greyson was born in the Midwest (Milwaukee) and did some serious theatre in the Big Apple. Years later, his fans would find out he was a guest in the studio where Orson Welles broadcast *War of the Worlds* in 1938.

Carl became a versatile announcer. He was already gifted with an extraordinary voice and leading-man looks that served him well on New York stages. By the time he ended up at WGN (1955), he was perfect for the new media Sheldon Cooper was creating. Carl worked on both WGN TV and Radio. He hosted *Night Beat*, which started about 1:30am after the late movie.

Audiences knew him as the soft voice and friendly face that delivered newscasts and introduced all sorts of shows. He was a new-media journalist. In 1962, Carl Greyson was recognized as the best news announcer by the *American College of Radio Arts, Crafts and Sciences*. Obviously, the people in the industry, and especially at WGN, held him in high esteem.

Sheldon Cooper was (and still is) a visionary and clear communicator. Everyone at WGN knew what (and who) he needed for the *All Time Hits* show. I'm guessing it was Carl Greyson who had the moxie and whimsy to suggest a meeting with Sheldon and that "screaming wildman" blasting rock-and-roll music toward the Lane Tech campus at lunch hour.

To say "the rest is history" is a disservice to both Sheldon and Carl Greyson. By the way, Carl hosted *Creature Features* (exactly what it sounds like) some time later and *The Three Stooges Show*, too. He knew how to deliver without taking himself too seriously. A—real entertainer.

Here's what makes Sheldon so exceptional: He shared his vision with everyone and welcomed their participation. The results were revolutionary. The entire WGN family did what the Screaming Wildman could never have done alone. Sheldon created the "vehicle" for the Buckinghams to gain prominence.

Carl Greyson and others in the WGN family got a chance to catch my rock-and-roll road show. Another WGN family member named John Opager gave the band an ideal name to combat the British invasion. Opager was a security guard at the station, but a valued part of the team.

As I mentioned, Sheldon shared his vision with everyone, and they responded in amazing ways. The Buckinghams and I give a respectful shout out to the late John Opager. Sheldon knew John's daily commute to work took him past the iconic Buckingham fountain. Little personal details add up to tremendous success in strange ways.

"I had a lot of freedom to create programming and I really like music," Sheldon sums it up. I'm glad I have the chance to tell him I still enjoy the "master" at work. He was in charge of this interview all along.

Life Begins at 90—Part I

We're at Ed Kelly's office on Lawrence Avenue. I brought you up to date the best way I know how. Sheldon could obviously do better. His entire day is a virtual "story board" with decades of memories and triumphs. I have no idea why he isn't the subject of many books, or why he hasn't written one himself. For that matter, I don't see why there isn't a statue of him somewhere.

OK, it's time to introduce Ed Kelly in the next chapter. I'll meet you all there at the end for our promised meeting and photo shoot.

Ed Kelly

When collecting my notes for this book, I remembered the impression Ed Kelly made on me. If you ever lived in Chicago, you'll recognize his name. I'm talking about the Edmund Kelly from the Seward Park area, the committeeman from the 47th Ward, and the manager for the last Richard J. Daley mayoral campaign. At the age of 91, he maintains a regular schedule (if there is anything remotely "regular" in most 90-year-olds). I spent over two hours in his office on my first overdue visit (another occasion where my book allowed us to renew acquaintances). I should have been doing this anyway, I know.

I can't believe how energetic and "rememberful" this guy is. I know there is no such word. Well, it's in the urban dictionary. I needed to make up a special word for a guy like this. Someone apparently beat me to this one anyway. I first met Ed Kelly when I was a young kid. We finally had the chance to relate as adults, on subjects that I wouldn't have cared about back then. He probably related these stories dozens, maybe hundreds, of times to others throughout the decades, but he was patient enough to indulge me.

Ed's dad was a salesman for the Pabst Brewing Company. His mom was a housekeeper. Not a homemaker. Just taking care of her own kids and household would have been too easy. If you grew up in his generation, or mine, you identified closely with either your Catholic Parish or your local park. Really, your street address was not even necessary if you were going to meet someone. That's why Ed Kelly (or I) will still tell folks "I was born and raised in Seward Park."

That would hold exceptional meaning for Ed Kelly. He was a young boy during the Great Depression. From 1930 to 1932, he would

A dapper Ed Kelly in his outer office gallery

change addresses due to the economic issues he and many of his friends faced. Kids spent so much time at Seward Park; where they slept made little difference to anyone. When the economics got tough for a particular family, a kid's friends might never know. Even during the worst times, there were opportunities to play every outdoor sport. When weather forced kids inside, they played volleyball, basketball, ping-pong, or checkers. They had a social network.

Poor youths had the safety of supervised non-school activities. Ed reminded me kids could learn how to shoot dice across the street. There were only wholesome activities on park district property. Have you heard the old-fashioned expression "we weren't choir boys"? Even if you were, it left you 23 hours each day to prove to yourself you weren't. Times, and people, were tough.

Can you see how hours melt away when each recollection triggers another? More grown-up discussions continued. Ed was a guard on his basketball team at St. Phillip's High School and won All-City honors. Afterward, he joined the Marine Corps. During World War II, he was an aerial gunner in a Pacific squadron. When the war ended, he went to DePaul University under the GI bill, I believe. He even did a brief stint as a professional basketball player for the Oshkosh All-Stars before he got serious about finding a "real" job.

An endorsement from a local ward committeeman led to a series of positions in the Chicago Park District. As he steadily worked his way up the ladder, his most rewarding experiences were working with kids. For some, that might mean teaching the mechanics of a good jump shot. For others (both boys and girls), it could mean learning a good ping-pong serve.

For all, it meant another form (or the only form) of stability in a chaotic and troubled childhood. He was proud to mention some of his students who enjoyed national recognition. Even now, he spoke fondly of guys like Harold Ramis (just think *Ghostbusters*) or Gene Siskel (famous movie critic). Who knew both of them would be part of Chicago's dearly-departed history (Siskel - 1999 and Ramis - 2014) while their mentor continues to "rock on"?

Any visit with Ed Kelly will touch on politics, then inevitably circle back to his efforts with the Chicago Park District. Later, I describe the photo gallery he has on display—autographed pictures of political figures. One features Mayor Richard J. Daley, scarcely minutes before he was forever lost to all of Chicago. Once again, we focused on the autographed pictures of sports figures that adorn the walls of his office and reception area. What's left to do? Set up a return visit. There is a lot more I need to put in my book. By now, I'm pretty sure that our Seward Park bond is destined to continue.

Our Return Visit

One overdue visit would lead to a much more timely one. This time Joe Pytel was with me. Not only is he an awesome Chicago music historian, he is a lifelong sports fan. He is a few years younger than me but still part of a generation that equally respects the sacrifices of famous folks and celebrates their accomplishments. The return trip to the Ed Kelly Sports Program office on West Lawrence Avenue was pretty smooth. The school kids were safely in their classroom while the Screaming Wildman was on the road.

We were about 20 minutes early. There is that "old school" mentality, a throwback to the days I promoted records and groups. You spent a lot of time waiting, but you couldn't afford to have someone waiting for you. As soon as we stepped into the outer room of Ed Kelly's office, he bounded out to meet us. Busy people have a sincere appreciation for people's time. Old busy people like us have a sense of importance in all activities. Chalk that up to respect, not urgency. I didn't have to introduce Joe. Ed Kelly grabbed his hand and introduced himself.

Amateur Boxing

During my first visit, there was a framed photo that immediately caught my eye. I want a dramatic build-up to this next section. I'm talking about the personally autographed photo of the most influential and talented boxer of any generation, Muhammad Ali. The story of their association, and later their devoted friendship, was the highlight of our visit. What did a guy like Ed Kelly do to make an impression on an international sports hero and humanitarian like Ali? Sometimes our friends tend to be too modest.

"Did I ever tell you I was a welterweight boxing champion in the Marine Corps during World War II?" he asked. See? He may have told other people, but not me. FYI, the welterweight class is between 140 to 147 lbs. Check out one of the current pictures of Ed Kelly that I included. He's not far over that weight right now, in spite of spending decades in the "banquet" environment of traditional public servants.

"There are two people who helped make the Chicago Park District amateur boxing program one of the finest in the United States back in the late '70s. First, there was Bob Walsh, general manager of WMAQ-TV Channel 5. He was responsible for giving indispensable television exposure to all Chicago amateur athletes. The second person was none other than World Heavyweight Boxing Champion Muhammad Ali," he continued. Okay, now I needed to hear more. Ed Kelly proceeded to set the stage for the resurgence of boxing in Chicago, then the emergence of his program on the national stage. Follow along with me. We're talking about the year 1968, to start …

"Both the Chicago CYO [Catholic Youth Organization] and Chicago Tribune Golden Gloves competitions were about to end," he started. I would have said they were "on the ropes," but Ed was serious here.

"I started boxing programs in 22 park district locations. That year, we entered 200 boxers and supplied the necessary referees and judges for competitions," Ed said. Amateur boxing was starting to move away from church gyms and into the public park fieldhouses. Maybe each parish found a different way to entertain the youth, like school dances with an energetic MC like the Screaming Wildman.

"Muhammad Ali purchased most of the equipment for each boxing center. At the time, he wanted to remain an anonymous donor. The Champ made a personal appearance at Bessemer Park [89th Street and South Chicago Avenue] to help kick off the program," Ed continued. Chicago Park District boxing continued to thrive after that. In 1978, Chicago's International Amphitheater (42nd and Halsted streets) hosted the 9th Annual City-Wide Championship title bouts before a crowd estimated at 7,500. At its peak, there were 28 park locations with a boxing enrollment of more than 6,000.

Talk about an after-school program! Lots of kids were tough. That is just as true today as it was in the '30s and '40s. One advantage we had (maybe it needs re-prioritization today) was a model for combining toughness and training. Music schools and boxing centers encouraged discipline and practice. You should have known I was going to make a musical reference somewhere. All competition makes us stronger.

Ed with Chicago Mayor Jane Byrne, Perry Como,
Ed with President Jimmy Carter and "The Greatest"

Ed Kelly saw continuing need for after-school activities. He attracted paid supervisors with boxing experience for the program. The health and safety of the kids was too important to be in the hands of unfocused amateurs.

"I called Tony Zale [former Middleweight World Champion in the mid-1940s] and asked him to be the head boxing coach. We hired many former professional and amateur boxers from the area to teach," Ed said. For the record, Tony Zale was born in nearby Gary, Indiana. Ed had skilled professionals teaching both the science and strategies of life through sports. If you want to get a feel for what kids of that era learned, just look it up online.

Thanks to Ed Kelly, NBC-TV began televising the Chicago Park District Boxing Championships. The publicity helped him to negotiate an agreement with the Polish Olympic team to box local champions at the North Avenue Armory. The Irish Olympic team made an appearance at Soldier Field in front of an ABC Wide World of Sports international audience, Ed told us.

Due to the Russian invasion of Afghanistan a year earlier, President Jimmy Carter declared the United States would boycott the 1980 Olympic Games held in Moscow. The politics would be sorted out elsewhere (not really, maybe never). Ed Kelly organized the Chicago Olympics, with competition throughout the city. The boxing event drew nearly 6,000 to Grant Park.

Ed Kelly influenced me and played a part in many of my activities throughout the decades. There is something about growing up in the same postal code with a guy that gives you a sense of belonging. For us, it was Seward Park (375 W. Elm) and St. Joseph's Church (1107 N. Orleans) in the area once known as Little Sicily. I've described my house as "across the street" from Seward Park. If you look at a map, you'll see the park nearly surrounded our segment of Elm Street. The fastest way to get to our church from my house would be through the park, past the gymnasium building. So much opportunity and temptation—all visible from my front room window.

The park district made other contributions to my life. I organized and found a sponsor for a semi-pro baseball team playing in what I call the "Latin Leagues" at Humboldt Park on North Avenue. This was just another once-in-a-lifetime experience I had in Chicago during that crazy and confusing time when the '60s spilled forward into the '70s.

No visit would be complete without the complementary tour of Ed Kelly's gallery. Photos of entertainers, sports heroes, and politicians adorned the walls of his modest office. I grabbed a snapshot of Perry Como, Muhammad Ali, and President Jimmy Carter. Chicago native Michael Flatley of Riverdance was also a "graduate" of the park district boxing program. Chicago Bears Gayle Sayers and Doug Buffone, media personalities Walter Jacobson and Irv Kupcinet, along with dozens of others, all had an unbreakable bond with Ed Kelly.

I consider him one of my mentors and friends. Once again, I'm grateful for his hospitality and his time. By the way, Ed visited regularly with the most famous boxer and humanitarian of any era.

Life Begins at 90—Part II

I don't think Sheldon Cooper or I were ever late for an appointment. Ed Kelly was already hard at work in his office when I rapped at his office door. Of course, Sheldon and Ed knew one another for years by name and reputation. Formally introducing them was a privilege for me. I tried to describe Ed's photo gallery ahead of time, but I could tell Sheldon was still impressed.

Their conversation flowed from one mutual friend or acquaintance to another, with minimal intervention by the Screaming Wildman. Joe added a little "color commentary" when someone hit an occasional name or date snag—not very often, of course.

We recapped the many highlights of my interview with Sheldon (or the other way around) on the way over. I snapped a picture of the memorial poster Ed had on his desk commemorating his friendship with Muhammad Ali.

I reminded all how independent programming media giant Sheldon Cooper helped change how the entire world viewed Chicago. Sheldon observed how television, radio, music, and the internet are intertwined. If we take the time, we can still see the unmistakable influence of Sheldon Cooper in modern media.

I understand Ed Kelly may one day have Seward Park renamed in his honor.

Guys, I'm honored and humbled to share this time with you all. Thanks.

Sheldon Cooper, Yours Truly,
Joe Pytel, and Ed Kelly
(September 28, 2016)

Muhammad Ali—
There's nothing else I could tell you about one of the most influential characters of my lifetime. I'll leave that up to characters like Ed Kelly.

There's a huge stack of chapters I need to go through at least once more before we print this book. I resisted the urge to pick this one up when I first heard of Ali's passing.

Now it's June 10th, the day of Muhammad Ali's memorial service and funeral in his Louisville, Kentucky, hometown. I'm thinking of him and his good friend Ed Kelly. This is a fitting time to give them both my attention and gratitude.

There are already too many folks I've mentioned in my pages who've passed since my project started. Life can be cruel.

Cal Starr

At the age of 85 (as I'm writing this in late autumn of 2015), Cal Starr recently completed a trip to Branson, Missouri, with a busload of his good friends and devoted supporters. Nothing seems to be holding him back. Aside from promoting a long list of country-and-western shows dating back to the '60s, he still regularly performs. If you ever get a chance to meet him, you'll be captivated by his voice. As an energetic performer, he obviously exercises it more than most of us. Anyone who talks to him on the phone places him in his early 30s, at most.

Our Storybook Meeting

Writing a book is a completely new experience for me. Really, I didn't think it was something I would ever have the time or patience to do. Conducting an interview was something I had to learn as well. Let's see, I'm supposed to ask a question and sit back (recorder nearby) and let someone else talk? I hope you realize the sacrifices I'm making for you all. It takes guts, or a sense of poor timing, to schedule a meeting in Chicago during the first full week of December. I was at my favorite meeting headquarters in the upper level of Mariano's Fresh Market at the corner of Webster and Ashland.

Remember, I'm never late for a meeting, especially when I'm the host. This is the ultimate sign of respect for my guests. I was dressed to introduce a performer. The stage was set for an ultimate showman. Cal Starr would prove to be one of the best and most meaningful interviews I would ever conduct. It required little effort on my part.

I noticed he commanded the stage the moment he stepped through the door. He continues to have a confident gait, and may have lost only a half-step, in spite of performing for seven decades. Today, he was ready for business. He brought a package of hand-picked posters, collected from his hundreds of promotions, as conversation starters. See how easy he made it for me? In his other hand, he carried a case with the C.F. Martin D-41 acoustic guitar some folks told him has one of the sweetest sounds ever produced. The resonance actually comes from the guy who plays it with skill and passion.

I met him halfway to our table and offered to help him carry something. I doubt anyone has ever touched his guitar case, or that it seldom leaves his side. I love a guy who demonstrates fierce independence, a warm smile, and a keen eye at the same time. He was also dressed for a typical performance and made his outfit look good, rather than the other way around. He set the posters down and affectionately laid his guitar on the table. I forgot to ask him if his guitar had a name. Maybe I'm not that good at an interview after all. It's probably named after a girl, given the way he treats it and "she" treats him.

"How do you want to start?" he asked me in true cowboy-styled manner over a cup of hot chocolate. Okay, maybe the chocolate wasn't a traditional drink. Wouldn't make for good lyrics, either.

"Well, I figure we'll lay out the posters like a gallery right here," I said. This would likely give me a place to start. That wasn't necessary. Cal Starr already had it figured out. He told his story in his own way at his own pace. This wasn't an interview: It was a concert.

I went down the row of posters and snapped a picture of each. We were plunging in before I finished. He's done this a time or two before. Why did I see a campaign poster among the concert playbills? See if you can keep up …

"Arthur Stallard was my dad. He ran for Congress as a Republican during the August 1944 primary," Cal began. We were going back to an era where folks backed up what they said with actual proof. Take this poster, for example. If you need more proof, you can find the record electronically. I wish folks would do some research on their own before taking any politician's word. Google "Arthur-Stallard-Kentucky" and you can actually read *Kentucky Votes: U.S. House Primary and General Elections, 1920-1960, Volume 3*. Or we can move on. Take Cal Starr's word as "gospel"…

"I played the guitar to help drum up votes for my dad," he modestly explained. His three sisters, younger brother, and he were obviously just enough support to get his dad elected as a state representative, with the young songwriter and entertainer serving as a page during his dad's term. The way I have it figured, young Calvin Stallard would have been around 14 years old at the time. The Hon. Stallard was probably too honest to capture a U.S. Congressional seat. However, his son was on his way to capturing the imagination and loyalty of a diverse musical audience. In his earliest days, Cal might have defined himself as a "country" singer because he grew up on a small farm in Kentucky, though he was born in my hometown.

Given that hard-working background, where and when do you think Cal Starr started turning heads and tuning ears to his own melodies? Of course, Chicago. More precisely '50s and '60s Chicago.

"Timing is everything," Cal reminded me. You're going to see that phrase a lot in this chapter alone. He paid his dues as an on-air personality at KFLA-TV in Shreveport, Louisiana. All the while, he envisioned success in his Chi-town. Stars (pun intended) aligned when his agent booked him at the historic Key Club near downtown Chicago. Soon after, he "springboarded" to Columbus, Ohio, to produce his first country-and-western concert, featuring Marty Robbins. From then on, he aligned the stars himself.

John Joseph Clem, nicknamed Johnny Shiloh, was just shy of 10 years old when his pluck and determination earned him a gig on the Union side of the American Civil War as a drummer.

"I wrote **Johnny Shiloh** and was fortunate enough to have the Jordanaires provide the background vocals. They were best known as the group that recorded with Elvis Presley. My song made it to No. 2 on the WJJD-radio Chicago survey. If the record was released on the Columbia Records label, it would have easily sold a million," Cal said.

At the same time, the Beatles awakened the industry. Country-and-western had 50,000-watt powerhouses like WJJD-Chicago reaching new audiences. Motown was hitting its stride. It was wild. There seemed to be room for everyone. AM radio was reaching diverse markets. Musicians seemed to have the understanding, tolerance, acceptance, and willingness to embrace other perspectives. Johnny Shiloh was the subject of a Disney film back in those days. All entertainment media looked as if they were working together.

Performing and Promoting

During the '50s and '60s, Cal Starr maintained an unbelievable performance schedule, approaching 300 dates yearly. At the same time, he recorded in Nashville and promoted some of the greatest shows throughout the Midwest. Even now, he is mindful and respectful of those who helped him forge his way.

"Ben Cowall from Columbus, Ohio, was a great promoter during that time and did a lot for my career from way back in the '50s," Cal mentioned.

The number of live performances moved to a more tolerable level in the decades that followed, and he was still putting together legendary shows. Our interview moved to another heirloom poster of his. By 1986, he was one of the most trusted and respected promoters of country-and-western music. Once again, he reminded me about that "timing" thing. There's more to just promoting a Loretta Lynn **Coal Miner's Daughter** concert.

"When her movie was released in 1980, she was in high demand everywhere," Cal said. Yeah, but it was no surprise she teamed up often with Cal Starr. If you looked at some of the other posters he brought for the interview, you would see why she would have confidence in him.

"Every concert or performance that I promoted actually happened. You know, in this industry, this was not always the case. All but one, in all of this time, lost a little money," he continued. Cal made sure that everybody was going to get paid. That included a payoff for the audience as well.

The Arie Crown Theater in the old version of Chicago's McCormick Place (before the fire) accommodated 5,029 paying customers, according to Cal. Who am I to doubt the memory of the promoter who regularly packed the house during country-and-western jamborees? Talk about an all-star lineup (all "Starr" lineup?). Captain Stubby was the MC, with a regular lineup including Ernest Tubb, partners Lester Flatt and Earl Scruggs, and of course, Cal Starr. Roy Stingley, Porter Wagoner, Ray Price, and Marty Robbins also appeared regularly during his productions.

I have to tell you, they knew how to attract world-class talent back then. Today, and even during the legendary Dick Clark tours of the '60s, there would be a single "house" band backing all of the acts. During a typical jamboree, the backstage area would be virtually "crawling" with musicians. The Texas Troubadours would back Ernest Tubb, and the Foggy Mountain Boys did the same for Flatt and Scruggs. Even Captain Stubby had the Buccaneers behind him. They had to be virtuosos to use instruments in musical comedy like Stubby and his crew did.

Hank Snow performed with the Rainbow Ranch Boys, Ray Price with the Cherokee Cowboys, and Mel Tillis with the Statesiders.

In total, over 40 Grand Ole Opry acts would benefit from Cal Starr's ground-breaking work. One name stood out among all the others on the promotional posters Cal brought. First, let me say the Sabre Room in Hickory Hills, Illinois, was one sought-after booking. Fans would see a wide variety of acts, from the Rat Pack crooners to rhythm-and-blues. Have you ever heard of a gal named Lori Stallard? I have, and so should you.

At a quite tender age, she appeared at the prestigious Sabre Room with the iconic Marty Robbins and his Tear Drops band.

Cal Starr's daughter would be known as Lori Lee Williams when I recorded **Diesel Cowboy** and a mournful rendition of **Kind of a Drag**, along with a few other songs I inherited from Lew Douglas. Don't let me get too far ahead of myself. Lori has her own well-deserved section in my book. Cal Starr and I both agree that Lori London (as she is currently performing) should be headlining her own show. You might think proud father Cal Starr would say that. The Screaming Wildman might be guilty of having only his self-interest at heart.

Remember, we are promoters and music professionals, first and foremost. Our job is to bring phenomenal talent to listeners of all ages and cultures. Would you believe an endorsement from one of the most accomplished musical composers and arrangers of all time?

If you didn't know about Lew Douglas, you had no right being in the music business. If I can speak for Cal Starr here as well (it's my book), guys like us also knew Lew as a partner and mentor. He was already seeking his fortune by setting songs to music, or vice versa, when Cal Starr was born, and I followed a decade later. When a guy like Lew tells you that the sweetest female notes he ever heard came from one Lori Stallard, take notice. He's wrapped notes and lyrics around voices like Pat Boone, Brenda Lee, pop singer Joni James, the Duprees, Marvin Gaye, Etta James, and Nat King Cole.

You may not realize it, nor did we until years later, but we were immersed in the musical scores of Lew Douglas. Have you ever noticed the music playing when the Three Stooges were revolutionizing comedy? Lew had a hand in it somewhere. Actually, you will notice that Moe, Larry, and Curly (among others) are categorized as musical comics for a reason. Lew also worked with Gerry & The Pacemakers, another group signed by the Beatles' manager, Brian Epstein. I can't begin to tell you how many ways Lew influenced decades worth of both aspiring and seasoned musicians.

You'll see Lew remembered fondly by Carl Giammarese of the Buckinghams, Denny Murray from the Lincoln Park Zoo, and Lori as well. He didn't recognize age, ethnic, gender, or musical factions. He only spoke in harmonies. He may be the only person in this book who influenced everyone else you read about here.

Recollections and Reflections

Okay, I know this is the Cal Starr chapter. It took me a long time to lead up to this, but here's why Cal Starr and I met, as if you didn't already know.

"I met Lew Douglas when he was at Mercury Records. He was the composer on songs by Marty Robbins and Ray Price, among many others," Cal started. When you spend so much time in Nashville, you get to know one another.

"Lew was such a great arranger, and I took him at his word about Lori's talent. Everybody knew and respected him. I don't think he ever would have associated with dishonest people," Cal continued. It's safe to say I knew about Cal Starr and his ultimately talented daughter long before I met them. Lew was such a good judge of both musical and personal talent, so I thoroughly liked them both before we ever met.

"Dan Belloc and Lew recorded Lori in Nashville some time before. I heard about this Carl Bonafede guy for a long time now. I gave Lori's number to Carl and they hit it off," he remembered. I really believe that people born in Chicago have a built-in comfort with one another. That's how we collaborated long before we ever met. I invited Cal and Lori to an oldies rock concert at the (old) Holiday Star Theater in Merrillville, Indiana.

Back to the Present

If this news came from anyone else, I wouldn't believe it. Cal Starr just released his latest album.

"Harold Bradley recorded with Elvis Presley, along with many of the top stars from the Grand Ole Opry, and is in the Country Music Hall of Fame. He is one of the nicest guys I ever met in the music business, or anywhere else for that matter. He never said a bad word about anyone. I read somewhere that he is probably the most recorded guitar player in history," Cal said. Harold was a session musician in Nashville for over 50 years. Who's gonna doubt that?

"Harold is 89 and I am 85 right now. This will be the first time either of us worked with just one other musician. *Together Again* contains 16 songs that we recorded in Madison, Tennessee, at the Hill Top Studio. There are

a few old-time standards," Cal explained. This would include **My Old Kentucky Home** and **You Are My Sunshine**—songs that invite everyone to sing along, no matter where or when.

"There's **The Battle of New Orleans** and one original Cal Starr song named **Cowboy Joe**. Are you ready to have me sing a little?" Cal asked, while looking for the guitar pick he slid into his pocket before leaving home. I bet that's part of his checklist before he goes anywhere: wallet, car keys, cowboy hat, and guitar pick. Just like any vintage artist, he also has a rack of CDs in his car for new deserving fans.

"You have another guitar when you go on stage, right?" I asked. I've seen it, but the folks who are reading this haven't, so I was asking him for you.

"Yeah, I have a Super Gibson 400 that goes back to around 1952. Still have the original amplifier, too. To perform, I have a new Bose system," he said. Okay, just as you probably guessed, you will see Carl Bonafede listed on eBay before you see that guitar. I'm afraid to know what I might go for on the open market.

Cal was ready to give me a few more tidbits of information. This was so cool because he was actually strumming while he laid it out for me.

I finally figured out why his voice was so strong and true. He was never talking during the entire interview, he was singing. The only difference: His guitar is no longer in its "holster." I managed to fire off a pretty good question, finally.

"Did you ever perform at the Grand Ole Opry?" I asked. Chances are, others may have asked that in the past.

"No, I heard that Roy Acuff thought about asking me when he was backstage at a concert while I was performing. I heard Roy never asked because I always seemed too busy," he answered. That might be the only regret in the illustrious career of Cal Starr. Well, it shouldn't be his regret, but that of dozens of acts he could have accompanied on stage. Maybe some current headliner will finally invite him. Cal's been around for most of the 90 years since The Opry was founded in Nashville. You'd think the longest running radio broadcast in U.S. history would have included a performance by Cal Starr by now.

"My dad passed at the age of 57, just like Marty Robbins," Cal said. Maybe he just revealed one of his secrets for maintaining a sharp mind. He connects bits of information to honor both his dad and long-time friends. I have a duty to pass this along to you, just as he recalled.

Cal is ready to perform for any and all gathered around. The acoustics in the upper area at Mariano's allowed his voice to resonate remarkably well. A couple of moms with toddlers perched in their shopping carts were just about to have a once-in-a-lifetime experience. Maybe I should put together a rooftop concert this summer with Cal, Lori, the Buckinghams, the Rail City Five ... sorry, I just can't help myself. I'm always promoting.

Believe it or not, I felt a hush fall over the room.

"I'm going to open up with a little bit of **Johnny Shiloh**," Cal started. He was in full concert mode. I was loving it. "Little Johnny Joseph Clem was the name that his pappy gave him. / He was too young to carry a gun, so he played his drum," he sang. APPLAUSE. Time to launch into a few bars of **On the Wings of a Dove**. Of course, he invited me to sing along with the chorus, as he must do with his customary packed houses. Nobody should turn down an invitation to sing with a country legend.

"… On the Wings of a Dove," we finished together.

"Who sang that again?" I asked.

"Ferlin Husky. Passed away in 2011 at age 85," he sang as his reply. He finished his set with another sing-along that was appropriate for anyone of any generation, if they can remember.

"… Please don't take my sunshine away," he concluded. Well, then don't leave.

I helped Cal pack up his posters and watched him while he lovingly slid the D-41 back home. That line sounds like it could be from an entirely different kind of book. No disrespect to Mr. Starr, but I'm proud of that line. I hope my editor won't toss it out.

I walked him back to his car, and he gave me a copy of *Together Again*, along with *Precious Memories*, a CD collection of inspirational songs. We wished each other safe travels. Easy to do, since we enjoyed April weather on this particular December morning. He brought the sunshine (he sang about earlier) with him. I forgot to ask him what he listens to in his car! I think he always hears music.

I'm so grateful I could introduce another quintessential performer. You don't need to be a country-and-western fan to admire guys and gals who take music to a new level. Check out Cal's bio clip https://youtu.be/l-uopiB5jZ4 or visit his website http://www.calstarrmusic.com/. You'll be glad you did. Once again, thank you, my friend!

Monster Entertainment

Mickey, Larry & the Exciters (1965-70)

Larry Alltop and Mickey Esposito put together a group that, I swear, was the most talented and entertaining I ever saw in my life. Larry was unbelievably acrobatic. We're talking about flips and karate kicks in front of a band that had flawless choreographic routines. Their dual lead vocals were every bit as good as those of the Righteous Brothers.

I first saw them in the lounge at Castaways Bowling Alley in Calumet City, Illinois. Long before the Exciters took the stage that day, the room was packed and the management had to turn people away. Mickey and Larry came out in orange suits while the rest of the band was dressed in black. Needless to say, they blew everyone away.

Not long after, I set up a recording session with them. With Lew Douglas doing the arrangements, I was sure **Stranded in the Middle of No Place**, https://www.youtube.com/watch?v=_bIW1_SMoKg, was going to be a home run. Check out that horn intro. You see what I'm sayin'? We're not talking about studio musicians here!

In 1960, I did a show at Eisenhower High School in south suburban Blue Island with the Four Seasons and Jimmy Peterson leading the Chicagoans. I never heard a better group than the Four Seasons until I heard Mickey and Larry. Thanks to the detective work by Joe Pytel, I was able to reach out to Larry Alltop and tell him in person.

Ballrooms and Bars

Once again, it's apparent we've waited too long to touch base. It would have been far better to see him in person. For now, we have to connect by phone. Nothing reinforces the bond between two people better than recalling our near-death experience. How about that for "openers"?

In 1969, I was driving Mickey, Larry, Paul (their drummer), and Paul's girlfriend back from a performance at the University of Wisconsin in Madison. It was the middle of winter, but I was cruising down I-94 at about 70mph when I hit a slick spot beneath an underpass.

We spun around three times and ended up in a ditch beside the road. Thankfully, everybody was okay. My shaken passengers were able to help me push the car back onto the highway, and we drove back to Chicago from there.

"I remember we talked earlier that day about Otis Redding and how he died in a crash near Madison," Larry mentioned. Yeah, his career was just taking off, but his chartered plane wasn't destined to stay airborne. Days before, Redding recorded **Sittin' on the Dock of the Bay**, destined to hit No. 1 the next year.

"We were promoting **Stranded in the Middle of No Place** at colleges. We were all young guys, and the crowds really liked us. The rest of the band would ride in the van with the instruments, and we would ride with you, Carl," Larry reminded me. You know what the Screaming Wildman says: The group that sways (off the road) together, stays together.

Mickey, Larry & the Exciters were one dynamic night club act. They would open for groups like the Mob, and later for Wayne Cochran and the CC Riders. Larry is ready for you all to know how the band came together.

"I had a group in Akron, Ohio, called the Pentagons. We did shows with Candy Johnson, who was famous for her roles in Beach Party films. We got an invitation to perform at the New York World's Fair," he started. To clarify, the event ran for two six-month seasons (mid-April through mid-October) in 1964-65.

"Candy Johnson and Her Exciters were doing multiple shows, seven days a week. This was just killing the band, and a few members were threatening to quit. I called my buddy in Akron for help, and he told me about a guy named Mickey Esposito," he said. Larry picked up a few more musicians, and the new Exciters concluded the gig in New York.

Just Getting Started

Mickey Esposito, Candy Johnson, and Larry Alltop spent considerable time in Spain after that. Once they got back to the States, the Exciters were ready to go it alone in New York City.

"I went to the Wagon Wheel on West 45th Street and caught a group called the Seven Sons. They were just about to break up. This was the last couple of nights of their gig. They asked me if I wanted to join them," Larry said. This has the makings of an exceptional story from an awesome duo. I bet you already know what's coming next.

"I told them my singing partner was right down the street at our hotel, and we'd be right back. Mickey and I had a hot routine at the time. We did some Righteous Brothers stuff along with other popular songs," Larry continued. Obviously, the crowd loved them, and it wasn't long before they decided to form a new group once the Sons officially dis-"banded" (pun intended).

The Exciters found a new drummer and began practicing in Knoxville, Tennessee. Before long, the group returned to the Wagon Wheel and began playing with Wayne Cochran in Pensacola, Florida. They started regularly booking engagements in Miami, New York, and back in Calumet City, Illinois.

As you may remember, Cal City was the south suburban birthplace of the Jake (John Belushi) and Elwood (Dan Akroyd) characters from *The Blues Brothers* movie. Belushi was actually born in the Humboldt Park neighborhood in Chicago. I think the characters in that movie were actually inspired by Mickey, Larry & The Exciters. Notice that I said "inspired," not "imitated." The Exciters literally "killed" everywhere they played, but there was a special bond between Chicago and the Boston-raised lead duo.

"The jackets for the Exciters were the same color as the scarves that Mickey and I would wear that day," he said. Sorry, Larry, I can't help myself. Besides the orange, you would see black, pink, and silver, among others. These guys might have liked clothes even more than I did, and still do.

They knew where to shop for a wardrobe, too. Smokey Joe's from Maxwell Street in Chicago was most likely the place where the zoot suit originated. Baby Huey and the Babysitters, the Jackson Five (where the members sang and danced in the store lobby during the early days), and Carl Bonafede were among the local (and steady) customers.

On any given day, you might see James Brown, Sammy Davis Jr., or Smokey Robinson pay a visit. I wouldn't be surprised if proprietor Morry Bublick was responsible for most of the dazzling outfits draped over all of Motown's male performers. From there, the comparison ends, according to the admittedly more handsome of their dual lead singers (wink) …

"We did karate moves, comedy, kicks, flips, and routines that included swinging microphones. That part of our act was so good that we actually got an endorsement from the Shure Microphone Company," Larry said. That mic was probably the most recognizable model in the music industry. You know, it was the one that would look like an orbiting wrecking ball in the hands of Mickey Esposito or Larry Alltop, or both simultaneously.

Success and Sustainability

It was easy to see why Mickey, Larry & The Exciters were in such high demand. If MTV had been around back then, a tune like **Save the Last Dance for Me** https://youtu.be/_S0yzRmSCpY would have been a global hit. I suggest that you stop reading now and check out this YouTube clip uploaded by Joe Pytel. You'll enjoy the vocal harmonies and varied wardrobes. The only thing missing is the video evidence. **Stranded in the Middle of No Place** did enjoy success in select markets, according to Larry.

"You know why that was, don't you, Carl? We could sell records wherever we performed regularly. Delray Beach, Florida; Salisbury Beach, Massachusetts; and the Flamingo Hotel, Las Vegas, Nevada shows would create demand at the record stores. We got a chance to share the stage with all of the popular acts of the time," Larry told me. The short list included Wayne Cochran and the CC Riders, Sly and the Family Stone, and the Platters.

If ever there was a band that was "too good" to be an opening act, it was these guys. They got the crowd so revved up that many of the headliners could seldom compare. Think about it. The Exciters would be doing flips and splits and comedy routines. There were four horn players stepping in up-tempo synchronicity and wearing the flashiest duds imaginable.

MICKEY & LARRY & THE EXCITERS

All of the guys in the band were great musicians and good looking. They would play at Club Laurel on North Broadway and then maybe George's Soul House at Milwaukee Avenue and Dempster Street the next day. We would see the same girls there.

"We weren't stars, but some people would follow us from state to state. Sparky, our lead trumpet player, came from Wayne Cochran's band. He was quite good looking, not as handsome as me, of course, and he seemed to have his own following. Mickey had jet-black hair and was really handsome," Larry mentioned. I was impressed by Paul, the group's drummer. He played the double-bass drum.

More Tales from the Road

We shared our memories about Wayne Cochran. Larry described him as the original blue-eyed soul brother. Wayne had that bouffant blond hair and big teeth. He was the ultimate showman, and he is still in touch with Larry. Wayne is now an ordained minister. Apparently, he's still in show business in a way. Just kidding, as God is my witness.

Cochran and the Exciters shared the marquee dozens, if not hundreds, of times. Even so, there was a night that stood out among all the others.

"We were in Miami when the Jackie Gleason variety show was celebrating an anniversary. He and all of his guests came to our show. We played in front of Jackie, Lucille Ball, James Brown, Bobby Hatfield [one half of the Righteous Brothers], and Joe Namath. After the show, Broadway Joe made it a point to tell us he thought our group outdid Cochran's.

"We thanked him, and I was glad he thought so. I don't think that Cochran ever had a bad day, and it would have been hard to compete with his 17-piece band," Larry said.

Mickey, Larry & The Exciters were far more than adequate competition, of course. They were accomplished headliners who just happened to go on stage before Cochran. Club owners finally realized that and split the two acts.

"Wayne would go on the road for a couple of weeks, and we would be left behind. We still managed to pack the room. When he returned, we would play a couple of weeks together. Then it would be our turn to play on the road for a while," Larry concluded. Apparently, you didn't get tired of that arrangement, and neither did the crowds or club owners.

I was the only one able to lure Mickey, Larry & the Exciters away from the ballroom circuit to do one-night engagements. I had them playing more intimate venues in Iowa, Minnesota, and Indi-

Larry Alltop—
We didn't mention our market in Massachusetts. We were so strong there, it would be a shame to leave that out. Club owners Brian Wallace and Henry Vara (known as the "King of Clubs") were two of our biggest supporters.

They booked the biggest performers of their time, like Frankie Valli and Kenny Rogers. The stars that came in – the entertainers that performed in those Boston-area clubs through the years: Wow!!!

ana. Was it my persuasiveness and charm? Only a little bit. It had more to do with the intoxicating prospect of landing the hit record we all knew the group deserved. Larry understood what I'm sayin'.

"I remember walking into a restaurant in Green Bay, Wisconsin, and hearing one of our songs playing on the jukebox," he said. Yeah, that showed you all were "hooked" by that point. You record, promote, tour, and mostly hope. Allstate Record Distributors paid for my trip to eastern parts of Illinois to promote in rural markets. Sadly, there are factors (other than remarkable talent) that determine the overall success of a group.

"Mickey Esposito perfected his low, gravelly voice long before anyone else," Larry said. There just happened to be another blue-eyed soul duo whose harmonious ballads had already been embraced by the industry. That crowded out everyone else when it came to selling records, according to Larry.

"Mickey thought the Righteous Brothers were the very best." Larry recalls. Everywhere I went with the Exciters, people would mistake their vocals with those of Bobby Hatfield and Bill Medley.

You know, Mickey, Larry & the Exciters did everything right, including the release of **Stranded in the Middle of No Place** under Twinight Records (sometimes referred to as the Soul of Chicago) label. They became so polished and popular that many headliners were reluctant to use them as an opening act. Many of those headliners somehow kept performing well into the 21st century.

I can't even imagine how many memorable moments this group created. I'm just glad to have witnessed a small part of it all.

The LARRY ALLTOP Show   CHAZ
    with the new EXCITERS   PRODUCTIONS

My interview with Larry Alltop ended with recollections of some other band members, like guitar player Les Strater and bass player Chad Bailey, who sounded like a cross between Ray Charles and Otis Redding. I hope I can talk to Mickey sometime in the future. Time to go for now.

"Thanks for thinking of me for the book. Love you, man," Larry said. Back at ya, Larry!

This just in: Mickey, Larry & the Exciters are mentioned in *The Studio 54 Effect*, an upcoming memoir by former owner Mark Fleischman.

The Cambridge Five

The Cambridge Five was one of the most talented groups I ever worked with. Just listen to the vocal work of Chuck Francour on **Heads I Win Tails You Lose** https:// youtu.be/a6s5UEZjr68. This is one of my favorite songs, written by the group's lead guitarist at the time, Mike Horton. Doug Gast was the founder, manager, and one-man horn section (trumpet and saxophone). Rounding out the original lineup were Rick Morgan playing drums and Denny Grounds on bass guitar.

By the time the group's ten-year run ended, the members were known as the Cambridge. That's what happens when you include a number in your name. Things get awkward when you add additional members to sweeten and strengthen your sound. When the Cambridge members decided to go their separate ways, Doug Gast was still on trumpet and sax. Don Cook (harmonica and congas) and Tom Stammich (saxophone) were the two lead singers. Ron Monsma was now the drummer and Bob Cotrell was on the keyboards.

Phil Everingham (lead guitar, banjo, steel guitar) joined original member Denny Grounds (bass guitar) to balance the string section, guitar that is. Chuck Francour returned for a while to sing with Stammich and Cook and enhanced the brass sound with his trumpet. Their very last performance, while still

Original Cambridge 5 at the Knights of Columbus Hall From left (standing): Chuck Francour, keyboards and lead singer; Mike Horton, lead guitar (RIP); Doug Gast, trumpet and tenor sax; (Seated): Rick Morgan, drums; Denny Grounds, bass guitar

at the top of their game, was in February 1973 at "my" Holiday Ballroom. Right now, I can't be sure I was aware of that fact at the time.

Yet Another Renewed Acquaintance

This chapter resulted from another overdue reunion thanks to investigative work by Joe Pytel. I'm really starting to regret my decision to avoid most electronics. The best way I know to honor the groups, promoters, DJs, and friends who enhanced my career is by writing this book. I'll leave it up to you all to determine whether I helped them as well.

Near the end of October 2015, I had my first conversation in decades with Doug Gast. He made heavy contributions to the following pages.

If you lived in this era, you know there was a lot of stuff going on musically. Music was the best expression of our feelings and those of our audience. You know, when bands could play five or six nights a week, that was a lot of pocket money for groups—and a lot of influence. Outstanding bands like the Cambridge Five could capture the attention and imagination of local crowds throughout the Midwest. Their records let them reach out nationally. I'm counting on the recollections of the guys (and girls) responsible for creating so many of my moments. Thank goodness Doug Gast has offered to help here.

The Midwestern Connection

Excuse me if I refer to the Cambridge Five (or Cambridge, if you prefer) as a Chicago band since they perfected the Chicago sound. South Bend is in the north central part of Indiana, much closer to the Michigan border than the outskirts of Chicago. On the map, it looks like a two-hour trip to the Holiday Ballroom on the north side, just down the road from legendary Wrigley Field. Given the choking traffic on I-90 westbound, you can safely calculate a trip from Doug Gast's hometown to a weekend gig at about three hours. He reminded me the band would "do" the Holiday Ballroom on the return trip from packing the house at Top Deck or the Black Knight in Lake Geneva, Wisconsin, on Fridays and Saturdays.

"Sometimes we would do a Top Deck matinee performance on Sunday and stop at the Holiday Ballroom on our way back," Doug explained. They were a group in high demand. Lots of big names would ask for them to perform with them. They kept their booking agent, Peg Richards, working at a feverish pace. Speaking of big names in Chicago, there was none bigger than Richard J. Daley. In 1968, the Democratic National Convention was held in Chicago. You might be too young to remember (I mean, you couldn't possibly be so "stoned" that you couldn't remember) there was heavy activity in Chicago due to war protests. Now you know the Cambridge Five played at the convention.

"Mayor Daley treated us as his own personal rock band. We were the ones he called to play at every one of his political events, wherever and whenever. I used to have some great conversations with the old man, Mayor Richard Daley, on stage and backstage. We performed at the Conrad Hilton right after Jack Kennedy was assassinated," Doug said. There were so many performers who not only let the show go on, but also pulled together shows to help soften the blow to their audience, despite being so hurt themselves. Music eases pain, whether you are listening or playing it. Maybe that is one of the reasons the original Mayor Daley regarded them so highly.

I said there was a lot of stuff going on then. None of us had the energy or time to keep up with groups between gigs. Now, we got a chance to see what life was like for folks who were working as hard as I was.

"We did a lot of fashion shows at McCormick Place and got to meet guys like Dick Cavett and movie star John Gavin (who was a real looker in person back then)," Doug said. I'm not going to waste space in the book to explain how important and cool these folks were. "Google" it.

"Performing near the Playboy Club in Lake Geneva, we got to party with the likes of football player Rosie Grier, and Animals lead singer Eric Burdon," Doug continued. There were comic acts at the Playboy Club at Lake Geneva, too. The Cambridge guys would hang with them all. You could learn to partake or learn how to avoid things that would ultimately sabotage a career. Doug reminded us there were groups and (mostly) guys who could "party." Before the 1960s, that word was a noun. Guys like us turned "party" into a verb. Many were one-man parties. When the crowds went home, the Screaming Wildman stood back and watched.

"I was pretty wild and crazy in those days myself, but I was smart and all about business first. Partying was secondary. No drugs were allowed when we performed before or during, a rule I enforced with an iron fist. In spite of that, all hell broke loose from me," Doug remembered. Next to his music, I guess we must have "clicked" while sharing the stage.

"Carl, I am glad you are still well and have been in my thoughts for decades. I used to make you laugh a lot since I acted crazy in front of you to the point of embarrassment. I made you laugh so hard in front of the girls who were stalking us at the Holiday Ballroom. That includes the women swooning over the musicians when we were all young and free," Doug mentioned. Oh, yeah, there was a lot of music, too.

Sex, Drugs, Rock-and-Roll. Yes, each in its place and proportion. Nobody denied the existence of temptations or the (sometimes unfair) influence they had over some folks. During our chat (interview sounds too formal), we still marveled at guys who were often wasted during a gig. There were a couple who escaped my detection until now. I'm not naming names here, just a little disappointed in some of them. I missed the signs from people I thought I knew. 'Nuff said.

Some guys joined musical groups to meet girls. Others left successful musical careers for those same girls. You'll meet some in this book. The same was true about female artists. I think I knew a couple. Don't ask me how.

More Cambridge Geography

I never waste a chance to pick the brain of a solid businessman and an awesome musical performer. Doug Gast revived his memories because he is still devoted to his group and the music community. You are in for an entertaining ride as you read on. If I said this someplace before, I apologize. I took great care to include as many outside references to the artists I want to thank in these pages. You will see hyperlinks and Q-R codes sprinkled through the text. I invite you to stop and listen. So does Doug. My close friend Joe Pytel deserves tremendous credit for keeping "my" music alive. Thousands of others have also taken the time to post videos in tribute to the era and the artists. You know what I'm sayin'?

What's in a name? I wanted to know how the Cambridge Five got their name. Well, there are five of them to start, remember. That's my attempt at a joke, sorry. I somehow remembered the group started out as the Tradewinds in 1961. Now for the "Cambridge" part, straight from Doug.

"It was the British sound and the groups like the Beatles and Rolling Stones that influenced everything. I wanted to give the group a name that sounded like they came from England. The Buckinghams did the same thing, didn't they?" Doug asked. Yeah, we did.

That's kind of funny because the English groups didn't name themselves that way. I searched for "the greatest British groups of all time." There were no group names with any references to England. Our naming strategy worked anyway.

Let's explore South Bend, Indiana, and the surrounding area, like the lower half of Michigan. Think of the area fifty miles north or south of I-90 between South Bend and Chicago. There was a lot of talent that influenced the music and the market. Doug Gast, the driving force of the Cambridge, is ready to make introductions. Their stories are intertwined with his group and the talent I booked for the Holiday Ballroom.

Doug also produced and promoted many events and concerts himself. He booked the Buckinghams, Cryan' Shames, Neil Diamond, and Eric Burdon, among others. He certainly has enough material to write his own book as you can see by how much he contributed to mine. Hint.

"Long before I founded the Cambridge Five, I performed with a great friend and classmate of mine from South Shore High School in Chicago. Corky Siegel is one of the greatest blues harp [harmonica] players of all time. He has performed all over the globe and is still touring regularly [http://www.chamberblues.com/]. He also played tenor sax and piano. He was half of the Siegel-Schwall band that toured all of the legendary rock clubs in the '60s and '70s. After I formed the Cambridge, he often traveled to South Bend and sat in on our sessions," Doug said. He provided a few more tidbits to tie regional music to national fame. This also illustrates how unfair the music business can be when it comes to the relationship between pure talent and fickle fame.

"Niles, Michigan, is only about 10 miles north of South Bend. Our band was really close to a guitarist named Tom Jackson. One cold winter, he recorded a song in his garage. The tape sat in a drawer at a local radio station for years. In the meantime, Tom would beg me to let him join our band, but we didn't think he was good enough. We really didn't realize what a good voice he had or how his biggest strength was writing original music," Doug explained. According to our mystery man's website (https://www.tommyjames.com/), a Pittsburgh DJ got an overwhelming response when he played Hanky Panky at regional dances. Radio stations soon began airing it. Tommy James and the Shondells became a national phenomenon.

There were a lot of great groups from the same Cambridge Five region. Doug Gast was handling all of the business stuff at the same time. The Cambridge Five were rockin' every place they played. Here's another band Doug watched take the big stage.

"Vince DiMaggio and the Princeton Five [Benton Harbor and St. Joseph, Michigan] recorded a song called **California Sun**. It was a terrifically clean and professional production. The Rivieras somehow heard about it and recorded their own version," Doug mentioned. Guess which one became a national hit? Right. Courtesy of Mr. Gast, here's more background about the region. Is there something about that number "five"?

"The Five Emprees released both **Little Miss Sad** (https://youtu.be/6zd4ncD-r08) and **Hey Baby** in 1965. Their lead singer was a guy named Don Cook. He was drafted and served several years as lieutenant, doing night patrols in the DMZ [demilitarized zone] in South Korea," he continued. Many of us forgot that some red-blooded American boys could be drafted and could serve in more than one armed conflict at that time.

"When he came out of the service, the Five Emprees wouldn't take him back and we let him join us. Now we had three lead singers and could perform any type of music out there, even soul. It took a little time for Don to get his recording voice back, but he was a great performer on stage," Doug said. Did he say three lead singers? Yes, there is more. Sometimes less is more. The Cambridge must have felt more was best.

"Our third lead singer was also from South Bend, Indiana. Tom Stammich sang soul like a real black man. He also played tenor sax along side my trumpet," he explained. True musicians say "black" in the most respectful way possible. We mean Tom sang from his soul. I'm not implying he could have endured the suffering and prejudice that gave breath to genuine blues. The Cambridge guys were gifted musicians with sensational stage presence. They had the persistence and professionalism to reach elite status. Was something still missing? Not according to their loyal fans, or me either. Could they get even better? Well, they did. Listen to this. I mean, keep reading.

"Phil Everingham, our last guitar player, replaced Chris Sands. He was light years ahead of the finest rock-and-roll guitar players. He could do everything, even more than Eric Clapton. Nobody could touch his abilities anytime or anywhere. He was also the finest and most dependable person and musician, off- and on-stage. Very loyal, and just the best guitar player anyone ever heard. He still plays to this day, including steel guitar," Doug said. He posted a YouTube

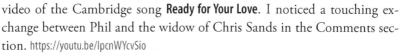

video of the Cambridge song **Ready for Your Love**. I noticed a touching exchange between Phil and the widow of Chris Sands in the Comments section. https://youtu.be/IpcnWYcvSio

Franky's Restaurant on caboose in Niles, Michigan.
The band in its final few years
(the tail end of the train and the band)
Doug Gast, trumpet and tenor sax
Denny Grounds, bass guitar
Don Cook, 3rd lead singer
Ron Monsma, drums
Phil Everingham, lead guitar
Tom Stammich, 2nd lead singer
Bob Cotrell, keyboards

Recording and Performances

In that era, exceptional musicians would often become great entertainers. In the Cambridge chapter, you're meeting guys like Doug Gast (the conscience of the group), who worked tirelessly to keep the band engaged and employed. Getting into a recording studio was a vital step to lasting success. The Cambridge may not have realized they were creating memories destined to last decades. When you hear their songs, you'll agree they did.

I've reconnected with guys who are still pursuing their passion. Many are still in their studios and offices. They are still interacting with fans of great music, our music. I want this book to help them connect with existing fans and make others. Lots of artists are posting YouTube clips themselves. If someone in the book recommends a clip, I try to accommodate them.

Artists and promoters developed a formula to satisfy an exploding market. There were hundreds of venues looking for new talent. First, find an accomplished group you could watch improve each gig. Someone uniquely positioned to do this would be DJ Dex Card. Aside from being a popular disc jockey on WLS 890 radio, he did hundreds of appearances at local dances. Eventually, he would employ hundreds of popular acts (and provide a springboard for some mega-acts) at his string of Wild Goose dance clubs. Check out his chapter for more.

Promoters like the Ed Redmond and Jim Bernard team at the Embassy Ballroom would also identify winning acts. Throw in the Screaming Wildman and Dan Belloc team at the Holiday Ballroom. You get it.

Next, we'd use established connections to get promising groups into the recording studio. Groups could seldom do this alone, no matter how much "brass" (not the musical kind) they displayed. That's where Dan Belloc and I served many groups pretty well, in my opinion. We would navigate the business end of things while the musicians could polish their delivery. Many eager and diverse groups found their way to 2131 South Michigan Avenue (the U.S.A. Records studio) just this way.

Finally, (if the fickle stars align) a group with freshly pressed vinyl could more easily shop their talent. Shop for what? For a DJ who may sneak the record past a difficult program manager to get some air play. You could also shop around for a producer/promoter who could represent the group. A promoter would need to log miles and endure rejections from radio stations in all markets. The more prestigious the venue, the more competitive the path.

There is no "finally" in this formula. Let's say your group has "arrived." What could possibly go wrong from here? In no particular order: Life on the road just got more complex. Popularity means some folks would have to abandon the security of a somewhat-steady day job, and their family, if they still had one by this time. The military draft was also a factor, especially during the era that we abandoned the use of the word "war." The name changed, but the devastation is very much the same to this day. Bottom line: In the best of times, you could count on lineup changes between records, and even between gigs.

In my line of work (actually my "calling") I tossed a couple of groups into the mix. I figured you may have heard enough from me for a while. You ready, Doug?

"We already had a strong connection with Jim Golden at U.S.A. Records. He was a good-looking guy. always wondered what happened to him," Doug said. See, I'm not the only one who gets distracted when I pour this all out in front of you.

"We released a single called **Oop-Oop-A-Do** on [Jim Golden's] Destination Records when we were known as the Tradewinds," he started. Go to Joe Pytel's YouTube video, **Floatin'** Cambridge Five, https://youtu.be/ssM3x1wBOSA. Joe explains the true identity of the artists. When you listen to the song, the historical inconsistencies are apparent. https://youtu.be/f2oKeOudY4E

As you will see, the Cambridge Five, later shortened to the Cambridge, teamed with Dan Belloc and his orchestra at U.S.A. Records to release a couple of singles: **Heads I Win / Floatin'** (USA# 850) in 1966 and **Keep on Running / I Hate To Laugh Alone** (USA# 875) in 1967. https://youtu.be/9xHml7GXXhw.

"Some of the original YouTube recordings were done with Dan Belloc and the Buckinghams at U.S.A. Records. Later recordings were done at Columbia Record Studios in Chicago with the Al Coyola Orchestra backing us," Doug explained. In the music business, timing is everything. Once you are with a record label, the breaks you get (or don't get) are seldom in your hands. Doug can tell you all about that.

"The Cambridge Five recorded **I'm Ready** at Columbia Records. The studio decided to shelve it for six months until they felt the timing was right. In the meantime, Rare Earth [at Motown, kind of] released what we think was a crappy garage version of the song, and it became an instant hit," Doug explained. The intro was most recognizable from the Temptations 1966 release. The original version was written by Smokey Robinson. The Temps took it to Billboard #29 and the Rare Earth version made it into the Top 5, if I remember. Even now, Doug Gast is still improving the sound of the group. That is true dedication to the craft.

"Joe Pytel is posting better-quality recordings of the group. Keep an eye out for the final recording of [A sides] like **Get Ready**, **Twine Time**, and **Keep On Running**. You'll also soon find **The Lonely Weekend.** It was recorded earlier but had the distinct Cambridge Five sound," Doug said.

Recollection Without Regret

Tons of memories flooded back from the times we shared. The Buckinghams performed many times with the Cambridge Five and became close friends throughout the years. How did Chicago groups like the Cryan' Shames, New Colony Six, Buckinghams, and Cambridge share the same stage so often and widely vary in success (measured any way you want) on the national scene? Nobody really knows. I'm so grateful, once again, for Doug's contributions to this chapter. I'm also grateful for his kind offer to keep us informed.

"I was tired, but it was a mistake to call it quits. Carl, with your help, Chuck Francour went to a group called Kracker and performed with them several years. Chuck still performs in Michigan and Florida. Remember that the Cambridge Five had four lead guitar players during their live performances and recordings. First, there was Dennis Sierens, then Mike Horton. Next, there was Chris Sands and then Phil Everingham. Horton and Sands played all of the lead guitar parts on the professional studio recordings. The taped live performances were done by Everingham. Sadly, Chris Sands passed away at the age of 62 in 2012," Doug said.

That reminds me, I have a few more recordings that I have in the works. Chuck Francour took the lead on **25 Miles** and **She's Coming Back**. Yeah, I forgot that this is Doug's forum. Our much overdue phone call led to more "what happened to" and "have you ever talked to" questions.

"Dex Card and I had lunch together, here in Florida. Tommy James married a gorgeous former Miss Florida and they are still together to this day. I've just been in touch with Carl Giammarese of the Buckinghams," Chuck said.

We went through so much together back in those times. Doug, you reminded me this group had a longer run than many of the other celebrated bands that we performed with and respected. This book gives us a chance to work together once again. Thanks for reminding me why it was all worth it!

A Brief History …

Trumpet and tenor sax player Doug Gast founded The Cambridge Five and acted as the group's manager. He recruited Chuck Francour, who played french horn in his high school band.

Chuck Francour was one of the original members. He first played keyboards and did not do vocals until persuaded by Rick Morgan, the original drummer.

Rick Morgan was an excellent marching band drummer. He left the band in the late '60s after graduating from Notre Dame University. Rick went on to Indiana University Law School in Indianapolis. He is still a practicing attorney in South Bend, Indiana.

Ron Monsma replaced Rick on drums in 1969 until the band disbanded in 1973. Ron's second love is painting. He presently paints portraits and teaches art at Indiana University in South Bend.

Cambridge Five original member Denny Grounds played bass guitar until the Cambridge disbanded in 1973.

Tom Stammich was the first genuine frontman and the second of three lead singers. After he joined the group in the late '60s, the group had to drop the "Five" in their name. His soul sound allowed the group to cover a wider range of songs. He also played tenor sax to complement Gast and gave the band an actual horn section when Francour revived his french horn play.

Don Cook, originally from the Five Emprees, joined the band as an additional lead singer once Francour left. He could work the crowd into a frenzy by swinging from a chandelier while singing and handing out drinks and beer.

Mike Horton was the original guitar player and was replaced by Chris Sands.

Phil Everingham joined the band in the late '60s and faithfully remained with the Cambridge for the longest time until 1973.

Bob Cotrell took over the keyboards in the late '60s when Francour left to pursue other endeavors. He did not sing lead but was a solid background singer. He remained with the group until the end in 1973. Bob Cotrell is still retired and now living in Niles, Michigan.

Throughout the years, Stammich and Francour would occasionally explore other opportunities and would then return to perform with the Cambridge.

If you've followed this until now...
The best-sounding and final makeup of the Cambridge went like this:
   Bob Cotrell on keyboards and organ. Don Cook as lead vocals, conga drums, and harmonica. Tom Stammich, a later but longer member, as lead vocals and playing tenor sax. Ron Monsma on drums and Phil Everingham on guitar.
   There were two original members of the Cambridge at the end of their run in 1973. Denny Grounds, bass player, is retired and living in South Bend, Indiana.
   "Denny can be regularly found sipping a beer at the Democratic Club in Roseland, a small burg to the north," Doug Gast, another original member, said. Good to know they kept in touch.
   Doug Gast, the founding member, played trumpet and tenor sax. He's been living in Naples, Florida, for the last thirty-five years. He continues to play trumpet and has performed alongside his son.

The Cambridge in the stairway leading to Don Belloc's office at the Holiday Ballroom
(Closest) Chuck Francour returning as 2nd lead singer; Bob Cotrell keyboards; Don Cook lead singer
(One Step Back) Doug Gast trumpet and tenor sax; Denny Grounds bass guitar
(Farthest) Chris Sands lead guitar; Ron Monsma drums

Performance Notes ...

For the last three to four years before the final gig of the Cambridge in 1973, the group played up to seven nights a week. After a matinee at Lake Geneva, Wisconsin, or Fox Lake, Illinois, the members would often take the stage at the Holiday Ballroom on Sunday night on the way home to the South Bend area.

They appeared throughout the Midwest with a number of famous artists. During their "golden" years, you would have seen their name on the marquee with Eric Burdon, New Colony Six, Cryan' Shames, Styx, REO Speedwagon, and Wayne Cochran & the CC Riders. Aside from numerous performances with the Buckinghams in Chicago, both bands left the crowds wanting more at Notre Dame University and other Indiana venues.

As you might expect, Doug Gast booked a number of shows in the band's home state. To name a couple, Neil Diamond in Fort Wayne and Rare Earth in South Bend. Baby Huey and the Babysitters from Hammond regularly teamed up with the Cambridge.

The Top Deck overlooking Lake Geneva and the Black Knight just down the road were among the group's favorite venues. Maybe it had something to do with the owners of those clubs and how often they would feud over who would land the Cambridge for a particular weekend. Both the Psychiatrist and Oliver's night clubs in Fox Lake, Illinois, often found themselves in the same dilemma.

Phil Orsi

I'm reconnecting with a lot of marvelous dudes who are still out there doing what they do, like me. Let me tell you a little bit about Phil Orsi. Then I'll let him tell you a little about himself.

Phil Orsi led a lot of groups who were inches (or seconds) from national fame. The frustrating thing for me (and even more so for them) is they shared the stage with so many hit makers. Members of those acts would be supportive and reassuring. Groups like the Beach Boys would be backstage hearing the applause and feeling the buzz the Little Kings would create.

New city, same lineup, same questions. Why hasn't a major label taken notice since the crowd is just lovin' everything that Phil Orsi and his band are throwing at them? Why do the Beach Boys have a contract with Capitol Records while the Little Kings are rockin' out on U.S.A. Records? Well, one group had Brian Wilson (OK, I answered my own question, kind of).

Really, there is more. There always is with the Screaming Wildman. Phil Orsi got to know the Beach Boys well enough to learn the harmonies of the Four Freshmen inspired the California-tanned version. As a side note: I think the Cryan' Shames were the Chicagoland answer. Their vocal blends were the envy of everyone I knew in the business.

I included a Cryan' Shames clip here. Close your eyes and listen. These guys were as good as any, and better than most. **Sugar and Spice** (on the Destination label) https://youtu.be/Fe7RlzkVS3U earned them a coveted Columbia contract. I intentionally tried to make that phrase sound like a song lyric.

I saw this happen in front of me on many occasions. It should have happened more often. Success should always last as long as memories linger. A number of factors affect the longevity of groups.

Take 1966, for example. The Beach Boys released the *Pet Sounds* album. Phil Orsi and the Little Kings released **Whoever He May Be** https://youtu.be/PDibecbaRw4 on U.S.A. **Sugar and Spice** by the Cryan' Shames would make it just north of No. 50 on the Billboard chart. There were other simultaneous events that would affect the make-up of some bands and the music they played. For example …

In 1966, the number of American troops in the Republic of Vietnam would more than double from the previous year (to well over 350,000). I think the kind of songs that an international audience wanted to hear also was changing. Remember, in 1960, the Beatles were starting their musical apprenticeship in Hamburg, Germany, when John Lennon was 20 and Paul McCartney was 18.

In the United States, guys 18 and above were required to register for the privilege of being drafted (the technical term was conscripted) to serve their country. Was it mere circumstance that allowed British groups to invade the American airwaves? Perhaps America was too interested in its own brand of invasion?

Remembering When

Obviously, it's been decades since we were all part of the most vibrant and turbulent era in American history. I'm continuously amazed at how much we remember once conversations get rolling. Here's what tumbled out of Phil Orsi's recollections.

"Carl, I remember you were managing the Centuries when I was playing with the Little Kings at the Vogue Ballroom," he started. Well, that's where we met. At the time, we were all occupied with making the best music possible and hoping to be part of the group who would make it big in the national market. We never had time to explain how they got where they were—until now.

"My father had an Italian food and liquor store. Around 1960, the original location [at 26th and Princeton] was razed during the construction of the Dan Ryan Expressway. The new location of Orsi & Sons was at 59 E. 18th Street," Phil continued. This was just a short distance from Record Row, between State Street and Michigan Avenue. That was nearly enough to get a guy interested in the music business. Of course, there was far more.

"Guys from Chess Records would stop at my dad's place for lunch. Muddy Waters would be in two or three days a week. I got to be friends with a lot of those guys," Phil continued. How could you not be inspired by conversations with living legends? Check out the sweet soul and

The original Little Kings, named after the comic strip (check out those emblems on their jackets) John Jackson, Clark Dufay, Phil Orsi, Steve Hamilton

falsetto lead on **Love Is Slipping Away**, written and performed by Phil Orsi
https://youtu.be/L_ObZy_LfKw.

Throughout this book, we're reminded how many bands would play five
and six nights a week. They would even do a couple of gigs some nights.
Not everyone could keep up that pace, so bands would break up and others
would evolve. Phil Orsi started the Little Kings in 1962.

"We started out as a four-piece band and ended up a trio. John Jackson was
on guitar and saxophone with Clark Dufay on lead guitar. Do you remember the
old comic strip of the little guy with the crown and cape? All of the guys had the
little king emblem on their jackets." Yeah, before folks got so crazy with lawsuits.
Maybe the King Features Syndicate was being tolerant and forgiving back then.

Whether he was performing as a solo act or with the Thunderbirds, Uni-Beats,
Little Kings, or Happiness Is, Phil Orsi was a class act. Well, the Little Kings
must have been, made apparent by the other stars who performed during those
shows. Yeah, I said it. Just because Phil didn't have a powerhouse label behind
him didn't mean he wasn't a star in his own right.

"We must have played more than a dozen times with the Beach Boys. They
always treated us well, even though they were a big national act. That was the
most fun I had," he started. There were many moments that must have come in
a close second.

"We played with the Dave Clark Five, the Kinks and Eric Clapton at the
Arie Crown Theater / McCormick Place. I can remember standing on stage just
as the curtains opened in front of 5,000 fans," Phil remembered.

"I was about 24 or 25 when the Little Kings were at their height of popularity. There is a picture circulating where the Little Kings are walking in the
middle of the intersection at 63rd and California. That's what I call a snapshot
of history. Look at those vintage clothes, cars, and instruments," he reminded
me. You can see them in a few of the YouTube links I included.

I got a van for the Buckinghams and Daughters of Eve (but no photos).
That's two reasons to be jealous of Phil Orsi, if I was that kind of guy.

Longevity Defined

Guys like us often discuss what longevity really means. The definition changes as time passes. Each group or performer needs to create their own. Through the latest technology (like YouTube) we are creating a market hunger, like a good promoter should. We still need to get the artists paid fairly. Premium subscriptions on Spotify or paid downloads from iTunes help us continue to do what we were born to do. It's nothing like the good old days of personality AM radio, but we have to use what we have.

The original production of those songs is seared into our old-timer memories. I mentioned my interview with (80-year-old) Ed Cody, and I could feel Phil's recollections aligning themselves. Perfectionists like Phil Orsi can recall most of their performances and every recording session.

"Ed Cody and I are good friends. I have pictures of the two of us taken in his studio. Of course, I also have photos of the Little Kings and the Thunderbirds," he told me. Thank goodness so many records and snapshots have survived. It took us nearly five decades to realize both the importance of every "player" and how the current musical generation can pay them tribute. We have to give them a "thumbs-up" in whatever social media platform you prefer.

Phil occasionally stops by Beverly Records and still marvels at the renewed market for vintage vinyl. Proprietor Jack Dreznes tells him some of his records are commanding a decent price. He also reminds us that vinyl is surging in the "Millennial" marketplace.

"A few years ago, I don't think I could have given my records away," Phil laughingly told me. I can feel he genuinely grooved during the era and was as thrilled as I am to have been a part of it.

The Dave Clark Five pose with the Thunderbirds in 1965. Phil is nestled in with the Brits, next to Dave, also John Russo on drums, Coy Lowehorne lead guitar, Ken Hoffmen on keyboards, Cal Clemons on horns.

"So many of the bands at that time were just regular people. Through a stroke of luck, they would land the song or two that would give them lasting fame and all that went with it," he said. We've seen it happen more than a few times.

Phil played regularly until the age of 50 and now jams regularly with his son and his band. Maybe that's not the kind of longevity he originally envisioned. However, this is really the only type that counts in the long run. You know, just having a long run to talk about means a lot at our age.

"Carl, you were always hustling to make things better for each group. You are my Italian buddy," Phil said. Well, I'm flattered he noticed how hard I worked. It was far easier to realize I was Italian. You know what I'm sayin'? Maybe some of these chapters will show how musically wealthy that era was. I'm happy to still be part of the ongoing story and grateful Phil Orsi is willing to share it with us.

Phil Orsi, Revisited

You know, once I really "got into" my book, I could feel all the good friends I acknowledged enjoying it as well. Many said how grateful they were that I included them. Well, how could I not? Once the first interview is complete, I've shared the rough draft with them. This proves that a Sicilian can actually listen as well as talk. Inevitably, there is much more to discuss. There are dates to nail down and more names to interject.

I'm hammering out the manuscript. I just try to let the folks involved talk about their own experiences. We may have been at the same events but had different perspectives.

I relaxed while interviewing folks for my book. They were all comfortable in front of a microphone. Phil and I had a good time reliving the moments we shared long ago. I sent him his draft so we might springboard into something else. Phil got things rolling during the early part of February 2016.

"Carl, you were such a hard worker, man. You were everywhere that we were: the Crystal Ballroom, Louigi's, the Holiday and Vogue ballrooms and Antoine's," he began. Of all the groups I worked with, Phil Orsi and the Little Kings were there at the top. I'm understanding more about why.

"How old are you now, Phil?" I asked. You can be blunt with a fellow paisano (that's the Italian translation for you all). We're Italian amigos.

"I'm 75," he answered. Hey, same as me, and I told him so. All of his guys were so much more polished and professional than groups like the Centuries and Pulsations. I got my groups, whose members had barely escaped high school, positioned to learn from musicians like Phil Orsi and the Little Kings.

Some guys got it and some didn't. That's partly why it took two groups to evolve into the Buckinghams. Both got a chance to learn showmanship from the other groups, if they were watching. It's one thing to practice music. It is quite another thing to inspire a crowd. I pressed on and asked Phil how many songs he recorded overall.

"I recorded 42," he answered without hesitation. He was waiting to tell you, but obviously was too modest. We briefly compared notes from Beverly Records about Phil's newfound popularity before our attention turned to one awesome engineer responsible for "tons" of that vintage vinyl. You know him.

"Ed Cody and I go back a long way," Phil remembered. I excitedly relived my recent interview with him, accompanied by Joe Pytel and Larry Nestor.

"Carl, I always admired your drive, man," he said. I think I understand the feeling behind the subtle shift in the conversation. We're still wondering why things came together for the Buckinghams and national fame eluded gutsy and talented guys like Phil Orsi.

"You got me thinking about Gary Loizzo" he said. He founded the American Breed, contemporaries of the Buckinghams, who made it big with **Bend Me, Shape Me**.

"That song is still being used in commercials, you know," he said. I sense he's not jealous, but honored to be part of that special era in our lives.

"I had fun. I'm still having fun." We'll meet again, I'm sure.

True to his music and the changing times: Phil Orsi is in the center, sporting the shoes, bell-bottoms, and hair.
Stan Tuma, Tony Petanado, Wolfman Jack, Larry Weimer

Postscripts

You know how you think of some things right after you hang up the phone with a person? I just thought of several ways that we can start our next conversation. Phil and I are not "email" guys. We would rather talk or meet in person. It's nowhere near as much fun to talk to someone if you can't see their reaction. Phil promised we will "break bread" soon.

Our next conversation might begin with stories about Officer Vic and all of the "personality" disc jockeys who made each dance an occasion. These guys did hundreds of appearances for charitable events. You know, when "real" charities and "genuine" celebrities donated their time and talent for the truly disadvantaged.

I know we're going to talk about all of our mutual friends and friendly competitors at U.S.A. Records. Most likely we will briefly acknowledge our short list of scoundrels that we encountered, too.

Among the best of the good guys, I'm referencing a couple for your entertainment and education. Gary Loizzo and (in an upcoming chapter) Dick Biondi are internationally famous, and my words would truly prove inadequate in the grand scheme of things. Just do your own research if you want to know more. In my opinion, you should. I think you'll find that Gary "bent and shaped" both Chicago and national music.

I included more links to Phil Orsi songs for your enjoyment.

Happiness Is https://youtu.be/GTZEaKuEnb4.

Loving on Borrowed Time (written by Larry Nestor) – Phil Orsi & the Little Kings https://youtu.be/1tO6hp1S0ms

Someone New – Phil Orsi and the Uni-Beats https://youtu.be/Z4jMJlOntbM

Sorry (I Ran All the Way Home) – Phil Orsi & the Little Kings https://youtu.be/NEO_JtFfsfY

Don't You Just Know It https://youtu.be/laumPMM1uaE

Stay – Phil Orsi & the Little Kings https://youtu.be/606kO_3_gew

Gary Loizzo

I mentioned Gary more extensively in my chapter about recording studios and engineers. He's another guy who never missed a beat (literally) while working with a diverse group of artists like Bad Company, Liza Minnelli, and Tenacious D.

Sadly, Gary passed away while I was pulling together my notes for this book. I included a link to a fitting tribute http://www.obitsforlife.com/obituary/1232413/Loizzo-Gary.php and included a scan of his remembrance card. I hope you feel that including it here is as touching and tasteful as I intended.

Ral Donner (1943-84)

This was another hard chapter to write, for reasons you will soon understand. Right up front, I guarantee everybody (with integrity and an ear for great music) is already a fan of Ral Donner. Note that I say "is" when I refer to him. An overwhelming number of people that I've interviewed recently have mentioned his name (fondly, of course). If you are less familiar with his work, consider yourself a fan-in-the-making.

During his induction into the Rock & Roll Hall of Fame in 1995, Robert Plant of Led Zeppelin cited Ral Donner as an influence. This is just another case where American markets somehow turned a blind eye to awesome talent. The British, however, knew how to capture the essence of rock-and-roll (really blues and soul) and package it for American consumption. The closest example here in the States would be Elvis Presley.

The King of Rock and Roll was the best-known fan of Ral Donner. They met in person at least a couple of times. I swear, you are not going to believe this. Presley once heard a Donner recording for the Gone Records label and mistook it for his own! Now you know what Ral sounds like. I refer to him in the present tense because his work is priceless.

I included a YouTube link to **Cinderella Twist**, https://youtu.be/pfBsfl2g0gU, from the 1962 movie *Dance Craze*. I wanted you to see a live clip of him. Somebody with better resources (and more patience than I) might be able to tell you how Ral (probably through Jim Lounsbury) got a chance to perform in this movie. This is certainly not the best example of his charisma and talent, but at least he made it to the big screen.

Do you know who else should be a fan of Ral Donner? Everybody who went to Taft High School. He grew up near the corner of Harlem and Devon, just a few short blocks away. See if you can follow me here. Jim Jacobs (of the musical *Grease* fame) was an alum of Taft. In the *Grease* movie, there is a scene with Johnny Casino & the Gamblers (portrayed by Sha-Na-Na members). The inspiration for Johnny most certainly came from Ral Donner & the Gents, at least in my book (pun intended). Jacobs and Donner were born less than a year apart, and the Gents performed at Taft, by many accounts.

I have to acknowledge Mr. Terry Wilson for jogging my memory on several fronts. For one of the most comprehensive accounts of the life and times of Ral Donner, I've included the link to his official Ral Donner website (http://www. thewick.co.uk/raldonner). As you will notice, this is a UK address. Once again, our European contemporaries seem to "school" us on our own music and artists. It's comforting to know Ral has 21st-century international fans. I just wish he received his deserved recognition decades earlier.

There were some very famous people who appreciated the immense talent of Ral Donner. Maybe the most notable was Sammy Davis Jr. How did young Mr. Donner even cross paths with a versatile and ground-breaking performer like Sammy? Only through his unprecedented commitment to young people. In the late '50s, even the prestigious Chez Paree nightclub sponsored a *Time for Teens* show to showcase young talent.

Crazier still (when compared to today), established entertainers would drop by to catch a few acts, and even perform themselves at times. That night, Sammy caught a young Mr. Donner performing a couple of Elvis Presley tunes. It could have been **Jailhouse Rock**, which debuted in 1957. No matter. Sammy Davis Jr. was significantly impressed.

In 1958, Ral Donner appeared at the Apollo Theater in New York. Can you imagine the kind of "soul" you need to influence that crowd? He was certainly one of the first Caucasian performers there.

I did some great and wild stuff at a very young age. I ran dances at the Swiss Hall and hosted my infamous cemetery dance as well. I sang with the Gem-Tones and recorded my first records. That doesn't even compare with playing the Apollo at any age. Ral Donner was 15 years old at the time.

Where did an impressionable Ral get so much exposure to soul artists? I don't think you need to look any further than one of my own mentors, Eddie Thomas. Remember that *Time for Teens* show I mentioned? Well, Ral's performances were enhanced by a group called the Medallionaires who (along with the Im-pressions) was managed by Eddie.

The crowds were loving the way Eddie's group complemented Ral Donner's vocal stylings. This was much like the Jordanaires, the group that provided the background vocals for many of Elvis's memorable recordings. The gospel back-grounds of both backing groups provided the soul and blues foundation that propelled both singers upward and outward.

I don't think Ral ever wanted to impersonate Elvis. I don't even think the crowds thought of him as an impersonator. More than anything, they just wanted more of that "sound." The truth be known, Ral was more taken with the sound and delivery of Jerry Butler from the Impressions. I included a link to **For Your Precious Love**, https://youtu.be/VndnTfW7Xyw, released in 1958 by Butler and the Impressions.

Ral was performing in his Baptist church choir at an early age. Butler literally exuded "soul," due in part to the poverty and prejudice that he endured in a segregated Chicago. I'm only guessing here because I didn't really get to know Ral Donner until much later in his career when his record labels abandoned him. More on that later.

I think record companies made it known they were willing to market Ral as a young Elvis. This would not be the case if he were known as a Caucasian Jerry Butler. Ral was neither. He was a consummate professional entertainer who could touch the "essence" of any audience. He drew his inspiration from groups like the Ink Spots, the Platters, and the Five Satins.

Ral recorded his first song when he was just shy of his 16th birthday. **Tell Me Why** (https://youtu.be/yOKrl9dOhFE) earned him a promotional slot on Jim Lounsbury's *Record Hop* TV show. Billboard and Cashbox were taking notice. He formed the Gents to back him up, and I started booking the group at my dances. In 1960, one of Ral Donner's biggest fans came to Chicago: WLS radio personality Dick Biondi.

Neither may have known about the other at that time. That would change before very long. **Girl of My Best Friend** was released by Elvis Presley in 1960. Shortly after, Ral Donner was incorporating that song into his act in and around Chicago. According to some accounts, Ral was reluctant to go "one on one" with the King (at least in the public's mind).

I was just an interested observer at this point. Of course, I was going to support any Chicago guy, just like all of Chicago does (I am reluctant to use the past tense). Even in the 21st century, Chicago needs to fight for rock-and-roll recognition. Ask Dick Biondi, or nearly anyone else in this book.

The first Ral Donner record on the Gone Record label (http://www.globaldogproductions.info/g/gone.html) was **Girl of My Best Friend**. Even the smallest labels could serve as the springboard for worldwide fame. The New Jersey (I mean really "new") band known as the Four Seasons released its first record on Gone. Ral charted, and they didn't. I wish I could find the YouTube clip showing the Gone Record label, but this one should work for you: https://youtu.be/FmPtApk1C1U.

Ral's version of the song was terrific, but that wouldn't guarantee it would get considerable airplay (if any at all). Unless someone else comes up with a better theory, let's use mine. Jim Lounsbury and Dick Biondi were already "up close and personal" with Ral Donner's talent and personality. Jim had him on his show as I mentioned earlier. Dick would have either seen him at dances or heard about him from other DJs.

Okay, I booked him myself and was aware of his immense following with the young crowd. I didn't have the ability to influence the Chicago market the way Lounsbury or Biondi could. Ral Donner was as modest as he was talented. Maybe it was a bit of a shock to him when his song continued to rise to the No. 2 spot on the WLS Silver Dollar Survey. I can't remember who was No. 1. My guess is **Poetry in Motion** by Johnny Tillotson or **Stay** by Maurice Williams & the Zodiacs. You know, **Shop Around** by the Miracles only made it to No. 2 at WLS. Man, there was a lot of unbelievable music back then.

The 50,000-watt WLS was beaming **Girl** daily far and wide and reaching markets only it could at that time. Dick Clark was as good at recognizing trends as he was at creating them. A couple of weeks after cracking into Billboard's Hot 100, Ral Donner was singing **Girl of My Best Friend** at his first appearance on American Bandstand. The song would top out at No. 19.

You Don't Know What You've Got, https://youtu.be/CQb8vywBsCA (I found a video displaying the Gone Label), was released in 1961 and climbed to Billboard's No. 4 position. Some people heard "Elvis" in this song. Remember, Ral was actually trying to capture the "essence and soul" of fellow Chicagoan Jerry Butler. Maybe Elvis was, too. Ever think about that before now? The WLS survey placed him at No. 3 this time. Chubby Checker's **Let's Twist Again** nosed ahead of him. This was pretty easy to look up. I'm wondering what I could have done with the internet magic back then! (Don't laugh!)

That second hit earned Ral another spot on American Bandstand. **Please Don't Go** (https://youtu.be/nvh3UD7RH8s) was the third single from the 14-track album released by Gone in September 1961. **Takin' Care of Business** sold well across the

United States and was touted by both the Cashbox and Billboard magazines. Ral Donner was emerging as a genuine "force" during the rock-and-roll era.

Popularity and Payoffs

The Top-40 radio format was really a new phenomenon in broadcasting. It was actually a survey of airplay (not necessarily sales). To put that a slightly different way, airplay would drive sales and not the other way around. I don't even know why I thought of this now. It was probably the references to Cashbox—the magazine and what it implied about revenue from the popularity of songs.

See if you can keep up with this, the way it's tumbling out of my head: Someone like Ral Donner was then more than just an artist, due to the well-deserved popularity of his songs. He was becoming a commodity. Nationwide, celebrity DJs clamored for his personal appearances. The radio stations (really their sponsors) were quite happy. Record companies were seeing their investment pay off.

Do you know where the majority of vinyl discs for popular records ended up during the '50s and '60s? Jukeboxes. (I'm too impatient to let you think about it.) Artists got paid a small percentage of each record sold. At least, they were supposed to.

The most popular records paid for themselves hundreds of times over (whenever someone dropped coins into the slot). Ungodly sums changed hands. Seldom would the right people get paid, in my humble opinion.

Hitting the Road

We're talking late summer of 1961 here. This would have been right before the release of *Taking Care of Business*. Ral appeared in the KQV (Pittsburgh) Radio Appreciation Day Show with nearly 20 popular acts like Frankie Avalon, Bobby Vinton, Gene Pitney, and Freddie Cannon. These types of shows were awesome in any location. In a smaller market, they were the only way artists could reach all of their fans.

Once again, the Top-40 radio stations could do a lot to drive sales. KQV was a relative powerhouse in the '60s. Near as I can determine, it only had 5,000-watts of power. Really, there were a couple of things that made it unique. First, it had three call letters. The King of the Quaker Valley was one of very few radio stations beginning with the letter "K" from the Eastern time zone.

At the four-letter stations, the "K" usually stood for a Kaiser Broadcasting affiliation. "W" was for Westinghouse to the east, except for WLS in Chicago, which stood for World's Largest Store (Sears). By the way, WGN (both radio and television) refers to the ownership of the World's Greatest Newspaper. At least, *The Chicago Tribune* is the most read in the Chicagoland area. Two fine gentlemen featured elsewhere in this book worked for the *Chicago Sun-Times*. Back to Pittsburgh …

KQV began marketing itself as the "Groovy QV." KQV had its own stable of personalities to promote rock-and-roll shows. Apparently, word got out across the pond because the Beatles performed in Pittsburgh's Civic Arena in 1964. From my era, Pittsburgh had a number of native sons, like Perry Como, Dean Martin, and Henry Mancini. All right, to my point …

Pittsburgh was a vibrant market. Kids in blue-collar families could afford a ticket to rock-and-roll concerts and purchase their own vinyl keepsakes. As we all know, radio stations were vital to record distribution. Pittsburgh, and every diner, gin mill, or restaurant in America (and overseas), had a jukebox getting plenty of use. The recording artists got a lot of exposure (but not a lot of cash, comparatively speaking).

Oh yeah, I almost forgot about one of the most influential developments in the history of music. You know what I'm talkin' about yet? You are going to kick yourself if you are nearly my age. On second thought, don't try to kick yourself.

You are probably too brittle! The transistor radio suddenly became more powerful, affordable, and portable. In 1962, my buddy Freddie Cannon released **Transistor Sister** https://youtu.be/oMsPENmI4WE. It was a light-hearted take on the awesome power that teenagers had (almost as much as disc jockeys). It was a fun time to be in the music business.

Ral toured extensively with Tony Orlando, Ray Stevens, and Bobby Vinton. He also recorded at Bell Sound Studios in New York City, met Elvis, and appeared on *American Bandstand* for the third time. Ral appeared on the cover of *Cashbox* magazine that magical year. Keep in mind, he was now only 18 years old.

Chicago Beckons

Back in our day, everyone had a favorite Ral Donner song. What does that tell you? It told me he was a serious, respected talent and a popular entertainer.

A couple of folks (like Dwight Kalb) who have their own chapters in this book shared Ral Donner experiences. Phil Orsi told me his favorite Donner song is **I Got Burned** (https://youtu.be/fBGc9cRA95k).

"I think Ral needed to do more up-tempo things as he did in live performances. The record companies had him doing too many ballads," Phil said. That's why live performances were so vital to a career. The record labels didn't want to mess up the "formula" once a recording artist had a hit. The live performances allowed artists to stretch a little. Phil would see artists up close and personal.

Let me give you a little background on another phenomenon of that magical era. Shows were big and featured multiple acts, with multiple performances each day. The big show at Medinah Temple (600 N. Wabash), that Phil is going to describe, featured appearances by Dick Biondi and Jim Lounsbury. It was sponsored by Pepsi-Cola.

"I was playing with the Don Carone (producer and orchestra leader) house band for the show. Dion, Brenda Lee & the Casuals, Johnny Tillotson, the Marvelettes, Freddie "Boom-Boom" Cannon, and Ral Donner were there. It was a frigid January that year, so the crowds were kind of sparse. Every night, Ral would turn in the greatest performance," Phil said.

Can you imagine Freddie Cannon and Ral Donner in the same show? I really loved them both, despite their contrasting styles. It was just good music. I actually recorded **Palisades Park** by Freddie. Bill Moore (whom I will also introduce to you) recorded me and uploaded it to YouTube (https://youtu.be/bxP9ltzmwHI). I did have a "crooner" side to me, though. A couple of folks

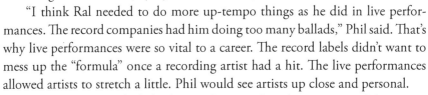

said I sounded a little like Paul Anka. Anyway, I don't think I could have done justice to a Ral Donner song.

One thing that makes a show great is the versatility on display. No audience wants to hear the same types of songs. Ral Donner could do ballads as well as up-tempo stuff and everything in between. I didn't find out until many years later that **(What a Sad Way) to Love Someone** (https://youtu.be/iOUZ4tai-ml) was one of Ral's personal favorites. Unfortunately, it never rose above No. 79 on the Billboard chart.

Ral continued to be a "force" while touring with the likes of B.B. King, the Drifters, Gladys Knight & the Pips, the Sensations, and Sam Cooke. Is there anything that could derail the Ral Donner Express? Nothing should have. Ral was 20 years old by this time and one of the most sought-after performers you could imagine. Shockingly, he would never crack the Top 100 again.

Without going into sordid details, Ral got into a dispute with Gone Records over alleged non-payment of royalties. Legal wrangling with record executives turned even uglier somewhere down the line. Other record labels seemed to be intimidated by New York musical power brokers and balked at offering Ral Donner a contract once Gone Records cut ties.

He did a brief stint with Reprise Records, which was also releasing songs from his mentor and initial benefactor, Sammy Davis Jr. For the next 12 years or so, Ral bounced from one label to another. Actually, that is not accurate. Ral just wanted to make music and get paid his fair share. His recordings and releases during that time reflected either the instability of a particular label or the dealings of the people working in the "underside" of music.

Some of the labels he worked with included Red Bird, Fontana, and (I think) Rising Sun Records, founded by Arlo Guthrie. Ral started recording at Universal Recording Studios in Chicago. He also started producing much of his own material and releasing it to Sunlight or Thunder Records (and Chicago Fire, his own label), among others.

I found a transparent-vinyl edition of **Don't Leave Me Now** on Star Fire Records. This disc is actually clear vinyl with colored chips pressed in. Ed Cody mentioned the technique during his interview. Chicago fans remained true to their local hero, and his records sold pretty well in the Chicago area. This wasn't quite enough to maintain contact with a worldwide fan base, however.

Ral Donner was true to his music and his supporters. To keep his creative juices flowing, he wrote a few jingles and songs for other artists. He also recorded a "live" performance of the Platters on his Chicago Fire label. As you might expect, there is a lot of Ral Donner unreleased material. Speaking of which …

Forever and Always

It's sometime in 1976, and Ral Donner and I are commiserating. Of course, there are no sure things in the music business. I'm pretty sure that both of us figured it would go a little differently for him since 1958 (at age 15) when he shared the stage with Chuck Berry, the Diamonds, Jerry Lee Lewis, and Buddy Holly and the Crickets at Chicago's Civic Opera House.

In a rare moment for Ral, he mentioned his confusion about staying relevant in the music business. I was having considerable doubts about my own career. For his sake and mine, I tried to find a suitable outlet for three tracks that Ral recorded at Universal in 1972: **Pittsburgh**, **Mr. Misery**, and **It All Adds Up to Lonely**.

 Those three, along with three others—**Wait a Minute**, **Greatest Moments of My Life**, and **Maria (Forever)**—are on two of my own greatest hits CDs. Check out **Maria (Forever)** on my Chi-Town label: https://youtu.be/HwOUqaJ8rq0.

Until then, I had no idea whether or not Ral would ever set foot in another recording studio. When Elvis Presley died in August 1977, Ral wrote **The Day the Beat Stopped** as his tribute and recorded it at Universal. Thunder Records released it the following year. Ral also recorded the double album *1935-1977: I've Been Away for Awhile Now*, in which he narrated Elvis's life story and performed dozens of Elvis's tunes.

It's kind of crazy how Ral Donner's career was permanently linked to that of probably the best-known performer in the rock-and-roll era. Ral provided the narration in *This Is Elvis*, a documentary created by Warner Brothers (1981).

The most tragic of parallels between the careers of Ralph Stuart Emanuel Donner and Elvis was their early departure from our world. In early April 1984, Ral passed away at age 41 after a heroic battle with cancer. If ever there was a guy who deserved to be interviewed for this book, it would be him. I hope these few pages satisfy his existing fans and create many new ones (as planned).

Lori London

Lori London is, far and away, the best singer I ever heard. She opened shows for country mega-stars like Mel Tillis, Ray Price, Mary Robbins, and Charlie Pride. At a Loretta Lynn concert, she left the crowd buzzing with her stir- ring tribute to country legend Patsy Cline. I included the link here so you can see what I mean. http://www.lorilondonmusic.com/patsy-cline-tribute

The Brooklyn Bridge (think, **The Worst That Could Happen**) and the Duprees (**You Belong to Me**, which charted at No. 7 in 1962) also engaged her to warm up the crowd for them. Recently, she performed at the historic landmark Tampa Theatre for a Christmas show and the Cuban Club in Ybor City (Tampa, Florida) for the annual Celebrate Sinatra event.

Her latest CD is called *Serenade*, a classic jazz and Broadway collection. She's been interviewed by John "Radio" Russell at WDCB 90.9FM (Chicago's Home for Jazz). You can occasionally catch one of her songs on his *Midwest Ballroom* show. Being a talented recording artist and performer would be enough for nearly anyone else. Of course, there's more.

Lori also appeared in the motion pictures *Sweet Home Alabama* (2002) with Reese Witherspoon and *The Terminal* (2004) starring Tom Hanks. She's also made radio appearances in Nashville and Philadelphia. In addition, she wrote and did voice-overs for WVLT 92.1 FM New Jersey radio ads. Recently, she was approached by a production company in Atlanta to write, direct, and star in a re-ality TV pilot called *Life With Lori*. I would call it *The Many Lives of Lori*.

Tripi Takes Flight: The Amazing Adventures of Tripi the Fly hit the Amazon® bookshelves August 12, 2016. This is the first in her children's series about a fly who can dance, sing, read, and write (just not fly). Read it to your children and grandchildren before Tripi's game and animated motion pic-ture hit the market! Maybe I'm getting ahead of myself on the last part, but I'm selling it anyway.

Some years ago, I compiled a CD under my Chi-Town label. Nine tracks are by my beloved Daughters of Eve. The other nine showcase the awesome and diverse talent of Lori Lee Williams, as she was known at that time.

Diesel Cowboys https://youtu.be/mjjkEerJj5A should have been her springboard for national recognition. Everyone who hears that track from her *Wreckless Heart* album wants to know more about that gifted singer. Popular journalist and host of the Saturday night Nocturnal Journal WGN (720AM) radio show Dave Hoekstra instantly became one of her fans.

Carl Giammarese of the Buckinghams was intrigued by her **Kind of a Drag** adaptation to a country lament http://youtu.be/m6vsaQSbM9o. I'm hoping Carl and Lori someday will perform a duet of that song (or any song, for that matter).

I continually thank two guys for introducing me to Lori. The first is Cal Starr, Chicago-born songwriter, recording artist, promoter (you met earlier), and her proud dad. The other is the dearly missed Lew Douglas, legendary arranger, composer, conductor, songwriter, and mentor to the Screaming Wildman. You're going to hear about Lew often throughout this book.

The Diesel Cowboy Days

Lew recorded young Lori in Nashville and raved about her talent and poise in front of everyone, including me. I promised him I would do everything possible to introduce her to everyone I knew in the business. After Lew passed away in 1997 at the age of 85, I acquired the masters from Lori's Nashville sessions.

I knew Lew would only introduce people when he was certain they would complement (and compliment) one another. That's why Lori and I "connected" the first time we talked on the phone. Years later, she was equally happy to meet me for a live interview and her own chapter in my book.

That's also why we talk about Lew Douglas all the time. It will make him happy we're still in touch. I bet that's also why we mention him in the present tense, since he is still with us.

Great to See Ya, Lori

I waited in my "mobile office" at Mariano's (Ashland and Webster). Before long, I saw the automatic door jump out of Lori's way as she scanned the room (like every professional performer does), then bound in my direction. We had to hug at some point, or we would have crashed together. People were watching.

I planned to open our conversation with recollections of Lew Douglas, but I came up with a friendly way to tease her instead. "You're still Lori London, aren't you? Every time I turn around, you've got a different name. You're always Lori sumthin' or sumthin'," I said.

How's that for openers? She laughed, of course, with her smile still shining while she formed her answer. Before that, I offered a little more, like I was doing a commercial.

"You were Lori Stallard, like I saw on your dad's poster. Lori Starr, like your dad. Lori Lee Williams, Lori London, you know, Lori Sumthin'," I said. I caught my breath, and my guest finally had a chance to reply.

"Oh my gosh, you are going to laugh. I was also Madison McQuade!" she chuckled. As I often say, it takes a lot to stop me in my tracks, but that got me laughing too hard to continue for a moment.

"That sounds like a name for a female gunslinger, doesn't it, Carl?" She's such a light-hearted soul. So easy to talk to, and even easier to listen to.

I mentioned that Joe Pytel uploaded a couple of Lori Lee Williams songs on YouTube. I figured you may want to have your own version, and I believe artists should be paid for their work. I also included an iTunes link to **Diesel Cowboys** (https://itunes.apple.com/us/album/diesel-cowboys-single/id1008525384). She knows it's my favorite song. I also love **A Whole Week of Mondays**. It's another one of the Nashville tracks I inherited and have on my CD.

"Yeah, that's another Lew Douglas song," she said fondly. "He is a phenomenal arranger and composer."

I reminded her he is a gifted judge of talent. We can't help but talk about him as if he were still here. I know that I probably told her this before, but I like repeating this for you.

"Lori, when Lew Douglas told me about you, he said that I wasn't going to believe what I was about to hear, and he was right. When I found out that you never took a single voice lesson, I could hardly believe it. We were both so sure a record executive would hear you and offer you a big contract," I said.

"Lew would put one finger up and tell me, 'It takes one person, just one, you know, the right person to make it all happen,'" she remembered. I still feel bad that it couldn't have happened the way we all hoped. Maybe I'm still the right person.

"You have a tremendous voice, and I can't believe that you haven't been discovered," I reminded her.

MADISON MCQUADE   A M A X

"Thanks, Carl. You make me cry," she said with delight. I know she means it in a good way.

Enter "Lori London music" into your web search window or use my hyperlink http://www.lorilondonmusic.com. If she doesn't change her name again, we're "golden."

I encourage folks to check out the **Diesel Cowboys** YouTube clip where Joe Pytel includes more photos than I can print https://youtu.be/mjjkEerJj5A. Once you fall in love with her voice, you can purchase one of her albums or individual songs on iTunes. Like I said, gifted artists deserve to be paid. You know what I'm sayin'? Finally, you can forward this link to someone eager to energize their live event. She's good enough to take Broadway by storm.

We discussed music trends and how the British bands all seemed to embrace country, R&B, and soul music. Maybe they were less afraid of different cultures. Maybe British groups forced Americans to appreciate, if not embrace, diversity.

Speaking of trends, we talked about our most recent recording sessions. Carl Giammarese created the instrumental tracks and I added my vocals. I mentioned he played every instrument on my latest CD. Lori handles things pretty much the same way.

"There are so many good tracks for sale. I just take them to my engineer and he lays down my vocal track. I usually get them done in very few tries," she told me. Only someone who has her live performance experience would ever be able to do that. I'll tell you something else. Only a true professional can learn to visualize her audience in the studio and project her feelings toward them.

"My *Serenade* album was done that way. How else could anyone afford to have an orchestra behind them? You just have to license the tracks before you release the CD," she reminded me. You make it sound so easy, Lori.

"You, Dan Belloc, and Lew were always looking out for me," she continued. Actually, we did that for a lot of people. None of them were anywhere close to her as far as talent goes.

Remember how I mentioned the Duprees at the beginning of Lori's chapter? Guess who foresaw the Duprees and Lori London sharing a stage?

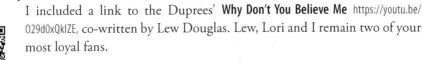

I included a link to the Duprees' **Why Don't You Believe Me** https://youtu.be/029d0xQkIZE, co-written by Lew Douglas. Lew, Lori and I remain two of your most loyal fans.

Influential Characters

Dwight Kalb

I'm sitting next to awesome drummer and rock promoter Dwight Kalb from CASK Attractions in early December 2015. Ordinarily, he would be capturing another landscape in colorful oil or acrylic in the Key West sunshine by this time. This year, he's still in town to answer (I mean fight) a Chicago summons issued while he was painting at Diversey Harbor near the Lake Michigan shoreline. He appeared to be deep-sixing his cigarette butts in an empty beer bottle nearby. Apparently, the law-and-order reputation of Chicago was at risk because some undercover female cop engaged him as he painted. After going on about his work and her own daughter's interest in art, she ripped a ticket out of her concealed summons pad.

Open container violation. Once his severe scolding (with court costs) was behind him, Dwight didn't plan to leave his Key West "headquarters" until spring had taken hold back in Chi-town. Unless, of course, he demanded a jury trial (if you can do that). It was going to be an amusing story for the snowbird set http://paperpaintings.growingbolder.com/celebrating-individuality/.

Could he pay his fine and forget the argument? Was there proof he didn't find that bottle rather than empty it? What would I do? It wouldn't even be about the argument. Sicilians were most likely conceived during some kind of squabble and very likely born the same way. For guys like us, it would demonstrate the lack of priorities for a court system that intends to prove its point and hassle a (perceivably) helpless mature man.

Okay, I answered my own question. "Free Dwight Kalb. Free Dwight Kalb." Join me if you want.

I'm anxious to introduce Dwight Kalb. I call him a true "artisan." Talented men wear their eccentricity with pride. A good heart and skilled hands make people overly cautious, if not jealous. Ask the Screaming Wildman. Dwight was an accomplished and sought-after drummer from an early age. He had a musical mentor he will honor later in this interview. He also had a student who got national—if not world—recognition.

I got to know him pretty well as one of the "pillars" at CASK Attractions. The "K" in CASK stands for Kalb. He has some great perspectives on being both an insider and outsider as a performer, artist, and executive. You have to be a little nuts (I mean eccentric) to take on that much. You also need to be brilliant to perform at an extraordinary level. That's what a genius does. A good friend also knows when to either encourage someone or kick their ass. I respect Dwight's decision on which was most needed at any particular time.

He brought a couple of packets with pictures, snippets, and a sampling of contracts to our reunion. While leafing through Dwight's remembrances, a couple of clippings caught my eye. I remember hearing about this when it happened, but I was busy doing my own thing. If not for the reminder, you would have missed a great story.

Dwight is quite the sculptor as well. A couple of his artistic pieces gained international attention. Iconic restauranteur Mel Markon commissioned him (in a way) to create a likeness of Brooke Shields. Rather than using wood or stone, his medium of choice was chopped liver. I included the *People Magazine* link to their archives for more details http://www.people.com/people/archive/article/0,,20081731,00.html. Some time later, Dwight sent a smoked-ham statue of Madonna to late-night

host David Letterman. The "Brooke" replica weighed a mere 30 pounds. Madonna was a monumental (pun intended) 180 pounds. Once inspiration took hold, his art went from appetizer to full buffet size. All art is supposed to entertain and inspire. His creations could satisfy hunger, too.

Dwight Kalb was (and still is) the best drummer I ever saw or heard. I am still toying with the idea of putting together a band. He would be at the top of the list of guys I would ask to join me.

"Yeah, I still play drums," he said. Brilliant and modest, to be sure.

There was something else he had on his mind to get things started.

"I knew I was going to meet you today, so I was going through my pictures. I haven't looked at my wife's photos in years. I got so emotional. It was really a bad morning for me," he continued. Once again, there is a little more to come later. I'm trying to lay this stuff out in some type of order. Let's just say Dwight's dearly-departed wife remains the deepest of his many passions. I'm convinced she still influences most of what he does today. That could inspire a song, don't you think?

The quintessential Dwight Kalb returned to the beat.

"I gave away my drums and quit the business because of some 'broad.' That was probably the dumbest thing that I ever did," he began. Obviously, she was not the person he would eventually marry. How is that quote for openers?

"She told me, if I didn't stop playing, she was going to leave. I taught Danny Seraphine how to play and gave him my drums. Yeah, the biggest mistake of my life. I would have been the drummer for [the group] Chicago," he explained. A lot of drummers could keep a beat. Only the great ones knew how to create one. Dwight describes the role of a drummer. I swear you will never listen to a single tune the same way once you finish this chapter. If you want more of this story, check out *Street Player: My Chicago Story*, by Danny Seraphine.

"I learned to play drums from Clayton Fillyau, who backed James Brown for many years," Dwight continued. The best drummers set the stage before the headliner takes over. Check out the YouTube clip of Brown's **I've Got Money** to marvel at Fillyau's work. https://youtu.be/L6I5_FxjIaQ. Yeah, lots of people, aside from me, think Mr. Kalb was that good.

In the early '60s, a four-piece band called the Kasuals got a reputation playing at Chicago dances and "tough" clubs in even tougher neighborhoods. Folks there viewed outsiders with distrust at best and contempt somewhere in the middle. That left plenty of room for old-fashioned ethnic hatred. The bands were just there to provide the soundtrack for any resulting mayhem.

I asked Dwight if he saw any fights when he played at Tuscany Hall on Grand Avenue. I already knew the answer.

"I remember the O'Shea brothers. They were all fighters: Brian, Rory, and Tommy. One day I'm up on stage and I have to jump in front of my drums to keep them from getting damaged. Rory was surrounded by a bunch of greasers. He managed to jump four feet up to the stage. I pointed him toward the open door facing the parking lot. I saved his life that day," he remembered. Being a musician was exciting enough. In some places, dances created just as many casualties as they did memories. You had to know when to watch or intervene. Mostly, you wanted to save your equipment—and your behind.

The Kasuals were tight and talented. I'll give you an idea of how they sounded right now. https://youtu.be/1OjevXJpjYI. Remember what I told you about "feeling" those drums? You shouldn't even bother to learn the mechanics if you don't have rhythm and soul in your rock-and-roll. When the legendary Dick Clark needed a backing band for his hand-picked acts in the Caravan of Stars tour, he chose Jimmy Ford and the Kasuals.

Maybe you didn't realize this, but this was an "actual" caravan. The performers traveled in a group—by bus. Depending on existing performer contracts, the rosters would change from one show to the next. We all thought we knew a lot about Dick Clark. He, as well as Dwight Kalb, Jimmy Ford, and everyone else on tour, had to be flexible and ready for adventure.

Remember, we said "bus tour" in multiple cities. That means places in the United States, both north and south in the '60s. You see what I'm sayin'?

"Dick Clark could have traveled in an air-conditioned limousine. Instead he traveled in the bus. He made it known if there were any drugs found on the bus, guilty parties got tickets home. He didn't care if your name was Diana Ross or Tom Jones, you were gone," Dwight said. I could see myself handling things the same way. Dick was determined to build both the image and reputation of his stars. Dwight didn't mention if anyone challenged that rule. It doesn't matter. Dick Clark made it clear nobody should expect special treatment.

The same applied with meals and accommodations. Some locales readily acknowledged the needs and rights of the entire touring company. I can just imagine how the conversation might have gone when people from the caravan were sharing space with a redneck. "What, haven't you ever been this close to a *musician* before?"

Jimmy Ford and the Kasuals walked up to a restaurant door and held it open for people like Dick Clark or Gene Pitney. The rest of their companions would start filing in. Ladies first. The Crystals, Dixie Cups, and the Shirelles. In no particular order, you'd see members of the Drifters, Coasters, or Reflections (Detroit-based group with equal success on both the pop and R&B markets— **[Just Like] Romeo and Juliet**: https://youtu.be/zX1-e0w3mUw) breaking bread with Brian Highland, Lou Christie, Johnny Tillotson, or Tom Jones.

"Imagine being on the bus in Montgomery, Alabama, in 1965 with the line-up we just mentioned. I spent days listening to the Drifters rehearse right behind me on the bus. We're in the hotel and I see Johnny Terry from the Drifters pinned up against a Coke machine by three rednecks. I'm ready to show what I learned in Chicago about defending the good guys. Right then, Dick Clark himself tells me to stand back and he gets the 'nuisance' removed," Dwight said. It turns out Johnny got to return the favor soon after, as Dwight describes …

Kasuals: Wayne Erwin,
Mike Sistak, Dwight Kalb,
Jimmy Ford

"We were on tour with Tom Jones when he had that ponytail. I was growing my hair long back then, too," he continued. Let me guess, Dwight, another welcoming committee from the deep south had a problem with long hair?

"I was already squaring off, just waiting for something to start. Johnny and quite a few others stepped forward, as a sign of solidarity. 'They have to go through me to get to you.'" Problem solved. Two-legged weasels don't handle pressure well.

If you understand anything about Dwight Kalb, you'd know his friends would have more likely been injured by Dwight himself as he clawed his way past them to take care of his own business.

Tales From the Tour

I guess we may have temporarily "Drifted" away (get it?) from the discussion of music for a time. Dwight did three consecutive 90-day tours with the Caravan. If he wants to tell you the thousands of stories that he compiled during those days, he can write his own book. For now, I want to pass along a couple that we shared during our interview. There were few fights among the folks on the tour. There was some needless drama, though, Dwight recalled.

"The Kasuals were informed (by Brenda Lee's attorney) that her backup group was called 'The Casuals' and Jimmy Ford's group would have to change its name. At that time, she was the 'Elvis Presley' of female headliners. The chances of winning a lawsuit against her were close to zero. Jimmy had to immediately find a new name to put on the marquee, or there would be none at all," he said. Apparently, the Kasuals had already been removed.

"That day, we're staying at the Executive Inn. Jimmy said, 'f*** it then. Tell them we're Jimmy Ford and the Executives.'" He was obviously more interested in music than marketing. Four-foot-nine Brenda Lee could obviously throw her weight around.

There's always plenty of love and excitement swirling traveling performances. During one episode of the Caravan (sound like a soap opera?), Dick Clark got a call from Motown's Barry Gordy.

"Gordy tells Dick there are three young girls who are going to be a big hit. Dick Clark originally told him there was no room on the bus. There really wasn't. Gordy assured him they were going to be great and would be working for $750 per week for those 6, 7 shows. At our next stop, we're all making room for the girls and Mama Ross, their chaperone," Dwight said. By now, you probably know who he means. Dwight Kalb was learning a little more about the business part of a musical tour.

"By the end of that 90-day Caravan, the Supremes already had three hits." **Where Did Our Love Go**, **Baby Love**, and **Come See About Me** were the first of five consecutive chart-busters for Diana Ross, Mary Wilson, and Florence Ballard.

"They were still making the same money at the end of that first tour," Dwight said. A contract was a contract. "We were all blown away by **Stop In the Name of Love**." It sounded like you were all becoming fans, and something more, Dwight.

"Major Lance [Chicago] and Diana Ross were becoming an item. Mary Wilson and I hung out a few times," Dwight added.

Dwight Kalb—
Over time, I became good friends with Tom Jones. One day he said to me (you know in that Welsh accent), "I heard that you used to play drums behind those strippers in the Cicero clubs." Yeah, Jimmy Ford and I would regularly play between 4am and 7am. I learned to play like that really well. Tom says, "I want you to play behind me when I do the bump-and-grind thing during my act." Sure enough, he gave me the thumbs-up and I did my thing. Jones offered me a job after the Caravan. This was in 1965. He offered me $350 a week and a room of my own to replace his current drummer on his personal tours. So, what did I say? No. I count that as one of the top three dumbest things I ever did in my life. In today's dollars, that would be $2,500 a week.

Touring creates a unique form of loneliness. The performers sing about their remedies for heartache nearly every day. Practice makes perfect. By the end of the tour, there was plenty of money (for some). There was definitely enough material for more songs.

"Clark made so much money that he split the final gate receipts with the band. For me, that meant $1,100 more dollars in my pocket for that last performance. In 1965, that was really great money," he said. A web calculation puts it north of $8K today.

Mutual Acquaintances

Dwight watched as things started falling into place for the Buckinghams. By then, he had given up the drums for that girl he referred to earlier. Three guys named Jimmy (Ford, Holvay, and Guercio) all played in the second touring lineup for the Executives. I'm so glad that Dwight met me for this interview. If not, you all might think I made this stuff up.

"Jim Holvay wrote **Kind of a Drag** about my girlfriend. She was still on his mind when he wrote **Hey, Baby, They're Playing Our Song**," Dwight reminded me. Wow, that's a painful way to be inspired. For the last 50 years, you may have thought "playing our song" recalled times for an actual couple. The next time you listen (like now https://youtu.be/bHV0T5REuVM), you'll know it describes a love never meant to be.

"**Susan**, the Buckinghams last big hit, was about her, too. That wasn't her real name, but everybody knew who this song was about," Dwight explained. At least everybody close to the Executives, and maybe the Buckinghams. This was one powerful couple. The male half was Dwight Kalb. His more seductive counterpart got one guy to give up the drums and another guy to pour his heart into some impassioned lyrics. I'm a little jealous of the guy and a little intimidated by the temptress.

Dwight was a helpless observer when the Buckinghams chose to "bolt" with James Guercio. It's sad how many times that guy's name is going to be mentioned in my book. It's not going to be bad, but fair (in my opinion). Dwight put things into perspective. I see where it might have been useful back then.

"They screwed you, Carl," my drummer friend started. That's what I'm sayin'! (Actually that's what I used to think, you'll see.) I used to book a group called the Missing Links, with a strong DePaul (student) connection. The musicians were all getting "tight." I was doing my thing (booking bands).

I should have known someone might take advantage of my trusting nature. Some promoter might call it an exploitable weakness. Such is the hard-core business end of music. I was a screamin' duck. An LA-based record company found lightning-in-a-bottle with a sensational group like the Buckinghams by signing them as their contract expired. Thanks for being here now, Dwight.

"True story. You taping this? One time Jimmy Guercio liked the girl I liked. We were both short and cute at that time. We would trade girlfriends on the road. Guercio wants my girl. Sure, take what you want. There were a thousand short girls. When you're a musician, you pick who you want. Girls were backstage in the hallway, waiting to get laid by the stars," he said. Naw, that really happened? Dwight, I think you're still cute (just not my type).

"Guercio was only an average bass player," the authentic rockstar continued. I think you said Guercio didn't have any imagination on stage, Dwight. I could have quoted you here, but I enjoyed saying it too much myself.

"He was great as far as the business went. When we went on the road, he wouldn't bring girls. He would bring books," Dwight added. So, some guys were actually more interested in *War and Peace* than whore and piece? I hope someone quotes me on this. Dwight, you bring out the nasty in me. We should start hanging out more often. Unfortunately, the biggest and cruelest joke would be at my expense. I'm over it, sort of.

The "K" in CASK

I joined CASK Attractions mostly because Willard Alexander became part of a painful past. The Mickey Call, Ted Allen, Marv Stuart and Dwight Kalb office did a tremendous amount of booking talent in the Midwest. I still have my personal list of the acts and clubs (and I'll share them with you later). I became the "legs" of the operation. I confirmed performers were on time, then collected any remaining fees from the host. I also knew most of the Musician Union guys who kept everything above board.

I didn't know the inner workings of CASK. But here's what I did know: Each of the partners managed their individual groups. In most cases, they acted as the exclusive booking agent, like I did for some groups at Willard Alexander.

The partners shared commissions when they matched others in the talent pool with events in the venue pool. CASK also had an arrangement with influential booking agents, like Ken Adamany in Wisconsin, to share commissions on successful matches with his own "stable" of talent.

Lots of people would call CASK and ask for Dwight because of his fair dealing and knowledge of the music business. He was constantly looking for promising acts and, hopefully, getting them on board. Who were the other guys and what did they do? Well, I know that Marv Stuart managed Curtis Mayfield. My editors reminded me Marv spoke for ailing Curtis at his Rock & Roll Hall of Fame induction ceremony many years later.

Dwight knows more. He broke it down in a way that I never could.

"Mickey Call reminded me of a *Goodfellas* type. He couldn't read or write, but he dressed like he owned a bank," he started. Dwight actually liked the guy enough to hang out with him. Humorous stories followed, like …

"Every time we'd go out to eat, I noticed he would always order the same thing I did. I finally figured it out," he chuckled. It was funny, but I learned what a great guy Dwight is. He didn't prey on someone with an obvious weakness, nor did he let the secret out (until 50 years later).

"We'd hang out at the Bitter End, where some of my paintings were. I started doing 'resin art,' illuminated stuff with fiberglass. I did a bunch of Dick Clark and members of the Rat Pack: Frank Sinatra, Dino [Dean Martin] and Sammy Davis Jr. Mickey would drive up in a Cadillac Eldorado and have manicured nails. Anyway, we were drinking or smoking, and he finally told what I already figured out awhile back.

"Too bad that stuff burned up when the place caught fire. If only it could have been removed before that. It could have been a nice addition to someone's private collection," he thought out loud. Thanks to Mickey, CASK had relationships with many Chicago clubs. Time to slightly shift directions.

"All of that fiberglass and glass stuff could kill you. I started painting instead. I call my business the Drawing Room." Dwight takes a short pull from the beer he bought in the market downstairs. They have a bar there, so it must be OK.

I mention Eddie Thomas several times in my book. He earned the love and respect of everyone in the music business. Dwight had a unique perspective on the way some artists and promoters were operating.

"I don't think Eddie Thomas was treated right. Marv Stuart wouldn't let me near Curtis Mayfield. I think he was worried that Curtis would like me to play drums for him. Maurice Jennings did the drumming and Joseph 'Lucky' Scott was the bass player on **Superfly**. That record made a fortune for Allen and

Stuart. Even Mickey got 'shafted.'" Oops, wrong movie/song reference there. **Shaft** was another song. One more song title describes the treatment of artists and promoters (**Ain't That a Shame**).

"I just had to get away from CASK," he said. I trust Dwight's judgment.

I'm not saying this actually happened (but could, under the right circumstances). What if the manager of a group (like Baby Huey and the Babysitters) requested $5,000 per performance from a booking agent? An agent might come back with sad news. He could get half of that, due to the alleged poor morals of the band. If someone were willing to demean their clients with the most vile (or racist) names they could muster, they might be able to pocket an ungodly sum which rightfully belonged to the artists. Thank goodness Dwight, Eddie, or I didn't know anyone like that.

Dwight and I talked about other talent we both booked at one time or another. One who stood far above the rest was Ral Donner. You already know about him if you started this book from the beginning. He was really "hot" property.

"We used to book acts at Pepe's on 63rd Street. I booked Count Basie at a place called the Cord & Blue," Dwight reminded me. We're not making this stuff up. Some people had clever names for their places of business.

"I would book Ral Donner, and we would improvise a band. I would play the drums and other guys would just 'jam' while he was singing. At the end of his set, he would get a standing ovation every time." Dwight Kalb and I were good judges of talent and always on the lookout. Sometimes we would strike gold. Often (without warning), gold would strike us instead.

The Chips

Dwight was in St. Louis during the summer of 1967 and strolled into a psychedelic bar. Actually, Dwight Kalb doesn't stroll, he strides. He steps into a room with a purpose, even before he knows what it may be. He was blown away by the act on stage.

"They were an all-girl band called the Hour Glass. Their James Brown act was just unreal. They would act like Wayne Cochran and tear the place up. The crowd would just go nuts. A very short time later, I became their booking agent, record producer, manager, and bodyguard," he said. Dwight brought me a promotional poster for the Chips (as they were now being called). The two at the top of the stack were Klayre Hartmann and Charlotte O'Neill. In the front row, we had Daren Pasterik (soon to be Mrs. Dwight Kalb), Sheri Hartman, and Aleat Maciejewski.

"Char played rhythm and bass guitar. Aleat was the drummer. We released a couple of records in 1968," Dwight added. I looked the tracks up for you.

 Break It Gently https://youtu.be/r2hFrgtoPaY / **Mixed-Up, Shook-Up Girl** https://youtu.be/aB6gcQWnigA was released on the Philips label in February. **When You Hold Me Baby** https://youtu.be/42Ta9iEESoO / **Dream With Your Eyes Wide Open** was released by ABC Records in November. I couldn't find that last clip. Sorry.

 Dwight and I covered a lot of ground that afternoon. Some of the time, we talked like devoted friends. Of course, we could have spent a lot more time together, and it would have gone by just as quickly. I really appreciate Dwight's efforts before our interview. I appreciate how tough it was with memories of Daren flooding back. I am even more grateful.

The next day, he called me with a few more details. I loved introducing Dwight Kalb in his chapter. This book is a lot more fun because of his unselfish contribution. He is one colorful character.

 "THE CHIPS"
The nation's No. 1 all girl band.

Personnel Mgmt.
DWIGHT KALB
312-787-8146

Industry Shapers

You'll have a greater understanding of how we built a music organization after you read this section. Maybe you would rather call it a coalition. I shouldn't call it a fraternity because there were a lot of females responsible for putting a creative spin on whatever we're calling the dawn of rock-and-roll.

Ooh, let's call it a tapestry (with no disrespect to Carole King and her Grammy-winning album). I'm quite a name-dropper, huh? By tapestry, I mean everybody in this chapter was a genuine musical force in their own area. They were free to reach across borders (and also music genres). That's another word I never thought I would use. See the sacrifices I am willing to make for you all?

To get a record produced, you had to deal with different personalities. If one person was less keen on a particular song or group, you could literally "pack up" and move elsewhere. Threatening to go elsewhere was sometimes enough to re-open negotiations. Things started heating up once a promoter, studio, or label started thinking about how much money they were going to lose if the project struck gold. My goal was to find a "home" for every song and performer.

I'm not the only person who did this kind of stuff. You have no idea how hard this chapter was to write. So many players. I don't want to forget (or slight) anyone. I just hope you enjoy what I have here.

Peter Wright

As near as I remember, Peter Wright was originally a horn player, which explains his interest in R&B. Being a musical performer gives you a unique perspective when evaluating talent. Eddie Thomas was a unique exception, although he was thoroughly exposed to music at an early age. See how easy it is to get distracted?

Let's classify Peter Wright as an independent record promoter, just to get things rolling. When he ran into obstacles, he took on additional roles to work around them. He got a lot of single records produced, on playlists, and into record stores. He worked with Dominic Carone for management/booking, much like I did with Willard Alexander.

He worked with the same cast of characters I've introduced throughout these pages. You know the "drill" by now: Pitch demos everywhere, oversee the production of masters and records to mass-produce while finalizing distribution plans. Depending on the size and influence of the labels, you would find yourself assuming many roles, remember?

Founding your own record label would eliminate a bunch of middlemen and streamline getting a song to the demo stage. The expense of recording and producing, however, would be yours alone. If you "really" believed you had something, it would be profitable. Guys like Peter Wright and I often thought it was worth the risk. Sometimes we were right.

Peter Wright started Quill Records as an R&B label. He was the main man, so when groups like the New Colony Six came along, he could immediately change the focus of the label and more easily sign similar acts. The label handled the manufacturing (Quill Productions) and could lease the results (demos/masters) to other labels.

Big labels had much better distribution options. If you could get any label to "buy" a song and assume the lion's share of the liability, the artists came along for the ride. When it came to promoting the record, it was always in your best interest to take the lead. You were most likely going to increase your profits because of your relationships with radio station on-air talent and management.

Only a flexible, innovative, and courageous mind like Peter Wright could put the pieces together for the New Colony Six. Heck, there were only a handful of people (like the Screaming Wildman) who knew what all of the pieces were. Once you knew, you were free to improvise. Picture a pickup baseball game. That's what producing a record for every new artist seemed like. Once the first one is done, you can improve on that by replacing a few parts.

Let me illustrate with my understanding of the New Colony Six story. Nobody other than Mr. Wright could have done this better. Six St. Patrick High School seniors crafted a name to "combat" the British (musical) Invasion by representing the "New Colonies" (get it)? Ronnie Rice was not an original member. Just throwing that at ya!

Quite unusual for any time, a few fathers of the group formed Centaur Record Corporation (later changed to Sentar because of legal stuff). As far as I can remember, they negotiated their own studio time. Of course, Peter Wright was guiding the process. The bandmates were free to make the best music possible while dealing with the inevitable lineup changes that all bands endure.

That's why you will see the distribution change from local U.S.A. Records (located right across the street from the legendary Chess label) to Philly-based Cameo Parkway. There are so many interesting facts on a record label; I bet you will never overlook them again. Ron Malo (legendary Chess engineer) has a production credit on at least one hit.

Oh yeah, this is the Peter Wright section. As I said, he had to make adjustments to create the best chance for success on each record. **I Confess** https://youtu.be/XIMO2CFmlx4 was the first single for the Colony. Peter Wright and Howard Bedno could certainly influence local airplay. The song peaked at No. 2 on the WLS Silver Dollar Survey. (**Lightning Strikes** by Lou Christie was No. 1 – wow, this internet thing just might catch on sometime!) On March 25, 1968, **I Will Always Think About You**, with Ronnie Rice on lead vocals, vaulted past **Lady Madonna** / Beatles and **Dock of the Bay** / Otis Redding. https://youtu.be/t1EEs__jJ0w.

If you check out the two videos, notice the Mercury Records label, with a Sentar Records Productions credit. Bottom line, Wright made a lot of careers by getting airplay and leveraging popularity to place songs on the Billboard chart just a few weeks later.

Peter Wright set musical wheels in motion throughout Chicago. The Exceptions were the biggest club band in the Midwest under the Quill umbrella. Their bass player was one Peter Cetera, the missing piece in the formation of the group that would be known as Chicago (Rock & Roll Hall of Fame – April 2016, at last). Marty Grebb, another former Exception, would later join the Buckinghams.

There was a very popular Milwaukee band called the Skunks at Quill. In 1967, they released a catchy tune on the U.S.A. label called **Elvira** https://youtu.be/ljRPuiVqE_Y. Fourteen years later, the Oak Ridge Boys topped the country chart and made it to No. 5 on the Billboard Hot 100 with the very same song. Peter Wright gave everyone their best chance at success. Could you say that he indirectly inspired the Oak Ridge Boys? Maybe I could.

I used to manage a group called the Delights (featured later in this book, of course). I eventually "lost" them to Peter Wright and Quill, who released **Just Out of Reach** on the Smash label https://youtu.be/0UNQo3RdlIM. Quill released an album called *We're Gonna Change the World*. This was a garage-band compilation that featured both the Skunks and Delights.

His newest adventure was called Twilight (then Twinight, soon after) Records. It specialized in R&B and soul music, but struggled because airplay was often limited to late-night hours. Donny Hathaway (best known for his work with Roberta Flack) got his start at Twinight.

Hundreds of acts owe a great deal to Peter Wright. He made a lot of ripples in Chicago's musical pond. Without him, things would have been far different, and by no means better.

Howard Bedno

This guy was everywhere I was, only he usually got there first. He's the main reason I named this chapter Influential Characters. Maybe some stuff got done in Chicago without him, but it wouldn't have been done nearly as well. Record promoters are constantly trying to find the best home for every song and group. It's a constant mix-and-match struggle.

Howard was born during the First World War and served his country during the Second. He was old enough to be my dad, but treated me like a friend. It was amazing how well he related to young artists. He had a particular fondness for the New Colony Six and my Buckinghams.

He had a passion for Chicago music and those who re-defined it. He took the news of the Buckinghams' departure particularly hard (but not as hard as I did). I think it had more to do with them leaving Chicago than Howard feeling a personal snub. He worked hard for every group willing to match his effort.

Howard was far and away the best promotion man in the business. Guys like Morris Levy (Roulette) and Jerry Wexler (Atlantic)—let's just say everyone— would immediately answer his calls. More likely, they would be calling him. If he liked a tune, it would, amazingly, be airing on powerhouse stations in a matter of days (in some cases, just a few hours). As an independent promoter, he found himself associated with Vee-Jay Records.

Let me just start with a little history here. Gary Indiana's Vivian Carter and James C. Bracken founded Vee-Jay (Vivian-James, get it?) in 1953. You might say they were worthy competitors of Chess. Vee-Jay had some noteworthy artists and would soon have an enviable distinction. Could Howard Bedno have anything to do with it? Even if you don't think so, you would have to admit he was quite a good-luck charm.

Remember, he was part of an older generation and would have a deeper appreciation for groups like the Dells and Spaniels. I was just a kid (even though I was starting to run dances and book bands) in 1956, the year Vee-Jay signed John Lee Hooker. I think Howard knew that blues, rock, and soul were going to fuse and saw the potential for "crossover" hits before anyone. There wasn't even a word for it back then.

 Vee-Jay signed Eddie Thomas's Impressions (with Curtis Mayfield and Jerry Butler). My best example of a crossover hit would be Dee Clark's **Raindrops** https://youtu.be/IntE69bFm9o. In 1961, he was one of the first major R&B singers to cross over to a pop audience. Finally, the commercial success began to match the artful soul sound. The song peaked at No. 2 on the Billboard Hot 100. Gee, Bedno was hanging around then, huh?

Shortly after, Gene Chandler hit Billboard No. 1 with **Duke of Earl**, released by Vee-Jay. OK, that was maybe the one song of the time that actually sold itself while Howard was on board. See if you can follow this next one …

Once upon a time (except this was a real-life fairy tale), there was a Caucasian R&B DJ named Dick "Huggy Boy" Hugg, who broadcast live from the front window of an all-night record store called Dolphin's of Hollywood. The West Coast sales manager for Vee-Jay gave Huggy a song "dub" from a New Jersey group. Right after he aired it that night, record stores were fielding requests for a record that didn't even exist!

Sherry https://youtu.be/7sJCYeG6be8 by the Four Seasons was an immediate smash for the Vee-Jay label. This was followed by another Billboard No. 1 called **Big Girls Don't Cry**. Both were featured on the first Four Seasons album released by Vee-Jay. The story gets better, if you can believe this …

With all the airplay the Four Seasons was getting, record companies were offering the upstart label other groups to put under its umbrella. There was a little-known group ready to "cross over" to the United States to try its luck. Yes, the Beatles released their first records on Vee-Jay.

Did you ever drive a car with the throttle stuck open? No? Good for you. You probably don't know how "record" (pun intended) sales and production needs for the hottest groups in the land can cause things to fall apart. I do. The awesome folks at Vee-Jay fell on hard times, partly due to production demands. Popularity has its pitfalls. OK, back to the guest star of this section …

There are so many stories woven into the "lore" that became known as Howard Bedno—you know, stories that become more significant after other things happen. For example, Surf Ballroom in Clear Lake, Iowa, might mean a lot of things to people. The Daughters of Eve and the Buckinghams played there.

In this case, I'm talking about the Winter Dance Party tour at the beginning of 1959. Who better to handle the promotion of a dance party in the frozen and forlorn Midwest, destined to begin at the end of January? By many accounts, Howard Bedno was the guy who toured the Chicago radio stations with Ritchie Valens to hype upcoming performances.

Mexican-American Richard Steven Valenzuela (born in the Pacoima neighborhood of Los Angeles) charted with **La Bamba** https://youtu.be/Jp6j5HJ-Cok the year before. This crossover hit, adapted from a Mexican folk tune, reached 20-sumthin' on the Billboard Hot 100.

Without a doubt, that song would have made it far closer to the top if the WLS Silver Dollar Survey had existed back then. The brilliant marketing and promotional campaign started in October 1960 during the Gene Taylor (7-9pm) show on weekdays.

WLS (and Chicago radio) did not merely reflect the overall numbers, they would be able to change them! Howard Bedno knew how to recognize a hit and get it on the air. The WLS signal could reach to Canada, depending on the time of day. The *Survey* would air when there was less radio frequency interference, and by 9pm, the record-buying public would be tuned in. I think **La Bamba** would have been an even bigger hit if he got the exposure a few years later on WLS.

Fate brought Valens and his hits to the world in 1958. In the early morning of February 3, 1959, known as "the Day the Music Died," his fans were galvanized by his tragic passing.

While writing this book, my contributors and I try to remember the first time we met. Sometimes we remember. Other times we remember differently. It is harder to remember the last time you saw someone, unless there is a spectacular event involved. That same tragedy pushes so many things into the background. For instance, the ill-fated tour that claimed the life of three popular entertainers (and their pilot) kicked off in Milwaukee. I didn't remember that. I looked it up.

Did it have to happen at all? If you read newspaper accounts, there are serious doubts. If it had to happen at all, think about the last performance of the Big Bopper, Buddy Holly, and Ritchie Valens. How much would be different if the inevitable took place somewhere else?

Instead of the Surf, we might be making a pilgrimage to the Fiesta Ballroom, Montevideo, Minnesota. The *Star Tribune*, the largest newspaper in Minnesota, would most likely be handling the publicity. Guys like Howard Bedno realized they might play a part in something that might have historic significance.

Howard knew which record companies would use their successes to bankroll other projects for up-and-coming artists. Being independent and righteous were just natural for him. Of course other promoters and record companies quickly learned how to create crossover hits. Most likely, they were influenced by both the personality and disarming drive of Howard Bedno.

OK, one more example. Sometimes there was no record label that could give the exposure or support to a particular group of artists. Maybe that's why Howard Bedno teamed with Eli Toscano to create Cobra Records. Eli owned a record store and TV-repair store on Chicago's West Side and already had the trust and support of the community.

The newly formed Cobra Records didn't waste any time. Eli persuaded Willie Dixon to join Cobra. With his guidance and talent, their very first release was a hit by Mississippi-born but Chicago-West-Side-raised Otis Rush. **I Can't Quit You - Baby** https://youtu.be/rpxNJcNRwFA reached No. 6 on the Billboard R&B chart in 1956.

There's a Led Zeppelin version of **Can't Quit You**, I'm told. Maybe the culture of American music back then (and maybe still now) is a little different than England's. How do we explain the ability of British groups to immerse themselves in R&B and hit the Billboard chart time after time in a style inspired by the USA? The British artists didn't invade the USA: They were invited by young people hungry for "earthy" music from their own unappreciated countrymen.

Howard Bedno could see it. Once again, a great reason to remain independent was to recognize trends, if not have a hand in creating them. Some people give partial credit to Howard Bedno for making **Dang Me** a crossover hit for country artist Roger Miller.

His next song was **Chug-a-Lug**. What's the first thing you think of when you hear that title? Howard could see how it would be endlessly played in every tavern jukebox across the country. In frat houses, this would be more than a song title: It would be considered a challenge, if not a command.

Howard Bedno is mentioned in *Spinning Blues Into Gold: The Chess Brothers and the Legendary Chess Records* by Nadine Cohodas, a Notable Book of the Year according to the *New York Times*. I think it is safe to say every artist in the business owes Howard a sincere thank you.

Ken Adamany

I found a rare video produced by Ken Adamany credited to a group called Cowboy Woman https://youtu.be/gaVkJY7BMfc. Some might say he and I are alike, except where we're not. I managed a few Chicago groups (and one from Milwaukee) in my time and got one group to No. 1 on the Billboard chart. I also worked for the Willard Alexander and CASK Attractions booking agencies.

Ken managed groups as well, like the Elvis Brothers and a group named Fuse (destined to become something far bigger) from Rockford, Illinois. They would eventually reach No. 1 on the Billboard chart. My friend Hank Zemola (with a chapter of his own) booked Cheap Trick (formerly Fuse) at his clubs.

I think Chicago would be willing to claim Cheap Trick as their own because of their music (that's Chicago the city, not the band). By the time you read this chapter, both Chicago (now I mean the band) and Cheap Trick were (finally) inducted into the Rock & Roll Hall of Fame (April 8, 2016). OK, that's where Ken and I are different, until the Buckinghams make it.

Ken was based in the Madison, Wisconsin, area. Of course, he booked a lot of his acts south of the border. Folks from the Badger State seldom visited the Land of Lincoln. It was the toll roads, I tell ya! They should have changed the welcome sign to *You are now entering the Land of Lincoln – Start Reaching for Your Change!* Things are much better now. Illinois will happily send you a bill.

Ken Adamany Music Enterprises had a virtual entertainment stable. I found his 1966 roster, which included both the Buckinghams and Daughters of Eve. CASK had a reciprocal agreement with him, so any bookings would make cash for both agencies.

I'm not saying all of these groups on the list were Ken's. If any were represented by another manager, they would do the math. There were a lot of un-fun aspects to the music business. Good managers and promoters let the bands just "rock" and they kept track of their "roll" (as in bankroll). The temptation to help ourselves would always be there. I'm proud to say most never did.

I included Ken's list for you. I thought it would be cool to jog your memory and give any members of these groups another chance to see their names in print. You can do your own research from there. I'm a busy guy and not getting any younger. You know what I'm sayin'?

I think you'll be surprised how many acts you will find online. These were originally on typewritten lists. You'll have to deal with any misspellings. I hope whoever originally typed this got paid what she was worth. Maybe that's another thing that hasn't changed either.

Ken Adamany Music Enterprises Limited – Serving the Midwest with Entertainment At Its Best … I think the Group listings imply who got paid what as far as commissions go.

Group A — the Disciples, the Legends, Shane Todd & the Gentlemen, the Van-Tels, Robbin & the Three Hoods, the Rocmans, Gidget & the Nu-Horizons, the Chevrons, Dee Robb & the Robbins, the Tremolons, the Rivieras

Group B — Playboys, Mystics, Bill & Bachelors, Nite Beats, Grethen, Vi-Counts, Juveniles, Sonic Sounds, Shattertones, Buckinghams, Knightranes, Daze & Knights

Group C — Tim Davis & Chordairs, Madadors, Pete & the Chevrons, Shafrels, Trade Winds, Nocturnes, Leopardess, Delmonts, Knightbeats, Impalas, Redwoods, Chessmen, Nomads, Phil & the Mystics

Group D — Neptunes, Morticians, Chastels, Calientts, Malibus, Esquires, Lancers V, Grapes of Wrath, Jaguars, La Sarres, Escorts, Casuals, Bossmen, Daughters of Eve, Porters, Odd & Ends

Group E — Chevelles, Invaders, Epics, Missing Links, Voodoomen, Ted & Tribesmen, (Konnt) Rate & Rayemen, Intrigues, Deacons, King George & Us, Sessions, Exits, Knights, Tempests, Embers

Dance Bands — the Bachelors, Johny Kate Orch., Marcatos, Squires, St. Gorden Combo, Jerry Jill Orch., Dave Remington, Red Hardy Trio, Middletons

Traveling Groups Available for Club Engagements (Number of performers in each act) — Speedy & the Alka-Seltzers (3), Terry Gale & the Storms (4), the Heard (4), Sammy McCue & the Legends (4), the Disciples (5), Bill & the Bachelors (4), the Warner Brothers (4), Bobby Jones & the Bygones (4), Tim Davis & the Chordairs (3), Dee Robb & the Robbins (4), Jules Blattner Trio (3), Kris & the Four Fifths (5), Myron Lee & the Caddies (4), the Pacesetters (4), the Gentlemen (5), the Daze & Knights (4), the Classmen (4), the Nite Caps (4), the Castaways (4), the Tempters (5), King Louis & the Laymen (5), the Pharaohs (4), the Galaxies (4), the Original Playboys (4), the Juveniles (5), the Van-Tels (5)

Special thanks – Ms. Jamie Tam for compiling and typing these lists.

James Marvell

This story might be the best proof of the theme I weave throughout this book. You never know—just act like it already happened. The follow-up on that is: Don't pass up any opportunity to display your talent, no matter how it looks, sounds, or even smells. Bear with me here.

Let's drift back to 1965. If you go to the electronic version of the U.S.A. Records discography (which I didn't know even existed until I started pulling this book together), you will see that my "formula" was hard at work. I remember including this link elsewhere, but I want you to verify what I'm sayin.' http://www.globaldogproductions.info/u/usa.html.

Remember, booking agents loved when a group had a "vinyl calling card." I strongly encouraged groups to get into the studio to make the audition process seamless when booking gigs. Where I saw groups with genuine talent and charisma, I offered to smooth out the process for them.

If you browse the U.S.A. Records discography, you'll see Phil Orsi and the Little Kings as early as U.S.A. #837 and #841. The first U.S.A. recordings for the Buckinghams were at the beginning of 1966: U.S.A. #844, #848, #853, and #860 **Kind of a Drag**. You'll see a few other groups mentioned in this book. This is more evidence of the "formula."

The Cambridge Five #850, #875, the Skunks #865 (**Elvira**, one of my favorites), the Screaming Wildmen #868, and Bobby Whiteside #879 are all in this book. I'm not saying I helped any of the others directly. The success of one group, however, propels everyone on the label founded by distributor Jim Golden.

I could promote all of these groups simultaneously at local dances, where the DJs made appearances. Kids at the dances created the demand for airplay or purchase from record stores. What does this have to do with James Marvell? Thanks for sticking around until now.

A group calling themselves the Skopes recorded U.S.A. #880 **She's Got Bad Breath** https://youtu.be/Wu6oc8XOhKM / **Tears in Your Eyes** https://youtu.be/ RzHaN-SMU_c. Of course, these are novelty songs. Thankfully, everybody expected this project to lead to better things.

Even the group name was crafted with a purpose. Everybody from that era remembers the mouthwash that made its *debut* (another word I might have said, but never typed—doesn't look right) in 1966. The spelling of the product was pretty close to the group name, or vice versa.

I suspect there were a few reasons why the radio stations balked at giving it airplay. The name-brand product was manufactured by a mucho-macho corporation (whose name I am afraid to mention) that advertised nationwide. The song may have been a national hit, had it not been suddenly shelved. Your guess as to the real reason is as good as mine, and I bet we're right.

Some said the song was in "bad taste" (with a straight face, if you can believe it). Nobody could have known how important those songs would be to everyone involved. The marvelously funny and frustrating thing about history is the creators are often unaware of its importance (and to whom it's important). Too much philosophy and too little music.

Buddy Good and James Marvell were a couple of high school buddies from Florida who sang and wrote songs. During the mid-'60s, they planned to start a band, get a manager, and pursue the dream of a lifetime.

Luckily, there were a couple of guys who dreamed about giving new bands the best shot possible. One was a guy named John Centinaro, who managed a record shop around Tampa. Buddy invited John to a garage rehearsal. The Skopes soon had a manager. Good (bass) and Marvell (rhythm) shared lead vocals. Along with Jimmy Pughdominick (drums) and Paul Paradis (lead guitar), they made their first recording.

Who else gave the Skopes a shot? Enter the Screaming Wildman. Well, I didn't actually enter. That would mean leaving home, and I was much too busy. Long story short (not easy for me), John phoned me for some help. I had no problem sharing "the formula" with him. We certainly weren't going to be in any type of geographic conflict (and it was the right thing to do).

John Centinaro and I were thinking about "upside" potential. The group showed promise. John co-authored the novelty song I mentioned. Buddy wrote the song that worked nicely for Side B. Everybody, including me, would gain valuable experience. We were all anxious to see if the band could establish both a stage and studio presence. U.S.A. Records had a new client.

If you check out the U.S.A. disc, you'll see John Centinaro and I share production credit on both sides. A half century later, we shared credit on a James Marvell accomplishment. He was inducted into the Independent Superstars Recording Artists Hall of Fame.

I proudly include the link for you here. https://whisnews21.com/2016/02/10/james-marvell-inducted-into-the-idss-hall-of-fame. It's great to be acknowledged for this small part of his storied musical career. There is one point to make about the leap of faith taken by both John Centinaro and the Screaming Wildman. After all of these decades, we've never met in person! So far.

When I started this story, I knew James Marvell as a man of many passions. Now (after finally reading what I originally wrote), I see he has a single passion expressed in many ways. Call it a musical ministry, if you will.

The drama surrounding the Skopes and their should-have-been hit proved to be temporary and invigorating. Getting a record banned (for lack of a better word) was the equivalent of a disc jockey getting himself fired. The publicity was worth it. The group changed its name. The Surprize released **I Will Make History** https://youtu.be/ilUGGh6sMB8 on the Cent (short for Centinaro) label, with writing credits to John and Carlos Zayas (actually Marvell—ask him why yourself).

I Will Make History was somewhat *prophetic* (still another word I never foresaw in this book). They did make history, just not as Surprize. I think they recorded at Tampa-based Charles Fuller Studios, and the only lineup change was drummer Roger Fuentes. Shortly afterward, Surprize disbanded and Fuentes, Marvell, and Good joined Mercy (founded by Jack Sigler Jr.).

Love: Can Make You Happy was written by Sigler (who also performed lead vocals). I included a YouTube clip from the movie *Fireball Jungle* https://youtu.be/j4A9Fffo-jM. Being part of the movie soundtrack is seldom bad. Too bad we only saw actors fronting the band. The B side of the Sundi Records single release is titled **Fire Ball**.

Love ... soared to No. 2 nationally at the end of May 1969. It doesn't really matter if the movie helped or not. The message was resonating. Sigler was draft-eligible and was most likely speaking for nearly every working-class family in the entire nation. I always like looking at which other hits were trending at the same time.

The Beatles held Mercy out of the top spot with **Get Back**. See, that wasn't a battlefield challenge, but rather a musical one. What else did the nation prefer at that time? **Hair** (Cowsills), **Oh Happy Day** (Edwin Hawkins Singers), and **Grazing in the Grass** (Friends of Distinction) is the answer. Apparently, nobody wanted to hear about more bullets being fired.

I almost forgot **Aquarius**, an eventual No. 1 by the Fifth Dimension, was in the Top 10 at the same time. The year before, their **Stoned Soul Picnic** pretty much summed up the desires of a war-weary nation. I may as well list the rest of the songs according to *Rolling Stone Magazine*: **Gitarzan** (Ray Stevens), **In the Ghetto** (Elvis), and **Atlantis** (Donovan): comedy, social awareness and whatever Donovan was thinking.

The William Morris Agency booked Mercy alongside the Association, Tommy James, and others. Buddy Good and James Marvell were ready to shake down (or shake up) musical and cultural boundaries, in their own way, of course.

While touring with Mercy, James and Buddy developed the Country Cavaleers brand of music (long flowing locks and James's signature rebel-banner guitar). Remember those times? Country singers were a clean-cut, church-social-looking bunch. Google a photo of Willie Nelson (circa 1970). Did the Cavaleers bring out the rebel in Willie? Probably not. It was most likely Willie's new friend (Leon Russell). I'm back now …

Again, John Centinaro saw only potential in the Country Cavaleers. Maybe our "Sicilian" reinforced an unbreakable bond. Enterprising people like John (and everyone else in this chapter) build on great relationships. To call them "salesmen" or "saleswomen" is kind of demeaning. They used their guile to create opportunities for their clients (more like good friends).

John Centinaro got them to Nashville, the next logical step for gifted and socially conscious musicians. I found an awesome link to *Hang on to What – The Strange Tale of the Cavaleers* by Edd Hurt (August 2014) http://www.furious.com/ perfect/countrycavaleers.html. I don't want to unfairly quote Edd, where he credits the Country Cavaleers with being pioneers of "outlaw country."

The next (and continuing to the present time) phase of his career may be best described as Christian Country. Now you've seen James Marvell shouldn't be characterized at all. Only he should proclaim the messages incubated during his teenage years near Florida's steamy Gulf Coast, or should I say "golf" coast?

The final James Marvell link is to **Only Christian Country** https://youtu.be/agX80Fd1ER0. You will see him perform the official (and only ever) theme song for the International Country Gospel Music Association (ICGMA). If some of you think he is one of the best performers I've introduced between the covers of this book, you'll be "preaching to the choir." I'm really enjoying this!

Conviction and integrity are the words that I was looking for when I wrote these last lines. How else do you describe the sizzling career of James Marvell and the way we were all mysteriously and permanently involved? Oh yeah, *grateful* works, too.

Bobby Whiteside

Bobby Whiteside has a varied and industrious career. You'll find him on the U.S.A. Records discography as a writer, singer, and arranger. He also had many roles at the evolutionary and revolutionary Chess Records. I swear, I wanted to include him in a dozen or so conversations with other folks in this book. This dude is in a class by himself.

I seem to remember he did a pretty good impression of Ricky Nelson, who started strumming and singing on *Ozzie & Harriet* (his parents' TV show). Some artists wait for that once-in-a-lifetime appearance. Ricky got a guaranteed slot nearly every week. In a distant second place, I nominate the Screaming Wildman for landing a consecutive 13-week stint for the Buckinghams on national powerhouse (even then) WGN. Where was I?

Some time back, I remember Bobby sending me something from a gig in Nashville. Phil Orsi, Bobby, and I were "everywhere" at once. There are better examples of Bobby's work out there somewhere, but I'm going to have to move on, so try **San Francisco Waits** https://youtu.be/jaALYcHyID, his Flower Power interpretation.

I describe Bobby as a musical *chameleon*. Believe me, I never thought I would be using this word in my book. How else do you describe a guy who specializes in adaptation? He knew when to blend into the background. Even more important, he excelled when he stepped into the spotlight.

It would have been a shame if I somehow left this guy out of my book. He may not be a "household" name, but within the industry, he's an unmistakable rockstar. Any one of the following would define a satisfying career.

Bobby is an accomplished piano, bass, drum, horn, and guitar player. Like so many Chicago artists, he has strong R&B roots. At Chess Records, he assumed either writing, arranging, conducting, producing, or engineering roles on many recordings. Etta James, Muddy Waters, and Minnie Riperton were just a very few of his clients and collaborators.

You'll find him on the Destination, U.S.A. and Mercury record labels from the early '60s onward. In 1974, Bobby recorded *Bittersweet Stories* at Curtom (Curtis Mayfield and Eddie Thomas) Studios. As far as I know, he is the only Caucasian artist with the funk, soul, and rock "chops" to crack the lineup. What could Mr. Whiteside do that could top that?

Well, in the early '80s, Bobby was working on advertising jingles with a guy named Richard Parker from Milwaukee. They wanted to try their hand at a pop song and put together a demo for **Comin' In and Out of Your Life**. As the story goes, this was no ordinary demo because it included a finished string arrangement.

Extraordinary work attracts extraordinary attention (at least in this case). Barbra Streisand released the Whiteside/Parker track as a single and included it on her *Memories* album. She recorded a couple more of Bobby's songs. I've been told Bobby did the musical arrangement and conducted the orchestra for one of her live performances.

He's worked with hundreds of recording artists on every type of project imaginable. He won Clio (advertising), Music City (Nashville), Windy City, and Cannes Film Festival awards, to name a few. Though he's been in Nashville for over two decades, he's still one of the finest representatives of Chicago music that I know. I'm more proud of him than envious, most times.

Recording Studios and Engineers

I'm going to reveal a secret I kept for my entire musical life. I really couldn't be two places at once! However, I was everyplace. Aside from running dances, I was proudly managing a handful of groups. I also played a significant production role on 225 or so 45rpm records. That's upwards of 450 songs in a span that lasted only around a decade. Let's call it the 1960s. I call it a "blur" at times.

Recording studios and record companies were running at full capacity. I'm going to give you a rundown of the studios where I, or the groups I represented, recorded their songs. The studio (and the engineer) were vital to record production, of course. From there, I had to worry about pressing and distribution.

Let me give you an example: The Daughters of Eve recorded at Ed Cody's StereoSonic or the iconic Chess Records studios.

A little Chess background: The Czyż brothers (Phil and Leonard) were Polish immigrants who found vast opportunity in Chicago music. In the entertainment business, it was often prudent to Americanize a surname to make it easier to pronounce. The company name might also create a broader market, in case there were prejudices that would make business more difficult. Choose whichever reason you like. Czyz became Chess.

I don't have a prejudiced bone in my body. That said, it never hurt to know the background of the folks running a studio for negotiation purposes. I told you I modified my last name for business reasons, didn't I? Buonafede became Bonafede.

Even I would stumble past the "u" when trying to work my name into a one-minute commercial spot. If I couldn't pronounce it, you couldn't either. By the way, "buona fede" translates to "good faith."

I've been a man of my word throughout my life. That was easier said than done in my line of work. I know it cost me money, but I never lost a friend by taking care of business my way. Where was I?

OK, back to the Daughters of Eve experience. I got them recorded at StereoSonic, where Ed Cody was both the proprietor and the engineer. At Chess, the chief engineer was a guy named Ron Malo. Both of them had a hand in dozens of legendary records. The Daughters of Eve and Buckinghams (when they were "my" guys and girls) can at least say the Screaming Wildman got them to the threshold of greatness.

After recording, the engineer works his magic to produce a final tape. This is used to create the "master" disc to actually press records from molten vinyl. The process was pretty much the way it sounded. Unless you got to see all of the process, it was hard to explain how many people needed to get paid before the artists themselves saw any money from record sales.

At StereoSonic or anywhere else, the studio got paid for their time and the engineer got paid for his. Because Ed Cody did nearly all of my commercials, I could negotiate a deal with him. We are still friends decades later, so it must have been fair.

The Daughters of Eve got to record with Ron Malo, who was in high demand. Chess wasn't about to keep guys like Chuck Berry, Muddy Waters, or Buddy Guy waiting, or somebody (like the Screaming Wildman) would pay heavily. The Daughters of Eve saved me so much money, it was uncanny. They were so well practiced from steady gigs that they produced many flawless tracks the first time through.

Now, we had to get the demo records made. That would take more time, money, and negotiation. There were dozens of record labels to choose from. Actually, it was more the other way around. The record labels could choose from hundreds of artists and managers anxious to make some sort of deal.

The labels would invest in the actual "mastering" and pressing of demo records. Naw, not really. Big labels only dealt in sure things. The artists themselves, along with managers, friends, and parents, would often pony up the required cash. Looking back to the '60s, I'm certain everyone would say it was worth it, no matter what the eventual outcome.

This left a lot of room for negotiation. Once again, let's use the DoE as an example. We recorded at either StereoSonic or Chess. Their first two 45s were released by U.S.A. Records. SpectraSound released the third. The final (and sadly, last) 45 was released under the Cadet label, sort of a subsidiary of Chess.

Here's where the Screaming Wildman had a distinct advantage in the Chicago market. I could play a demo at the dances I was running. Big-name disc jockeys making guest appearances would listen to the recordings. Even better, they could immediately judge audience reaction. The disc jockeys (and WLS or WCFL) were constantly on the lookout for the next big thing.

Of course, the chances of making it big (however groups defined it) were pretty slim. For as long and hard as I worked, I consider myself eternally blessed to watch one group make it to No. 1.

There were several bands who had fabulous musicians, looks, and charisma. Somehow it didn't always strike a chord (get it?) in the vinyl or AM-radio world. If MTV existed in the late '60s, the Daughters of Eve would be national (if not global) stars. They had a mature stage presence with spot-on Marsha/Judy vocal blends (and they were all accomplished musicians). I swear, they probably inspired groups like ABBA and the Bangles. You know what I'm sayin'?

If the formula for being "discovered" included hanging tough and having a good time, I had it covered. Getting paid real money (at least enough to keep bill collectors or parents happy) created staying power. I did my very best.

While I was hosting the dances, I was booking acts for the Willard Alexander Agency. We encouraged the groups that worked with us to get a demo record made. The sales weren't as important as securing gigs. For talented (yet undiscovered) groups, that would pay far better than record sales. For groups that broke big, that was just as true.

Decent pay would allow groups to plug along until their big break (with obscene pay) came along, or didn't. Regardless, it was a great time to be a musician. Actually, it was awesome. I was the first one to ever use that term.

Ready, Go!

Bill Hall and Stu Black were two great engineers at Hall Recording Studios on South Wabash Avenue. That's where the Gem-Tones recorded their songs. That's also where I recorded **Were Wolf** and **A Story That's True**.

Let me see if I can weave a pattern into my experiences with Boulevard Recording Studios at Dearborn and Ontario. Howard Bedno was a dynamic music promoter and co-founded Cobra Records (who recorded Buddy Guy among others) in the late '50s. The Cobra label used Boulevard to record. Howard proved to be vital to the success of both the Buckinghams and New Colony Six.

I did some of my earliest commercials at Boulevard. I also got Tom Thumb and the Four Fingers, founded by Alan and Bob Campbell, recorded. They were one of the best groups I had heard back then. I want to remind you, I was hosting dances and evaluating talent in the mid-'50s. I was around 15 years old and already playing with the big boys.

Balkan Recordings was on South Archer in Chicago. Back then, it was a Polish neighborhood. That won't matter to you. As I mentioned, that fact may be important to me during negotiations. I wish I could remember the name of the engineer. That's where I recorded Larry Nestor's **Baby Sittin' Blues** https://youtu.be/ BWgYPdi-P_Q. Jimmy Peterson (the Mob) was also a regular session musician on my stuff.

In the early '60s, the hippie movement was starting to evolve into a genuine culture in Chicago's Old Town neighborhood. Bob and Jack Weiner opened Sheldon Recording Studios at 1700 Wells just a few years before that. They were the guys to see for creating record masters. That's where I recorded Larry Nestor's St. Louie Here I Come https://youtu.be/FA-hJUzWkVk and The Good Old Days released on the U.S.A. Records label. I actually worked at Sheldon for about three weeks. I'm guessing there wasn't enough variety for me.

In the early 1960s, Ed Cody (who has his own chapter) took over Hall Recording and named it StereoSonic Studios. He and I logged hundreds of hours together with my commercials, the Daughters of Eve, some Buckinghams, and hundreds of other tracks I recorded for fledgling acts.

Sometime around 1961, I took the Centuries (who would eventually morph into the Buckinghams) to Nationwide Recording Studios, inside the St. Lawrence Insurance Building at 4851 N. Western.

I'm getting a little sentimental as I recall this. I had many recording studios willing to schedule time for me. Independent labels would spring up overnight. After I got a group recorded, I would shop the tracks around to the guys I knew from various labels. I'm not saying that my own Chi-Town label was born this way (but you might). OK, back to the recording studios, and some of the guys (and girls) who made them buzz.

My mentor and business partner, Lew Douglas, and I would trek out to Des Plaines, Illinois, to record Frank Pisani at Custom Audio Studios. I included a link to Candy and Me https://youtu.be/bwxmfwHn_Q8 from Joe Pytel's YouTube channel.

There is so much history on this clip you would not believe it. You could listen, watch, and read all at once.

I forgot what timeless productions we put together there. See if you can keep up with it all. Frank was a master impressionist and singer. Lew Douglas was a legendary composer and arranger. Sue Garrett (credited on Candy and Me) was a student of the awesome Ed Cody and would emerge as an engineering "force" of her own. Candy was written by James Holvay (think, Kind of a Drag) and his collaborator, Gary Beisbier.

We even did better than this in another session at Custom. Pisani was once again the lead vocalist on Happy Ending, Go Now, and Little Serenade. We used Dick

Justin and his singers while Lew Douglas arranged the orchestra pieces. We used all 16 tracks, and I think the engineer was a guy named Jim Vareneski. This was a 3-Deal Music project on my own Chi-Town label around 1976.

Know what? You will see Pisani credited as Pizani in some places. I think he found that using the "z" created a more authentic pronunciation for non-Italianz. See what I mean? Of course, there was no mistaking his country of origin, so what's the harm?

I think it was 1969 when a guy named Marty Feldman founded Paragon Recording Studios on Fulton, just west of Halsted. His teacher and mentor was none other than the legendary Malcolm Chisholm from both Chess Records and Universal Recording. Marty worked with a lot of Chicago-based blues, soul, jazz, and rock artists, including the Screaming Wildman.

Speaking of Universal Recording, it was located at Walton and Rush. It was founded by another legend, Bill Putnam, the designer of the modern engineering console. We might call Bill the "Isaac Newton" of recording. Think how impressive that name (really both names) are going to look in the index of my book. Slick, huh?

Next to Ed Cody, I would have to say my most memorable work was done with Ron Malo from Chess Records on South Michigan in Chicago's historic Record Row. He worked on both Buckinghams and Daughters of Eve recordings, among many others.

One of the drummers I used during many recording sessions was the dad of RCA Recording Studios' engineer, Brian Christian. Brian was a talented engineer who worked with Bob Seger, the Ides of March, the Guess Who, Alice Cooper, Ramsey Lewis, plus the Tufano & Giammarese Band.

My long time friend Phil Orsi reminded me of another studio I overlooked. The recently departed Gary Loizzo (January 2016) from Gary and the Nightlights and the American Breed (you know, **Bend Me Shape Me** https://youtu.be/zarsqZCX08Y) founded Pumpkin Studios. Gary was a grammy-nominated recording engineer, who worked with the likes of Styx, Survivor, and REO Speedwagon.

The Screaming Wildman recently celebrated 50 consecutive years with the Chicago Federation of Musicians. As you may already know, I'm still working on various projects at Steve Yates Recording http://www.steveyatesrecording.com. I'm proud to say I have several audio and video projects in the works as I am writing this.

I dropped in on Steve while I was writing this segment. Of course, I found out he's been too modest to share a couple things until now: Steve was quite a good musician himself and a member of the last act to record with Ed Cody at StereoSonic.

Bill Moore is a photographer and video artist. He and I just hit it off from the very first day we met. We've spent hours reliving my stories and reviving my brand of music. I never thought I would be recording anything new at my age. Bill helped me understand how to develop an internet presence on YouTube.

He's been generous with his time and patient enough to coach me on the potential of internet marketing. I encourage you to explore the diversity of his work on his YouTube video channel. You will see more of "yours truly" and other fascinating folks from his extensive travels https://www.youtube.com/channel/UCXxUa-jeNyZpTJNaZpElQ1A.

The Chicago music tradition is wide, deep, and endless. I bet you would agree it's also vastly underrated. I learned the very reputation of a recording studio rests heavily on the shoulders of its engineers. I've had the unique pleasure of working with many of them as collaborators and friends.

It's humbling how they welcomed me through their doors the same way they did internationally famous acts. I hope you're inspired to explore their stories further. I'm not going to pay someone to print them out for you here. Money doesn't grow on trees, though it does grow *in* trees.

'Nuff said.

The Ultimate Social Network

Dick Biondi

Dick Biondi first hit the airwaves at WCBA in New York back in the mid-'40s, then helped usher in the rock-and-role age a decade later. By the time he moved to Chicago at WLS 890AM Radio in 1960, he was already a sought-after radio personality. He would soon become the nation's No. 1 disc jockey, averaging an incredible 60 share of the radio audience. The first DJ to play a soon-to-be-legendary Beatles song was none other than the already legendary Dick Biondi. (http://www.947wls.com/dick-biondi/)

In 1963, he went to KRLA in Los Angeles, where his syndicated program reached well over 100 stations. The Dick Biondi Road Show introduced dozens of Southern California acts at school dances and record hops.

After the Buckinghams released **Kind of a Drag**, I traveled across the country to persuade influential DJs to play it. One of those was Dick Biondi. I was kind of a pitbull promoter, before anyone knew those were dogs. I wasn't vicious, just tenacious enough to guarantee my groups got every opportunity they deserved.

WCFL/Chicago lured him back for nearly five years until WNMB/North Myrtle Beach, South Carolina, added him to their lineup. In 1984, Biondi again returned at Chicago's WJMK, 104.3FM, and helped orchestrate their transition from country to vintage rock-and-roll—and emerge as a serious WFYR rival.

He was among a group of legendary disc jockeys featured in a Rock & Roll Hall of Fame exhibition in 1995. Three years later, he was inducted into the Radio Hall of Fame. After a half-century captivating audiences nationwide, Chicago named the alley south of the old WLS studios "Dick Biondi Way."

At the age of 79 (2011), he was inducted into the Southern Tier Broadcasters Hall of Fame. He is still working into his 80s, on weekdays from 11pm until 2 am at 94.7 WLS, playing classic hits.

Dick's Promo Poster
(50 Years in Broadcasting)
Chicago's Classic Hits – 94.7 WLS

I was fortunate enough to work closely with a number of DJs who had a significant influence on the music industry. It didn't hurt to be associated with a number of radio stations that ranged from 50,000-watt titans like WLS and WJJD to 5,000-watt stations like WCFL, the "Voice of Labor," that began playing Top-40 hits.

Guys like Dick Biondi and a stable of other on-air talent harnessed the power of the teenage demographic and influenced the entire Chicago music culture. It took a coordinated effort to book teen dances at churches, ballrooms, and schools, then promote them on the radio. Guys like me capitalized on the charisma and enthusiasm of household names like Dick Biondi for extended duty. They'd make personal appearances, then introduce the "live" performers who, at that time, were close enough to touch.

Dick Biondi was always one to "mix it up" with his adoring fans and the acts he introduced. He was always promoting talent and hoping to increase fan reaction. All of those schemes didn't have the expected results.

For instance, the story goes he once got Elvis to autograph his shirt while he served as MC at a Cleveland concert. Dick made the huge mistake of mingling with the crowd afterward and ended up hospitalized when female fans pummeled him in their (eventually successful) attempts to rip the priceless souvenir from his back. This is just one example of the sacrifices artists, promoters, and DJs made to create unique experiences, day in and day out.

Biondi was fired for telling a dirty joke (at least by mid-'60s radio standards) and was then "exiled" to California, or so the story went. Controversial (and frequently fired) DJs have greater mass-market appeal, depending on the rebelliousness of their actions. I stayed in touch with him and came to understand that he longed to return to a mainstream market.

"Do you think you will ever come back to Chicago?" I asked.

"I'd sure like to," he said. We never gave up hope.

WCFL was just getting off the ground, trying to compete with WLS. I knew the WCFL program director, Ken Draper. I mentioned Dick Biondi wasn't very happy. Shortly after our conversation, he called Biondi and got him back on the air in Chicago in an after-midnight slot.

A Personal Visit

Even if you've been on a first-name (or first sight) basis with the legendary Dick Biondi for decades, it is hard to get an appointment with him. He's still streaming to an international audience. In spite of our countless conversations over the years, my mind was still racing with anticipation. I was trying to organize my thoughts around my book project.

Should my mind wander, there are plenty of familiar stories to fall back on. I jumped on the CTA Brown line at Armitage and stepped out at State and Lake, then shuffled down to street level across from the WLS studios, 40 minutes later. Guys my age (and that of my gracious host) know that commuting, Chicago-style, is the best way to get things done. Aside from the parking expense, time is even more precious. I saved a lot on both.

Sadly, this was the evening of the Virginia news crew shooting. I could sense the security guard at the door was going to eye everyone suspiciously. He was courteous enough as he ushered me into the waiting area. He didn't need a memo to remind him kooks come in all sizes, with varying degrees of fire power. I saw this while waiting for Dick Biondi. I make it a habit to arrive early for every appointment. I knew Dick was cut from the same cloth.

Another well-recognized media figure (I won't reveal the name so as not to embarrass her or him, or reveal which media) drifted through the lobby, past the waiting area. Instinctively, I shouted out the person's name in recognition. In another era, or maybe just a single day earlier, this person would have returned a heartfelt wave. Today, I saw terror in his/her eyes, before their "filters" confirmed I was a familiar (and hopefully, still harmless) face. They nodded, kept moving, and anxiously eyed the next security portal while watching for any sudden movements.

Dick Biondi bustled in shortly afterward (about 10 minutes early for our appointment). "Bustling" is another lost art, in my opinion. It's not like rushing, or the panic-driven gait of pseudo executives. He paced forward with purpose in every step.

Even though we'd soon be seated in a comfortable meeting room, the interview began the second he saw me. We were in full conversation as he strode toward me to shake my hand. He waved his security fob to unlock the door, hold it open, and punch his floor into the elevator panel. No time for uncomfortable silence during the ride upward.

"Dick, I heard you tell the story about some guy trying to shoot you. Can I use it in the book?" Maybe this wasn't the right time, given the circumstances of the day. Facts are facts, and the question didn't seem to affect him at all.

"Yeah, I don't think we ever got the whole story about why the guy was so mad. He had a gun and was going to shoot me. Officer Vic saved my life." Folks from that era would know Vic Petrulis was very popular with WLS listeners and made many personal appearances at record hops. Fewer knew the beloved safety announcer and traffic reporter was an active member of the Chicago PD. Maybe the shooter didn't know (not that it would have mattered). Officer Vic was a cop, protector, gentleman, and a trusted public figure at the same time.

"Vic saw the gun was already cocked, vaulted toward the shooter, and put his finger between the firing pin and the hammer," Dick explained, in a way that showed how true professionals behaved. No shots fired; suspect neutralized without mayhem; and two immensely popular and unassuming individuals carried on with the day's activities. That was an awesome story. Now we were ready to begin our "formal" interview.

"Wild Itralian" Revelations

After all this time and many mutual experiences, I'm still finding out more about Dick Biondi. He did a radio commercial at age eight and apparently felt at home in front of a microphone since 1940. In 1946, he was hired as a go-fer at a local radio station. A short time later, he became the PA announcer for a Yankees farm team during the next two seasons (1948-49).

He spent a considerable amount of time with the legendary New York Yankee lefty Whitey Ford (who was quite possibly only four years older). Whitey is still alive as I write this. Baseball legends retire early. Rock-and-roll legends can pursue their passion for more than three generations.

"I thought we are talking about Carl Bonafede, not Dick Biondi," he jokingly reminded me. Well, it's my book, so I can go on about how we witnessed the evolution of Chicago rock-and-roll together.

"I called The Hall [Rock & Roll Hall of Fame] and talked to some kind of manager there," Dick said with a chuckle. The only thing that his legions of listeners have missed for all of these years is the sparkle in his eyes while he is working, or building to the punch line in one of his marvelous stories.

"Yeah, I'm part of the Hall of Fame and I don't want to be," he continued. I may be paraphrasing here.

"No Chicago (the group), no Cryan' Shames, New Colony Six, Ides of March, you guys are all idiots!" Dick scolded. I know I got "idiots" right in that quote. At least, the Impressions represent the Windy City. I agree with Dick Biondi: Midwestern groups are under-represented in the HOF.

"Coastal" groups of questionable credentials seem to be honored in great numbers. Guess what? Since our interview, and maybe because of Dick Biondi's gentle reminder (rant), Chicago and Cheap Trick have been newly honored.

The rest of our meeting started to blur as I tried to relate my recent experiences with others interviewed for this book, like Eddie Thomas and Jack Dreznes from Beverly Records.

"I still have 3,000 pounds of records stored from my days at North Myrtle Beach," Dick mentioned. We recalled our first meeting when a young Carl Bonafede tried to get a popular disc jockey named Dick Biondi to play **Were Wolf**.

Dick showed me the framed plaque commemorating the launch of WLS with the inaugural lineup: Mort Crowley, Jim Dunbar, Art Roberts, Bob Hale, Sam Holman, and Dick Biondi (in the 9-to-midnight time slot).

Dick was quite generous with his time. He spent nine days in a cage with a chimpanzee as a charity stunt (during the time of his California exile). The year afterward (at the Hollywood Palladium), he was dunked 1,800 times to benefit the American Cancer Society.

Of course, Dick Biondi had a few celebrated run-ins with radio station management (which prompted an immediate change of locale). Dick reminded me he worked in (and was invited to leave) a Cincinnati station before his stint in North Myrtle Beach, returning to Chicago "for good" (for the good of all of us) during the Jane Byrne mayoral era (1979–1983).

Is Dick thrilled with his current 11pm - 2am stint? Well, you don't last seven decades without a positive attitude.

"Hey, where else can a guy get paid for working three hours a day?" he joked. Well, when you are fielding calls a full four hours before going on the air, the man is earning every penny, just as he has since his first gig in 1940. Dick Biondi did the very first rock-and-roll show at McCormick Place.

"Fats Domino was the headliner. There were 13 acts in total," he said. Dick seemed to recall as if no time has passed at all. I hope WLS understands they have one of the last living rock and roll dinosaurs on the air, and still one of the hardest working of any era.

"Because we are streaming, I have listeners in Beijing, China, and Holland. Lots of folks in Chicago who leave the swing shift or start the graveyard shift catch me during one of their drive times. Hey, do you still have the suit?" he asked. He teased me about my hand-crafted checkered suit that I regularly wore to introduce both the Daughters of Eve and Buckinghams.

"Yes I do, and it still fits me pretty well," I answered. Do you notice how Dick always shifts the center of attention to his audience? Compare his method with that of current pseudo-celebrities clogging the airwaves.

Finally, we talked about the origin of what I'm now calling the "Chi-town horns." Like the intro to **Kind of a Drag**, I didn't think there was anything like it. In fact, it was somewhat controversial at the time. Clark Weber told me it was one of the main reasons he doubted the song could become popular. It was too loud. We concluded the best representation of Chi-town horns would be the iconic introduction on **Vehicle** by Ides of March. I asked if Dick knew the story about the "focus group" (before there was such a term maybe) debut of **Vehicle** for a Chicago audience. Jim Peterik came to the Holiday Ballroom accompanied by his future wife and asked me to play it. Of course, it was a smash right out of the box, and the Ides were on their way.

We stopped by his modest office cubicle on our way back to the elevator. Of all the personal-appearance photos Dick Biondi could have displayed, he chose one from the dance he hosted at Dunbar Vocational High School in the mid-'60s. The school was at 3000 S. Dr. Martin Luther King Jr. Drive (or South Park Way as it was known back then).

The urban segregation practices in large cities like Chicago "contained" the African American population into tight geographic areas under the guise of urban renewal. In the photo I mentioned, Dick Biondi was the only one we could call "of Caucasian persuasion." In that snapshot, we could clearly see how only the music mattered to anyone there. The kids at the dance were thrilled by a visit from a genuine, caring Chicago celebrity.

If you ever get a chance to stand in front of the photo like I did, you'll feel the warmth literally pour out. I got an even greater insight into Dick Biondi—the man—and a dear friend to us all. He's a character with flawless "character."

Dick Biondi—
Carl was the hardest worker and the greatest-ever promoter in the Chicago music scene. He often went without, to get his people recognized and paid. Everyone who mentions Carl agrees that he is the best. Just the things he did for local talent at the Holiday Ballroom alone are legendary. While I was in California, Carl Bonafede spent three days there to "lobby" for airplay of a tune called *Kind of a Drag* by the Buckinghams. By the time he left, it was blaring from speakers all along the West Coast.

I don't ever plan to stop broadcasting. Chicago is absolutely the best place in the United States for radio. One reason is because Carl never stopped either. If there is anything that you want to know about Chicago rock-and-roll, Carl is the guy to ask.

Lucky Cordell

There are tiny slivers in your lifetime that might make decent stories. Sometimes it takes decades to make you realize how significant those experiences were. I've been waiting years (or in the case of this book, pages) to tell you about Lucky Cordell and the WYNR phenomenon. This is one chain of events nobody could have ever predicted. The memories we created together in that narrow time frame were as indelible as they were impossible to comprehend.

I worked as a janitor at the WYNR radio station back in 1963. To me, it was always important to *be* somewhere and be doing *something*. I was well-positioned to observe how opportunities sometimes create themselves. It was just necessary to put them into motion. By devising my own Screaming Wildman spin, I could have fun, make money, and create something that might last a lifetime. Maybe the brief history of WYNR will give you some idea of how this all wildly played out. Was I in the right place at the right time? As it turned out, I was in the best place during the *only* time. You'll see what I mean.

In 1962, WGES was acquired by a dude named Gordon McLendon, who is credited with developing the Top-40 radio format. The newly named WYNR (for "winner") 1390AM retained its primarily black audience at the outset and steadily added a multitude of white listeners. Thanks to charismatic and personable radio talent like Yvonne Daniels (a pioneer in Chicago radio) and Dick (The Wild Child) Kemp, this 5,000-watt upstart was challenging the status of 50,000-watt Chicago radio giants WLS and WCFL. Rebellious and impressionable teens were exerting newly developed power by turning their AM dial.

While emptying trash at the station, I struck up the first of many conversations with Mr. Lucky Cordell. He was a leading R&B DJ dating back to the '50s. If I recall, he came from WGRY (Gary, Indiana) to this fledgling and already influential Chicago station. This may have been his first experience with a Top-40 format, but his ability to move an audience was already legendary. He was called the "Baron of Bounce" for a reason. If you were in the entertainment business like me, you had a high regard for all types of music. I always considered DJs and other on-air talent as inspirations, rather than competition.

That must have been Lucky's philosophy as well. When I took some of my dance flyers to him, he seemed to show a "knowing" interest, almost as if he recognized who I was. I'm trying to recall our exact words as he contemplated my latest proposal to an elder (and distinguished World War II veteran).

"I'm looking for a DJ at a new dance venue, and you are the hottest guy around," I said. Lucky nodded slightly as an invitation to continue. This guy didn't get this far (and endure this much) to let someone waste his time. His interest must have been genuine.

"There's this place called Luigi's Banquet Hall on the corner of North and Rockwell. I've been working on this for a while. We can have the place from 7:30 to 11pm, sometime in November. I'm thinking Thanksgiving Day. November 28th," I continued, and he contemplated.

"And you want me to be there?" Lucky said, maybe just to politely let me know that he was listening.

"I'll take care of all of the arrangements, like security and advertising," I pressed on, as if he had already agreed. He didn't need to know I still needed to negotiate with the folks at Luigi's. They didn't need to know I hadn't landed a popular DJ, much less who it would be.

"And you want me to be there?" Lucky repeated. He seemed amused, but was thoroughly thinking it over. This would be an audience he never yet experienced in Chicago and most likely anywhere else. I think we both visualized an energetic and receptive crowd, if we could make this happen.

"Think about it and let me know," I said. Lucky knew I would be back to work tomorrow and would surely ask him about his decision. I sensed he also knew I would be going forward, even if I needed to find another DJ to pull this off.

"Okay, if you get this set up, I will be there," he said. From there on, all of our discussions were about making this a memorable dance. He chuckled when he found out my on-air friends at WLS were promoting the dance. We were looking forward to Thanksgiving night, November 28, 1963, at Luigi's. It would be rebellious, irreverent, and such a perfect '60s teen-aged event.

Tragedy and Healing

At 1pm Friday, November 22, 1963, President John Fitzgerald Kennedy was pronounced dead at Parkland Memorial Hospital in Dallas, Texas. The entire world was shocked and disillusioned. That weekend was nothing more than a blur, with one surreal event stacked upon another. The ceremony and protocol of a military funeral, coupled with mourning a man most of the nation embraced, took a toll on us all. On Monday, November 25, the eternal flame marking the JFK burial place had been lit.

I figured every person in America was just as exhausted as I was. It was Tuesday, two days before a Thanksgiving holiday that nobody could ever anticipate or forget. Was there ever a chance we would cancel our much anticipated (and publicized) inaugural dance at Luigi's? Not really. We had no idea how the entire thing was going to go, even before the unthinkable tragedy and the aftermath was still unfolding.

One thing was certain. We were all eager to find out if anyone would feel like dancing. Thanksgiving Day coming so soon after the tragedy was probably a good thing. It forced many of us to go through with our plans and resume some semblance of normalcy. The NFL Green Bay Packers and the Detroit Lions played to a 13-13 tie that afternoon.

Music people thrive on uncertainty. People like Lucky Cordell and I are actually driven to create unforgettable experiences. By Thursday afternoon, we were anxious to see if anybody was going to join us at Luigi's. No matter how many (or how few) people were going to show up, they were guaranteed to get our best. I don't even want to preface that with "under the circumstances." We wouldn't let the acts of others determine how we acted ourselves.

For nearly all of the 600 or so teens who showed up that night to either enjoy themselves or comfort one another, this was their first Lucky Cordell experience. Needless to say, there was no way he would ever disappoint. He made a lot of new fans and listeners that evening. He even introduced a young lady (whose name I wish I could remember) to the crowd who taught them the very latest "street" dance steps. Lucky and his guest stayed to the very end, and refused to collapse into a puddle of exhaustion until the very last of the party-goers were safely on their way home.

We continued the dances each Thursday for more than three months. Lucky, and the multiple acts we were able to attract, made Luigi's a most successful and popular destination. Within a short time, the dances actually started to become "too" popular. We provided more than adequate comfort and safety within the banquet room itself. As it turned out, the impact on the neighborhood was less favorable. Eventually, the kind and accommodating folks at Luigi's needed to respect the wishes of the immediate community, or risk their reputation.

The regular dances ended before spring of the next year. WYNR underwent much more radical changes shortly after. The station that revolutionized the Chicago Top-40 landscape resumed an R&B format for a scant few weeks. In September 1964, they changed their call letters to all news WNUS. Other notable talent at the station included Big John Evans, Bruce Brown, and Floyd Brown (who worked several dances with me afterward).

Hard work and perseverance create successful outcomes, no matter the circumstances. For pulling together one Thanksgiving dance (following one of the most noteworthy tragedies in America), so many incredible things needed to happen. It's just freaky. WYNR existed for hardly two years. Staffed by primarily R&B on-air talent, they challenged, if not temporarily dominated, their well-established and even better-funded Top-40 competition. Lucky and I never worked together again. It never had anything to do with our respect for one another. Fate threw us together. It also ripped us apart without explanation or apologies.

Lucky Cordell's Passing

Shortly before I edited this chapter, I heard Lucky just succumbed to injuries sustained during a fire at his Chicago South Shore home. Even at the age of 86, he left us way too soon, and certainly not under the circumstances I would have chosen for such a great man. He has my gratitude for the indelible mark he made on my career. May he forever rest in peace.

More About Moses "Lucky" Cordell
Lucky has been honored by The HistoryMakers® - The Nation's Largest African American Video Oral History Collection.
www.thehistorymakers.com/biography/lucky-cordell-40
    If you want to hear the voice of Lucky Cordell in 1963, precisely at the time he and I worked together, here's a YouTube® audio clip
https://youtu.be/N5uGCWMj1lQ.

    Lucky worked at several radio stations as a disc jockey before taking a position at WVON (Voice of a Nation). He worked his way to General Manager in 1970. Under his leadership, the ratings and advertising revenue steadily increased.

    In the early '60s, the station had merely 250 watts of power, just enough to influence the south and west sides of Chicago. It was said that Barry Gordy of Motown sent all records he produced to WVON first. This was the station where a young and talented Don (Soul Train) Cornelius perfected his most recognizable speaking voice.

Dex Card

Was there ever a more perfect name for someone in the entertainment industry? This faultless advertising tag was actually his given name. It's safe to say the innovation was the handiwork of his parents. However, Dexter Card would be responsible for shuffling and dealing his way through the music business. That's why I'm thrilled to have his contribution here.

Think about this. Another elder statesman of the rock-and-roll era at the heart of this book still indulged me with an interview. I don't want to give too much away before I formally introduce him to you. I'm not sure how many interviews Dex does now. But I can guarantee he is just as graceful with his words and praise as always.

Every disc jockey I've talked to still has the cadence and delivery that stimulates an audience, even if it's a single listener. Dex also has taken care of his instrument, somehow. His golden tones are still as vibrant as those of folks decades younger. I guarantee his voice can whisk you back to the decade you choose.

"Actually, I was a smoker during those times and just lucky that it hasn't caught up with me somehow," Dex revealed. When I think about all of the smoke drifting around at concerts or record studios, it's surprising any of us survived this long. This must be luck, more than lifestyle. The chances are a little better than having a hit record, however.

I bet he's answered the question about landing at WLS thousands of times. A true professional and warm human being, he gave it another go.

"I was doing the morning show at KYW in Cleveland. Ron Riley and I worked together there before he landed his gig in Chicago. Ron suggested that I contact [WLS Program Manager] Gene Taylor when word got out that Bob Hale would be leaving the afternoon time slot," he started. Apparently, there are other kinds of jockeying at radio stations.

"We did a little phone negotiation, and I sent him a demo tape. Soon after, we met face to face and he offered me the slot," Dex continued. As others have said, you have to work your way into Chicago. For a kid born and raised in Portland, Maine, that was no easy feat. WLS now had showmanship and personality in one tidy package. It sounds a lot different to hear him tell it …

"I was glad to have that job, too. WLS was a phenomenal station. They had a 40% afternoon market share, where the norm was 6-7% back in 1964," he said, revealing a shrewd business mind. You could say he knew dollars made sense. Remember, that was nearly 25 years before the **Dollars Make Sense** song, released by hip hop artist Jay Rock in 1999.

OK, I got you to the time when Dex Card landed the afternoon time slot on the weekday WLS Silver Dollar Survey.

"My show was pretty systematic, if you remember. I would start at 2pm and play the top 30 songs in Chicago and work my way up to number one for the finale," he reminded me.

This is really where radio personalities, promoters, managers, record companies, and booking agents started working closely together. I guess you could say I was sort of a radio personality since I was a familiar voice on the radio. Unlike Dex, I would never earn a time slot, especially if it meant leaving my hometown. Working side by side with radio royalty would be reward enough for me.

Maybe his listeners would assume he just cruised northward on Lake Shore Drive from the WLS studio in the shadow of the Wrigley Building once his shift ended. Here's where the worst-kept secret of the Chicago music scene is once again revealed.

"I would head to the London House after work while I waited for the traffic to die down," he recalls. That's where promoters and managers just happened to congregate as well. If it happened to be at just the time radio personalities left work, it was merely a coincidence.

"I want to attribute our longevity to the time we spent at the London House," Dex said with a long laugh. I mean a deep-throated baritone that stopped me in my tracks. Dex readily admits being into his eighties, with a voice that all generations would rightfully envy. I didn't mention it during our interview, but I couldn't ever associate his voice with his legendary crew cut.

Showmanship and Sincerity

Dex Card was the kind of guy who could display the honorable traits in the subtitle above. He would seize an opportunity and mold a product that would benefit everyone. I'm a guy who believes in generating a heathy profit, as long as it's shared with all concerned.

"There were record shops on nearly every block and several in each shopping center," Dex continued (when I let him). The disc jockeys (I prefer radio personalities) were whipping up a vinyl recording tsunami. I never thought I would be using that word in my book, either. In the '60s, nobody in America ever knew that was a word (otherwise, I would have used it in my advertising).

Guys like Dex would be hard-pressed to determine whether they were satisfying a market or creating one. I guess we all just decided to roll with it. People would "track" their favorite songs as they worked their way up in the WLS survey. That would trigger more record sales. For local groups, it would mean more bookings for musicians and requests for personal appearances by DJs.

I was booking talent, managing bands, hosting dances, securing guest appearances (at the London House, sometimes), and marketing the whole mess. Of course, securing big-name guest DJs meant they and their station would be promoting my dances on the air. Nobody was interested in any more than their fair share of the profit (at least not guys I worked with, especially Dex).

He and I both focused on the opportunities for talented groups. Since it seemed to take a good deal of extra effort to get national exposure for Chicago groups, we were willing to do whatever it took. Jerry Germansen from the Delights and John Poulos from the soon-to-be Buckinghams asked me to be their manager. That also meant acting as their booking and recording agent. Dex Card never needed persuasion when it came to helping local bands.

Everyone benefitted every time a DJ mentioned their list of upcoming appearances. At the Holiday Ballroom, we would regularly attract crowds approaching 700, week after week. DJs welcomed the opportunity to mingle with the crowds and just maybe discover a national sensation.

The Wild Goose Phenomenon

His popularity and charitable appearances made Dex one of the most trusted celebrities of the era. I'm still in awe of the things he accomplished after leaving his regular stint at WLS. Can you imagine creating an even more successful gig for yourself after that? It took exceptional talent and dedication.

I sort of crashed during the '70s. I had no "roll" left after the Daughters of Eve and Buckingham "rocks" left bruises, but thankfully no permanent scars. For Dex Card, those were rich and rewarding times in unimaginable ways. Many folks had a front-row seat for a new era of music he promoted.

"After leaving WLS, I did my own syndicated radio show from a studio I constructed in a spare bedroom of my home," Dex began.

Sharing the marquee with the Buckinghams in 1966 (Courtesy of Jerry Germansen from the Delights). How's that for an entertainment package?

He also put his natural talent and charisma to work by building teen clubs and promoting rock concerts.

"My very first teen club was in Waukegan. I found someone willing to salvage the wood from an abandoned bowling center in exchange for the labor. I set up a stage and installed some lighting, then booked the Cryan' Shames as the opening act. The place held 1,500 and they drew a capacity crowd. My greatest pride was seeing Chicago groups like the Shadows of Knight, Buckinghams, and the New Colony Six gain recognition," he continued.

"I helped discover Styx. Do you mind if I share that with you?" he asked.

Do I mind getting an inside story on one of the best groups the Chicago area ever produced? Here's a little info I want to lay out before turning things over to Dex once again. Roseland area Dennis DeYoung (vocals, keyboards) joined brothers Chuck (bass) and John (drums) Panozzo to found a group known as TW4 when Dex first invited them to his Wild Goose clubs.

Their record-breaking performances would make Dex a ton of money and eventually attract the attention of Wooden Nickel Records, according to bass player Chuck in his 2006 autobiography *The Grand Illusion: Love, Lies, and My Life With Styx* (available on Google Books). Yeah, the mega-band Styx got an unbelievable boost from the Wild Goose venues and the tireless promotion of Dex Card. I thought my studying days were behind me.

Dex reminded me there were six or seven Wild Goose clubs in the Chicago suburbs, and he started producing rock concerts at college campuses in the Midwest.

"After a couple of years in the concert business, I was doing swell enough to leave my syndicated show," he continued.

"I hired Styx to open concerts for Canned Heat, whose first album was released shortly after their appearance at the Monterey Pop Festival in 1967. Styx released a record called **Lady** and I started using it in my commercials and promotions.

"I started headlining them and continued to use the record. **Lady** was the most requested record at WLS and finally broke into the Top 10 nationally. I ended up doing 63 concerts with Styx. I did their first downtown show at the Auditorium Theater. Of course, we booked national acts in my clubs but took great pride in presenting Chicago groups." Dex paused for a moment, like he did on the air when he wanted a point to sink in. Maybe he was just handing me an opening, as if I needed it before now.

I'm outraged when a record can be popular in Chicago and fail to get airplay in national markets. Chicago groups had great talent. We are a political town but still seem to grapple with the strategies or politics of the music business. Once Styx left Wooden Nickel and moved to A&M Records, **Lady** (penned by Dennis DeYoung for his wife) finally got national airplay and reached No. 6 on the Billboard chart in 1975.

Dex Card used that awesome rock ballad in advertising spots for the Wild Goose clubs and practically everywhere else. That unmistakable piano intro literally set the stage for Styx https://youtu.be/QumxOQganfo. I think it is one of the most recognizable songs in music history. Whatever Dex and Styx were selling, we were joyfully buying.

Since I started laying down this chapter, I'm reminded the first WLS Radio broadcast of a rock concert was Styx at the Chicago Stadium in 1978. Dex was just getting warmed up.

"Can I share another story with you?" he asked me. Sure, I was tired of talking anyway (we all know how far from the truth that is).

"I was dropping off one of my commercials at WCFL Radio, and the program director approached with a song he wanted me to hear. Apparently, these guys stole the show at the Fort Lauderdale music festival and wanted help getting on the air. As soon as I got home, I found out who represented them and booked Three Dog Night for dates beginning in 1970.

"My summer venues were primarily ice-skating rinks. When they started playing my joints, they were getting $1,500 per night. By the end of my tour, they were getting $15,000," Dex told me.

There's no need for an encore after hearing the role he played for a group with more than 20 hits on the Billboard Top 40. Because we are talking about the legendary Dex Card, of course, there was far more.

"I got into the concert business around 1968 and did it for about eight years," he started. The teen clubs had apparently run their course as well and Dex was ready for a new outlet for his promotional skills.

"I started buying radio stations. My first was in Kenosha, Wisconsin. Racine and Appleton followed soon after," he told me.

Recollections and Regrets

There is only one regret he thought worth mentioning. It's one I can easily understand—retiring too early.

"I'm still in touch with Ron Riley and Clark Weber. Clark just retired, and I'm the oldest of the three," Dex lamented. It sounded like a request for a do-over.

If I'm reading this right, we both stepped away from the daily grind when it wasn't as much fun. There's no way to remain active in the business and avoid the hassles. Dex traded the Wisconsin winters for Sunshine State humidity and alligators. There was too much hands-on required from a radio station owner. I'm guessing that's why he didn't buy any down there.

Dex modestly recollected the encouragement and direction he gave to other emerging radio personalities. "Chicago" Eddie Schwartz hosted a late-night program at WIND (560). His shows were lively, educational, and inspiring. He regularly conducted forums on genuine issues, like racism and poverty (subjects that revealed the intellectual side of graveyard-shift listeners).

WCFL DJ, promoter, and fellow radio station owner Jim Bernard had an invaluable teacher in the person of Dex Card.

"I think Jim may have been more interested in how I handled business at the Wild Goose than the musical acts. All I did was urge him to pursue a career in radio," Dex said. Thank goodness the Dex Card blueprint for success found its way into capable hands. Thank you both, guys. Compliments flow like water as time melts like ice in springtime (poetic, huh?). Dex respected my loyalty and ability. It was clear that he was a tremendous Cryan' Shames fan.

"They would have done even better under your management, Carl," Dex said. He is awfully good at creating smiles and good wishes to this day.

Good disc jockeys and other radio dudes have an internal clock that tells them when it's time to wrap things up. Some guys, like the legendary Dex Card, poured their heart and soul into entertaining others. It's human and healthy for us to want more.

"I haven't been in contact with many groups since my retirement. I still have a couple of daughters in the Chicago area. They took me to an outdoor Buckinghams concert in Northbrook. The band acknowledged me from the stage. It was a pleasure to hear the applause," he said.

I could have shoved these last Dex Card thoughts into the preceding paragraphs somewhere, but the old fashioned *P.S.* works here:

"The Beatles, and the rest of the British Invasion, created a very exciting time for musicians. The Motown sound and West Coast groups like Jan & Dean and the Beach Boys made it a great time," Dex recalled. We agreed music has disappointed us since then. Maybe technology has messed things up for musicians.

"There just aren't as many groups that excite people," he concluded. If there is anyone who can chart a (forward) course to better times, it's Dex Card. Thank you once again.

Jim Bernard

See that photo of Jim Bernard behind the mic at WCFL Radio in Chicago? Disc jockeys were among the most versatile and expressive people on the Chicago-land music scene. They even did "live" commercials, sometimes during song introductions. Or they would use popular songs as the "backdrop" for their commercial scripts on behalf of places like World Wide Auto Transmission on Cicero Avenue. I remember Jim would even poke fun at his own delivery while on the air. I suggest you try to read copy, often with a minimal script, or none at all, to understand what talent it takes to keep a program on course. These guys were a lot like orchestra conductors, with the additional talent of wielding their own (voice) instrument.

Let me try to fill in the last 50-some years for you all. Jim Bernard Hebel and his partner and collaborator, Ed Redmond, were running regular dances at the Embassy Ballroom (Fullerton and Pulaski) in the '60s. As I mentioned before, this was during the "golden age" of teen venues. There were dances nearly every Friday, Saturday, and Sunday.

You might say we were friendly and respectful rivals. At that time, there was plenty of work for bands, DJs, and promoters. Anyone I was lucky enough to include in this book will tell you this was a stressful and competitive business. You had to hustle to keep your nose above the water line. This means you had to log your time at the London House (Wacker Drive and Michigan Avenue) to mingle with the big-name DJs. Likewise, it didn't hurt to get on a first-name basis with the luminaries from Chess or Vee-Jay Records from Chicago's legendary Record Row on South Michigan Avenue.

Blue-Collar Media

As Jim reminded me, his first real job (at 18) in the music business was at Chess Records, where the Rolling Stones recorded **2120 South Michigan Avenue** (the Chess studio address) among other tunes in 1964. Lesser known by the world, but better known by those of us who lived and breathed Chicago music, the Daughters of Eve and the Buckinghams recorded there as well. As a matter of fact, landing a recording session there, among the greatest rhythm-and-blues artists of any century, was in itself an envied accomplishment. If you were lucky enough to work closely with their much-admired (and envied) engineer, Ron Malo, it would be so much better.

Jim and I were captivated by both the music and the artists who performed it. At an early age, we were convinced this was going to be our calling. The emergence of the Beatles led to the formation of thousands of garage bands, practically overnight. As a result, there was no shortage of venues to play. Musicians and singers began to mix, mingle, and collaborate. Bands reconfigured, defined and re-named themselves. Artists were exposed to a new type of rhythm-and-blues, carefully crafted to appeal to a much broader base. Somehow, the Beatles' **Rock And Roll Music** proved more palatable to a certain sector of the record-buying public than the Chuck Berry version, written and recorded in a less-enlightened 1957.

In the early '60s, record producers and promoters, disc jockeys, radio stations, ballrooms and nightclubs, musicians, vocalists, writers, and a rabid audience created a "perfect storm." Sorry for the overuse of that term, but I think it really applies here. Jim Bernard—his beloved business partner and collaborator Ed Redmond, Dan Belloc, Jim Lounsbury, and many of the other folks who are mentioned in this book—saw the building power, energy, and height of the tidal wave. If you wanted to be part of the music scene, you were going to either drown, or learn to "hang ten." I'm proud to say that everyone in this book was a surfer.

I think Jim may have been the one to say "we had many of the same experiences without being in the same room." That creates a bond that can sustain you through all kinds of times. That "common ground" approach, particularly in a hard-working town like Chicago, allows us to resume our relationships even though decades have passed. Often, we were so busy catching the same wave we probably didn't realize we grew up in the same (60614) postal code until years later. Without having much time to look around, he and I were competing, and this respectful rivalry enriched everyone.

If I booked one of the hottest acts getting Chicago airplay, the groups themselves started to look around for who else may be able to book them during the same road trip. Then, it would be a race to line up a disc jockey to appear at the advertised event, and the same jockeying (pun intended) for the hottest on-air talent would ensue. Often, the record-buying, and fiercely energetic, teen crowds would have us working 20-hour days. This was all to satisfy a crowd that sometimes made us feel like Seymour from *Little Shop of Horrors*. We would do anything for our all-consuming love interest, and they knew it.

Let's keep with that surfing analogy a little longer. While we were treading water to catch the next wave, Jim may have had a better sense of wind and climate than most people. He was an accomplished entertainer and did many things his peers would someday envy. One of these was being a WCFL disc jockey in a rabid Chicago market, with a lineup that included Bob Dearborn, Dick Shannon, and the nationally famous Larry Lujack. Doing this, without sacrificing his relationships or integrity, is something I really admire. He also taught school and did a good deal of European travel (before "I was too old to enjoy it," he would later tell me). In the rock-and-roll business, he may be one of the best educated, traveled, and "grounded" of us all. Some would say he had a "dream" life. However, there are a few scenes in that dream I would not discover until much later.

Everyday America

Cresco is much closer (one hour) to Lacrosse, Wisconsin, and Rochester, Minnesota, than it is to the capital city of Des Moines, Iowa. So, what does present-day KCZQ-FM 102.3 "Super C" Radio (a 3,000-watt adult contemporary station nestled into the northeast corner of Iowa) have in common with a 50,000-watt powerhouse like Chicago's WCFL back in "the day?" That would be Chicago native and Lane Tech / Chicago State graduate Jim Bernard. While many of us chose to ignore the inevitable "winds of change," he was ready to capitalize on his experience and realize his lifelong dream: to own his own radio station in a vital, but relatively small, market in rural America.

I think he would say that he was "large," and even more importantly, trusted enough in a Chicago powerhouse environment to witness a lot of

Posing with Crystal Gayle (sort of) during the '80s at country powerhouses WJJD and WJEZ

significant things go down. He was also just "small" enough to take this experience and craft a sustainable future without damaging his reputation or pocketbook. Many of his contemporaries were not prepared for being (last surfing analogy) swept out to sea or foundering in the shallow water. Never one to do things halfway (I would say half-@ssed), he bought a string of radio stations. He understood that keeping a radio station "in the black" (which he did from "day one") requires building and maintaining relationships between his listeners and advertisers.

OK, one more surfing analogy: Jim Bernard Hebel (he uses his full name in the Chicago market so "his people" realize he made it) and I actually drifted together due to an uncanny set of circumstances. When Ed Redmond passed away in 2007, Jim helped found a scholarship fund with the proceeds of Ed's extensive record collection. One of the companies he contacted turned out to be Beverly Records. When my name came up, Jim learned they had me on "speed dial" before there was such a thing. Actually, I still have the same phone number from back then. If you have one of my old promotional pieces, or business cards, you already know how to get in touch with me. I've come a long way, without going very far (geographically, at least).

Tales from the Surf Ballroom

Most people remember the Surf Ballroom in Clear Lake, Iowa, for one reason. It was the venue for the last performance of the legendary Buddy Holly, Ritchie Valens, and J.P. "Big Bopper" Richardson before they died in a plane crash on February 3, 1959, en route to Moorhead, Minnesota. Many folks don't realize it, but the Surf Ballroom has been continually operating for more than 55 years since then (https://www.surfballroom.com/index.html). I had been traveling with a bunch of folks, including Joe Pytel and the Beverly Records crew, to the Winter Dance Festival on "the day the music died," according to Don McLean's celebrated **American Pie**. Since our reunion, I've been interviewed on local television and heard my records played on Jim Bernard's "Super C" station. You never get tired of hearing "your" songs blaring from someone's (anyone's) speakers. The magic endures even as the years pass.

While pulling together the material for this book, I've unearthed a bunch of things that somehow tie a lot of my career together, in ways I never could have predicted. Once you dig into the history of the Surf Ballroom, before or since the tragic events that put Clear Lake, Iowa, in the conscience of rock-and-roll America, you will notice the long list of legendary performers who played the famous venue. Maybe aging rockers are "collectors" (or packrats, because "you never know"). I still have the booking contracts from my days at Willard Alexander. Anyway, I started compiling a list of venues for the Daughters of Eve touring schedule for this book and I came across "Surf Ballroom - Daughters of Eve - Sunday, 4-28-1968." The girls, my girls, gutted out a genuine rockstar schedule. If the music gods had been kinder, they'd still be playing today.

Jim kept only a single station from those he originally acquired (the one with the best reception). Here's what it sounds like when he explained the radio dynamics of rural America: "I'd be happy with 10 watts if I could transmit from the top of the Hancock Building in Chicago. With our antenna, KCZQ-FM 102.3 Radio can be heard in the parking lot of the Surf Ballroom." His community trusts him to create a shared playlist on its behalf. Think of Chicago-flavored FM album rock and you might feel at home listening to awesome instrumentation and vocals that missed the mainstream because of the overly commercial Top-40 format.

Let me know the next time you hear anything by Heartsfield (most likely formed at The Earl of Old Town on Wells Avenue) http://www.heartsfield.com. The reassuring strength of "your" radio station (if it is run by Jim Bernard) means they're playing tunes from the artists whom you treasure but have nearly forgotten. You may develop a yearning (I don't know if they say "hankerin'" in Iowa) for a tune by Aliotta, Haynes, and Jeremiah, who were launched in the Old Town (say, North and Wells) section of Chicago. (https://youtu.be/0saZiLV7-7E). Their **Lake Shore Drive** was one of the signature songs made famous by Chicago media personality Eddie Schwartz on late-night Chicago radio.

Cuban band Kracker—**Because of You (The Sun Don't Set)** (1972) https://youtu.be/MqNime_-XPU—found favor with Keith Richards and Mick Jagger. I think it's partly because of the Rolling Stones' close ties with Chess Records and their appreciation for Midwestern music.

Moving Forward, While Looking Back

It's funny how an endless stream of memories seem to spill out whenever Jim Bernard and the Screaming Wildman collide in northeastern Iowa. We're also still giving each other friendly advice. When I got a look at Jim's extensive gold and platinum record collection, I suggested he display it more prominently. By my next visit, I saw something like the rock-and-roll shrine that I envisioned. Hours seemed to melt away as we talked

Jim Bernard Hebel—
My wife Sandy reminds me that I was "one cocky SOB" during my disc jockey days. The same thing could be said for Carl Bonafede, in the most affectionate way. For most people, promoting was a job, and it showed. Carl loved it. He was the premier hustler – promoting every waking moment. Everyone in the music scene agreed that the Screaming Wildman was a "Piece of Work." Everywhere I've seen him introduced, he's received enthusiastic applause.

around his dining room table. He made a good point about our having many of the same experiences, just from different perspectives. One of his unique accomplishments, which anyone would crave, was landing that disc jockey gig at Chicago's WCFL. Jim reminded me you don't become a household name with the 2-6am time slot.

That's one reason I couldn't hope to imitate him. I would have been too homesick to function. As he reminded me, "You have to work your way back to Chicago." That required landing gigs in Saginaw, Michigan; Indianapolis; Milwaukee; and others too numerous to mention. Dex Card opened the door for Jim at WCFL in a way, but not before he did his "time" in lesser markets. Too much stuff would be out of the Screaming Wildman's control to pull it off.

In no particular order, our discussions included: Dex Card and the Wild Goose teen club ... conversion of the Old Century (Clark Street) and Music Box (Southport Avenue) theaters to music venues ... the American Breed, Gary Loizzo, Styx ... Jim Golden (U.S.A. Records) ... the Rotary Connection ... Jim and his wife Sandy's herd of breeding horses ... comparing our list of "scoundrels" in the music business (we all knew!) ... Chicago's Bob Hale hosting the last show by Buddy Holly at the Surf Ballroom ... upcoming appearances by Brian Highland, Frankie Avalon, Lou Christie ... Ides of March ... Willie Dixon, Chess Records, Rock & Roll Hall of Fame ... Bernie Allen...

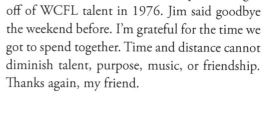

WCFL Jocks Say Goodbye on 3-15-76. (http://chicagoradioandmedia.com/multimedia/audio/1497-wcfl-jocks-say-goodbye-031576)

We also talked about how often radio stations switch formats, even with legendary jocks still in their talent stable. I found a clip of the sign-

off of WCFL talent in 1976. Jim said goodbye the weekend before. I'm grateful for the time we got to spend together. Time and distance cannot diminish talent, purpose, music, or friendship. Thanks again, my friend.

Jim in his "Super CFL" promotional beach hat (around 1976)

Beverly Records

I'm renewing acquaintances I let fall into disrepair. My closest friends will tell you I prefer close contact. That's why I prefer to visit people in person, rather than just call them. Here is where I apologize for not being very responsive to telephone messages. Sometimes the technology frustrates me. Most of the time I'm just exhausted from my daily routine.

Part of the reason I am writing this book is because so many important people in my life never knew much about one another. The best example I can think of is one Mr. Eddie Thomas. Everyone should know him, and so, even before circulation of the final version of this book, I've shared his chapter with many others. I'm seeing so many of these chapters intertwine. I'm keeping my editor busy. Here's another example.

Vintage Vinyl

This chapter took shape in late August 2015 when I visited Beverly Records on South Western Ave. Chicago natives are aware many of the 77 Windy City neighborhoods are named for streets. Others describe the industries important to working-class people who made them vibrant (like the Pullman area, where railroad cars were manufactured). The Beverly area is one of the most racially and ethnically diverse neighborhoods in all of Chicago. This is further proof that music can be a unifying force (even more so than sports, my other passion).

I was among her first (1967) customers when Christine Dreznes (soon to be affectionately called "Mrs. D") first opened Beverly Records. Today, I'm meeting her son Jack at their "flagship" (and now only remaining) location. I was early for our meeting (as usual), and Jack was already there before regular hours. We had some time to reminisce before the steady stream of customers began.

I was a regular visitor (yeah, I bought stuff, too) through the years. Beverly Records also served as the backdrop for a flattering piece *Chicago Sun-Times* columnist Dave Hoekstra wrote about me awhile back.

Carl Giammarese from the Buckinghams and Debi "Drums" Pomeroy from the Daughters of Eve were among the celebrity sightings at Beverly Records through the years. Today, I was meeting Susan Rakis, the current road manager for the Buckinghams. You will see her posing with the album cover from one of her favorite groups and the "single" 45 that was responsible for her favorite gig, maybe next to her Girl Scout work.

By now you can see I write the same way I talk. One thing leads to another, and there doesn't seem to be a beginning or an end, once I find myself in the middle. We started our interview with a few "snaps" of Jack's mom and dad. Their memorial photo near the rear of the store still overlooks the packed rows of shelves. A record store is like a portal to the past, don't you think?

"Mrs. D" was a true entrepreneur, long before I knew there was such a word. Hard-working folks with Midwestern values made this city great. Christine was gifted, innovative, and energetic. While raising two fine men, who would also work in the family business, she started a gift, candy, and novelty store serving local school children. http://www.beverlyrecords.com/

She soon added phonograph records and costumes to her offerings. Even though we had dozens of conversations over the years, I found out something new about Christine Dreznes today that made her even more endearing, and shrewd in my eyes. Back in "the day" when 45rpm vinyl ruled, record distributors would make their rounds at "mom and pop" stores (another term I cherish, and miss). Establishments sold records on a "consignment" basis. Agents of the record distributors would drop off the Top-40 singles, collect cash for sales, and remove the records that toppled off the chart.

In working-class neighborhoods, kids had to earn their money before adding songs to their collection. Some kids couldn't afford a particular record before it fell out of popularity. The distributors' minions already had carted them away and replaced them with those getting airplay. There were also cases where cherished records would get damaged or lost during informal record parties. Whenever boys got involved, fights broke out during the testosterone-fueled encounters girls love to create. Just kidding. Now you know why I never "domesticated" myself. Who would want to be known as "Mrs. Screaming Wildman" anyway?

John and Christine "Mrs. D" Dreznes

Speaking of girls in more loving terms, they were notorious for playing a favorite record until the grooves wore through to the flip side. There, I gave you an innocent and endearing reason why records needed replacing. Mrs. D to the rescue! This was a stroke of genius and a need nobody was addressing. I'm jealous and grateful at the same time. The next time a record minion (probably a nice enough guy) stopped by, she offered to buy his older records (at a discount, of course). To save labor and hassle, most readily agreed.

As she readily admitted years ago, "I didn't know the difference between the Monkees and the Beatles." Christine did, however, always have a kind word for her young customers. She eventually taught herself which records had lasting value. Before long, her husband John, sons Jack and Randy, along with several others were serving the music community at four locations during the '70s and '80s. It takes great patience and perseverance to simultaneously create a market and passionately satisfy it for some 45 years.

Many businesses stumble when a second generation assumes management responsibilities. The name of the store says it all. Beverly Records was an established community service, intended to last for generations. As a lasting tribute to Christine and John, the beat goes steadily on. Jack Dreznes put his encyclopedic knowledge on display for me and continued with his grateful clientele. While we talked music, he "punctuated" our discussion by slapping down the relevant album cover in front of us.

When I mentioned I went to Cooley High School (long before the movie came out), there was the album cover, in its re-released (due to the popularity of the movie) glory. I mentioned the accomplishments of my dear friend Eddie Thomas and his promotion of Jerry Butler's career.

The discussion turned to the subversive methods needed to introduce diverse audiences to passionate soul artists. Jack tossed down *Aware of Love*, a Jerry Butler album. The cover features a thoroughly enraptured Caucasian couple. Back then, the only way Cooley High (and Cabrini-Green) graduate Jerry Butler would be welcomed into many households would be under camouflage.

We discussed the resurgence of needle-on-vinyl and how emerging technology found its way into newly released material. *Lazaretto,* the "Ultra LP" from Jack White (the White Stripes), is a great example. The album is something you both listen to and experience. It engages his audience and might be an engineering marvel. There are hidden tracks, locked grooves, and a holographic angel hovering above the spinning disc. One track plays from the inside out; the other plays outside in. This is better seen than read: https://youtu.be/59782bpPUgk

I know. If you still think listening to albums with friends is a "passive" experience, a technologically advanced record may not be your first choice. But, what if groups from our day released re-engineered tracks that appeal to younger audiences—this millennial demographic? More people should be hearing the same music that delighted and inspired us. I don't think this book is a vanity or nostalgia piece. I want to strengthen the bonds between generations and cultures the way we used to—through music.

OK, this is a concept I need to wrap my mind around. Tell me if I'm wrong (and I will most likely argue with you). In my earliest days of making records, we cranked out vinyl "calling cards" for hopeful groups.

Many of the groups I mention here (myself included) consider it somewhat of an honor if their work is captured and distributed on a CD (you know, new media). I'm told young people are gravitating toward phonographs as their "new" media. Oh, to think I might make a record again!

In my lifetime, we might see groups gain popularity from CD sales. Pressing cutting-edge vinyl afterward may be considered the new pinnacle of success. What goes around sometimes comes around, in great and unexpected ways.

I won't ever get too technical (because I can't), but an "earthy warmth" surrounds folks who listen to vinyl. Engineers would call it tone or depth or "compression" or some such. I like my definition better.

Susan Rakis remembered a time when Carl Giammarese wanted to cover an "oldie" while on tour, and she called Jack. After hearing a few bars, he identified the needed track and proceeded to play the record so Carl could jot down the lyrics and cover it at his next performance.

I love getting folks together to renew acquaintances and share a few laughs. Somehow, we always managed to learn more about one another.

Everyone in this book is far more than an "extension" of time long past. We're still committed to producing the best music possible. I've met new folks willing to work as hard as we did to further the cause. As always, I'm grateful to Jack (and his loving family) for the Beverly Record brand of hospitality.

Jack, Yours Truly, and Susan Rakis at
Beverly Records in Late August 2015

"Susan" 45rpm Record Jacket –
Courtesy Beverly Records

Close to Home

Larry Nestor

Google (I never thought I would say this) "Prolific Creativity." You'll see a variety of articles and blog posts. Some of them are quite good, actually. What you don't see "yet" is anything about Larry Nestor. I don't even know where to begin when it comes to my relationship with him, and he to his many fans. He wrote and I sang **Baby Sittin' Blues** https://youtu.be/BWgYPdi-P_Q, released on the Impala Records label in the early '60s. He was born in 1940 (same as the Screaming Wildman). He probably wrote more than 1,000 songs to date. As I mentioned in Ed Cody's chapter, Larry was arranger, producer, and of course, staff songwriter for soul label One-derful! Records. Yes, the "exclamation" was part of the trademark and logo.

A gifted, award-winning author and playwright, he teamed up with Gary Peterson on nine published musicals, with *Good King Wenceslas* being the last to date. I'm impressed with all of his titles and wide range of interests. His inner child is always on display in the most appealing way possible. I don't know anyone else who could write an instructional piano book for children called *How to Tickle the Keys with Ease*. Check it out.

This is from the same guy who wrote **Countin' My Money**, which I just recorded this year. He also wrote every song on his 2014 *Christmas in Chicago* album. I recommend the first track, **Santa Doesn't Smoke Anymore**, available from the Microsoft Store.

Okay, I get it. Music and creativity are not bound by outdated distribution methods. The artists have to be at least comfortable, if not thrilled, with the compensation. Larry's *Play Piano Play* album is available on Google Play, along with a variety of others. I'm going to do the same thing myself, once this book hits the shelves. I've been told it may only be on a virtual bookshelf. I'm creeped out.

Larry also did a brief stint on keyboards with the Buckinghams. That's a good example of what I did back then. I made introductions (with occasional suggestions) and let groups work things out for themselves. Many artists strive for "one big chance" for fleeting fame (not nec-

essarily riches). If you've been reading any other part of this book, you know what I'm sayin'.

Larry wrote dozens of songs that should have been hits. Sometimes the greed of record distributors, or the lack of vision by promoters, stack the deck against guys like him. However, Larry Nestor is still playing long after others cashed out. I'm told internet demand creates better Google scores. There's a chance the next time you search for "prolific creativity," you might see a familiar name.

Interview and Reunion

The live interviews I've done should help make this book popular. Everyone has a different perspective on the same events. It gets interesting when we explore the many things we have in common. Before long, an interview becomes more like a rambling conversation. That's the way I like it.

As you already read, Larry Nestor jumped at the chance to tag along during my interview with Ed Cody, the legendary engineer. I'm blown away by how often I use the *legendary* word. Everyone in this book deserves it. It's too embarrassing to tell folks some things in person. I'm a guy, first and foremost. See, I would never use "foremost" in a conversation. Now, I'm ready to introduce you to "my" version of Larry Nestor.

Larry directs a string overdub session at the Steve Yates Recording Studio

"What was our first record back in 1961, Carl?" Larry opened. We're not really playing cards, but a good conversation should go like that. You know, everybody gets a turn. Remember, I recorded **Baby Sittin' Blues** by Larry Nestor on the Impala label. You might say it was a novelty song, destined to make me world-famous and propel Larry to national stardom. It's still a novelty song. We're both still waiting for those other things.

It's more important to note our first collaboration started a lifelong friendship and stoked our creative passion. In **Baby Sittin' Blues**, you might notice I was perfecting my Paul Anka delivery. Found on the B side, **I'll Know Then** is one of my own compositions. I'm pretty sure I was shooting for the Julius LaRosa sound.

Larry was already deeply committed to his music. I'm blown away when I think of how much more there is to know about a person.

"I wanted to be a songwriter from a very early age," Larry started. Okay, the fact he knew where I was headed in this interview was uncanny. There is such a word as "canny," but I never used it. I bet you never did either.

"When I was little, my dad wrote a cowboy song. I was exposed to the great radio music of the '30s and '40s every day. I started to get serious about songwriting when I was 17," he continued. We got off on a tangent about Larry's copyrighted music, like **Shy Guy** and **Split Personality**.

"**Shy Guy** was recorded in 'Buddy Holly' style. The Garrett Sisters from River Grove were our backup singers," Larry said. I knitted this chapter together both before and after our visit with Ed Cody, where we discussed the writing process. Getting your thoughts to flow while a blank piece of paper stared at you required technique and discipline.

"I remember paying 50 cents to ride a Trailways bus from Grand and State in Chicago to my home in River Grove," Larry said. I trusted him to weave this information into our discussion of songwriting. It also gave some insight into his early days before he could afford a car.

"You had time to write a song during the trip. Sometimes I would be caught without a pencil. I had to keep repeating a song over and over in order to remember every word," Larry revealed. Yeah, inspiration can strike at any time. You sometimes need to adapt and be grateful.

Small World, Big Audience

Guys like us have to keep moving constantly. Creative juices keep flowing when we are on our feet. Lots of people have the mistaken notion about opportunity knocking. You can wait a lifetime for that mythical rap on your door. What if opportunity interrupts you while you are already knee deep in other endeavors? Guys like Larry Nestor are adept at modifying their vision to appeal to a wide variety of tastes.

"I began writing for musical theatre in 1980 and really love it. It's the best entertainment and gives you maximum enjoyment for your dollar. I'm working on an animated musical project set in both present time and 15th-century Scotland. King James II bans the game of golf because his bowmen are practicing their swing and not their marksmanship. It's really an anti-war statement," he said. See what I mean? In capable hands, every concept is possible and attractive enough to get support from well-known, yet unlikely sources.

"I was contacted by Sir Sean Connery regarding the script. I believe he can be persuaded to voice the role of the king, provided he didn't have any singing parts," he told me. Larry (verbally) introduced me to Angus and Bonnie MacBump, two protagonists in the musical.

Larry also performs for senior citizens—the best audience in the world, he promised. Larry doesn't include us in that group. Yeah, I figured we're not really going to get old until maybe 85 or so. In the meantime, if people want to throw

that "senior" label on us for food discounts and such, a buck is a buck!

"We actually did a show at Ed Cody's residence not long ago," Larry remembered. Maybe he was just looking for a way to wrestle the conversation back from me. So Ed and Larry were already reunited in a way.

"I've played duos with my fabulous drummer son, Tom, when he can break away from his work in St. Petersburg," he said. It's easy to see how Larry could musically inspire his own child. He's done it for dozens at a time.

I'm reminded of the passion it takes to look for gigs after finishing your "day job." Larry Nestor often has several jobs at once (all in music).

"In 2002, I had the pleasure of traveling to London, Ontario, to see the world premier of *A Tale of Two Cities*, for which I wrote the songs. Gifted playwright Gary Peterson adapted the script and well-known arranger and jazz keyboard player Frank Mantooth (RIP) did the musical arrangements.

"The play was directed by a super-talented young woman named Frances Patry. I stayed with the Patrys and had a Cole Porter weekend," he said. I guess that's how lyricists described a weekend of celebration.

Here's an example of the rambling conversation I mentioned earlier. We went back to the mid-'60s and Larry's time at One-derful! Records and his relationship with co-founders George and Ernie Leaner. I remembered Russ Vestuto made the original introductions and Larry came aboard.

Alvin Cash & the Crawlers made it close to the top of the Billboard R&B chart with **Twine Time** (https://youtu.be/SXneqm3g7Kc) just before. When you check out the clip, you'll see the label needed a lyrical boost. It's also a great example of how and where a gritty kind of soul emerged. There are not many instrumental tunes that could get people moving whenever the song aired, but this was certainly one fine example.

I imagine the One-derful! label had every intention to compete with Vee-Jay and Chess Records. To attract and develop new talent, the Leaners "leaned" on the creativity of Larry Nestor. Just like other creative forces with other labels, Larry found himself in many production roles. Once again, I'm going to set the stage for the times. Larry and his collaborators captured so much emotion with their productions.

I'm going to introduce you to a great talent who far too few folks have heard. Beverley Shaffer sang **When I Think About You** (https://youtu.be/F41Dhpzd5mE). As the song lyrics suggest, love should be wedding bells and wishing wells. Now, compare that with the most soulful war protest song that I have ever heard in my life. Larry arranged, conducted, and co-wrote (with Shaffer) on **Where Will You Be Boy?** (https://youtu.be/9SurKSlaTzk).

Many times before, I've invited you to pause and enjoy the songs I'm describing. This time, I want you to close your eyes and drink in the seductive soul of Beverly Shaffer. See what I mean? This is 50 years later and I am hopelessly in love with this lady. I think she has greater vocal range than many Motown divas. Once again, Chicago artists and labels poured themselves into songs like this. They deserved worldwide recognition.

Now you got me started, and this was supposed to be Larry Nestor's chapter. Where were we? Larry co-wrote (with James L. Jones) **I'm So Tired of Being Lonely**, sung by the Sharpees. He also worked closely with Otis Clay on a number of projects while at One-derful!

There are so many folks in this book who worked with Larry in some way. Here, I introduced folks who are not part of my own circle. If I was ever inclined to be envious of anyone, it would most likely be Larry Nestor. I'm really grateful for his contributions to this book (but most of all, to our Chicago songbook).

About Otis Clay–
While editing this chapter, I found out Otis Clay passed away in early January 2016 at age 73. C'mon guys (and girls), this bad news is starting to hurt.

Larry and I visit the Steve Yates Recording Studio on the same day as our interview.

The Lincoln Park Zoo (1965-70)

Here's yet another group that features the signature Chi-town brass sound, killer arrangements, and unbelievable vocals. The Lincoln Park Zoo deserved a major-label contract and national recognition. Sadly, there's no such thing as a moral victory in sports, or in the music world. Their lead singer provided the vocals (without credit) on a hit from another group. The Screaming Wildman has to assume a good deal of guilt for that situation.

Some people gave me a lot of credit for the time and attention I gave these guys. They had no shortage of fans, and my only regret is that lasting success somehow eluded them. However, I'm really excited about the way this chapter came together. Drummer Denny Murray made awesome contributions, and the entire book is better because of them. There's no better way to tell their story than to use his words and photos. I get to butt in wherever I see fit. It's sort of my book.

History

In the mid-'60s, a group of musicians from the southwest side of Chicago got together to play rock-and-roll music. At first, they called themselves the Classic VI. Throughout this book, I mentioned why it's never a good idea to use a number in the name of the group. That left no room for expansion, if and when the time was right.

The group was influenced by pop, jazz, and classical styles of music. The Ventures were a very strong influence on guitarist Wayne Nykodem and bass player Arvy Tumosa. Denny Murray and his brother Tommy were influenced by vocal groups like the Four Seasons and the Lettermen, as well as big band, jazz, classical, and soul artists. The group would later evolve when trumpet and piano player Kenny Miller and tenor saxophonist Bob Walicki joined them. Tommy Murray also played trumpet, creating a unique three-horn section. From 1967 onward, the group called themselves the Lincoln Park Zoo.

Most groups were going for the British rock sound. This new "fusion" group nailed down the intricacies of genuine soul music. They concentrated on strong vocals and complex harmonies. At the outset, the group covered popular songs.

Before long, they gained recognition for creative horn arrangements to go with those killer vocals. The Zoo members were schooled musicians and performed a wide variety of songs few other groups would attempt. Their repertoire grew as much as their reputation when they began writing original material. As Denny will tell you, there were a lot of considerations for making the group more marketable. These were not only musical choices.

Denny Murray

"We all grew our hair long to satisfy the music industry. Some parents were not too happy. But we were hungry for success," Denny began.

Right from the beginning, I thought they had a legitimate shot at landing an album deal with a major label. Maybe that happens all the time in a totally fair and objective world. Nonetheless, the '60s were a fun time for Chicago rock. A good group could find gigs at dozens of venues. Zoo leader Denny Murray sought out agents, clubs, and promoters. I'll let him take over for a while …

"I don't quite remember my first meeting with you, Carl, but our paths somehow crossed at nearly the same time Jimmy Peterson entered the picture. Jimmy was a great club entertainer, pianist, composer, and arranger. He heard our group and was blown away. Most of all, Jimmy was captivated by brother Tommy's singing skills. He had a super vocal range and a falsetto that hit the stratosphere. You immediately recognized his talent," Denny remembered.

Yeah, the Zoo worked with Jimmy and produced several singles. The first was **If You Gotta Go (Go Now)** https://youtu.be/hkwFUR8o7c0. The B side was a hip instrumental called **Love Theme From Haight Street** https://youtu.be/7iKnCik_xDM. The Lincoln Park Zoo was well on the way to success.

"Jimmy placed the single with Eddie Mascari from Mercury Records. We were excited with the DJs' positive response to the A side. Several stations played our song, but there were no significant sales. The Willard Alexander Agency soon had us playing all around the Midwest," Denny continued. Yeah, I really liked these guys.

Tommy Murray

The Lincoln Park Zoo was opening for several national acts, including the Grass Roots, Lemon Pipers, and the Spencer Davis Group. We also had them playing at ballrooms and colleges around the country. It seemed only a matter of time before they would capture the attention of a national audience.

"You and Dan Belloc started financing future Lincoln Park Zoo sessions. We respected his success with the Dan Belloc Orchestra and your ability to attract big crowds at the Holiday Ballroom, Carl," Denny continued.

The Lincoln Park Zoo was gaining some traction, but overall success was still eluding the group. Jimmy Peterson got them back in the studio and cut some great tracks, including **The Greatest Moments in My Life**, **Symphony of My Soul**, and **Alice in Wonderland**.

Wayne Nykodem

"We are especially proud of these songs. Jimmy Peterson did a great job both writing and arranging. They were big production sessions that showcased Tommy's singing and our vocal arrangements. **Alice in Wonderland** is a magical track. **Moments** and **Symphony of My Soul** were both picked up by U.S.A. Records, with no sales to speak of," Denny painfully reminded me.

"**Alice in Wonderland** was probably too hip for the two-minute pop song world and was never placed with a record company," he said. It was certainly ahead of its time.

"Carl, you didn't give up on the Lincoln Park Zoo and kept looking for new songs from publishing houses. Your success with the Buckinghams and reputation gave you access to some heavyweights in the industry. Remember, you and I flew out to New York and met several big shots, including Morris Levy, from Roulette Records. Some of them showed interest. In retrospect, we should have followed up with those guys," Denny said. Yeah, there were a lot of huge companies expecting artists to return, once they had a sure thing.

Their Mr. Norm radio commercial played a major part in the Buckinghams' early success. I wanted do something similar for the Lincoln Park Zoo. Burton Shoes was a well-known Chicago retailer, and I was right about turning over some of the artistic control to the Zoo.

"We arranged a cute jingle based on the Nancy Sinatra hit **These Boots Are Made for Walking**. My cousin Barbara Lawless sang the lead. The Zoo got great publicity, and the commercial played for almost two years on WLS and WCFL. We got a nice fee for arranging and playing the commercial and received residual checks every 13 weeks," Denny reminded me.

I always did my best to get bands played and paid. Commercials spots are no match for cracking the Billboard and Cashbox charts, of course. In 1968, I approached the Zoo with

Arvy Tumosa

several songs written by Linda and Keith Colley, a successful wife and husband songwriting team. I was hooked on two in particular, **Playgirl** and **Shame Shame**. The Zoo focused heavily on writing their own material. We agreed performing original material was a critical factor for getting an album deal with a major label. The group and I had different opinions of "whose" material was most likely to produce the hits we all craved.

"This was a contentious issue for the members. You really pushed us to record those two songs, Carl. Denny, Tommy, and Bob Walicki believed in you—you had an ear for picking hits. The Lincoln Park Zoo did not record either song. As history shows, your instincts were right," Denny remembered. Guys, if there was ever a time I wanted to be wrong, it was then (and still now).

I eventually got the Zoo to record a few songs that found their way onto vinyl. Some of these were major productions with additional horns and strings. The first couple were released on the Twinight Records label. We weren't able to catch

Denny Murray— For the Record (pun intended)
This story needs to be told. Brian Lake was *NOT* the lead singer on *Playgirl*. The music track was recorded by Thee Prophets. Tommy Murray sang lead on *Playgirl* as well as *Shame Shame*. Carl originally approached the Zoo members in early 1968 with the two songs. The reluctance by some Zoo members to use other writers' material was a lost opportunity and strategic mistake. In August 1968, Carl and Dan called Denny and Tommy pleading for help. Thee Prophets cut the track for Playgirl a minor third too high for the band's lead singer. The rhythm tracks were complete. The horns and strings were overdubbed and paid for. Carl and Dan were in a pinch.

Tommy and I agreed to do the session. We spoke with Bob Walicki, who agreed to help with the background vocals. Our decision was based on our friendship with Carl, thinking it may open other doors for the Zoo.

The session was held August 28, 1968 (which happened to be same night of the riot at the Democratic National Convention). Ed Cody was engineer for the session at StereoSonic Studio located at 226 South Wabash. After Tommy completed leads for both songs, our eyes started tearing and our throats got sore. Tear gas had crept up the elevator shaft from the riot activities. We came back a week later to overdub the background vocals. Tommy, Bob, and I arranged and sang the backup vocals.

Months went by and, to our surprise, *Playgirl* by Thee Prophets is on the air waves in 1969. *Shame Shame* was recorded by a group called the Magic Lantern and hit #29 on the *Billboard Hot 100* chart in late 1968. This was a painful experience for the three of us. For Tommy, it was especially difficult hearing his voice on WLS and WCFL and receiving no credit for his creative work. Thee Prophets also got an album deal. The Zoo had written over 100 original songs, ready for recording. It's all history and nothing can change the past.

In late 1969, Carl called me again, seeking Tommy's help. Tommy and I initially laughed at the request. We asked Carl and Dan for a huge advance to even consider going into the studio. Carl and Dan were not happy with our request. We thanked them, said goodbye, and hung up the phone. Thee Prophets never had another hit.

a break in the marketplace. We tried everything to showcase the powerful and diverse talent of the band.

"**Kissy Face** was a pure bubble gum song written by Wayne Nykodem. The lead was sung by the entire group. You and Dan Belloc financed these songs," Denny mentioned. The group thought I had an ear for great songs. I knew how talented these guys were. Then, they got the attention of a musical mastermind.

"Arranger Lew Douglas entered our lives. He was an accomplished musician with great credentials, like doing arrangements for the great Billy May Orchestra. He won numerous awards for productions with Patti Page and the Tommy and Jimmy Dorsey orchestras. Lew also wrote scores for TV shows like *Batman* and *The Green Hornet*," Denny pays a fond tribute. Best of all, Lew did the arrangements for the Lincoln Park Zoo songs that I just mentioned.

"Lew was a funny guy. One day we were discussing our arrangements and he expressed his need for the group to write 'pop' songs. We were writing a lot and listened intently to the advice of a seasoned pro. Lew told us to forget writing musical masterpieces.

"He shouted, 'Write the next Tommy James hit like **Mony Mony**.' Lew sort of danced a bit as his emotions got stronger. Then he blurted out, 'Forget the masterpiece, write me a great piece of shit. The public wants that crap—not Beethoven.'

"That was the essence and secret of 1960s popular music, expressed by a real musician. Needless to say, we all laughed but understood the message he tried to get across. **Kissy Face** was created as a result of Lew's persuasive rant," Denny recalled how often they all laughingly repeated this story through the years.

I provided links so you can first listen and then track down the originals for your own vintage vinyl collection. By the way, Sambanette was the only polka-type song that I ever recorded.

Kissy Face https://youtu.be/gTlu0oCVNnI

My Baby Can Do It https://youtu.be/ux8iu12tJXY

Sambanette https://youtu.be/fOMQJW_BVH0

You're My Inspiration https://youtu.be/wf9ff_SNBzg

I Still Want You https://youtu.be/A8vxWPuykKM

It All Adds Up to Nothing (sorry ! – didn't find it)

Moving On …

Producer Jimmy Bryant entered the Zoo's lives in 1969. Denny met Jimmy at Beacon Artists, an agency booking gigs for the Zoo. Jimmy was a hot record promoter, having success with super acts like the Fifth Dimension and Gordon Lightfoot. He was also managing and producing a local group called the Neighborhood. Jimmy heard the Zoo and liked the sound and original material.

"We recorded two songs at RCA Studios. Brian Christian engineered the session. Jimmy placed **Woman Don't Let Me Down** and **Zoo's Blues** with FONA Records. WCFL and Milwaukee's big rock station were ready to play **Woman** …. WLS was a go if WCFL and Milwaukee got things rolling. Jimmy was close to getting a Bill Gavin pick on the song. Our good friend Dick Biondi at WCFL was a supporter of the Zoo and the song," Denny recalled. Even when legendary disc jockeys became fans, it was often not enough.

"Our hopes were high, but it was not to be. WCFL agreed to start playing the song, but the current general manager lost his job at the last minute. Management turmoil at WCFL stalled our record, and the other stations would not move forward. Yes, timing is everything. There are no words to describe our disappointment. The Rock Gods prevented success for the Lincoln Park Zoo," Denny concluded.

Gone, But Not Forgotten

Denny is quick to acknowledge contributions from the band members, particularly those who can no longer share their memories, at least not in this world.

"Bob Walicki was a premier tenor saxophone player. His life was music. He was a student of legendary saxophone player and teacher Joe Daley. Bob received his draft notice in the late '60s. As an alternative to getting embroiled in the Vietnam conflict, he enlisted in the Army and wound up playing in their band. When Bob returned to civilian life, he briefly opened a recording studio. Then he changed course with his music career and received a degree in Communications from Northwestern University. Bob died tragically on April 15, 2001.

"Jerry Kowalczyk was a member of the Zoo for about a year. He was a prodigy on the Hammond B3 organ and a clinician for a major organ manufacturer. Jerry moved to Boston and joined a great show band called the Mason Dixon Line. While driving to a performance, he was killed in an auto accident on the Boston Turnpike," Denny sadly remembered the date and time.

The Lincoln Park Zoo was truly a family—a labor of love. The band members worked hard to create quality music and make performances memorable.

"Our many fans were so very faithful. We continue to thank them for their wonderful support. The life of a musician is not easy. Our parents made it much easier and were an integral part of our success. They let us pursue a dream so many folks were trying to realize. Unfortunately, none of our parents are still around to share these memories. They truly believed in us. On behalf of all Lincoln Park Zoo members, let's stand up for our wonderful parents. *That's all folks!*" Denny concluded. Once again, thank *you* Denny, for your candid insight.

Final Words

Denny compiled the discography that follows. The Lincoln Park Zoo was truly one of the most talented and versatile groups ever recorded. As you read earlier, they opened for a number of famous groups. I'm positive that each was as impressed with the Zoo as I was and that national success was inevitable.

The Cowsills were one group that recognized the Zoo's talent and would eventually collaborate with the band. At least the Zoo would be part of a (too) long-awaited album release. I'll leave it up to Denny and the rest of the Lincoln Park Zoo to describe their relationship with me. I hope they still consider me a devoted fan.

Lincoln Park Zoo Members
Denny Murray: *Drums, Percussion, Piano, Vocals*
Tommy Murray: *Trumpet, Lead Vocals, Guitar*
Wayne Nykodem: *Guitar, Vocals*
Arvydas (Arvy) Tumosa: *Bass, Vocals*
Bob Walicki: *Tenor Saxophone, Vocals*
Kenny Miller: *Trumpet, Keyboards, Vocals*
Jerry Kowalczyk: *Hammond B3 Organ*
John McGuire: *Guitar, Vocals*
Vic Rochkus: *Guitar, Vocals*
Matt Cufferin: *Trumpet*
Bruce Otto: *Trombone*
Dick Schaeffer: *Bass*
Herb Brokop: *Keyboards*
Tom Foyer: *Reeds*

LINCOLN PARK ZOO

U.S.A. RECORDS
**The Greatest Moments
in My Life – A side**
USA 912, 111968-A
Composer: James Butler/Peterson
Recorded: 1968
Studio: StereoSonic Studio
Engineer: Ed Cody
Producer: James Butler/Peterson
Lead Vocal: Tommy Murray
Background Vocals: Denny Murray,
Tommy Murray, Bob Walicki, and
Kenny Miller
Symphony of My Soul https://youtu.
be/6N2g89hqK9c– **B side**
USA 912, 111968-B
Composer: James Butler/Peterson
Recorded: 1968
Studio: StereoSonic Studio
Engineer: Ed Cody
Producer: James Butler/
Peterson
Lead Vocal: Tommy Murray
Background Vocals: Denny
Murray, Tommy Murray, Bob
Walicki, and Kenny Miller

Mercury Records
If You Gotta Go (Go Now) - A side
72708, 1-40552 MRC
Recorded: October 1967
Composer; James Butler/Peterson
Studio: StereoSonic Studio
Engineer: Ed Cody
Producer: James Butler/Peterson
Lead Vocal: Tommy Murray
Background Vocals: Denny Murray,
Tommy Murray, Bob Walicki, and
Kenny Miller
**Love Theme From Haight
Street - B-Side**
72708, 1-40553 MRC
Recorded: October 1967
Composer: James Butler/Peterson
Studio: StereoSonic Studio
Engineer: Ed Cody
Producer: James Butler/Peterson

Album
**The Cowsills Plus The Lin-
coln Park Zoo**
(Mercury)/Wing SRW-16354 (1968)

FONA Records
**Woman Don't Let Me
Down – A Side**
Fona 317
Composer: Denny Murray, Tommy
Murray, Wayne Nykodem, and
Arvy Tumosa
Recorded: June 1969
Studio: RCA Studios
Producer: Jimmy Bryant
Engineer: Brian Christian
Lead Vocal: Tommy Murray
Background Vocals: Denny Murray,
Wayne Nykodem, and Arvy
Tumosa
Zoo's Blues – B Side
Fona 317
Composer: Denny Murray, Tommy
Murray, Wayne Nykodem, and
Arvy Tumosa
Recorded: June 1969
Studio: RCA Studios
Producer: Jimmy Bryant
Engineer: Brian Christian

Kapp Records
Playgirl – A Side
K-962, K-11510
Composer: Linda & Keith Colley
Recorded: August 28, 1968
Studio: StereoSonic Studios
Producer: Carl Bonafede and Dan
Belloc
Arranger: Lew Douglas
Lead Vocal: Tommy Murray
Background Vocals: Tommy Murray,
Denny Murray, and Bob Walicki
Shame Shame – B side
K-962, K-11510
Composer: Linda & Keith Colley –
Knox Henderson
Recorded: August 28, 1968
Studio: StereoSonic Studios
Producer: Carl Bonafede and Dan
Belloc
Arranger: Lew Douglas
Lead Vocal: Tommy Murray
Background Vocal: Tommy Murray,
Denny Murray, and Bob Walicki

Album
Playgirl, Thee Prophets
KS-3596
Recorded: 1969
Studio: StereoSonic Studios
Producer: Carl Bonafede and Dan
Belloc
Arranger: Lew Douglas
Engineer: Ed Cody
Lead Vocal: Tommy Murray
Background Vocals: Denny Murray,
Bob Walicki, and Tommy Murray

Twinight Records
My Baby Can Do It
Twinight 127
Composer: A. Anderson & M.
Panayotovich
Recorded: October 1969
Studio: StereoSonic Studios
Producer: Carl Bonafede and Dan
Belloc
Arranger: Lew Douglas
Studio: StereoSonic Studios
Engineer: Ron Malo
Lead Vocal: Denny Murray
Rhythm Guitar, Vocals: Vic Rochkus
Kissy Face
Twinight 127
Composer: Wayne Nykodem & Arvy
Tumosa
Recorded: October 1969
Studio: StereoSonic Studios
Producer: Carl Bonafede and Dan
Belloc
Arranger: Lew Douglas
Studio: StereoSonic Studios
Engineer: Ron Malo
Lead Vocal: Denny Murray, Tommy
Murray, Wayne Nykodem, and
Arvy Tumosa
Rhythm Guitar, Vocals: Vic Rochkus

Not Placed with Label
Sambanette
Composer: ?
Recorded: October 1968
Studio: StereoSonic Studios
Producer: Carl Bonafede and Dan
Belloc
Arranger: Lew Douglas
Lead Vocal: Denny Murray, Tommy
Murray, Wayne Nykodem, and
Arvy Tumosa
Rhythm Guitar, Vocals: Vic Rochkus
You're My Inspiration
Composer:?
Recorded: March 2009
Studio: StereoSonic Studios
Producer: Carl Bonafede and Dan
Belloc
Arranger: Lew Douglas
Engineer: Ron Malo
Lead Vocal: Tommy Murray
Background Vocals: Denny Murray,
Wayne Nykodem, and Arvy
Tumosa
Rhythm Guitar, Vocals: Vic Rochkus
It All Adds Up To Nothing
Composer: ?
Recorded: March 2009
Studio: StereoSonic Studios
Producer: Carl Bonafede and Dan
Belloc
Arranger: Lew Douglas
Engineer: Ron Malo
Lead Vocal: Tommy Murray
Background Vocals: Denny Murray,
Wayne Nykodem, and Arvy
Tumosa
Rhythm Guitar, Vocals: Vic Rochkus
I Still Want You
Composer: ?
Recorded: March 2009
Studio: StereoSonic Studios
Producer: Carl Bonafede and Dan
Belloc
Arranger: Lew Douglas
Engineer: Ron Malo
Lead Vocal: Tommy Murray
Background Vocals: Denny Murray,
Wayne Nykodem, and Arvy
Tumosa
Rhythm Guitar, Vocals: Vic Rochkus:
Alice in Wonderland
Composer: Sammy Fain & Bob
Hilliard
Recorded: 1968
Studio: StereoSonic Studio
Engineer: Ed Cody
Producer: James Butler/Peterson
Lead Vocal: Tommy Murray
Background Vocals: Denny Murray,
Tommy Murray, Bob Walicki, and
Kenny Miller

The Rail City Five

These guys and I go back for pretty close to three decades. They were very popular locally and played at many Chicago-area clubs and festivals. While putting this book together, I got a chance to introduce songwriter and keyboard artist Paul J. Mally to a few other people collaborating with me. From the first day I saw the Rail City Five (a tribute to our hometown—also known as the Rail City), I was impressed with everyone in the band. They wrote as well as they performed. We've been in regular contact all these years. I've dropped by Paul's office at Top Dog Disc pretty regularly. I ended up recording five of the band's tracks on my compilation CD, *5 Decades of Musical Memories - Chicago*, on my Chi-Town Records label.

Thank goodness Paul offered to fill in details about our first meeting and lots of stuff that happened afterward. I remember Paul was working in his dad's shop, and I came in to get 8-tracks created. Mid-'70s recorded media turned out to be a blip on the recording radar, between vinyl records and the compact disc. Paul and I got around to talking about his band and how they put together some cash from playing gigs. They got some fantastic demos recorded at Pierce Arrow Recorders in Evanston, Illinois.

He remembers the studio was located in a converted Commonwealth Edison power plant. Despite the outside appearance of the facility, the band knew they were among highly regarded professionals. That is where the group met engineer Gus Mossler, formerly the staff engineer at RCA Records. Gus's first gig was recording Elvis Presley. Among his many credits, he also engineered **Sweet Jane** by Lou Reed.

Photo by Paul Natkin (courtesy of PJ Mally)
L-R: Steve Chiappe - drums (standing)
Carmie Zack - vocals, bass
Ron Matthews - guitar
Greg Waldron - saxophone (with hat)
Paul (PJ) Mally - keyboards, vocals (arms crossed)

After one of the Rail City Five sessions, the band members met Cheap Trick (recently inducted into the Rock & Roll Hall of Fame) waiting in the lobby to record. Both Robin Zander and Rick Nielsen were very supportive. Those encounters are priceless, especially when a new group is hoping to build a loyal (or rabid) following.

Steve Chiappe was their drummer and Carmie Zack was their lead vocalist, bass player, and songwriter. Paul J. Mally was on keyboards and Ron Matthews was on guitar. Greg Waldron did vocals and played saxophone, keyboards, flute, and guitar. I still say today – Paul wrote a sure-fire hit called **Made in the USA**. It would become another great song withheld from the public due to a series of unfortunate circumstances.

Seems there was a guy named Bruce Springsteen who released **Born in the USA** in June 1984. Even though Paul's masterpiece was copyrighted some time earlier, the Springsteen tune became the cornerstone track of a 30 million worldwide seller (and anchored his two-year tour). The Rail City Five had little chance to get airplay for a track with too similar a name. It wasn't meant to be. Paul remains philosophical (the Wildman—not so much).

Check out **Life's a Catastrophe**, written by Carmie Zack https://youtu.be/8VeUBlG4nSA, and **Drivin'** (another written by Paul https://youtu.be/UhpzNOZ7FkM). These are more examples of proven and accomplished musicians for whom the stars failed to align. This was particularly true of many Chicago bands hitting the music scene in the 1970s and beyond. If some celestial creature dropped the Rail City Five in front of me 20 years earlier, I'm feeling the outcome might have been far different.

Back then, I could spin a demo for a DJ and get his opinion. Even better, I could see his reaction. When I pitched a song face to face with record executives, I could "read" their reaction. It made all the difference in the world in the negotiation phase. The '80s "punk" movement seriously hampered the marketability of the Rail City Five. Accomplished musicians and their passionate compositions were no longer highly valued. To hear him say it …

"In the punk era, anything more than two or three chords was completely uncool," Paul Mally reminded us all.

The guys definitely paid their dues when juggling jobs, college classes, and gigs at Quiet Night (Belmont and Sheffield). According to Paul, it was a major "hassle" (the best '60s word ever) to get his piano up the long staircase leading to the stage. The Rail City Five regularly played Huey's, Tut's, Iron Rail, and Thirsty Whale (River Grove). Beginnings (Schaumburg) was actually in a strip mall but was still an amazing venue. Paul reminded me about other circumstances that factor into a group's ability to draw an audience. Even the government seemed to conspire against Chicago and the rest of Illinois.

Along with many popular bands, the Rail City Five was rockin' Illinois clubs, where the drinking age was 19 for beer and 21 for liquor. The National Minimum Drinking Age Act was passed in 1984. Take it, Paul …

"Illinois raised its minimum drinking age back to 21. The Wisconsin border was a mere 90 miles away, with the drinking age still at 19. Club owners could no longer fairly compete for the best talent, and many were forced to close," as he re-lives the painful history. Wisconsin raised its drinking age two years later. Chicago music (and the musicians who supplemented their take-home pay with weekday gigs) would never recover.

Of course, the Rail City Five trekked to places like Hooker Lake Inn, Twin Lakes Ballroom, and Majestic Hills at Lake Geneva, Wisconsin. The band also recorded at Royal Recorders in Lake Geneva. There was friendly competition between bands in the same predicament: work, school, practice, and scratching out a gig or two in the hometown. Once in a while, someone would express interest in Rail City Five original songs. For instance, Jim Peterik, from the Ides of March (**Vehicle**), and later Survivor (**Eye of the Tiger**) showed interest in songs like **Life's a Catastrophe**—you know, stories we all understand.

I can't say exactly how or when Jim heard tunes from the Rail City Five "playbook," but Paul gives me credit. As he knows, I won't leave my house without my CDs on hand—always promoting. Paul always reminds me I was one person who never gave up on his band. He recently told me a story about one of those defining moments for band members.

"More than twenty years ago, I was making deliveries for my dad somewhere in Northbrook and stopped at a fast-food drive-through window. A couple of cars ahead some blonde chick in a red convertible had our song **Drivin'** blaring from her speakers. I wanted to follow that car to ask where she got the recording," he chuckled. I just thought of three or four reasons to follow that car. Paul was obviously being more professional and focused at the time.

Every time I talk to Paul, I unearth another story from one of the Rail City Five founding members. He used to be in a band with a few guys living near Cook County Jail. That's not the story—at least not *this* story. They did a gig at Oak Street Beach, or more literally, *on* Oak Street Beach. Take it, maestro …

"We dragged my Spinet piano, with microphone pickups inside, right onto the sand. We were all young so nobody thought about putting any plywood boards underneath. We were probably only 50 feet from the water, and the lifeguards seemed more fascinated than concerned about, well—you know. When anyone touched a microphone—it was a 'wow,'" as if Paul was reliving the moment that voltage coursed through his body. At that precise moment, Nikola Tesla would have been more useful than Ludwig van Beethoven.

Here's still more stuff I didn't know about the Rail City Five. Paul mentioned some of the band's promotional pictures were taken by a genuine photographic superstar. Paul Natkin just posted a blog entry about the Chicago band era (http://blog.natkin.net/back-to-the-1960s/) while I was working on this chapter. Most folks are familiar with his iconic images, including the Bruce Springsteen cover photo for *Newsweek* in August 1985. Paul Mally remembered Natkin had an exhibit at Elmhurst College back in 2013.

Natkin's experiences could fill a book, but he'll probably never stop taking pictures long enough to write one. He did, however, collaborate on *The People's Place*, a book about soul food restaurants, with another of my favorite guys, Dave Hoekstra. That's another thing I'm realizing: Lots of the people I know already worked with one another. I hope younger readers take inspiration from the characters I introduce.

The Rail City Five performed at Chicagofest in 1983, during the last year of Chicago Mayor Jane Byrne's administration. That fact seemed to be burned into Paul Mally's memory, so I'm mentioning it here. Take it, Paul ...

"There was an audition for local bands to perform that year. The top two would get to take the stage. The top honor went to some alternative band from Milwaukee, Wisconsin. The next slot was awarded to the Rail City Five. We got to open for the Turtles." Paul jokingly recalled that "open" only meant his band was the last group to perform before the main attraction was set to go on.

The stage was set up in the parking lot outside Soldier Field. Of course, the Rail City Five just wanted to hang out with the Turtles after their set. Unfortunately, making sure all of their equipment was safely "swapped out" took a lot of time. Paul has a better story about that, and didn't want to get into it here—that's what Facebook is for. The Turtles had the audience packed so deep, the guys from the Rail City Five barely caught the performance from the very back of the throng.

Moving Forward

Journalist Dave Hoekstra was very impressed with the Rail City Five, once he heard their tracks on my CD. He interviewed Paul and gave them a complimentary review in the *Sun-Times* Show Section, dated October 10, 2010, in his article about me.

Hoekstra also played **Made in the USA** during my (and Carl Giammarese from the Buckinghams) segment on his *Nocturnal Journal* program that aired on February 21, 2015. Once again, there is nothing like hearing "your" music blaring from speakers. This time, it was nationwide on WGN radio. It's never too late or too often when it comes to these guys. Dave mentioned that the song had striking similarities to U2 songs.

We briefly talked about "what if" scenarios connected to **Made in the USA**. In the new era of "searchable" content, perhaps an Indie filmmaker would be interested in using it for his or her soundtrack. At the very least, we agreed we need to work on (legally) getting the song into circulation. Sadly, the time when I could circulate among DJs to get songs evaluated has long past. But with a worldwide market (and hunger) for influential lyrics, I can see the Rail City Five gaining a new and highly informed audience.

Paul once told me, "If our band had only met you earlier" and "you are the only one who never gave up on us."

All I can say is "let's see how far we can go from here!" I have no intention of giving up, and we know we can't go back. We already know "life's a catastrophe." Maybe we can still nudge a few catastrophes into alignment.

Paul Mally—30+ Years With the Screamin' Wildman, Carl Bonafede
If you are lucky in your life, you will encounter some truly unique and
colorful people. And if you are really lucky, a few of those gifted people
become your supporters and friends. Carl Bonafede is one of those.

I think I first met Carl in the early to mid-eighties. At that time, I was
starting a rock-and-roll group with some friends – all of us from Chicago.
Like thousands of other musicians throughout the world, we had high
hopes of multi-platinum records, concert tours, even a video on the then
new thing called MTV! Eventually, we came up with the name of our group
– The Rail City Five. Five musicians and Chicago was the railroad hub of the
nation – well, you get it.

Everyone in our group grew up listening to all of the classic (and soon
to be classic) rock and pop bands of the '60s and '70s: the Stones, the
Who, Bob Dylan, the Animals, local heroes Cheap Trick, and later, early Tom
Petty, Bruce Springsteen, and of course, the Buckinghams! Eventually we
started recording some of our own tunes and playing at a ton of clubs and
fests. After a while, we were on a roll!

And then, lightning struck! During this time, I was also working at my
father's business. We manufactured 8-track and cassette tapes. One day,
Carl walked into our office to place an order. In the course of our conversations, our mutual interest in the music business came up. Little did I know I
was already talking to a legend!

Carl took an interest in our band and in our original songs. He always
encouraged us. One song that we wrote, called *Made in the USA*, is still one
of his favorites. Every time I see Carl, he tells me, "That song should be a hit
record!" And he should know, having guided some of the classic groups of
the '60s to the top of the Billboard charts.

Did we end up as rockstars, playing those mega stadiums and selling
millions of records? Well, like so many others, the answer is no – BUT not
for lack of enthusiasm or persistence by Carl. Because Carl was the one
person who ALWAYS believed in us. And to this songwriter, if he says your
song is a hit, that's enough.

The Lot

My Daughters of Eve were playing a gig in Hastings, Nebraska, in 1968. In a parallel galaxy, during the year we both called 1966, a group of Hastings High students started practicing regularly and snagged a few gigs. They eventually became known as the Lot and attracted huge crowds in Kansas, South Dakota, Colorado, and numerous places closer to home. They had a manager named Nick Kallos. That sounds quite a lot like the evolution of the Buckinghams, except for one thing: Enter the Screaming Wildman.

I could have sworn there was a dude named "Kannassas" or something in that Hastings story. Anyway, the word was out about my success with both the Buckinghams and the "Daughters." I was still working with Willard Alexander at the time. As I mentioned earlier, every demo record made it easier for me to book groups at dances. Many events had celebrity disc jockeys doing live appearances. The stage was set (pun intended) for DJs to discover new talent and maybe persuade a program director to give the song some airplay.

Because of my track (no pun intended) record, I could help groups secure valuable recording slots within high-demand studios like Ed Cody's StereoSonic. I'll leave it up to you to decide whether it made any difference as far as access to the recording studio goes.

I never saw the Lot perform before they packed into their '55 Chevy (according to their Facebook page) and headed toward Chi-town, StereoSonic, and the Screaming Wildman. We recorded **Loving You Is All I Do** https://youtu.be/skjvWJqiazQ, **Call Me Your Baby** https://youtu.be/5TG6rPFQyME, **Write A Letter** https://youtu.be/P-hl9cpfgjA, and **Ann** https://youtu.be/QQMCZ7da7iM.

The magical moments during that session occurred strictly by fortunate accident. Abner Spector (Chess and Cadet Records) happened to be at StereoSonic when the Lot and I got down to business in the studio. Abner fell in love with **Loving You Is All I Do** and offered to lend a hand in the production of the song. He seemed driven to create memorable music in true "Chess" fashion. Ed Cody did the mixing, with Abner enhancing many of the individual tracks.

Every song sounded better than any of us could have hoped. Through the magic of the new technology I am slowly learning to accept (and maybe will one day love), you can hear what I'm talking about. Thanks to the continued diligence of Mr. Joe Pytel, you'll be treated to a photo gallery as well.

When you listen to **Loving You Is All I Do** (this is the ideal time, while I'm thinking of it), tell me that the intro starts out much like **Get Ready** by the Temptations. Check out the Cadet #5613 record label. Take note of Mike Smith, the lead singer, guitar player, and songwriter. Yeah, I'm credited as the producer, but that's not what I want you to take away from this.

Faith and hope (or you could say "fate") caused the original Kallos-Bonafede collision in Hastings. When the band set out for Chicago, there was no way they could know that two sides from a blossoming singer/songwriter from Nebraska would end up on the Cadet/Chess label, or that Abner Spector would labor behind the scenes to give their tracks a better shot at success. Any other day or any other time, maybe not … you know what I'm sayin?

I saw many bands experience their shining moments. For some, it was a killer recording session with the hope of national exposure looming. Fame is just as elusive as it is intoxicating. Love and life add to the uncertainty and really stack the odds against success. We were lucky to witness the romantic times where bands like the Lot would flourish, however briefly.

This was countered by the uncertainty (if not terror) of seeing bandmates and family members shipping off to a war zone, when they should have been planning careers, families, or a rock-and-roll tour. The Lot was no different. Their makeup and mentality were affected by the departure of guitarist Dick Kluver and manager Nick Kallos, called to duty in Southeast Asia.

According to their own accounts, Mike Smith (lead guitar), Ace Kluver (bass), Jim Casteel (drums), Craig McDowell (organ), and Randy Marshall (tambourine) hung together until around 1968. Some fifty years ago, I tried to do "right" by you guys. I hope you still feel the same when you see this chapter.

The Ides of March

The original four-piece band organized in Berwyn, Illinois, and officially became the Ides of March in 1966. You have to consider them a Chicago band since they all grew up a few blocks from Austin and Roosevelt (next to the Oak Park and Cicero suburbs and Chicago's Austin neighborhood). See, I'm trying to give you a geography lesson, followed by a little bit of history. The more you knew about people the better you could promote them.

1960s Berwyn was an overwhelmingly blue-collar, Eastern European area, with hundreds of single- and two-story bungalows. With that conservative background, you might expect dwellings to lack imagination (and you would be so wrong). Many homes featured detailed oak woodwork, stained glass windows, and brazenly colored glazed brick exteriors and tile roofs.

The Ides of March were equally talented and daring. They built a signature brass section that defined the Windy City sound with the release of their megahit record **Vehicle**. I can't wait any longer to share it with you. As I'm putting the finishing touches on my book (and particularly their chapter), this YouTube clip https://youtu.be/_EBMo8xHGNs is approaching two million views.

The city of Chicago, Screaming Wildman, and other loyal Ides of March fans still proudly watch **Vehicle** maintain international and multi-generational hit status. I'm not going to repeat anything their legions of fans don't already know in these couple of pages. Someone should write a book about them (they have too many pending engagements to write it themselves). I barely have the time or patience to finish my own.

Here I focus on my relationship with the "Ides" and Jim Peterik, their charismatic and talented leader. See, you are not going to read anything like that on their website (Jim's too modest, grateful, and focused). I'm going to proudly tell you about my recollections while the band struggled to make a name for itself, right after becoming the Ides of March.

Let me get this out of the way upfront. I knew how busy Jim was when I contacted him for a quote I could use in my book. Within minutes, I got the heartfelt reply that you'll see later. My purposes were kind of selfish. You'll also read how he and the Ides of March work tirelessly for the disadvantaged. I'm going to reveal a little bit about myself here. I need a little bit of recovery time after finishing each chapter. Everyone I've contacted has been so generous with their time and praise. I'm moved in ways you can't imagine.

Most people would agree that I was (and still am) noticeable and approachable. I offered advice to artists with the talent and desire to take their craft to new levels. The music business was (and is) just as ruthless as it is unfair. People who sought my opinion would get the straight story.

I'm flattered that someone like Jim Peterik would come to me for help. Before the debut of **Vehicle**, the Berwyn group had a handful of singles on the Parrot label but no offers to compile an album. In 1968, things started to heat up after the group recorded a single on the Kapp label. A short time later, they landed a contract with Warner Brothers Records.

Vehicle (by many accounts, the fastest-breaking song in the history of the label) propelled the group to top-tier status (like opening for Led Zeppelin, Jimi Hendrix, and Janis Joplin). In 1973, the band members went their separate ways, until their beloved Berwyn offered them a chance to reunite in 1990.

Jim Peterik—
Carl Bonafede was one of my favorite people as a young and green member of Berwyn's own Ides of March. We looked up to him for sage advice and his unfailingly realistic assessment of our chances in the real world of rock-and-roll.

"Jim, remember – there's a boy in every basement practicing his ass off to be better than you. So you better be better than him!"

I took his advice to heart. In early 1970, I showed up one night at the Holiday Ballroom with my then girlfriend Karen. I had a hot acetate under my arm of a song the Ides just recorded. Without hesitation, Carl said he would give "Vehicle" a spin when the crowd started filing in.

He was true to his word, and suddenly I heard that now iconic horn riff blasting through the Altec A800s. This was the first time the public got the chance to hear it.

The response was good, and when the song reached number one, Carl loved to remind me of its premier.

Carl, I'm sure I thanked you through the years for all you did for me and 100 other Chicago bands. But one more time – thanks for your grit, your determination, and your love of the human spirit that makes us who we are.

You are a true street fighter and pioneer. Keep fighting the good fight.

My hiatus (how do you like that fancy word?) from nearly everything musical roughly corresponded with the "Ides" breakup, so we fell off each other's radar. Jim Peterik was just getting started. He founded the band Survivor and co-wrote all of their platinum hits, including **Eye of the Tiger** (the signature song of the *Rocky III* movie).

After their reunion, they released three albums in the 1990s and returned to national touring at the turn of the 21st century. The "Ides" established a scholarship fund at Morton West High School in Berwyn, where most of the founding band members went to school. Since 2005, they've performed at Chicago's Holy Name Cathedral 6pm Christmas Eve Mass and raised funds through sales of their *Sharing Christmas* album.

I marvel at the success of the people I've known. Maybe some groups would "hang it up" after having a street named after them. The former Home Avenue between Riverside Drive and Cermak Road in Berwyn is now Ides of March Way (site of J. Sterling Morton West High School).

The Ides of March (http://theidesofmarch.com) roll onward after 50 years. I'm proud to say a "live" Chicagoland audience first heard **Vehicle** at my house (the Holiday Ballroom). Jim Peterik and the Ides were destined for greatness no matter what. I was thrilled to be a witness.

A Word from Our Sponsor ...

You've seen little shameless advertising to this point. On the next page, I show you the 32 tracks I have on my Musical Memories CD. I used these songs as the framework of many chapters (or so I want you to believe)!

Working with these artists was a sincere pleasure. I was told it would make for a sloppy book unless I put each artist or group into a specific category. I hope you (and they) agree with my choices.

I managed to get many quotes (except for the dearly-missed Ral Donner, among others) from nearly every group or honored guest for your reading pleasure. I can still picture Ral rockin' the house.

The following is better than just a blank page – don't you agree?

5 Decades of Musical Memories - Chicago
Carl Bonafede CD – Chi-Town Records – While Supplies Last!

Songs	Writers	Publishers
Daughters of Eve		
1) California Sun (2:03)	J. Jones-H. Glover	Lloyd & Logan Bub BMI
2) Respect (2:09)	O. Redding	East Pub L. Co-Time Music BMI
3) Land of 1000 Dances (2:20)	C. Kenner-F. Domino	Anatole Music-Thursday Corp BMI
4) Just Like Me (2:11)	R. Day-R. Hart	Marcas Reg Music BMI
5) Midnight Hour (2:05)	W. Pickett/S. Cropper	Cotillion East Music BMI
6) Hippy Hippy Shake (2:00)	C. Romero	Licensed under EMI Records-EMI
Rail City 5		
7) Drivin (3:48)	P. J. Mally	Sparysongs BMI
8) Made in the USA (3:26)	P. J. Mally	Sparysongs BMI
9) In the Night (2:50)	P. J. Mally	Sparysongs BMI
10) Life's a Catastrophe (2:50)	C. Zaccaria	Sparysongs BMI
11) Midlife Crisis (3:44)	C. Zaccaria	Sparysongs BMI
Ral Donner		
12) Pittsburgh (2:30)	Dick Hamilton-Hugh Heller-Jacques Wilson	Brief Music BMI
13) It All Adds Up To Lonely (2:26)	Public Domain	Search Pending
14) Maria (Forever) (3:53)	D. Ragonal-Lew Douglas	Maryon Music ASCAP
15) Wait A Minute (2:22)	A. Campbell	Maryon Music ASCAP
16) Mr. Misery (2:26)	L. Nestor	Va-Pac-B. B. Marks-BMI Maryon Music ASCAP
17) Greatest Moments of My Life (2:49)	J. Butler	MRC Music BMI
Lincoln Park Zoo		
18) I Still Want You (2:03)	Milton-Drakb	Trusty Pub BMI
19) You're My Inspiration (2:04)	J. Butler	MRC Music BMI
20) Sambanette (2:28)	Public Domain	Search Pending
21) Kissie Face (2:20)	Public Domain	Search Pending
Mickey, Larry & the Exciters		
22) Save the Last Dance for Me (2:20)	Doc Pomus-Mort Shuman	Rumbalero-Progressive BMI
23) Stranded in the Middle of No Place (2:27)	Stevenson	Mikim Music BMI
24) You Don't Know What You Mean To Me (2:26)	Eddie Floyd-Steve Cropper	East Cotillion BMI
25) Don't Let It Slip Away (2:03)	J. Butler	MRC Music BMI
Delights		
26) Gonna Find Me a Woman (2:00)	Public Domain	Search Pending
27) Long Green (2:17)	Lynn Easton	Burdette Music BMI
28) Every Minute Every Hour (2:18)	Public Domain	Search Pending
29) Just Out of Reach (1:58)	Public Domain	Search Pending
Fabulous Centuries		
30) I Love You No More (2:13)	Geoff Boyan	Deb Music BMI
31) Yeh It's Alright (1:54)	Geoff Boyan	Deb Music BMI
32) Mr. Norm's Grand-Spaulding Dodge Commercial	(The Buckinghams)	

Closest to Home

The Delights (1961-66)

The Continentals printed their first business card in the spring of 1961. They advertised "music for all occasions" and listed Gerald Germansen as the primary contact. At age 12, he was the youngest member of the group and headed for Gordon Tech as a freshman in the coming September. In many ways, his professional career was very much like mine. His folks hosted the Saturday practices for the bandmates from the American School of Music on Armitage Avenue, just west of Humboldt Park.

Barry Plost, 14 (Von Steuben), played the trumpet. Rudy Salas, the 14-year-old drummer, attended Marshall, and Norbert Soltysiak (12, and headed for Weber) played the saxophone. Just like me, "Jerry" adopted a different professional name (Screaming Wildman was already taken) and kept the Continentals engaged with local gigs.

The Music Man Contest was sponsored by Webcor-Richards Music Corporation. In 1962, The Continentals advanced to the regional competition by taking first place at the Goldblatt department store at Pulaski Road and Madison Street. Jerry captured second place himself with his accordion medley.

Shortly afterward, the Continentals auditioned for Ron Terry's Amateurs contest at the Aragon Ballroom. A few days later, they competed "live" at WGN studios (the springboard for the Buckinghams in their rise to the top of the national charts).

Success is seldom possible without change. The Delights (Germansen and "Nibs" Soltysiak teamed with Gregory Grimes, Vincent Schraub, Robert Buff and Luis Sanjurio) continued to develop their personal style and increase their popularity. WLS disc jockey Don Phillips and

Jerry Germansen (keyboards, vocals)
Luis Sanjurio (bass, vocals), Bob Buff (drums),
Vince Schraub (guitar, vocals)
Greg Grimes (RIP) (lead vocals, saxophone)
Norbert Soltysiak (saxophone, vocals)

I started fielding requests for them at dances we were running. I became their personal manager, and Willard Alexander was now their booking agent.

The years 1964 through 1967 were furious for everyone involved in Chicago rock-and-roll. My groups were at the vortex of the most fabulous time of my music career. I must have been watching myself during some type of out-of-body experience when I think about an "average" day. The Delights were a big part of that.

I'm working as a booking agent with Willard Alexander during the day. At least a couple of days of week, I'm the MC for dances at Antoine's or the Holiday Ballroom with popular radio disc jockeys like Don Phillips, Dex Card, Ron Riley, Art Roberts, and WVON's Lucky Cordell. As if that weren't enough, I'm setting up recording sessions for the Buckinghams, Daughters of Eve, and Delights at legendary studios like Chess Records on South Michigan avenue. **Long Green** — https://youtu.be/uQevZZ6iX9Y

I stumbled on a group of guys who were already in the capable (though youthful) hands of an entrepreneurial mind like Jerry Germansen. He immediately reminded me of a younger version of, well, me. He swapped his accordion for an organ, which was subsequently stolen from his truck while parked in front of his home. I imagine he longed for an instrument that was more portable. The keyboard player needed to rely on the kindness of strangers if his bandmates were unavailable. One of the greatest quotes I got from Jerry dealt with the overall mobility of a garage-style band. "I'm willing to play for free," Jerry explained. "I just want to be paid what it's worth to haul my s**t from one gig to the next!"

During the '60s, the entire country supported a generation of potential rock-stars. There was a multitude of opportunities to hone your skills in front of live audiences. I fondly remember so many establishments willing to open their doors. I'm also reminded the same is no longer true for today's youth.

I have a more complete list of the places I personally entertained, MC'd dances, or booked local and national talent. For now, let's say that each venue went out of its way to provide a safe environment and was constantly competing with every other. People like my collaborator and friend from the Holiday Ballroom, Dan Belloc, concluded that a safe environment was essential. Then we turned our attention to whether it could be profitable. It proved to be both, once priorities were established.

The disc jockeys were relishing their local, and sometimes national, celebrity. They were willing to "mix it up" with their fan base after their radio show was over. They had some influence at the stations and might occasionally "lobby" a program manager for airplay. Others might have designated hours each week when aspiring talent could bring a demo tape and get a (sometimes brutally) honest opinion of their work. Some lucky folks would actually get a chance to lock eyes with their idols, in the hope that they could evoke some positive body language.

What was my role in all of this? The Screaming Wildman would be driving the moving studio that I described earlier to all of the high schools. I'd be handing out promotional fliers, free tickets, and sometimes records, as close to a high school campus as the police or school officials would tolerate. Then I would wrap up my work for the Willard Alexander Agency, which also booked talent for the dances at the Holiday Ballroom or Antoine's, to name a couple.

On dance day, I would be at the venue around 6pm or so. This would give me time to help coordinate security and set up my area if I was the MC. For the Delights, I would make sure the group's equipment would be set up and handle any needed introductions to radio personalities. The crowd started gathering at 6:30 and doors would open around 7pm. There would be three and a half hours of activities, from 7:30pm until 11pm, or so.

Afterward, I'd help the band pack up and say goodbye to the guest DJs, who would often stay around until the conclusion. Many times I was too "stoked" (to use a term that I wish was available then) to sleep. I would instead go to record an advertising spot or two for one of the radio stations I was working with at the time. Some may say that I didn't keep regular hours. I prefer to think that I was available at practically any time of day or night to help my groups and my associates get the recognition that they deserved.

Now, I'm back to recording the Delights. We recorded four sides together at Chess Records, where I once again had the privilege of working with Ron Malo on their cover of **Long Green** by the Kingsmen who took it to No. 4 on the Billboard Hot 100 in 1964.

This kind of lays out the method for getting out a 45rpm single vinyl record during the height of the garage-band era. Here you can see the process and the pitfalls, encapsulated in my experience with the Delights

The Actual Fan Club Button
from Jerry's Personal Archive

and repeated, for better or worse, with other groups I've managed or promoted. Once we record a "side," we have to work with a capable (in the case of Ron Malo, awesome) engineer with a label willing to handle both the production and distribution. The bigger the label, the more people they have on staff to promote it. That's why you will see many of the records I produced for a single group distributed on more than one label. It comes down to negotiating for the best deal possible for every single record.

Often my own Chi-Town label wasn't big enough to handle every aspect since I was already working constantly to get my groups this far. The entire process is pretty accurately summed up by the last two sides I recorded with the Delights. The title **Every Minute, Every Hour, Every Moment** (written by Grimes) epitomizes our struggles together. On the reverse side, **Just Out of Reach** (the cover of an obscure song released by the Zombies in 1965) sounds a little like our mutual understanding that the Delights were destined to evolve in a way that I could no longer enhance or control. This 45rpm became a Quill Records Production, released on the Smash label.

In 2009, Quill produced a compilation Orange Vinyl LP called *We're Gonna Change the World!* featuring a number of garage bands like the Gents (with pre-New Colony Six vocalist Ronnie Rice). The Delights may be the best R&B/British-style fusion band you ever heard. Both of those tracks appear on the record. By the way, the front cover photo on the limited-edition LP was none other than the Willard Alexander publicity photo for the Delights when I managed them. You know the one, with the leopard-skin jackets.

I'm so grateful to Jerry Germansen, who lent me his scrapbook. There is even a Delights fan club button, complete with a picture of the group. As he mentioned in his note when he shipped them to me, "These have not been out of my possession for over 50 years … but for Carl Bonafede …" I am touched and honored.

Jerry Germansen—
The best times were playing shows with other groups. We often jammed with them before or after the shows.

I remember a show at Kane County Fair Grounds when the venue flooded and the show was canceled at the last minute. The covered stage was dry. We were set up to play and decided to jam some. There was a new group that had just released a first 45. *Bluebird* was the A side. Their drummer joined in as we played *I Ain't Gonna Eat Out My Heart Anymore* by the Young Rascals. Then a guitarist or two joined in. That group turned out to be Richie Furay, Stephen Stills, Neil Young, Dewey Martin, Bruce Palmer, Jim Messina, Ken Koblun, and Jim Fielder, playing as Buffalo Springfield at that time.

We also played with the Mamas and Papas, the Guess Who, the Association, Sam the Sham and the Pharaohs, Cream (Eric Clapton), and many more.

We did record with Ron Malo, the same engineer who recorded the Rolling Stones, at Chess Records in Chicago.

The Hudsen Bay Company

You know, Hudsen is spelled with an "e," meaning an *even* more sophisticated sound. The group recorded only one single under the Smash label: **I See Her Face** (https://youtu.be/p66i1BoFm9I and), written by Vince Schraub, and **You**, written by Greg Grimes.

 The members were exactly the same for both the Hudsen Bay Co. and the Delights: Bob Buff (drums), Jerry Germansen (keyboards, vocals), Greg Grimes (lead vocals, saxophone), Luis Sanjurio (bass, vocals), Vince Schraub (guitar, vocals), and Norbert Soltysiak (saxophone, tambourine, vocals).

Norbert (Norb) Soltysiak later joined the Hardy Boys, a band that released two LPs on RCA as a tie-in to the TV show of the same name. The Delaware label also released the song **Long Long Time** by A.J. and the Savages.

Jim Holvay

I swear, you are in for a treat in this chapter. "Jimmy Soul" Holvay was one of the first guys I contacted for a contribution to my book. This is also among the last chapters I put together. Go figure. Since he came on board so to speak, I've been trying to mash in as many of the colorful and talented characters I have had the privilege to know.

When a guy writes a song, he doesn't know who it will stir up, or when. Holvay had no idea that the Screaming Wildman would eventually take notice or that the marketplace was eager for fresh material that wasn't Beatles based. It takes an accomplished musician to get melody and poetry to play nicely together.

I'm glad I waited to put this Holvay stuff together because I learned so much about creating chapters. I feel a little more capable of giving him well-deserved credit for the fuel that took the Buckinghams to the moon. That would make me the rocket booster—you know, the vehicle that helped them break free of everything that holds all of us down in some way.

As you all know about rocket boosters (even those of us who couldn't wait to get out of school), they are destined to be cut loose once they've served their purpose. See, I couldn't have made those types of comparisons last year. Anyway, there are other worthwhile observations I'm making as my words spill out. Pretty good, don't you think? I'm trying to piece together what happened and find reasons why it did.

I think the most serious (and gifted) rock-and-roll songwriters of their time were piano players. Think Brian Wilson, Carole King, and Jim Holvay. Hey, I can compare George Gershwin to Holvay if I want. It's my book. Of course, you might be able to list many exceptions to my rule. If you plunked down the cash for your own copy of my book, feel free to argue away (and thank you).

Now for the treat I promised you. I'm going to let Jim Holvay do some of the talking from here on. He certainly has enough material to write his own book. I suggest he try it while seated at a piano keyboard.

Oh, yeah. One other thing. I'm going to let Jim talk directly to you with minimal input from the Screaming Wildman. Maybe.

"The first time I encountered Carl Bonafede would have been in 1960, when he was singing with the Gem-Tones at one of the Jim Lounsbury record hops at the Willowbrook Ballroom. The guy sounded just like Paul Anka and had an incredible stage presence. Though I was only 14 years old, I was already a musician, with a recording session on my meager resume. At least, it gave me the courage to introduce myself.

"In some ways, I may have been emulating him without knowing it. During my remaining Lyons Township High School days, I played with and recorded a couple of songs with the MayBees and met my long-time collaborator, Gary Beisbier.

"I graduated in June of 1963 and joined the Chicagoans shortly afterward. That August, I was at another Lounsbury event at the Blue Moon Ballroom in Elgin, Illinois, where Carl was again performing. Jimmy Peterson, the frontman and lead singer of the Chicagoans, already seemed to have a relationship with Carl and Joe DeFrancesco, another Chicago promoter.

"By the end of the year, Clark Weber, program director for WLS (890AM), had just heard (and actually named) our instrumental track, released as **Beatle Time**. Because of his relationship with many influential disc jockeys, Weber among them, Carl Bonafede may not have actually known me. It was more important he knew 'about' me at this point," Jim opened.

I think you'll see writing credits for Holvay, Beisbier, and Peterson for **Beatle Time**, released by the Constellation Records label. And now he continues …

"A high-register trumpet player named Jimmy Ford led a group called the Kasuals. They built a solid reputation with a guy named Bob Ahert, the Chicago head of the William Morris office. They secured a job as the backup band for an upcoming 1964 Dick Clark Caravan and were now known as the Executives," Jim related. Legal wrangling was behind the quick name change. See Dwight Kalb's chapter for more insight.

"Jimmy Ford recruited Gary Beisbier and me for what would be known as the Executives #2 tour band. In the summer of 1966, the Executives were playing as the backing band at Dick Clark Teenage

The Chicagoans

World's Fair at the International Amphitheater at Halsted and 42nd Street on the south side of Chicago," he told me.

There is another theme in my book about these days and times. Because of the war raging in the Republic of Vietnam, creative, talented (and patriotic) guys were forced to stay enrolled in college or face a future even more uncertain (and dangerous) than that of a traveling musician.

"I was dinking around on a spinet piano in a music practice room at Lyons Township Junior College and wrote **Kind of a Drag**. I wasn't sure Carl remembered I was a songwriter until he asked if I had any tunes.

"Yeah, I do have something, and Carl asked when he could hear it. I remember cutting a demo of the song on acoustic guitar between shows," he recalled.

History Redefined

I'm tempted to say the rest is history. Actually, there are so many intertwined histories to even get to this point I'm beginning to believe less in fate and more in chance. Let me review before I turn things back over to Mr. Holvay as I (sort of) promised.

Let's begin with the record label responsible for Jim Holvay's emergence. Ewart Abner (former president of Vee-Jay), Bunky Sheppard, and Art Sheridan (owner of Chance – home to the Moonglows and Chicago's own Flamingos) started Constellation in 1963. Chicago R&B artists Dee Clark and Gene Chandler were responsible for the bulk of the earliest releases from the new label at South Michigan Avenue in the historic Record Row area.

During one tiny sliver of the Beisbier / Holvay timeline, they wrote a tribute instrumental to the Beatles. It was recorded by chance during the last few minutes of a demo session for a female artist. They shipped the entire session tape to Chicago promoter Joe DeFrancesco in the hope he could land a contract for her. As it turned out, one of those tracks caught the attention of one, and then another, of the most influential players in the business at that time.

Bunky Sheppard, well known for producing Gene Chandler's **Duke of Earl** and most likely the reason both now were with Constellation, invited Joe to come along to the WLS Christmas party (with the tape, of course). As you remember, legendary Clark Weber was the program director at the time. What better second opinion could you get when it came to evaluating talent?

If I was in that exact situation, I wouldn't go to a Christmas party in Clark's house (actually it was only a suite in the WLS empire) with gift-wrapped trinkets, candy, and nuts. I would go with media-ready demos and a proven plan of action. According to one of the main players in this story, the girl who had her hopes pinned to this recording session was a Leslie Gore sound-alike. Apparently, her voice or the songs she chose (or both) proved unremarkable.

Here, I can speak from my own experience and for others who've shared theirs in this book. That's not saying she wasn't talented or endearing. It was saying that she wasn't going to be marketable in the foreseeable future, if ever. However, the instrumental track at the very end created a flicker in Weber's eyes. Here's the conversation the way I understand it. I'm sure DeFrancesco might have spoken that evening, but not here.

"Who's the band?" Weber asked.

"The Chicagoans," Sheppard answered.

"I like it. What's the name of the song?" Clark asked, taking the reins.

There was no title, just a catchy melding of Beatle-esque chart-busting facsimiles. (I learned how to manufacture words that probably won't offend anyone.) Really, the title wouldn't have mattered. Weber named the song **Beatle Time** and christened the group the Livers (short for Liverpool). https://youtu.be/RZJL4eZZOYg. Remember, this happened in the last week of 1963. Does this make Clark Weber a visionary and a man of action? You are free to draw your own conclusion, of course. Holvay and the band were getting deserved recognition. The indignities of immediate re-branding were a small price to pay. The Kasuals became the Executives in a virtual heartbeat under harsher circumstances.

Let's break down this series of events and how it fits into broader history: the Beatles emerge in the U.S. on Vee-Jay Records with little fanfare; JFK is assassinated and the world mourns; Christmas and the Beatles were destined to usher in a year of healing and hope; Clark Weber is introduced to the Chicagoans; **Beatle Time** is released by Constellation Records and WLS starts playing it; Ed Sullivan welcomes the Beatles on February 9, 1964; **Beatle Time** makes it to No. 15 on the WLS list of top Chicago hits.

Do you see why this chapter was so hard for me to write? I'm so lucky and grateful for my life and the things that happened. I'm starting to marvel at how much was completely out of my hands. I was certainly doing my own thing and quite competently, if I may say. Sure I can—it's my book. Of course, the presidential tragedy was a horrendous thing. This also is not the only place you'll read about it and how we found a way to push forward.

Were the Beatles the most available salve to heal the country? Would their popularity and acceptance have been different if not for the worst days in most people's memory? That's not the point (now that you are expecting me to make one soon). I'm grateful and mystified at the same time. I needed to put together the circumstances that allowed the Screaming Wildman, Buckinghams, and Jim Holvay to share a defining moment or two.

Soulful Songwriting

It takes a special kind of person with the talent to both reveal their own soul and reach into another's. Doing it within the time constraints of AM radio proved impossible for all but a few. Hey, I wrote songs that were somewhat popular. Take my tune **Margie Cha-Cha**, for instance. It was fun describing how she drifted into my life. Why she didn't stay (or wouldn't leave) was the kind of story most of us wanted to hear. Raw strands of emotion, knit together with melodies, could sustain the message when the words began to fail. That's Blues and Rhythm. It's Soul (with a capital S). I'm glad I wrote this down!

OK, we're back to this timeline again. Groups like the Executives, and others you found on my pages, were accomplished and entertaining musicians who had genuine life experience. I could only hope my newest generation (like the Pulsations and Centuries) would learn something. Would they ever be able to write songs? Maybe, just not within the time frame I saw in front of me. To take advantage of the tremendous marketing potential of the evolving Buckinghams, I needed to find original material for them to perform.

"I went to see the Buckinghams at a record hop and thought they were horrible," Jimmy Soul said in earlier interviews. Maybe he showed it, too. It didn't stop me for a second. I was on a mission. I heard (and knew) he was a songwriter. This stuff gets around. I asked what he had for me (in a kind, Screaming Wildman sort of way).

"I've got something called **Kind of a Drag**," Jim told me. Remember where I mentioned (or he did) about that Dick Clark Teenage World's Fair gig where he was playing?

"I cut a demo on acoustic guitar between shows at the Amphitheatre for Carl, and I thought that was that," Jim has related in lots of interviews. The Screaming Wildman was never one to let anything sit. Neither was the author of the tune that defined a handful of careers, especially mine.

The Mob Evolves

Jim Holvay wasn't inclined to wait around to see if his lyrics were going to resonate. He prepared to launch his dream band. I'm going to borrow a few lines from the band's story. I invite you to read the online version yourself. I hope they think about doing a book. A year ago, I would never have said this, believe me.

Holvay was inspired by an old gangster movie called *The Mob*, showing on WGN. The band would dress in stereotypical pin-striped suits, black shirts, and white ties with a carnation in their lapels. The music and presentation would be revolutionary. Most groups had four of five guys, max. The Mob would have a full-sized horn section (they said full blown, I didn't want to take any credit for their pun) and a virtual mob on stage. Holvay and collaborator Mike Sistak presented the concept to Jimmy Ford and Gary Beisbier, and the nucleus formed. Once again, that came from their narration. Let me refer you to their online story here. http://www.themobmusic.com/MOB_story.html

I took a little credit for the big horn sound that grabs your attention at the start of Jim Holvay's **Kind of a Drag**. In the Buckinghams' chapter, you'll read these were "tracked" with the help of Dan Belloc and his orchestra from the Holiday Ballroom.

Don't get me wrong, Holvay, the Buckinghams, and Screaming Wildman deserve their fair share of the credit for capturing lightning in a bottle. To this day, I try to recognize everyone who got the song to the top of the Billboard chart. I now declare the sound was inspired and perfected by the Mob. We were more like the marketplace test pilots for the horn intro which (I like to remind everyone) did not sit well with trendsetters like Clark Weber.

Intersecting Circles

I was looking for a way to describe the free flow of concepts, sounds, and even personnel that started out as the Jim Holvay story. I managed to follow a few detours and emerge where he, the Mob, Chicago (the band and the city), and Blood, Sweat and Tears (the band and the pitfalls of the music business) all merge.

Chad and Jeremy was a gifted (British Invasion) duo using the Mob as their opening act and backing band. The Mob was also playing nightclubs from one end of the country to the other. At Wine and Roses in Schiller Park, Illinois, word reached Jim Holvay about one of his heartfelt creations:

"You remember that song you recorded for Bonafede? It's on the radio."

"I turned the radio on in the kitchen," said Holvay.

I've heard it said he thought it sounded cheesy. Thank goodness cheese was selling well at that time. Shortly after that, my circle nearly detached from those of the Buckinghams and Jimmy Soul. I wouldn't have traded the experience for anything else.

I'm grateful for my contribution to the Buckinghams' only No. 1 hit. I celebrate Holvay's others on their behalf (**Don't You Care**, **Hey Baby: They're Playing Our Song**, and **Susan**). The story behind each is well worth exploring.

The same could be said for a few entries in the Chicago (the group and the city) songbooks, thanks to Jim Holvay. He would modestly give the credit to others. I'll leave that up to him.

> **Jim Holvay—**
> Despite writing three songs that the Buckinghams parlayed into million sellers, I never entertained becoming a full-time songwriter. Trying to, as Lou Rawls once told me, have "all of the stars in the universe ... line up just right" and pen that next big hit wasn't for me. I wanted to be on stage, out front, playing my guitar.
> "I wanted to be a star and get the women."
> *– From a newspaper interview*

The Buckinghams (1964-present)

There were actually four talented groups I worked with on a regular basis: P.C. Limited (represented by CASK Attractions), the Facts of Life (Mike Carioscia), the Fabulous Centuries, and the Pulsations. Dan Belloc and I were in the right place to watch the Buckinghams' story unfold. I'm introducing lots of other key contributors to the Buckinghams' success and popularity on the following pages. In case you didn't already know, here's a quick refresher.

The Buckinghams gained notoriety as "Chicago's answer to the British Invasion" when **Kind of a Drag** (U.S.A. Records) topped the national charts in 1967. It knocked the Monkees (**I'm a Believer**) out of the top spot. It would take no less than the Rolling Stones' **Ruby Tuesday** to unseat our group. That same year, *Billboard Magazine* called the Buckinghams "the Most Listened to Band in America." According to *Cashbox Magazine*, they were "the Most Promising" vocal group of the time.

Did the Buckinghams members fulfill that promise? In the following months, they released 45rpm singles **Don't You Care**, **Hey Baby, They're Playing Our Song**, and **Mercy, Mercy, Mercy** on the Columbia Records label, along with **Lawdy Miss Clawdy** (on U.S.A.) and others. The Buckinghams were a marketable success after the (Columbia) release of the *Time and Charges*, then *Portraits* albums. Not bad for a group of guys barely old enough to take a (legal) drink.

We're going to start our story with the way the Buckinghams, deservedly, made the transition from "band" to "brand." In 1966, before hooking a mega-label contract, "upstart" U.S.A. Records released *Kind of a Drag*. This album (every song recorded at the legendary Chess Studios in 1965) set the stage for awesome events. Rather than waiting for certain stars to align, we all took note of the stars that were already in place and made a "go" of it, or at it.

WGN-TV Appearances

It was 1965 and Sheldon Cooper, program director at WGN-TV, needed acts for the new *All Time Hits* show. Singers and dancers would perform popular musical tunes from stage, movies, and radio. After the Pulsations' audition, Sheldon awarded them the gig, though it was later quoted they were the "least worst" of the groups he auditioned. All is forgiven.

Everybody is a critic. Few folks had the power to change (or end) careers. An endorsement from one of the most respected and envied pioneers of television would soon be enough to take a local band to the pinnacle of music success.

The WGN family liked the group more than they let on, but didn't particularly care for their current name. Before we started taping, at the suggestion of John Opager, a WGN security guard, we changed it to the Buckinghams. You'll find a heartfelt tribute to him after his passing in 2012. (https://www.facebook.com/notes/carl-giammarese-singersongwriter/in-loving-memory-of-john-l-opager-jr-1943-2012/474239429288363)

Not only did this sound like a great name to combat the British Invasion of musical groups, it reinforced the Chicago connection to Buckingham Fountain. After each member voted "yes" (these guys were a democracy), we headed straight to the fountain for that iconic photo shoot. Say what you want about this gig, it was 13 solid weeks, two songs a week, at the WGN mega-station, airing on Tuesday nights from 9 to 10, *in color*!

Back then, people had to make a (sometimes painful) choice about what they were going to watch since video recorders were science fiction at the time. I remember *The Fugitive* was one of the heavily rated shows in direct competition with WGN in that time slot. That same year, the very popular *Adventures of Ozzie and Harriet* show (springboard for rock-and-roll pioneer Rick Nelson) was entering its 14th season. It was time for some new blood. It didn't matter to the guys, or to me, that we were viewed as newcomers. They were being introduced as "Rock-and-Roll Royalty" by WGN. The guys looked slick and sounded great. People were watching and talking (this was the genuine social media). The group was determined to make the best of it. At least, some of them would.

Once-in-a-lifetime opportunities are entwined with grim realities. The music business was fickle and confusing during the best of times. For blue-collar families with draft-eligible boys, the realities were terrifying. Bandmates were subject to the whims of a detached government. If you catch some clips of the fledgling Buckinghams, you'll see George LeGros sharing lead vocals with Dennis Tufano for the first three weeks of their breakout WGN performances. After George answered the call of his noble country, Dennis took the reins for the majority of the singing.

By the time the group's game-changing television gig ended, Curt Bachman was replaced by Nick Fortuna on the bass guitar. Carl Giammarese (lead guitarist), John Poulos (drums), and Dennis Miccolis (keyboards), who posted the YouTube® clip I found here (https://youtu.be/DksBxZezUuE), were eager to see what type of music and madness were in their future. At least, I thought so. Dennis was replaced, for a short time, by Larry Nestor and finally by Marty Grebb on keyboards and vocals. Would the stars align for the Buckinghams? Maybe. It was my job to coax as many humans as possible to help out. Lots of stuff was happening at once, and this book wouldn't be one-tenth as interesting unless I let some of the real players add their experiences and feelings.

"Mister Norm" Commercials

On my (*Five Decades of Musical Memories From the Windy City Chicago*) CD, I included a clip of the Buckinghams' radio ad beaming all over the country at the same time the band was appearing weekly on WGN.

Carl Giammarese arranged the commercial for Mister Norm's Grand-Spaulding Dodge, which became the highest-volume Dodge dealership in the United States. Was it Mister Norm's mechanics, who could tune a factory 383-cu.in. V-8 (delivering 180hp) to an unbelievable 325hp, or was it the appeal of the new darlings of the airwaves? You decide. I already did.

Mister Norm (Kraus) opened Grand-Spaulding Dodge in (I think) 1962 and built his business by appealing to young car buyers who craved speed and performance. Only a hip and hard-driving group would be able to get his message across. This was another match that somehow defies explanation, even now.

The Falling Pebbles

One of the sides the Buckinghams recorded was an instrumental called **Virginia Wolf** (https://youtu.be/O-IVIVKjPEs). It was released as a single along with **Lawdy Miss Clawdy** on the Alley Cat label. I guessed its pseudo name was supposed to be a "take off" on the Rolling Stones. You'll see Ron Malo and yours truly on the production credits. I have to give a lot of credit to John Poulos for the idea. This got a lot of exposure for the group by getting even more of their music out there. This was a great example of the collaborations and alliances it took to get a single record to the marketplace. This also gave me leverage to find every recording a home.

Legacy-Type Stuff

On Friday night, May 29, 2009, I had a reunion of sorts with the Buckinghams when the band performed at the Genessee Theatre in Waukegan, Illinois. My good friends Pat De Luca and Joel Bierig accompanied me to see the Buckinghams perform, along with the Ides of March and Ronnie Rice from the New Colony Six.

We had a great time. I hadn't talked with them or seen the group perform in some 20 years. Carl Giammarese invited me to the performance. He mentioned he was putting together a biography, and he wanted me to come out and see him play. Since then, you could safely say we've been collaborating. OK,

I gave you the condensed version. He and I got together over coffee at one of his favorite places and hashed out our account of the (50 years) Buckinghams' ongoing story.

Carl Giammarese Interview

I was tooling down the Eisenhower Expressway to meet him at a Starbucks just outside of Chi-town. See how I worked my record label name into my book? Always marketing. Why was I requesting an interview? We kind of knew the history. Heck, we lived it. Because of this "book thing," I needed help refreshing my memory. Maybe we could compare notes, and I might make this story more understandable by using nearly the same English that you do. You know what I'm sayin'? That's the last time I'm allowed to use that expression for this entire chapter. This is hard work. I hope you think it's worth it.

I got to the coffee shop only a couple of minutes before the "other" Carl. It reminds me of the times I spent idling outside Lane Tech with the rest of the band packed into my old station wagon with the equipment hitched to the trailer behind us. On a week day, we'd be headed either to the suburbs or to Antoine's ballroom just to our east on Addison Street.

On Fridays, we were most likely headed west to the Kennedy Expressway, destined for some Wisconsin teen club or banquet hall. So here's a little bit of nostalgia for those who grew up in this era. In addition to the music from one of the greatest music periods of all time, the drinking age (for beer) was 19. Eager crowds awaited both.

That drinking law was great for getting the Buckinghams bookings. The Willard Alexander booking agency loved the group, at least at that time (more about that later). But the agency wasn't responsible for getting the group across the border, ready to perform, packed up afterward, and chauffeured home. That was left up to the Screaming Wildman.

Don't get me wrong, I loved every part of it. I especially took driving seriously. I got to know everyone's parents well enough to build a trust I would never betray. Not everyone could (or would) do that.

When I arrived at Starbucks, I took a seat facing the door. Maybe that was the "Sicilian" inside me. Really, I was just looking forward to seeing him again. I was worried I might have misunderstood his directions. During my whole life (and career), I would be at least 20 minutes early for appointments. That gave me plenty of time to worry about everything else.

Finally (in Bonafede time), I saw him striding toward the glass doors. He gave me his Carl Giammarese smile and extended his hand. He does the same thing for his fans. He treats all of us like we are somebody special.

It was October 20, 2015, and Carl G. was wearing Cubbie Blue. We were hoping the first Wrigley Field playoff game between the Mets and Cubs would go differently than the ones in New York. We needed to stop Mets second baseman Daniel Murphy from dismantling our team single-handedly. By this time he had homered in his last four post-season games. That included the clinching games against the Dodgers and the first two games against the Cubs. By the time I got around to editing this chapter, I'm reminded we didn't stop either the Mets or Murphy. That dude homered in every single game against the Cubs. The rest was sad, and continuing, history.

Now, I let one of the founding members of the Centuries give me his perspective. At the beginning of this chapter, you've seen my recollections. Wherever Carl Giammarese's memory proved better than mine, I made the appropriate corrections. The Centuries were gaining a following in the Morton Grove area. Bass player Curt Bachman approached me about getting the group a gig at the Vogue Ballroom. This was the biggest stage (and audience to match) for the group at that point.

"The first song that we ever played was the instrumental theme from the Outer Limits. You know, doo-doo, doo-doo, etc.," he reminded me. I wondered what the words looked like on the sheet music. Anyway, the rest of the set went extremely well and the crowd was very receptive. All of the guys seemed to feel they had something important going. I booked the Centuries at other places like Antoine's, along with a couple of dances at some Italian joint on Chicago Avenue in an Italian neighborhood. How long was it before the Centuries decided to approach me with the offer to manage them?

"For me, it took all of 10 minutes for me to make up my mind!" Carl told me. Do you how hard it is to write about a conversation between two Carls? I knew that he didn't mind repeating the last statement on my behalf. We started to roll forward with our conversation as if it were no longer an interview.

"Remember, we were going to call ourselves the Kingsmen?" the young Buckingham asked. Another group just released that instant hit called **Louie Louie**. Of course it sounded like "loo-why loo-why," if you sang it right. That band name was off the table. Centuries it was.

As two guys who have a long history together, our conversation took unexpected directions. We'll get back to the timeline, after we throw in this sidebar.

"You know we did **Louie Louie** for an encore at our recent Buckinghams performance," Carl said. Maybe I'll call him "G" for the rest of this chapter. I'm getting tired of typing.

"Really, did you sing it?" I asked.

"I sang just one verse."

"Did you understand the words?" I played the 45 at one of my dances with the turntable at only 33rpm. There were allegations about obscene lyrics. That controversy created a lot of bookings and sold a lot of records.

"If you look up the verses online, there are no dirty parts. There were about 25 of us on stage, including Rick Derringer from the McCoys (**Hang on Sloopy**)," Carl told me. Gawd, you should see the chick dancing in that YouTube® video (https://youtu.be/_FdV1dFvKA8). I'm glad some bands have live footage from that era. When you get guys from all of those groups together in a public broadcasting venue, the stories flow and crisscross constantly.

 "I think you are supposed to sing the words so that nobody understands them," Carl continued. That reminded me of Elton John, Michael McDonald, and every rapper I ever heard. Not that I ever heard that many.

We're back to the part where G reminded me why the Centuries wanted the Screaming Wildman to represent them.

"You got us exposure all over the city. I kept thinking back to my first dance at the Holiday Ballroom when I was maybe 15, a few years before I formed a band. I was inspired by the pretty girls and impressed by the musicians. I wanted to be part of all of that. I remember seeing Lou Christie. Thanks to you and the Willard Alexander booking agency, the Centuries would have the solid representation," Carl said.

I don't know if this is the right place to mention how Carl Giammarese began building his dream (or realized that he could start rearranging the stars to his advantage). I came on board after the Centuries did the heavy lifting required to launch a band. Talented drummer Gerald Ellarde (Carl's cousin) was teaming up with Niles West High School classmate Nick Fortuna. Curt Bachman would play bass and share vocals with Gerald. Carl would play lead guitar. There was no shortage of gigs for guys willing to pay their dues.

The Centuries became the "house" band at the Holiday Ballroom after I began representing them. Willard Alexander was capitalizing on the group's growing reputation and booking them at the Aragon Ballroom, or with Ed Redmond and Jim Bernard at the Embassy. I was way too busy to keep track of everything going on with the band. Eventually, I learned Curt Bachman was leaving the Centuries for Saturday's Children. This won't be the last time we'll mention him in this interview. Let's just call him restless, and leave it at that.

The British invasion inspired all Chicago groups. The music was only going to get better with the competition for gigs and girls. Remember, this was also prime time for "personality" radio. The disc jockeys would make personal appearances, discover local bands, and lobby WLS and WCFL program managers to play their records. There was no written formula, of course, but it went much like this: Form a group, get gigs at dances, catch the eye of promoters/DJs/managers, record several tracks in a studio, press a demo record and get it played at dances, beg radio program managers to give new groups an opportunity, and use the new popularity of the recording for more gigs, etc.

Just as the Centuries were hitting its stride, a group called the Pulsations was evolving in much the same way. I began booking them at the Holiday Ballroom and nearly every place the Centuries played. Who's telling this story now, my guest, or me?

Drummer John Poulos founded the band (another similarity to the Centuries) with keyboard player Dennis Miccolis, featuring dual lead vocalists Dennis Tufano and George LeGros and bass player Curt Bachman. Here's a great spot for Carl Giammarese to pick up the story.

"I'm backstage at the Holiday Ballroom, hearing Tufano and LeGros doing both Everly Brothers and Righteous Brothers covers through a locked stage door. I was banging away, trying to get a glimpse of them, but it was so loud, nobody heard me. John Poulos was already trying to get me to join their band," Carl started. I wasn't aware of this at first. Bands merged all the time. I should have known earlier since they were both "my" bands by then.

"George and Dennis took me out for a milkshake to convince me to play lead guitar for the Pulsations," Giammarese remembered how it went for him. Sometimes we forget that these guys were just barely out of high school. In Carl's case, he was still going to Lane Tech. Business decisions were often finalized over milkshakes, french fries, or some other hideous food combination. Okay, whatever it took to reach the final decision, the Pulsations had a new guitarist.

"We are now a six-member band (LeGros - Tufano - Bachman - Poulos - Giammarese - Miccolis as lead vocal, lead vocal, bass, drums, lead guitar, and keyboard, respectively). Poulos asked the Screaming Wildman to manage the new Pulsations as well. Carl, you had the energy and connections to get us plenty of work. I remember making $200-300 a week working after school and weekends. I also remember going from an A average to a C during my last year of school," Giammarese said. There is no success without sacrifice, I guess.

Like I said earlier, an interview can become a conversation once the formality wears off. The downside is the interchange starts to lose direction. I'm responsible for at least half of that here. Near the beginning of this chapter, I talked about my station wagon with the gear hitched behind. This is the perfect time to sidetrack, or pull off the road, literally.

"I'm driving down the road with youz guys," I said. I might as well capture the dialogue as accurately as possible. "We were heading to some place in Wisconsin and the engine overheats," I said, handing off to Carl.

"You jump out of the driver's seat and throw open the hood," he continued. That's just what any screaming wildman would do. All of the Buckinghams have since heard (and told) this story for decades. Some of you may be aware it wasn't all that glamorous or fun getting to gigs. Thank goodness, there are stories like this you can count on to break the monotony.

"Now, with steam still coming out, you twist open the radiator cap, and it blows up in your face," Carl said. I should have known better. Maybe the guys in the Buckinghams may not have. They cut too many classes while pursuing their musical dream. I gave them a quick course in the laws of physics and driver's education. Thank goodness, they didn't need to do any first-aid. They may have cut that class as well. The funny part is nearly over. Carl was ready to wrap this up, but those are not tears of nostalgia in his eyes.

"Every time we are together that story comes up," Carl said. I didn't think of a joke about the "Steaming" Wildman until just this minute.

"Nick gets a real big kick about that, even now," I said, after one more parting shot. "It's been 50 years, and my eyebrows are now just growing back." I made this up. I've had eyebrow implants for a long time.

Herb Gronauer and I were lining up a bunch of gigs in the tri-state area (Illinois, Wisconsin, and Indiana). Now we're back to the 13-week WGN *All Time Hits* television show. In my all-time hits boxed set, I have a DVD with a bunch of those shows. If you watch them in order, you'll see the gradual transformation of the group. Actually, it wasn't so gradual. There were some radical, even life-altering changes. It was a new band with a new name.

"On the very first show, we had on gold lame suits with pompadour greaser hair," Carl recalled. The Buckinghams were introduced as "rock-and-roll royalty." The other acts on the show could be described as contemporary, even conservative. The Buckinghams were issuing a direct challenge to the British groups. WGN management thought this was possible by having the group sing Beatles tunes, go figure.

"After a couple of shows, you'll see John Poulos with his hair combed down and wearing a John Lennon cap. Then Curt Bachman became more Beatles-looking. LeGros, Tufano, and I still maintained the greaser look," he continued. Slow converts. At this point, it couldn't have gone better. Actually, it could always be better for working-class kids with the prospect of being drafted into armed conflict.

"George told us he had bad knees and there was no way that he would be drafted. Nearly overnight, I recall waving goodbye to him at the train station,"

Carl continued. On the fourth show, you'll see Dennis Tufano as the sole lead singer. I don't remember having to explain the changes to the WGN management. Good thing, since I would have to understand it myself. Curt Bachman would end up quitting again.

"I still don't know why he left in the middle of the biggest break you could have had," I lobbed the question in Carl's direction.

"At the time, we all thought that he was continuing to look for the next big thing. He confided to me much later that he thought, with George gone, there was no longer a unique aspect to the band with a single lead singer. In the meantime, Nick Fortuna from the Centuries was playing in some band on Mannheim Road and switched from rhythm to bass guitar. In the fourth WGN show, we're a five-man band and Nick has replaced Curt."

That wasn't the only thing going on during that time. Willard Alexander (actually Herb and I) was promoting the band everywhere. The Buckinghams recorded a commercial for Mr. Norm's Grand-Spaulding Dodge located at (you guessed it, Grand and Spaulding avenues) just southwest of Humboldt Park in Chicago. Now we have nationwide exposure on television and radio. In exchange for our work on the commercial, Mr. Norm donated a turquoise van with "The Buckinghams" painted on the side.

"That turned out to be a big mistake having the name on the side," Carl said.

That van got stolen, along with all the band's equipment, not long after the Buckinghams piled in for the first time.

"Where did it get stolen? Was it in front of my house?" I asked.

"No, it was in front of Dennis's house," Carl reminded me. It was later found abandoned, I think, on an expressway somewhere. It wasn't vandalized, but the equipment was gone. The Buckinghams were so popular at that time that even the theft of their equipment turned out to be great publicity. Who would have made that known to adoring fans? (wink) Anyway, there was a huge response on their behalf. The Buckinghams were soon fully equipped once again, thanks to public donations. We stray a little off topic once again. My kind of conversation.

"Clark Weber got in touch to congratulate me on our recent WTTW show," Carl shared a tidbit.

"Did I ever tell you that Clark Weber didn't want to play Kind of a Drag because he thought the intro was too loud?" I asked. I ask him every time.

Carl Giammarese—
One of the reasons we wanted to work with Carl Bonafede was because he had so many connections. There were Dan Belloc (Holiday Ballroom), Paul Glass (U.S.A. Records), and Howard Bedno (a hard-working promoter and big fan of ours). Carl would do anything to promote us, including marching with a sandwich-board in front of the band in a Thanksgiving Day parade. We could always count on him. He had a high-performance engine, and he is still hitting on all cylinders.

I took the guys down to Smokey Joe's or someplace like that to get them matching suits. These were the kind with collarless (Beatles-type) jackets. I got the very same one for myself to wear at their (or should I say "our") next appearance.

"We hoped to surprise our audience with a new look. There you were, wearing the same outfit when you introduced us," Carl reminded me. It was a good thing I was so lovable and useful. The Buckinghams were actually too tolerant.

"We were starting to look beyond the WGN show," Carl continued. Carl and I weren't quite ready to break away from WGN recollections just yet though.

"The Buckinghams shared the dressing room of Ringmaster Ned Locke," Carl explained. Chicago folks from that era remember him as the lovable, smiley guy who introduced the acts during the iconic *Bozo's Circus* kids' show, airing every weekday at noon.

"I tried on his top hat once, and the brim dropped down to here," he said while pointing to his chin. We also mentioned a couple of local stars, like Frazier Thomas and Ray Rayner (my personal favorite). Ray was on the air, literally hosting kids' programming morning, noon, and afternoon until right before dinner. He also wore an umbrella hat at times. He may have been my inspiration.

Remember, the Buckinghams were airing weekly on WGN. Willard Alexander was having the easiest time booking the band, thanks to All Time Hits and the Mr. Norm commercial. All that was missing was a hit record to get them national exposure. Thank goodness Carl Giammarese was with me. We were working together again. It felt good.

"Remember, we were the unofficial 'house band' at the Holiday Ballroom, playing every Friday night. Dan Belloc, the owner/big-band leader, was thinking the same way," he said. I think it's cool that this young Buckingham had his head on straight. During our interview, I was reminded how much he respected (if not worshipped) guys like Dan with an accomplished musical history.

"Dan Belloc wrote a pretty big musical hit called Pretend that was sung by Nat King Cole," Carl said. I looked it up later and saw that Lew Douglas also was listed as co-writer. This time, I didn't want to break the thought pattern. After all, Carl was generous enough to sit down for this interview.

"The Buckinghams wanted more. We didn't want to be thought of as just a 'cover' band. We wanted to record some original material. That's when Dan Belloc and you negotiated with Howard Bedno and we got four tracks recorded: **I'll Go Crazy**, **I Call Your Name**, **I've Been Wrong** (https://youtu.be/voob_RhagFM) which the Hollies released, and **Kind of a Drag**. As a cover band, we were doing everything from the Beatles to James Brown," he continued. Yeah, getting a studio to record songs is one thing, but getting a record company to release them was another.

Oh, another thing: "There was a group that you wanted us to listen to. We would finish our gigs and find where [the group] the Big Thing was playing," Carl said. I think I can weave this all together, if you hang with me.

Recording Kind of a Drag

The Buckinghams were the first Caucasian group from Chicago to record at Chess Records in its 2120 S. Michigan Avenue studio on the near-south side. I will emphasize "from Chicago." Other groups discovered the richness and depth of blues and soul before their American counterparts, like the Beatles, and one led by Mick Jagger (age 23 at the time). It was hard for all of us to get down to business when the Rolling Stones slid out of their session right before us.

We were in the midst of rock royalty in the once-prominent Prairie Avenue residential district, dotted with decaying mansions in various stages of disrepair. Most current residents had given up hope of meaningful employment. This was likely the Buckinghams' first excursion to "the other half" of Chicago. Getting a Chess recording session and having master engineer Ron Malo mixing it together was a privilege. There was educational value in the trip as well.

Creating the Chi-Town Sound

Chi-Town Records just happens to be the name of my own record label. You want to make somethin' out of it? Okay, the point of this segment was how many things aligned in order to create a classic springboard for the Buckinghams. Some folks credit me with adding the horns to the intro of **Kind of a Drag**. Well, you can't have the idea without virtuosos who can play and arrange them. Remember, the Holiday Ballroom had just that. It generously opened its doors to teens out of respect for music. Thank goodness, some rock groups had the good sense to respect and appreciate it.

"Dan Belloc had a trombone player named Frank Tesinsky who arranged the **Kind of a Drag** horn track after listening to the vocals and music. It featured a trombone, go figure," my guest of honor said. Carl Giammarese is both a musician and a magician on his own recordings. He reminded us the term for enhancing tracks is called "sweetening." It had been going on in the ballroom era since the dawn of recorded music. In the rock-and-roll era, sweetening created a bold and brassy sound that attracted both audiences and record companies.

With **Kind of a Drag**, we had all of the necessary components for a hit record. The original lyrics by James Holvay were sung in a slower tempo. I held a tape recorder mic in front of him so the Buckinghams could hear it for the first time. As mentioned, the original vocal and musical tracks were recorded at the Chess Records studios. The original orchestral tracks came from Frank Tesinsky (who also played on Woody Herman pieces). The final mixed recording came courtesy of legendary engineer Ron Malo. At my suggestion (at least I'll take the blame, if not the credit), we wanted to slightly increase the tempo of the final release.

"One fascinating facet of Ron Malo's work was his ability to increase the tempo of the songs on a reel tape without changing the key. Ron managed to do it on **Kind of a Drag**. Miraculously, it was still in the key of G. Maybe he regularly did it for R&B songs," Carl said. Well it was new to us, and it was working. There was nothing left to keep this song from becoming a nation-wide hit. Well …

Releasing Kind of a Drag

Imagine the excitement for all of us responsible for producing **Kind of a Drag**. Maybe this wasn't our record after all since the record label had the final word. Let's say the owner of the record label had the final say. He didn't consider the artists whose blood, sweat, and tears were in this song. More on that later. In-stead, he listened to the promoters and disc jockeys (actually, the radio stations) who stood to profit from its release and distribution. https://youtu.be/B9bjHw6BOBk

There was this "timing" thing that record labels needed to fret over. My job was to look at it from the performer's side and persuade, remind, and fight for the Buckinghams. There was growing frustration with U.S.A. Records just sitting on it. At dances, folks were constantly raving about it.

"You always hear about the 'garage band' era. Where we come from, all of us were basement bands," Carl G. said. Maybe the really awful musicians were ban-ished to the garage. Remember, most of those old-fashioned garages were not connected to the house and had no heat.

"We practiced a lot at my house until my folks got tired of hearing us and then either Dennis's or Nick's folks would step in. The Tufano and Giammarese families would never tire of hearing that song. My mom always loved it and knew it was special. We practiced it all of the time and played it live. Everybody loved it. It was too expensive to do that intro at our live performances before that song became a hit. After it went to the top of the charts, we still didn't add horns. That was a mistake. We don't make that mistake anymore," he continued.

"What provided the breakthrough as far as getting airplay?" I asked.

According to Carl Giammarese, the horns were one of the deciding factors.

"In that day, AM radio was everything and program directors would get hundreds of records to review. Only a handful could ever make it into the playlist. If the intro didn't grab their attention in the first few seconds, it would literally be sailing toward the rejection pile," he said. For some of the records, that was the only perverse entertainment the vinyl discs would ever provide. I bet many great songs had a slow intro or just caught the "main man" on the wrong day.

"Even today, I hear from past program directors and they still say they loved that intro," Carl continued. I couldn't contain myself here: Clark Weber insisted that the **Kind of a Drag** intro was too loud. Once the rest of the world embraced the song, WLS eventually had to give Chicagoland what it wanted.

"Overall, WLS was very supportive of local groups and did their best to give worthy songs regular play. Years later, Paul Shaffer [David Letterman Show] would tell me that he could get the WLS signal in Thunder Bay [Ontario, Canada]," Carl said.

We finally got Jim Golden and Howard Bedno to release the record. I think the most favorable results came from Arkansas and Boston. Not everybody was on board yet, though. John Poulos and I did a road trip to Los Angeles, where Chicago legend Dick Biondi had been temporarily banished, to get it played out west.

"We would buy the latest copy of *Billboard Magazine* and scan the Bubbling Under section," Carl told me. Our efforts would eventually produce the best result possible. Well, some people got paid, and others got "schooled." In any case, it was all worth it. The fact that we are still talking about it now is payment itself, sort of.

Adios, U.S.A. Records

As Kind of a Drag surged up the charts, it was time to take another serious look at the future. While we were at it, we needed to look at the past. Did we have the time and energy required to produce a second hit, given the waiting game we played with Kind of a Drag? The current U.S.A. contract was complete. There were many things I could have done better. First would be getting Buckingham parents' signatures on U.S.A. paperwork. At the time, it didn't matter since all parties fulfilled their obligations. At least the legal ones.

There were some flaws in my plan to move forward, and they were apparent to everyone. The Buckinghams were still below the legal contract age, and each needed to sign another agreement. There were conflicting opinions on how popular **Kind of a Drag** was. This translated into how much the performers were going to be paid. Somehow, the song surged to the No. 1 position without selling a million units if we were going to believe the U.S.A. bean-counters.

"**Kind of a Drag** paid us $8,000 apiece," Carl said, providing the objective accounting on this one. If we use 1970 dollars, adjusted for inflation, it's about $50K or so. Really, though, it was not about the money, but more about evaluating the best offer available for the next contract. U.S.A. Records was not measuring up. Maybe I didn't see it all then. The best offer I could pull together was not going to be good enough in the long run.

Bottom line: the Buckinghams had the No. 1 song in the nation and no record contract. Other record companies and agents would be eager to represent them if they wanted to make a jump. You know where this is going.

Breaking Away

The Buckinghams needed to make a decision on the best way to move forward. I can't remember when the term "one-hit wonder" was first used. My (for now) young Chicago band had no intention of spending any time on the sidelines. The decision weighed on everyone, as Carl reminded me.

"I hardly ate or slept for a week. My dad kept reminding me about that 'loyalty' thing, as only a Sicilian could. I was only one-fifth of the band," he said. The guys had a few things to consider. The U.S.A. Records and Carl Bonafede team produced notable results, but was that good enough?

"U.S.A. did not 'work' the record enough," Carl explained. We have the kind of relationship that lets us be honest.

"A No. 1 record should have, at least, earned a spot on Dick Clark's *American Bandstand*. There were no teen magazine stories," he continued. They thought that Willard Alexander (or Herb Gronauer and I) wasn't planning to do anything different either. A guy named James William Guercio had been hired at Columbia Records as a producer. Some time earlier, I talked to him about working together on a project or two, but we could never reach an agreement.

Guercio was associated with the big Columbia label, and legendary Clive Davis was at the helm. The potential to take the group to new heights would be far greater with a new manager. The Buckinghams made a decision to go with Guercio. Eventually, I would agree with

My plaque showing Kind of a Drag at the Top Spot on the Billboard Chart the group's decisions. At that time, however, I had to grapple with the indignities of being fired. Guercio offered me a cash interest in the future success of the Buckinghams. I just didn't like the way he approached me. I had my pride if nothing else.

Thankfully, I did have more than just my pride. I had the Daughters of Eve that was destined to leave an indelible mark on its fans, myself included. I continued to follow the success of the Buckinghams with a combination of sadness and admiration (maybe a little envy, too).

National Recognition Continues

The Buckinghams and I accomplished so much together. I wouldn't let my feelings for Guercio dampen my hopes for the band's success; however, I did have to watch from a cautious distance back then.

"Even with you sitting right next to me, I have to say that going with Guercio was a good move for the Buckinghams," Carl started. I appreciate his honesty, and he made a number of good points.

"The William Morris Agency took over, and we were marketed far better. Things were happening really fast. That first year, we played close to 300 dates. Columbia had distribution hubs nationwide. They would meet the artists in limousines and take them directly to radio stations for live interviews," he continued. Yeah, I could see why the Buckinghams would think that was better.

As far as the "limo" thing, record companies were actually spending the artists' money. In the long run, the Buckinghams were paying for their own ride. Sorry, I'm just ranting out of jealousy. We got sidetracked a little and our conversation temporarily shifted to a lineup change for the Buckinghams.

"Miccolis no longer fit, and you suggested Larry Nestor as a substitute. That lasted for about a month. The only contribution that he made was introducing us to [let's just say bad habits]," Carl said. We weren't talking about music then, I'm sure.

"We found Marty Grebb from the Exceptions, a far more musically sophisticated group. Peter Cetera [later in the group Chicago] was their bass player at that time," he continued. Musically, the Buckinghams were as strong as ever. The band's decision to change labels (and managers) did not sit very well with many DJs and promoters, however. For some reason, many of them were angrier and felt more insulted than I did. Howard Bedno was far from happy. (Gary) Ebbins-Guercio Associates was actually the management company, and it was attracting a lot of attention.

Back in Chicago, DJs and program managers were threatening to boycott the Buckinghams songs. This wasn't in the interest of good business. We couldn't understand the reason for it. Was Guercio somehow viewed as an outsider? Was his partnership with Ebbins, who clearly had no ties to the Buckinghams before that, a distraction? Did the media and promotional "hierarchy" in Chicago feel betrayed by the Buckinghams? **Don't You Care** was the first single by the Buckinghams released on the Columbia label. Kind of takes new meaning, huh?

The Chicago media was the last to respond to the Buckinghams' sure-fire hit. The rest of the nation responded appropriately. True fans of the Buckinghams (and of music) never wavered. Obstinate Chicago jocks and promoters were eventually compelled to be sensible.

"**Don't You Care** became too big of a hit for anyone to ignore. It ended up at No. 6 on both the Billboard and Cashbox charts. We tried to keep our relationship, but you and Guercio couldn't push past your differences," Carl explained. Who? Me?

A Most Successful Run

A continued relationship with the Buckinghams would have been distracting and stressful at this point. Besides, my work with the Daughters of Eve was going to take a good deal of my time and energy. As it turned out, the Buckinghams were right to pursue another offer. Was their path the best one possible (you know, with Columbia, really Ebbins-Guercio)? As much as I would never have admitted it at the time, yeah, it was. You can't dispute the results.

"Shortly after we released Don't You Care, the Ebbins and Guercio team broke up. They asked the Buckinghams to choose between them. Ultimately, the Buckinghams chose Guercio because he was the music man. Ebbins was (at one time) the manager for actor Anthony Quinn," Carl expressed. Musically, it seemed that my "rival" was shaking things up with the Buckinghams, as Carl explained.

"Guercio had us mimic the Johnny 'Guitar' Watson version of **Mercy, Mercy, Mercy**, and the song ultimately went to No. 5, making it our most successful record next to **Kind of a Drag**. He reached out to James Holvay for two more other songs. **Hey Baby, They're Playing Our Song**, and **Susan**," Carl said. Both singles just barely missed the Billboard Top 10.

Television appearances were also piling up for the group. The Smothers Brothers, Jerry Lewis, and Joey Bishop shows were a few we discussed. Yeah, the Buckinghams also finally got appearances on *American Bandstand* and the *Ed Sullivan Show*. Now, I'm the one wondering why it took so long for the *Ed Sullivan Show* (the most sought-after spot in the entertainment world) to come calling. The Buckinghams performed **Susan** on the Sullivan show in 1968. The music world was ready for more things "Buckingham."

The decidedly ugly business side of the Buckinghams brand became a problem. Relationships affected profits, and trust affected relationships. Profits also affected relationships and trust. Hit records can create a good deal of wealth for authors and publishers of music. Managers and promoters profit much less so. Artists profit the least. I would rather write a hit than sing one.

If a manager or artist wanted to markedly boost his or her profits, getting credit as an author of even a marginal recording could help you score high on the profit side of the ledger. For some, that was the only side that counted. The relationship between the Buckinghams and Guercio lasted only 18 months or so. I'm not going to say that I know why.

He closely aligned himself with a couple of other famous groups. Both of them (Blood, Sweat and Tears / Chicago) had pretty intense horn intros in their signature songs. Columbia tried to find a substitute producer for the Buckinghams, but nothing seemed to work after that. There were other factors that contributed to the band's (50 years and counting) history. I'm grateful that Carl was willing to fill in a few gaps in this part of the story.

"On the *Mercy, Mercy, Mercy* album, there is a song called **It's a Beautiful Day**. I think it was the best thing we ever did. It was written by John Turner, our keyboard player at the time," Carl said. I regret not asking him which song meant the most to him.

Sustainability

There are so many things that have to be in place, and stay in place, to sustain a career in the music business. Producers, promoters, radio stations, and studios were in a constant cycle of re-invention in the late '60s, just as they are now. So many things happened "for" the Buckinghams to get the band where it is now. Once the members had a chance to look around, they could see how many things were also happening "to" them. Carl gave me some perspective on the factors that caused the breakup of the Buckinghams.

"Columbia could not find a producer who was a good fit for us. They were just no longer paying attention. With the advent of FM radio, more diverse acts were emerging. Since the Monterey Pop Festival in June 1967, the listening audience craved acts like Janis Joplin and Jimi Hendrix. Clive Davis was signing these types of acts. Groups like the Beach Boys, the Turtles, and the Buckinghams were becoming far less of a factor," Carl explained. In ultra-commercial AM radio, songs could be dismissed for being too long. They could also be discounted for being too controversial. In my opinion, AM radio wanted only proven hits.

Maybe the Top-40 format was beginning to keep new acts out of the market because the management was too conservative. Soon counter-culture became the new culture. This was also at the height of the Vietnam conflict (war). The folks at AM radio were still getting their way, sort of. They were now playing only commercially proven hits. They just couldn't be counted on to present new acts to the marketplace. Call it what you like, album, extended play, or theme music was created for the FM band. It really pains me to say this, after all of these years, but I couldn't picture the Buckinghams as a counter-culture or pro-test group. Neither did Columbia, I guess.

I'm not dismissing the talent and dedication of the Buckinghams, of course. Both individually and collectively, I would kill (well, not literally) for the op-portunity to collaborate with them anytime. Actually, I did. More on this later. Carl Giammarese and Dennis Tufano, actually all of "my" guys, were far from being through, thank goodness.

"Lou Adler was the founder of Dunhill Records. He took an interest in the Giammarese / Tufano singing and songwriting duo on his new Ode Records label. Even though he was so successful, he was one laid-back kind of guy," Carl said.

Lou Adler was one of the producers of the Monterey International Pop Festival. He had a good sense of how to marry the '60s and '70s. I think he found it easier to signify his "transformation" by selling Dunhill Records and founding Ode. He ob-viously thought highly of the former Buckinghams, given the talent he assembled.

"Carole King (*Tapestry*) as well as Cheech and Chong were on that label. John Poulos was our manager. Unfortunately, we did a lot of covers and were unable to write hits. In those days, I also wrote and sang around 300 commer-cial jingles to keep the creative juices flowing," he continued. Thanks, Carl, for keeping the "feeling" alive.

I mentioned the recently departed (2014) Mayor Jane Byrne a few times in my book. Her predecessor was actually responsible for the first Chicagofest the year before she took office in April 1979. It was held at Navy Pier and it lasted a full two weeks. As you might imagine, there was a call for hundreds of acts by me-dia sponsors. There were several live broadcasts from blues, jazz, comedy, rock, country, and classic rock stages.

One admission ticket, which couldn't have been more than a few bucks at that time, got you a choice of entertainment for the entire day. The main stage seating approached 30,000. This was similar to the annual audience size of the Vogue, Embassy, and Holiday ballrooms, compressed into one narrow slice of mid-summer fun.

Bands that were emerging, reuniting, or currently at the pinnacle of popu-larity would all be playing somewhere. Radio stations and sponsors were dying to present a new lineup. The new mayoral administration was keenly aware of opportunities to make Chicagofest a world-class event. I couldn't say who planted the idea for a Buckinghams revival, but Carl Giammarese was ready to relate his experience.

"John Gehron was the program director at WLS at that time. He asked me if the band would consider a reunion at Chicagofest. Nick and Dennis were on board. Marty was playing with [the group] Chicago at the time," Carl said. The city was more than ready to hear their favorite Buckinghams hits performed live once again.

"Twelve thousand fans packed the roof stage, and the response was tremendous," Carl told me. This was the start of something good. I was working as an armed security officer at that time and was lucky enough to get a gig at Chicagofest. There I was, in full uniform, protecting the Buckinghams in a new way.

"Everyone in the band kind of saw Carl Bonafede at the same time, *with a gun!*" Carl recalled. From that glint in his eye, I could tell he was having a little more fun with me. Of course, I would never have considered shooting one of my beloved Buckinghams, or (nearly) anyone else. Just kidding. I want you to consider me as a person of high caliber. Sorry, I couldn't resist.

The Buckinghams were reunited. Original members Giammarese, Tufano, and Fortuna were igniting crowds with the same music that used to bring people to their feet at the Holiday Ballroom. During our interview, I reminded Carl that both he and Nick Fortuna met future brides there, too. Their relationship with me was somewhat longer, but of course, not more meaningful.

Sometime during the resurgence of the Buckinghams, Dennis Tufano left the group for the last time.

"Dennis told me that he didn't want to be a Buckingham anymore," Carl told me. He headed for LA, for reasons we could only guess. Carl went on to put things into perspective. I'm starting to think it would take a few, or more, decades to understand what happened and why. So, Dennis left, 50 years after we created a brand called the Buckinghams.

"One of the good things Guercio did was to not put emphasis on individual members of the group. The public wanted to hear the music, and the lead singer was not as important as the sound and the feelings of the audience. When '60s nostalgia started heating up, we were able to re-record the hits and perform them live. Now, the Buckinghams perform maybe 40 dates in off years and 75 or so at best," Carl said. Everybody is getting along as well as we always hoped. Tufano is also singing Buckinghams hits on his own, and the rest of the band is finding a way to coexist amicably.

"Dennis is doing guest appearances at musical venues and performs a few songs. The Buckinghams are doing a full 90-minute show. We invited Dennis to perform at one of our shows, a benefit for the ailing Marty Grebb at the

Arcada Theater [in St. Charles, Illinois]. He also joined us at our WTTW performance due to air soon," Carl mentioned. This was a wild lineup, with the Cryan' Shames, New Colony Six, Shadows of Knight, American Breed, and the McCoys.

Finally, we discussed the impact of modern technology on the music industry. It seems there are so many ways to distribute music without compensation for the artists. I'm only guessing, but listening to the Buckingham hits on YouTube (with a big thanks to Joe Pytel for keeping all of "our" music in circulation) may lead to an increase in demand for more live performances.

We also talked about abuses of the digital podium. Online pundits and self-proclaimed voices of the public think it's their duty to attack some of our best memory makers. Of course, they are poor examples of journalists (not to mention human beings). I hope that you will find my few pages accurate and uplifting. Most of all, they are truthful. If there are any inaccuracies, they are certainly unintentional.

Carl did mention one of his antagonists by name. Lots of people know his name and reputation. I won't dignify him by scribbling his name here.

Finally, Again

I'm proud to say the "two Carls" worked together in 2015. Giammarese recorded my latest CD *57 Years and Still Going*. It's a collection of classic hits, like **Lydia the Tattooed Lady** (the Groucho Marx song) and **Sara Lee**, one that Carl had never heard before. We even did a mini-tour together. It was a one-night-only appearance on Dave Hoekstra's WGN 720 Nocturnal Journal radio show on February 22, 2015. Search for Hoekstra-Bonafede-Giammarese for a link to the show.

Forward to the 41:30 mark and catch a great acoustic version of **Don't You Care** by one of the founding members of the Buckinghams. At 48:00, you will hear

my rendition of **Things**. You will also hear **Made in the USA** by the Rail City Five, coming in at 52:30 minutes. I can't stop promoting. I'm telling you, we pulled off a pretty great interview with Hoekstra that's well worth your time. When was the last time you thought about the Lincoln Park Zoo (I mean the musical group) besides in this book, of course? Since that interview, I'm thinking about

Yours Truly and Carl Giammarese

them all the time. Maybe I should have included this segment at the very beginning of this chapter to save you some reading.

During that 20-minute interview, we touched on many subjects relat-
ing to my 57 years in music. Carl got a chance to mention the *FlashBack*
(Buckinghams hits) album released in 2015. I included a link to the iTunes
store here for you: https://itunes.apple.com/us/album/flashback-2014/id883662258. See, I
am still promoting, even though you might think that I hate technology.
All of my groups deserve audiences from all generations.

We wrapped up the Hoekstra interview with my rendition of **Countin'
My Money** written by Larry Nestor. You may remember he did a brief stint with
the Buckinghams.

I think Hoekstra put us last in his show lineup because of my reputation for
commanding an audience. You know what I'm sayin'?

I enjoy and appreciate this crazy time, now that the Buckinghams and I commu-
nicate more regularly. This book thing has me thinking about and doing things
I never dreamed of doing. We concluded our interview with a picture of Carl
and me. Notice that I am wearing "the suit" that Dick Biondi referred to in his
interview—just one more thing that we briefly discussed.

I'm claiming the Buckinghams was responsible for creating what I call the
Chi-town sound—you know, that horn intro that Dan Belloc and his orchestra
developed for **Kind of a Drag**. I'm not saying other groups imitated it. Let's just say
the Buckinghams inspired other groups to incorporate some heavy brass in their
recordings. Remember earlier we talked about one of the favorite groups of the
Buckinghams named the Big Thing? They evolved into Chicago. The sound of
the two groups suggests a certain something.

There is common ground, if not a clear path back, to Dan Belloc and other guys with "orchestral" experience. They were the true pioneers when it came
to taking bands from the garage to the main stage. To me, the best example of
that influence is the incredible intro to **Vehicle** by Jim Peterik and the Ides of
March. C'mon, you know it.

Dennis Tufano

I hoped to get a live interview with the original lead singer on every Buckinghams hit. Dennis Tufano was performing at the WGN TV studios on the
Midday Fix http://wgntv.com/2016/03/09/midday-fix-dennis-tufano-performs-live/# program to
promote his performance for the benefit of the Taft High School art and music
department on March 12, 2016. Check out the link because there is a lot
more information about the history of Taft High School.

For example, it was the alma mater of Terry Kath, who played with Jimmy Ford and the Executives and then later with the Missing Links. He was most famously known as the "bandleader" of the Chicago Transit Authority, later shortened to just Chicago. There were some deep DePaul University roots there as well. As you may have read, I still live in the heart of the DePaul neighborhood, or the University lives in mine. Take your pick.

In this book, we talked a lot about the great ballroom and teen-club music venues. Just as important (probably more important) were the Chicago Public School performing arts programs throughout the city. Of course, academics were at the heart of the program for lots of folks – maybe not me (definitely not me)—including many athletes and musicians.

During the 1960s, teens were virtually immersed in music. At Taft, as well as at every public school, you could learn by day and practice music every afternoon and evening. I guess that was true in some Catholic schools, too. Dennis Tufano was an alum of Gordon Tech (as it was named at the time). I guess you could call that the Addison Street connection. The WGN studios were right there, too.

Ral Donner, the singer with the voice like Elvis, was only a couple of years younger than me and started his freshman year at Taft High School in 1956, as I can remember. That was the same year Elvis released **Heartbreak Hotel**. Ral made his rock-and-roll debut at a Taft High School dance that same year.

I guess I could start just about anywhere and connect to practically anyone else in this book. Right now, we're looping all of my recollections through William Howard Taft High School. In fact, two of my closest friends and business partners taught at Taft. One was Dan Belloc, from the Billy May Orchestra and owner of the Holiday Ballroom. Frank Pisani, a consummate entertainer, was the other.

Anyone lucky enough to spend time with either of these two guys learned business, critical thinking, and improvisation along with their special "sharps and flats" exercises. No matter what type of work you intended to do in life, high school years often provided the soundtrack.

Speaking of soundtracks, you are going to love this, I promise. Taft alum Jim Jacobs collaborated on a play named *Grease* about high school students during the rock-and-roll era that I remember best. The movie set for the mythical Rydell High was Venice High on the west side of Los Angeles, but I'm convinced the inspiration was, of course, Chicago's Taft High School on the northwest side of Chi-town. Jacobs' collaborator was a guy named Warren Casey from the Chicago Playwrights Center. I think Casey also had some Second City improvisational training, but don't hold me to it.

Let me think. Who do I know to best connect a world-famous musical play and movie back to Taft High? That would be Dennis Tufano! Earlier, we talked about the internal factors that split the Buckinghams apart. I certainly didn't want to waste the precious time I had with Dennis in our telephone interview, so we picked up after the time that Marty Grebb and Nick Fortuna drifted away and Carl Giammarese and Tufano formally ended things.

> **Dennis Tufano—**
> Carl, you were essential to our success. You pretty much discovered us, promoted us, helped us get our stuff together, and carried the torch for us all the way. You gave us our start and found the way to keep us out there.

"I did a little acting and had some small TV parts in LA. Even after we revived the Buckinghams in Chicagofest, I was still focusing on my solo career," Dennis reminded me. That's how he once again found his way back to LA.

"I co-wrote and performed (with singer Mindy Sterling) the original title and first season theme song for the *Family Ties* television show. I joined Olivia Newton-John on tour to sing a couple of duets with her," he continued. I included a link to a live performance of **You're the One That I Want** from *Grease* here: https://youtu.be/LO8rQ9WpeCM.

We discussed how fans are sometimes confused about Dennis's ties with the Buckinghams. Though he is no longer a part of the "official" group, his audience enjoys the music and the memories from the time they broke big.

The Tufano Show at Taft featured songs from three different phases of his career. We heard the tribute to Bobby Darin and tunes from the *Grease* songbook. Most dear to my heart was the career-launching and show-stopping rendition of the Buckinghams' **Kind of a Drag**.

I'm proud of the small part I played in the varied career of a talented guy like Dennis Tufano. He, likewise, has influenced many people during his theatrical, film, commercial, radio, television, and recording projects.

At the risk of my eyes completely puddling up, I have to acknowledge Dennis's call out to me from the stage at the Taft High benefit concert.

"Carl, if it weren't for you, I wouldn't be up here right now. God bless you, my friend!" he said. I would be lying if I didn't tell you how touched I was by the response of the crowd. If you check out the Dennis Tufano Facebook page, you'll see a picture of Dick Biondi and yours truly at the concert as well. Good times.

> **Nick Fortuna—**
> Out of all of the people who have worked with the Buckinghams, Carl Bonafede was the hardest worker. He put more time, energy, and more of himself into making the Buckinghams what we were and what we are.

Dennis Miccolis

This book is full of memories and apologies, as you most likely know. I mentioned the Buckinghams' original keyboard player earlier and posted his YouTube link. I'm sure every member of the group could write his own book (but not until all of them stop making music—perhaps never).

Dennis suggested I include a photo of the defining album cover with that pose in front of Buckingham Fountain. If you remember, I would never pass up a bargain (nor will I now). I included a different link (https://youtu.be/1FlqSenFxEc) to that signature song showing a multitude of Buckinghams photos. I saved myself a couple of pages and you a couple of pennies.

Dennis Miccolis—
Carl, I remember driving with you after our performance at Comiskey Park with the Beatles (43,000 screaming fans and probably our biggest audience ever). You had a red-plastic toy phone sitting on your console, and you told us it was functional. All of a sudden you picked up the phone and started talking into it. We all laughed about that for a long time.

You used to call me Mickey so that, when you were talking to Dennis, we all knew you meant Tufano and wouldn't get us confused. I gave two weeks' notice and left the band after I got my 1A draft card.

I later became a Chicago cop. I really wanted to play jazz, so Carl was correct when saying I no longer fit. I worked in law enforcement, but music has always been my first love. I still wish the remaining original Buckinghams members—Dennis, Carl, Nick and I—could get together for a reunion show in Chicago.

Pat DeLuca with good friend Susan Rakis (road manger of the Buckinghams)

Pre-Concert Get-Togethers
Carl Giammarese, Yours Truly, Nick Fortuna, from the Buckinghams, along with good friends Pat DeLuca, Editor Joel Bierig

Ides of March and Survivor Singer/Songwriter Jim Peterik

John Poulos and George LeGros

It's easy to get caught up in the moment and forget major contributors to my life (aside from the book project). Let it continue to be known – there would never have been a Buckinghams without drummer John Poulos. He personally recruited Dennis Tufano and George LeGros as the dual lead singers for the Pulsations.

He and I had a deeper relationship because we often talked business in addition to music. John matched my commitment to the Buckinghams and deserves the largest share of credit for assembling the band. I wish there truly were "rock gods" I could blame for the breakup of the Buckinghams.

Even more so, I wish there was someone to blame for John missing the Buckinghams' reunion concert at Chicagofest 1980. From the day I learned of his passing just shy of age 33 in the spring of that year, each day since is tinged with sadness. That becomes a genuine tug each time I see the Buckinghams on stage.

I'm including a YouTube link to **I Should Have Known Better** https://youtu.be/CDQ_L80-V8o, performed by the Buckinghams on Sheldon Cooper's *All Time Hits* show that aired on WGN-TV. The song title says a lot.

As you read earlier, George LeGros left for military duty just as the Buckinghams were poised to break into the big time. It was easy to get caught up in those unbelievable good times.

But, during every performance, George's absence was far more than just "a drag" for the band and for me. It doesn't get any easier as time goes on.

George played in several bands throughout the years. He is among the many guys I didn't keep close tabs on, much to my regret. Sadly, I missed my final chance much earlier than anyone expected.

"Vintage" George LeGros

Time gets away from us all. I relived the shock and sadness of George's passing at age 56. Could it really have been 15 years ago already? He was one of the founding members of the Buckinghams. His talent–and especially–his sacrifices, make him a significant contributor to my story.

Footnotes

I included a couple of links to the Missing Links. True to their promise, the Missing Links provided additional (no longer missing) links to the reasons why Tufano and I are once again sharing time together.

Even someone like Guercio has helped us bond together, for reasons that we've already mentioned. If that's what it took to once again put us under the same roof, so be it. I'd much rather think that it was Ron Malo (Chess), James Holvay (songwriter of **Kind of a Drag**), or the dozens of other folks mentioned in this chapter. Thanks for hangin' in for the last 50-sumthin' years.

Missing Links overview: http://www.60sgaragebands.com/missinglinks.html

Missing Links story https://youtu.be/Oo45vPfUiao

Appendix - U.S.A. Records

There is a lot of information out there … if you know where to look and what to look for. Here's all of the stuff I did for and with the Buckinghams on the U.S.A. label (http://www.globaldogproductions.info/u/usa.html). Man, you just go to the link and search. Actually, once you are on the web page, you can just hit Ctrl+F to find the term you are looking for. This is so cool. Here's the history of the Buckinghams at its original label in printed format.

U.S.A. Records presents the Buckinghams

844   The Buckinghams
        I'll Go Crazy / I Don't Wanna Cry – 1966
848   The Buckinghams
        I Call Your Name / Makin' Up and Breakin' Up – 1966
853   The Buckinghams
        I've Been Wrong / Love Ain't Enough – 1966

860   The Buckinghams
        Kind of a Drag / You Make Me Feel So Good – 1966
869   The Buckinghams
        Lawdy Miss Clawdy / I Call Your Name – 1967
873   The Buckinghams
        Summertime https://youtu.be/MgMNQv6UwY8 /
        Don't Want To Cry – 1967

Personal Manager
CARL BONAFEDE   THE BUCKINGHAMS   W/a   WILLARD ALEXANDER INC.
                                         New York · Chicago · Atlanta
                                         Beverly Hills · London

The Daughters of Eve

I put off writing this chapter until nearly every other one was finished. I'm glad I waited. For what it's worth, I'm a slightly better writer than I was at the beginning. My real reason, as you probably already guessed, was my fear these memories would really weigh on me. In the following pages, you'll find my fondness for the Daughters of Eve has increased. My sadness still lingers between the lines.

I found myself organizing the chapters of the book as "before or after" the Daughters of Eve. I'm going to refer to the band as DoE at times. I write better, but my typing is still awful. A doe is defined as the female version of many species. Musicians are unique species. The coolest musicians and singers are DoEs.

The Daughters of Eve defined my entire career in many ways. Thank you.

With the Buckinghams on solid ground (talent, popularity, and unlimited potential), I started to give serious thought to creating an all-girl band. I saw the them as the perfect complement to the male talent that I booked at my events.

Did you notice I said girl *band* and not group? I wanted seasoned performers who could hold their own musically. They would also need the female version of the Everly Brothers' vocal blends. I had to be sure they wouldn't melt in front of an audience or freeze in the recording studio. They would also need to routinely leave a crowd shaking their heads in amazement.

Oh yeah, they would be kids the same age as their audience. Maybe we didn't talk about it anywhere until now. Chemistry is a really important factor in forming a new band. I guessed (and hoped) auditions would also uncover other potential band members. At the risk of spoiling my own chapter, I got my wish.

I planned to get national recognition for this monster group and wanted folks talking, buying records, and requesting (if not demanding) more.

This was far more than a dream: It was a plan that I could deliver. Remember, I worked for the Willard Alexander booking agency at the time. There were dozens of dances, teen clubs, and ballrooms in the Chicago area alone. Let's call it the Tri-State area. Wisconsin and Indiana were less than an hour from the Screaming Wildman headquarters.

My super group would wow the crowd on Friday and Saturday nights and be back sleeping in their own beds at a reasonable hour, at least for musicians. Their parents wouldn't need to worry any more than usual. I knew the market. I just needed to assemble a group that would thrill the audience.

In the Beginning ...

I'll get to the Bible-like reference in this chapter later. The word "audition" sounds intimidating—because it is. I'd been performing since age four or so. I knew the pressure and ways to overcome it. I was looking for people who could handle an audition and look (and actually start to feel) the way an audience expected.

I didn't have a formal office (with a secretary I would have to pay). Kids and parents would need to lug instruments and set up. I didn't have the patience or time (still don't). I'd rather check out a band already in action. I could evaluate the members' talent and the way they moved an audience. Since I was building a band from the bottom up, I would hit the road to find musicians where they practiced. The ideal time would be right after school.

Back then, most kids were under the watchful eye of a responsible adult, usually mom. I was being auditioned at the same time. I was always professional and courteous when conducting professional business. That still meant I wouldn't hesitate to use the Bonafede charm when needed. If her momma says no ... daughter won't go!

Taft High School is on the far northwest side of Chicago near Bryn Mawr and Harlem in the Norwood Park neighborhood. At my dances, I announced the start of auditions for an all-girl band. I knew how fast the news would travel. I was getting hundreds of kids at dances every night. I figured a lot of "hopefuls" would get in touch.

My ideal choices would already be in a band of some sort. Marsha Tomal and Judy Johnson were already singing with a group. I drove to Marsha's house, where her band practiced, to see how the band played and sounded.

They were both practiced musicians and sounded unbelievable together. Judy sang in a higher range and Marsha's voice was the perfect complement. I was already anxious to get them both into a recording studio. Before too long, I would introduce them to the rest of the world. Yes, I said world. I'm just as excited now as I was then. I'm going to finish my introduction and turn things over to some of the original bandmates to fill in more details.

Debi Pomeroy was only 15 years old, and Marsha (the on-stage spokesperson for the group) was maybe a year older, just like Judy Johnson. Andee Levin was the most "tender" teenager in the group. She was barely 14 when we started playing serious gigs. By my recollection, we thrilled the audience in nearly 35 states. Many people thought the group was merely a novelty act until the girls brought fans and skeptics to their feet.

We were fortunate to live at a time when there was tremendous investment (both time and money) in young people. We went from teen clubs to ball-rooms, from high schools to civic arenas, and from drive-in theaters to military installations. I, like nearly every member of the audience, cherished the time we spent together.

On the practical side, we needed to release a 45 rpm record, and it was up to me to "lobby" (another technique I mastered before it was reserved for political reasons) disc jockeys to get us a fair amount of airplay. Part of the problem was the DJs at first dismissed the Daughters of Eve as a gimmick. Once they saw the effect that the four rockin' teenagers had on an audience, the DJs became fans.

Fortunately, there were a number of personalities I could count on to tell it like it was. Folks like Ron Riley and Joel Sebastian, to name a couple, were able to get an audience moving at dances and listening during their shows.

Debi Pomeroy

I'm so glad this book gave me the chance to renew acquaintances. I was able to get Debi's thoughts down on paper a while back. You know how hard it can be when your relationship started with an impressionable and fragile kid on the one hand and a manic, though well-intentioned, older brother type on the other.

I can finally let some of the actual members tell their story in their own words. Of course, I get the chance to step in once in a while. You know what I'm sayin'? I didn't know, or remember, that Debi was never at any of my dances. I knew her older brother, Dustin, played rhythm guitar in a band called the Dirty Wurds—you know, the kind of name that a minister's son can be proud of. Debi was playing guitar in her boyfriend's band, the LA (Loyola Academy) Classmen. The band members liked her so well that they renamed themselves "Debi and the LA Classmen." If someone wanted to think the "LA" in a surf band stood for Los Angeles, they were welcome.

Debi was also organizing her own folk-type band with a girl named Andee Levin. Now the curtain rises for the next scene. What is this, a screenplay?

"A guy named John Damascus saw me play drums in our basement where my brother's band stored their equipment. I told him I never played along with other musicians. He told me to just watch him to see how it was done. He was a friend of Marsha Tomal from Taft High School. John came up to me between our classes at Senn and asked if I wanted to audition as a drummer for a new girl band," Debi reminded me. I learned there's a Catholic saint named John Damascus who made contributions to the world of music. Now, you know, too.

"Around 2002, I remembered everything when I did a Daughters of Eve interview for Spectropop (http://www.spectropop.com/DaughtersOfEve/). At the 50-year mark, my memory is not as good. John Damascus helped me set up for my audition. I would supply the beat for **Twist and Shout**. I was ready for my chance," Debi reminded me. Marsha and Judy were "all in."

Here's how this came together, as far as I remember. Marsha told me she might have a drummer. I went to the Pomeroy house to see this tiny girl sitting behind her borrowed drum kit. I was blown away by her audition. I said, "We need to get you your own set of drums." That was my clever way to tell her she was on-board. I also said "we" need to get you a set of drums.

I'm sure the Rev. Ralph J. Pomeroy and his wife, Dorothy, already knew about our audition beforehand. It wasn't going to be a complete surprise if their talented daughter decided she was no longer interested in folk guitar. She now saw herself as the anchor for a unique and talented group (who just happened to be girls) ready to set its world on fire.

This may have been a hard sell if I were talking to any other Lutheran minister. It was not so much when talking to a true community activist and mentor for countless teens from nearby Senn High School (Ridge Road and W. Ardmore), where Debi was a sophomore. In the '60s, the neighborhood was a little grittier than others.

There was little difference between the Pomeroy household and its ministry. The family members opened their doors and hearts to all, caring for dozens of foster children and ultimately adopting three. I call the entire family "class acts"; however, there was no acting involved. Maybe Rev. Ralph saw me as a music evangelist or something. Whatever we discussed must have worked, huh, Debi?

"My dad took me to Drums Ltd. on Wabash Avenue in the Music Row area near Chicago's downtown. Everyone was familiar with Ringo's drum kit, and that's the model I chose," Debi said. Luckily (for me and the future Daughters of Eve members), the Pomeroy family felt I had only the best intentions for the band members. That didn't mean this was smooth sailing from this point on. Some folks lose out, and others bow out. This would not be the last time as the band took shape.

Debi Pomeroy—
Thank you, Carl, for coaxing my parents into buying me a drum set and for your faith in me as the drummer when I never played drums. I would never have experienced this fascinating life had I not met you and the girls.

"Judy and Marsha already had a drummer in their band. For some reason, she didn't like you, Carl," Debi reminded me. I got over it in a big hurry. I don't think Debi was too broken up over it either.

Once we found a bass player, we could launch our nameless band. A short time later, I thought our girl group was complete. The girl I hired to play bass was a little unfocused, for lack of a better word. She failed to show up for an important practice at Bethany Lutheran Church.

Debi had the hassle-to-move new drum set (not that Marsha's Farfisa organ would be much easier to transport). Between that and my missing bass player, let's say I was a little agitated that day. You might say I was a little demonstrative, too. Do I need to remind you I was known as the Screaming Wildman? Later, one of the girls would describe me as ranting and raving, as if they had no experience with an adult expressing displeasure. Although with Rev. Ralph for a dad, maybe Debi hadn't.

A couple of Debi's friends came over to watch them practice that Saturday. I didn't really mind. The group could perform together in front of a meager (at least for now) audience.

Practice was on hold, and I was operating at a higher decibel level than they expected. The group was bummed and frightened. Then, this girl with long, red hair, dressed in black, stepped forward.

"What if I fill in 'til she gets here?" she asked.

It takes a lot to stop me in my tracks. Marsha and Judy recently did it, as well as Debi "Drums" Pomeroy. I liked the way this new kid jumped in. I found out later she assumed the peacemaker role in public and at home. I don't think anyone spoke while she slipped the bass guitar strap over her shoulder. I could tell it felt a little unnatural. She let her rhythmic talent take over. That other girl never did show up. It didn't matter at this point. I didn't wait for practice to end.

"Would you like to be in a band?" I asked.

She may have hesitated slightly. Maybe she envisioned a career more in tune with her folk music background. Maybe she needed to discuss things with her folks first. The group launched into another song. By the time it ended, all four (make it five) realized how well Andee fit in. Unanimous decision, right, Debi?

"Shortly after that session, Andee's dad bought her a Hofner bass guitar like the one Paul McCartney made famous. It was hollow-bodied and lightweight, with a thin neck, ideal for female hands. We practiced at my house or Marsha's house," Debi reminded me. We had a complete band.

None of us would be anywhere without the sweat and sacrifice of parents (including mine). Debi wasn't old enough to drive yet. Maybe her family was used to a ministry lifestyle, in which all kinds of people came to their door (and sometimes stayed beyond their welcome). Marsha's folks were extraordinarily hospitable. I was a good test for them when we held practice at Marsha's house.

None of the girls had their own "wheels" yet, so an average day for the band was bound to interfere with family life for everyone involved. We'll revisit this "parent thing" when it comes time to explain or defend myself.

There was a bunch of stuff going on from my side, so naming the group was nearly the last thing on my mind. Of course, it would be great to come up with a name that I could begin advertising. There was excitement radiating from the girls, and new fans were anxious for the band to assume an identity. The origin or evolution (my apologies to the dear reverend) of the name is a bit hazy. It likely emerged from the Pomeroy household, perhaps from a number of simultaneous contributions. We've had 50 years to think back on it, and the bandmates offered their perspective as well. Here's my best interpretation.

Some dude named C.S. Lewis penned and published *The Chronicles of Narnia* fantasy novels. They were a big thing in the '50s (and for every generation afterward). Apparently, we welcomed other English imports besides musicians. These books weren't part of my reading list in high school, not that it would have mattered. Well-read and academically gifted students in the '60s would be very familiar with the references to human children as "sons of Adam" or "daughters of Eve" in *Narnia*. Talk about name recognition—brilliant. That's a British term as well, I'm told.

Who suggested the Daughters of Eve as the name of the group? Was it Debi's boyfriend as an underground reference to a fantasy world? Was it Reverend Ralph, who might have used such a reference while inspiring his flock? This was a perfect name requiring no further explanation to either the "churched" or un-churched. The Daughters of Eve were ready for the world—and the world would soon be thrilled with them.

My favorite picture of the original lineup.
Debi Pomeroy, Judy Johnson, Marsha Tomal, and Andee Levin at the Lake Michigan shore.

The first non-ballroom Daughters of Eve gig was in February 1966 at the annual McCormick Place auto show. The place was packed. The crowd was buzzing with anticipation. Even non-Sicilians agreed this was a "primo" debut with an audience to match.

"You could tell they hadn't seen or heard anything like us before. They responded like we were the Beatles. I wish I still had the song lists. It was clear Marsha was the 'Paul McCartney' of our band. She was just gorgeous—a real guy magnet," Debi said. Glad you said it, Debi. It might sound creepy coming from me.

Given the number of teen clubs springing up overnight across the country, I knew there would be no problem booking one of Chicago's hottest new groups. Some might have thought the Daughters of Eve was a novelty act or just some extension of a music school recital, until they saw the band play or heard the girls sing. I said Marsha and Judy were the female Everly Brothers. Soon, other people were saying it for me. Check out **Don't Waste My Time** (https://youtu. be/0d7GBvTtk9k). Okay, you can tell how wound up this chapter has me.

"We used different songs to open a set, like **Black is Black** from Los Bravos. **Time Won't Let Me** by the Outsiders was another favorite. **California Sun** (https://youtu.be/sLFRoeUhKBQ) was my personal favorite because of that heavy drum solo," Debi continued. We all knew DoE was ready for both the road and the recording studio. What could possibly go wrong? Well, nothing the girls did. They didn't need stress, just gigs and industry exposure. I may have contributed to our problem.

"For a while, Judy's mom would kind of treat us like pawns in a chess game. She would yank Judy out of a gig at the last minute and leave us all in tears. Andee's dad would sometimes get into it with you. It would be hard on us all. You had the best of intentions and always got us paid," Debi said. Yeah, I would never allow anyone to question my intentions. I really don't think parents questioned my motives, just my methods. How I helped the Daughters of Eve fulfill its destiny is still open to interpretation. There's a little more about this later. It's time to talk about making records.

The girls were great entertainers and musicians. This was rare in the music world. The Beatles were great, by all reckoning (even mine), but the Rolling Stones' vibe drove audiences wild. The band's swagger dripped onto every track they made … then oozed from our speakers afterward. Between the two most prominent representatives of the British Invasion, which is still rockin'? Right! That's how I felt about DoE. I could see them staying around for a long time.

When the Daughters of Eve set up in the Chess Records studio, the girls had each song nailed down. They had already performed them in front of audiences until they were absolutely flawless. Once the tape started rolling, this was just like another performance for them. We recorded the musical and vocal tracks *at the same time*. Yeah, you read that right. I didn't have to waste time (and Screaming Wildman money) hiring studio musicians or laying any useless tracks. In two "monster" sessions, we did *eighteen* complete sides.

Here's the double-edged sword threatening the completely innocent DoE members. Their records sounded exactly like their performances. From a "production" perspective, this was good. From an originality standpoint, it wouldn't get them national recognition. Many thought I was not aggressively seeking original material for DoE (as I did for the Buckinghams).

I went by gut instinct when it came to choosing which songs would satisfy the market. Because U.S.A. Records was my go-to label, I didn't have to search for production help. I had to figure out which songs should be engineered, produced, and distributed for public consumption.

Any record release meant a "bump" in popularity and increased booking requests. Live performances had people raving about the Daughters of Eve. The band's first release covered two already popular tunes. **Hey Lover** https://youtu.be/ZD80-NpfDU4 is called wickedly groovy to this day. **Stand By Me** https://youtu.be/uEfc2Vr2ieA struck a chord (pun intended) because a male soul singer originally took it to the top of the charts. Those lyrics inspired movies, righteousness in classrooms, and valor on the battlefields. This was clearly a good choice for DoE, from my perspective.

Sought-after vinyl laid the groundwork for gigs and kept them at home during school time. I now had original material from a local writer ready to roll out to the marketplace: **Symphony of My Soul** by Chicagoan (geographically and professionally) James Butler.

Near as I figure, I caught flak from a DoE parent or two about mishandling my managerial duties. Was I paying them fairly? Well, a goodly (or should I say comparable) sum went to the young artists for live performances. The booking agency and event management agreed on the contract price. The booking agency and the manager got paid, too. There weren't many folks to compare me with. I didn't double dip. I arranged to get paid last, if at all.

With record production, once again, I followed the conventional norm. I'm not saying it was "right," just conventional. Songwriters would make a lot of money from a hit. Record labels had the biggest risk and took a goodly sum to record, produce, and market a vinyl disc. Companies with past hits could leverage their profit by taking a gamble on unproven artists. Small record labels didn't have that luxury. Even mega-label artists got very small percentage of sales. The smaller the label, the smaller the paycheck for the artists, though the percentage was the same for both.

I've said this other ways before, but this ties it all together … I used records to land

Andee Levin—
Thank you, Carl, for choosing me to play bass for the Daughters of Eve. This really changed my life and ended up becoming a part of my permanent identity.
I appreciate all that you did to put the band together, to record us, and to promote us.

gigs. That was the most reliable way to sustain a group and get folks paid. I saw one of my groups "break out" and was certain I could do the same thing the same way. This time I was working with an even more dynamic and exciting group called the Daughters of Eve.

When emotions ran at their hottest, rational discussion of the strategy and realities of the music world didn't resonate with all parents. You'll find many examples of these same brutal and fickle forces still at work today: If only … fill in the blank with your own group, manager, label, producer, promoter, distributor, radio station program director, etc. We didn't even talk about pressures the artists faced. DoE created fun and excitement for every audience. Unfortunately, the girls were experiencing far less of that themselves.

If it were solely up to peacemaker, devoted daughter, and talented bandmate Andee Levin, she would have taken to the road with the other Daughters of Eve members. I couldn't see a way to resolve my conflict with Andee's dad. Replacing her was the healthiest decision I could make for the band's sake. Their talent put them far ahead of most groups. Their struggles and lineup changes would be the only "ordinary" thing you would ever be able to say about the Daughters of Eve.

I knew this would be just as hard 50 years later. I hope you all appreciate it.

Building a Tour

We needed a new bass player on short notice. It seemed the best place to look would be at either Taft or Senn. Debi, Judy, and Marsha made the recruiting far easier. Debi remembers …

"I think Marilou Davidson was one of the LA Classmen's girlfriends. I didn't even realize she played guitar then found out she played bass," Debi said. I remember Marilou was a very good musician. We were in a hurry for someone to step in. Problem solved, sort of. DoE still had typical teenage pressures. I had to constantly remind myself they were *real* daughters, plus students, siblings, and girlfriends.

Add "blossoming rockstar" to that mix, and smart (maybe not me) people could see the pressure rising. With the Daughters of Eve on stage, the girls had the same ability to escape as their audience. Reality has a way of crashing the party.

Marsha Tomal—
We did amazing things, made good money, and traveled around as 16, 17, 18-year-olds. We attempted to have a normal life with school and boyfriends.

Carl would make up stories and make us laugh. There was a girl duo named the Two of Clubs, and Judy and I would sound like them when we covered a tune called *Walking Tall*. Carl would tell audiences that Judy and I used to be called the Two of Clubs.

He would do things like that. We would play at clubs in small towns, and the crowds loved him and us. We'd be signing autographs. How many teenagers would be doing that, besides us?

Marilou Davidson (kneeling left) Joins DoE

"We needed to be the first act in the lineup at places like Antoine's Ballroom on Wednesdays since we had school the next day. I didn't much care for school. On the other hand, Marsha was the total package. She was an academic and cheerleader," Debi said. Marsha was also a gifted musician, vocalist, and unofficial leader of DoE, both on- and off-stage. This was supposed to be the part where we talk about Marilou Davidson, but it seemed she left the band nearly as quickly as she joined.

From what I understand, none of the band members have been in contact with her, either. I don't know which facets of her life commanded more time and attention than she was able to give her adopted group. Based on what I (still) know about the music business, her decision to leave was most likely not only hers. This is one of the most mysterious and sad things about our whole story. If I had anything to do with her departure, it will be news to me. I would still love the opportunity to find out.

Except for sad circumstances surrounding our bass players, things went exceptionally well after the band's formation in December 1965. The next year, "my" groups (the Delights, Buckinghams, and Daughters of Eve) were often performing together and packing local clubs as well as those in surrounding states. At the beginning of this book, I mentioned Bon-Bon's drive-in and my personal record for the biggest crowd (and disruption of Norridge).

In 1967, upstart U.S.A. Records released another DoE record with **Symphony of My Soul** https://youtu.be/NdKKuN8sAFI (an original song from James Butler) on Side A. **Help Me Boy** (a take-off on the hit by the Animals) was on the other side. Butler also was credited with production.

Early that same year, U.S.A. Records had the top-selling single in the nation with the Buckinghams' **Kind of a Drag**. Painfully and (as it turned out) inevitably, the Buckinghams bolted for greener pastures. The show needed to go on for the Daughters of Eve. Unfortunately, I was unable to put on a brave face for them. I'll let Debi tell you …

"We already knew the Buckinghams had broken ties with you when we arrived for our next gig at Antoine's. You only wanted them (and us) to be famous. We saw you crying and smashing Buckinghams records in the office. I remember you telling us 'I want youz girls to sign with me right now! I don't want to lose you all!'" Debi said. Yeah, that was a very vulnerable moment for me. I bet this was the only time I even used the word "vulnerable" since then. It's uncharacteristic for a Screaming Wildman. I threw my heart and soul into the DoE tour. The music gods left me alone for a while.

I never let my guard down when it came to protecting the girls. Their parents left them in my care for days on end. If it weren't for the hectic booking schedule for the Daughters of Eve, I may not have been able to put the "sting" of losing the Buckinghams on the back burner. It was still visible, just not cool enough to put away. See? Now back to the finest and most wholesome foursome I ever knew.

At least one of the girls' moms would act as a chaperone during some of the earliest overnight trips. As time went on, the girls got comfortable with the performance and travel routine. The moms eventually saw me as a protective big brother and became more comfortable leaving their daughters in my care.

I built a lot of safeguards into the travel schedule. The DoE was safe (even safer) than the girls might have been at school. For starters, the girls were all quite protective of one another and were never alone with me or anyone else. Really, they spent a lot of time sleeping while I drove between gigs. Bob Bebanko would ride shotgun and serve as the roadie at each venue. Glamorous, huh?

"Carl, you were such a funny guy and told us all kinds of jokes to keep things loose and keep us from getting bored. Spring break, summer vacations, holidays, and weekends, we would be on the road," Debi reminded me. Yeah, I always had the best intentions for "youz girls." None of us noticed just how famous they had become. I had to constantly keep them under my watchful eye.

"Marsha and I became close friends when we roomed together on long road trips. We would get into some harmless mischief, like sneaking out of our room—you know, kid-type trouble. Other times, we'd all bunk in a single room like a slumber party," Debi said. That worked for the girls, of course. I slept when and where I could. All of my waking moments were pretty intense on performance days. The only times I could relax were when the Daughters of Eve were actually on stage. I got used to watching one flawless set after another. The crowd reaction was something I savored. You don't get tired of that. Nor should you ever take it for granted.

Playing teen clubs was a refreshing break for all of us. There was no liquor available for sale, so the girls had a safe rest area between sets. In other places, the performing and backstage areas were out of bounds for teenagers. There was no chance any of the DoE would get into any "real" trouble. Often there was just too much physical distance between them and my attentive eyes. I learned to "read" crowds from an early age. Fortunately (for potential culprits), I never unleashed the Screaming Wildman on anyone. Even now, I would spring to their defense in a heartbeat. Yeah, "spring." I would summon the strength somehow.

Road Warrior

Lori Wax and the band sort of found one another, and she made an immense contribution to the Daughters of Eve as our third (and longest standing) bass player. All of our recording sessions were complete. We released (original composition) **Don't Waste My Time / She Cried** on SpectraSound in 1967, then (original composition) **Social Tragedy / A Thousand Stars** on Cadet Records in 1968.

 None of us ever imagined they would never return to the studio together as the Daughters of Eve. It was far better we didn't know. There's a line in **Social Tragedy** https://youtu.be/pWh9CouYtlY about not letting "it" slip away. Sometimes, we are forced to helplessly watch while it happens. When you got to this line, didn't your eyes "puddle up" a little (like mine)?

I dug out my original DoE booking slips to help remind me just how intense this extended tour was. I'm starting to realize how much of a hardship I placed on the girls and their families. Debi also jogged my memory. At first, traditional ballrooms were our primary venues.

Just as the Daughters of Eve started sizzling, teen clubs were popping up everywhere. They modeled themselves after shows like *Shindig*, *Hullaballoo*, or Dick Clark's *Where the Action Is*. Check out some of the YouTube clips from that era, and watch how much emphasis they placed on dancing.

This new breed of club owners didn't need the hassle of securing a liquor license (or even furniture). As long as they worked with proper union labor to erect a safe stage, with certified electrical hookups, owners could start hosting dances in record time (pun intended). The focus was on open space for movin' and groovin' and little else.

Lori Wax turned in one tight performance after another, and the band had more stability than ever. Good thing because I booked the girls solid. At the end of this chapter, you'll find a list of performances (like the Surf Ballroom) including dates.

Lori Wax (second from right) now on board

Multiple Appearances

Touring took a toll on all of us. Remember, I was booking agent, manager, record producer, promoter, chauffeur, and chief chaperone at every gig. Because the girls were under age for liquor consumption, even in such "enlightened" states as Wisconsin (drinking age 18), they had to remain separated from their fans, or I'd face some sort of bureaucratic or police complications.

Day after day, we piled into our brown van with the Daughters of Eve banner on the side (who thought about taking pictures?). Thanks to Mr. Norm's Grand-Spaulding Dodge (where the Chicago address is part of the name), we got a discounted rate on our wheels. Founder Norm Kraus frequently heard the Screaming Wildman personally read his advertising copy on national radio stations, including 50,000-watt Chicago powerhouses.

Here are just a couple of places we made multiple stops: Golden Horse Shoe in Lebanon, Kentucky (Saturday, May 11, 1968), Lamplighter Club in Salina, Kansas (Saturday, February 3, 1968, and Thursday, May 2, 1968), and Cotillion Ballroom in Wichita, Kansas (Sunday, February 4, 1968, and later that year in mid-June). Once again, none of us could have pulled this off if not for Bob Bebanko, our durable and dependable road manager.

Debi Pomeroy —
Between sets, we would stand backstage and marvel at how the kids would be dancing while Carl was spinning records. He was far more than a booking agent, promoter, and manager. He was really a great entertainer. He loved it when we would back him up on stage while he sang songs like *Hot Pastrami* or *What'd I Say*. He booked us in some great rooms, including the Kinetic Playground on Clark Street in Chicago.

Another one of my favorites was Sandy's Escape in Omaha. It was two stories and no alcohol. It reminded me of the Like Young Club in Old Town where my brother used to play.

Supporting Our Troops

While the Daughters of Eve actively toured, the United States was still embroiled in heavy military conflict in the Republic of Vietnam. Our military base appearances were quite meaningful for both the performers and their audiences.

The group was greeted with the very same fervor the Beatles experienced when first landing on the American continent. There were even instances of fainting during their performances. Each DoE concert had serious rock-and-roll and its share of bittersweet memories as sadness mingled with madness in what we called the "real" world back then.

In 1966, combat training escalated at Fort Campbell, Kentucky, and Fort Riley, Kansas. The Daughters of Eve created thousands of fond memories on its personal tour of duty. This section reminded me how busy and dedicated the girls were.

The earliest gig I have on record was at the National Guard Armory in Kingsford, Michigan (on a Saturday, August 1966). On extremely short notice, I booked the Daughters of Eve on Thanksgiving Day at the National Guard Armory in Concordia, Kansas (Thursday, November 23, 1967). The girls and their families deserve credit for their sacrifices. During that Midwestern winter, we had two performances at the National Guard Armory in Iron Mountain, Michigan (Friday-Saturday, January 27-28, 1968).

For some uncanny reason (musical and political historians might someday be able to tell us why), at the height of popularity for the Daughters of Eve, the number of U.S. deaths during the conflict also peaked: by some counts, 1967 – 11,363 / 1968 – 16,899 / 1969 – 11,780, or nearly 40,000 deaths all together. During those same years, it seemed like everyone was in a band, or knew several people who were. Likewise, everyone knew several casualties of war, either through service or devastating loss (often both).

Several military installations booked repeat performances by DoE. The girls made each of those unique and special. I only mention a few here. Once again, I say they served their country well.

On February 21, 1968, I penned a contract for three performances at the NCO Club at Fort Leonard Wood, Missouri (Friday-Sunday, March 1-3). That gave us only a one-week notice. Most young men conscripted (drafted) into the U.S. Army received their basic combat training there. The year before, over 100,000 completed the 10-week course as fit-for-combat soldiers.

The girls played for the guys at Forbes Air Force Base in Topeka, Kansas (Sunday, May 5, 1968). They were among the first deployed in the Vietnam War and among the last airmen to engage in combat there. DoE sandwiched two performances around the Memorial Day holiday that year at two National Guard Armories in Rapid City, South Dakota (Wednesday, May 29, 1968), and Moorhead, Minnesota (Friday, May 31, 1968).

The Daughters of Eve had two performances at the NCO Club at Hunter Army Base in Savannah, Georgia (Wed-Thu, June 5-6). Army helicopter pilots were trained there. We left Hunter the next day for the NCO Club at Fort Rucker in Alabama for consecutive performances at the U.S. Army Aviation Center (Friday-Sunday, June 7-9). Because additional facilities were needed, the Army Aviation School at Fort Rucker was operating beyond full capacity.

During the Vietnam conflict, Fort Rucker's 1st Aviation Brigade had well over 20,000 soldiers assigned. They were credited with perfecting helicopter warfare. By the end of the American involvement and the fall of Saigon, the brigade logged more than 4 million sorties.

Breaking Up

Dr. Seuss describes my feelings about the Daughters of Eve phenomenon: "Don't cry because it's over, smile because it happened." If I had the power to do it all again, we most likely would end up in the very same place. I may have tried to play too many roles and actually diminished the success or longevity of the group.

In any case, I had only the very best intentions for the Daughters of Eve. Marsha and Judy (whose vocal blends could positively **never** be replaced) were planning their weddings. Marsha joined the discussion at this point. Ooh, she mentioned things we would have done differently, like someone would have been following us around with a movie camera.

"Carl, I know you wanted us to be as big as the Buckinghams, but once they left, your heart wasn't in it," she bravely started. I'm just grateful I wasn't the reason for the breakup of the group. Of course, nobody else in the group was responsible for my shattered dreams, either.

My rockstar dreams started in the '50s. Times and people were tough, but the country (overall) found a way to give us a clear path forward. I'm going to say the harsh realities of the late '60s swallowed us. Marsha wanted to be with her boyfriend (tough enough, given our DoE performance schedule).

Thousands of young people wanted to take their commitment to the next level. In another place and time, Marsha and her new husband could have made a home in Chicago. He and the Screaming Wildman would have argued regularly about her DoE schedule, but we'd be back in the studio. He would have been welcome to tag along (maybe I could have gotten some sleep and he could have driven the van). Or …

"I went with my husband, now stationed in the Philippines. I thought the Islands would be like Hawaii. It was more like a third-world country. When he went to Vietnam, I pretty much got left behind," Marsha recalled. "Leaving the Daughters of Eve was terrible."

I should have known how many sleepless nights she endured. Not because she was uncertain about the right thing to do, but because her friends (and the Screaming Wildman) would be disappointed.

"I knew Judy wanted to get married, too. She could have stayed in the band. She still lived in the same neighborhood," Marsha offered. Okay, time for the Screaming Wildman to set the record straight.

Marsha Tomal—
Carl is a pretty creative and amazing guy. He had us doing things nobody else would be doing. A girl band playing their own instruments in a recording studio was pretty non-traditional. He got us good original material and had an ear for what would work with the group.

He was a hard-core manager – out there all the time promoting us. We never got a chance to perform on a variety show, but recording at Chess Records and touring the United States was a great experience.

I don't remember our last gig. It was just too terrible to leave the Daughters of Eve.

If Judy was the rhythm, Marsha was the soul. There was no going on without her. She is much too modest to entertain the notion, but the rest of us knew it was true.

I'll forever blame the war (or whatever we want to call it) for the breakup. When I think about the thousands of lives that were shattered during that era, I once again feel selfish.

Can You Believe?

I'm touched (but you already knew that). No, I'm grateful that "youz girls" were so willing to be part of my book. I'm glad I got most of you together while I'm still on the green side of the turf. While we pieced together the Daughters of Eve chapter, Andee and Lori already made casting suggestions for the story when it becomes a screenplay.

Marsha (Lucy Liu), Judy (Lady Gaga), Debi (Jody Foster), Andee (Sandra Bullock), and Lori (Sheryl Crow) would once again rock the house, the way I always dreamed. Who would play the Screaming Wildman?

Nobody asked me. Someone (who wanted to remain anonymous) suggested Joe Pesci. "Not the *Goodfellas'* Joe Pesci, but more like *Cousin Vinny*. They're still toying with the concept. Lori came to my defense, I think …

"Honestly, if Carl was crazy, we would have killed him and stashed his body deep in the bowels of the Palace Hotel in Pender, Nebraska. He had to be a bit of a manic to manage a bunch of unruly princesses known as Youz Girls—that should have been our name!"

The Daughters of Eve created a lasting impact on the music scene, but more so on my life. No day goes by without me thinking of them.

Andee Levin—
To have the experience of bonding and making music with these talented girls, recording at the renowned Chess Studios, and of course, to have the experience of my grandchildren's smiles and wide eyes as they listen to the songs that I played. Very few women my age can say they had these events in their history.

Debi Pomeroy—
I can't remember our last performance. I must have blocked it out of my mind. I was heartbroken when the band broke up, a fish out of water – totally lost.

I never knew how much the band influenced people until I got a computer and discovered so many people looking for the Daughters of Eve. Carl, thank you for giving me the best teenage years ever!!!

The Wildman—
I just found out Andee and Lori regularly correspond. Our first and last bass players never met one another (yet)! The Daughters of Eve continue to create timeless bonds. You know what I'm sayin'?

What's Shakin'?

Just about everything I have is shakin' at this point. As you must have guessed, the Daughters of Eve members immersed themselves in real-life stuff for a half-century. Debi, Andee, and Marsha are now in the Pacific time zone. Lori is in the Eastern time zone while Judy and I remain in the Chicago area. I hope we someday hear from Marilou.

You know, when you put so much of yourself into your music, it puts something back into you. I can't take credit for the musical addiction DoE satisfied in its own way in the decades that followed.

Debi and Andee were interviewed on KUSF (November 2009) about their experiences. I included a link for you here: https://youtu.be/Kxl7_qLeqiM.

Lori and Debi played in countless bands through the years and keep their Facebook® friends up to date. Andee taught hordes of youngsters (a few at a time, thank goodness) to play piano.

The Daughters of Eve story has lessons for us all. That's why I laid it out in front of you. People can instruct you on the mechanics of your chosen instrument. Your passion and discipline seep into every cell in your body. DoE and everyone between these covers (seductive, huh?) changed the very chemistry of people surrounding them (most of all, me). They're here for me now because I was there for them then. We're still here for one another, and for you. I have to soon let go of this chapter, or nobody's gonna ever see it.

My book gave me a good reason to catch up with Marsha. I saw how my faith in her was justified, just like the admiration of her fans and bandmates. She wasn't done with music, by any means. The music world would be thrilled to have her in front of a microphone once again.

Of course, I'm giving you the condensed version. The extended story will most likely come out in the movie we discussed. Marsha logged some time with Baby Huey and the Babysitters. See, back when I still thought of myself as a chaperone or big brother, I wouldn't allow myself to see her as the sultry and soulful artist she'd become.

Marsha joined her parents in Hawaii and played with the Hank Jones Trio. She spent time in Europe and later moved to northern California. She played with a girl band called Broad Daylight, with gigs in Idaho, Montana, and the Rocky Mountains area. Fast enough for you? I'll slow it down so you can savor the best part. You'll be impressed, though not really surprised. I promise.

Filthy McNasty's LA bar on Sunset Blvd. was a popular hangout for the biggest-name entertainers like Mick Jagger and Elvis. When the bar closed at 2am, many headed to an after-hours club in north Hollywood. Richard Berry and his group (now including Marsha) entertained there regularly. Berry wrote and released **Louie, Louie** in 1957. https://youtu.be/z-2CKsaq5r8

Marsha learned more about the filthy, nasty music business as well. **Louie, Louie** was one of the most recognizable rock anthems in history. Berry wouldn't enjoy either the celebrity or the royalties. At the club, Marsha caught the eye (or, most likely the ear) of another great performer. Etta James, who grew up with Richard Berry, invited them both to tour with her.

They played in San Francisco (with activist Angela Davis attending). Afterward, they went to the Cool Jazz festival in South America as R&B entertainers, just as Etta's popularity was waning and the gigs began drying up. Marsha took the theft of her equipment as a sign and made a career change.

She studied psychology and is currently a licensed psychotherapist. Once again, the Screaming Wildman may have inspired her in some way! She spent the last 27 years working with a behavioral medicine center, taught some college psychology courses, and is now writing a parenting book. Hey, I know some people in this book business now. Let's talk!

The Daughters of Eve biggest gig to date: February 1966 at the McCormick Place Auto Show. Thank goodness Andee's dad had the foresight to hire a professional photographer. Live performance photos are extremely rare.

Of course, they were booked solid at local dances from the very start.

Photos provided by Andee

Recordings and Releases

We started playing gigs with a solid catalog of songs that fit nearly every mood or venue. By design, these were solid tunes that were familiar to a live audience. That's the kind of tightrope act we were forced to perform. The radio market wanted new material, but audiences wanted familiar stuff, leaving them comfortable enough to appreciate a solid performance. Our first release had proven tunes that blossomed into an energetic and growing fan base for the Daughters of Eve.

U.S.A. 1779, 1966.

HEY LOVER:

Debbie Dovale, from the Pittsburgh, Pennsylvania, area, was only 12 years old when the song was released in 1963.

STAND BY ME:

Ben E. King wrote this song, along with Jerry Leiber and Mike Stoller. It was released in 1961.

Produced by Carl Bonafede and Ron Malo.

The next release contained an original song credited to James Butler, who is also known as Jimmy (or James B.) Peterson from the Chicagoans. As you might remember, bandmate James Holvay wrote a few songs for the Buckinghams. I won't say that this song was written specifically for the Daughters of Eve, but the tight vocal harmony of Marsha and Judy made it sound as if it were. Bassist Marilou Davison had replaced the extremely popular Andee by the time we released our second single.

U.S.A. 891, 1967.

SYMPHONY OF MY SOUL:

Written by Chicago songwriter James Butler.

HELP ME BOY:

It was a hit for Eric Burdon and the Animals earlier in 1967 as *Help Me Girl*.

Produced by Carl Bonafede and James Butler.

Change is inevitable in the music business, and the Daughters of Eve sported a new label for its next record. Lew Douglas, Dan Belloc, and I founded Spectra-Sound Records. We followed our new formula for record releases, by pairing a new song from John Serafini with a twist on the Jay and the Americans release of **She Cried** that reached #5 on the Billboard Hot 100. The rigors of the road claimed another bass player. Fortunately, Lori Wax immediately stepped in to relax a hectic situation.

SpectraSound 920, 1967.

DON'T WASTE MY TIME:
> Written by John Serafini.
HE CRIED:
> It was previously a hit as **She Cried** for Jay and the Americans in 1962.
> Produced by Carl Bonafede.
> Engineered by Ron Malo.

Still more changes for the group and me. The popularity of the group kept us touring while the fourth and (unexpectedly) last 45rpm released by DoE got deserved airplay from our Cadet (Chess) release. Who knew? Kathy Young and the Innocents took **A Thousand Stars** to the top five on the Billboard Hot 100 while she was only 15 years old. On the same disc, the Daughters of Eve introduced **Social Tragedy**, another new James Butler song. I later recorded Ral Donner on the same song and renamed it **Don't Let It Slip Away**.

Cadet 5600, 1968.

SOCIAL TRAGEDY:
> Written by Chicagoan James Butler.
A THOUSAND STARS:
> First recorded by the Rivileers.
> Produced by Carl Bonafede.
> Engineered by Gary Knipper and Ed Cody.

I so wanted the girls to be famous. I hope this chapter reminds them they were, and still are. You'll find most of these tracks on YouTube or one of my CD collections. I just bundled them here for you. Start out with the classic tune by Paul Revere and the Raiders. **Just Like Me** http://youtu.be/fKuwZ8slp1l has a great photo gallery as well.

California Sun / Respect / Land of 1000 Dances / Midnight Hour / Hippy Hippy Shake / Symphony of My Soul / Stand by Me / Just a Little / Hey Lover / Help Me Boy / Social Tragedy / Don't Waste My Time / He Cried / A Thousand Stars in the Sky / Midnight Hour

Daughters of Eve Performances (partial list of road trips)

Sat - August-1966	National Guard Armory - Kingsford, MI
Sat - 7-22-1967	The Farm Bureau Building - Mt. Carole, IL
Tues - 7-25-1967	Eagles Ballroom, 440 N. Wisconsin - Berlin, WI
Fri - 9-1-1967	Kon-Tiki Teen Town (agreement made 10 days earlier) - Fairfield, IL
Sat - 9-9-1967	Harmony Recreation Center, 605 Main Ave. North - Harmony, MN
Sat - 9-23-1967	Exposition Gardens, Opera House - Peoria, IL
Sat - 9-30-1967	The White Rabbit - Niles, MI
Sat - 10-7-1967	Dance-Mor Ballroom - Swisher, IA
Fri - 10-27-1967	Turner Hall - Watertown, WI
Sat - 10-28-1967	Masonic Temple - Dixon, IL
Thu - 11-23-1967	National Guard Armory - Concordia, KS
Fri - 12-15-1967	The Downers Grove Center - Downers Grove, IL
Wed - 12-27-1967	The Club 18 - Mt. Horeb, WI
Thurs - 12-28-1967	The VFW Hall Youth Center, Elm Hi Street - Edgerton, WI
Fri - 12-29-1967	The Hullaballo Club - Dubuque, IA
Mon - 1-1-1968	Rothchild Pavillion - Rothchild, WI
Fri - 1-5-1968	The Place, 632 Plymouth - Grand Rapids, MI
Fri - 1-12-1968	OHr Place - Deerfield, IL
Sat - 1-13-1968	The Prairie Moon Ballroom - Prairieburg, IA
Fri-Sat - 1-27,28	National Guard Armory - Iron Mountain, MI
Fri - 2-2-1968	The Firebird Inn - Hastings, NE
Thurs - 2-8-1968	The Varsity Club, 1920 Ward Avenue - La Crosse, WI
Fri - 2-9-1968	Christ Church, 470 Maple Avenue - Winetka, IL
Sat - 2-10-1968	St. Rita High School - Chicago
Sat - 2-10-1968	St. Rita's High School, 6310 South Clearmont Street - Chicago, IL
Sun - 2-11-1968	Juliana Grammar School, 7142 North Osceola - Chicago, IL
Fri - 2-23-1968	The Field House, Parson's College - Fairfield, IA
Sat - 2-24-1968	University Center Ballroom - DeKalb, IL
Fri-Sun - 3-3-1968	NCO Club at Fort Leonard Wood - Missouri
Tues - 3-5-1968	G.T. Club, 5002 East 6th Street - Topeka, KS
Fri - 3-8-1968	Fairfield Auditorium - Fairfield, NE
Sat - 3-15-1968	St. Ignatius High School - Chicago
Sat - 3-16-1968	The Club 18 - Mt. Horeb, WI
Sun - 3-17-1968	Polar Country Club - Polar, WI
Fri - 3-22-1968	Park College, The Commons - Parkville, MO
Sat - 3-23-1968	Coliseum Ballroom - Benld, IL
Sat - 4-6-1968	T.J. Sokol Hall, 12th and Normal - Crete, NE
Sun - 4-7-1968	Pollyanna Rte 33 South - Effingham, IL
Fri - 4-12-1968	The Place - Grand Rapids, MI
Sat - 4-13-1968	The Platters Club - Cadillac, MI
Fri - 4-19-1968	Fake Sams Joint, Main Street - Hillsboro, IL
Sat - 4-20-1968	Marrillville High School (agreement made 3 mo. earlier) - Marrillville, WI
Fri - 4-26-1968	Skylon Ballroom - Hartington, NE
Sat - 4-27-1968	Elm Ballroom - Syracuse, NE
Sun - 4-28-1968	The Surf Ballroom, 460 North Shore Drive - Clearlake, IA

Wed - 5-1-1968	Renfroes Club - Emporia, KS
Fri - 5-3-1968	Me & Eds Nite Club - Manhattan, KS
Sat - 5-4-1968	City Auditorium - Oakland, NE
Sun - 5-5-1968	Forbes Air Force Base - Topeka, Kansas
Fri - 5-24-1968	Prairie Moon Ballroom - Prairieburg, IA
Sat - 5-25-1968	The Pollyanna, On Route 33 - Effingham, IL
Wed - 5-29-1968	National Guard Armory - Rapid City, SD
Thurs - 5-30-1968	Lisbon Park Pavilion - Lisbon, ND
Fri - 5-31-1968	National Guard Armory - Moorhead, MN
Sat - 6-1-1968	Holly Hock Ballroom - Hatfield, MN
Sun - 6-2-1968	Dons Ballroom - Ghent, MN
Wed-Thu - 6-5,6 - 1968	NCO Club at the Hunter Army Base - Savannah, Georgia
Fri-Sun - 6-7,8,9	NCO Club at Fort Rucker - Alabama
Mon - 6-10-1968	Phillips Roller Cade - Decatur, AL
Fri-Sun - 9-16,17,18-1966	Gun Club - Cottage Grove, WI

Photos provided by Lori.
(left) Cotillion Ballroom, Wichita, KS
Marsha took this picture of Lori,
and insisted on an action shot.
(right) Golden Horseshoe – Lebanon, KY

Unknown Dates -
The Varsity Club - LaCrosse, WI
The Place - Grand Rapids, MI
The Vets Club - Pender, NE
Firebird Inn - Hastings, NE
Municipal City Auditorium - Burlington, IA
Rhinelander Memorial Building - Rhinelander, WI
Central YMCA, 915 W. Wisconsin - Milwaukee, WI
City Auditorium - Oakland, NE
Elm Ballroom - Syracuse, NE
Sandy's Escape, 6031 Binney Street - Omaha, NE
The Top Hat Club, 273 East Court St - Kankakee, IL
Frog Hop Ballroom - St. Joseph, MO
The Hulabaloo Club - Bubuque, IA
Me & Eds Nite Club - Manhattan, KS

Autographs

I hope to collect autographs from all six Daughters of Eve. This space is reserved for them.

Safe at Home

Junior Arzola

After music, sports would be my next biggest love. I was a decent ballplayer in my time. By the end of the 1960s, the music business just kicked me around pretty good. I needed a break from the craziness. Actually, I just needed a different kind of insanity to keep my competitive juices flowing.

One of those diversions, which soon became a passion, was bowling. Even though I often bowled on a team, I considered it an individual sport. There will be more about that later. On the other hand, competitive baseball gave me both individual and team experience. It was good to be outdoors for a change.

On the baseball field, the Screaming Wildman could still do everything he did best. I could still serve as master of ceremonies during a game. (In baseball lingo, I was team manager.) On the baseball diamond, all eyes would still be on me several times during the course of a game. This was much like a DJ gig.

I met an entirely new group of people who shared my somewhat-controlled aggression. Here's the real cool part: I played with an unbelievable number of folks just about as crazy as I was. While doing interviews for this section, I was surprised how many of them also had musical connections. One of my former teammates still lives in Chicago. Ours is the longest *continuous* relationship I have in my life.

I occasionally talk with most folks in this section. Interviews are completely different. I found out many interesting things about these guys because I took the time to finally ask. They are all rockstars in their own right. We got a chance to talk about what we did and how it made everyone's life better.

There's only one place to get the ball rolling. Nah, that's bowling. In this section, I want to "lead off" with that longtime friend I just mentioned.

The Spark Plugs

I'm sitting near the customer counter at Southport Security just west of Belmont Avenue in Chicago http://www.lockshop.com. Three stools in front of the workbench make it look more like a bar. The hospitality is very much the same as a barber shop. It's a great place to trade stories and people-watch.

I've visited owner Otilio Arzola Jr. hundreds of times through the years. We've got a regular routine whenever Junior has a room full of customers. At full

Screaming Wildman volume, I re-enact my US-30 dragstrip commercial. Everyone growing up in the '60s is familiar with my "Sunday-Sunday-Sunday" opening.

Since I memorized my script back then, many of the top dragster names tumble out without hesitation. High-fives, laughter, and fond memories follow in abundance. I'm a willing entertainer. Today, things were slightly different.

I conducted my interview while customers were shuffling in and out. Nobody seemed to mind. I didn't realize one of his "counter men" was also a superb Chicago athlete.

Bobby Merk played guard for the Gordon Tech (now DePaul College Prep) basketball team. He also played Windy City Softball at Clarendon Park, where the players are among the very best in the city. He supplied more details on the cast of characters we introduce in this section.

Junior just reconnected with Jim Cooper, a utility catcher on our baseball team, and he was on hand today. The collective experiences from our neighborhood and the Latin Leagues in Humboldt Park made this chapter more rewarding than I could have ever hoped.

Play Ball

I planned to just start my interview anywhere and let the history flow out. Whether we move backward or forward in time is not as important as getting it all down. Once you read this, organize it in your own mind any way you want. We're trying to remember who played where on the team.

"Our first baseman was Armando DeGuzman, remember, Bob?" Junior started. He always wore those fancy hats before he changed into his uniform.

"Armando always dressed really nice. Still does. I see him once in a while," Bobby answered. See how well this works?

"I thought he played ball at the University of Illinois, Champaign," I said.

"Naw, he played at Southern Illinois University in Carbondale, Illinois. Same as me," Junior corrected me.

"Were you on the same team?" I asked. That's something I never asked until now. I should have known it was an impossibility.

"He was already out of college before he played for the Spark Plugs," Junior said. Most of the team, as well as the rest of the league, formerly played high school, college, or minor league baseball. Because he had exceptional talent, Junior started playing for us when he was 15, or three full years younger than the minimum age.

Yeah, we lied about it on the roster. It was easy enough to do. It didn't have anything to do with him being long-haired, Latin, or lanky. He could track down balls in center field, hit with some authority, and steal bases. Maybe he moved so fast that the other team didn't notice he wasn't even shaving yet—our team didn't either.

"Armando and I were the only Latin players on the Spark Plugs," Junior reminded me. That, I certainly knew. The rest of the teams in the league were well aware of that fact, too. One was sponsored by the National Puerto Rican Congress. Any time they lost to us, it hurt their team and national pride.

Don't get me wrong, the players and their fans never threatened us or anything like that. "Congress" just wasn't used to losing to anyone. The Spark Plugs played hard but didn't take themselves too seriously.

Some entire teams were overly sensitive when things didn't go their way. Our team had lots of guys who could never be intimidated because they were just talented and goofy enough. We spent some time trying to "position" the rest of the guys we could recall.

A couple of them deserve their own section, and you are going to learn more about them a little later. Some of the others were Al DePisa, Bobby Woods, and the Mazurek boys (Johnny, Greg, and Bill). Unique to the Spark Plugs, we had a Star of the Week. That meant we would recruit guys (literally off the street in the neighborhood) to keep from forfeiting a game.

Some of them were really talented, like George Garland, a lefty who could really crush a baseball. He had a good nature, with an intimidating build.

As I mentioned earlier, we started in the middle of the story. The 60614 postal code encompassed a number of different neighborhoods. In the late '60s and the '70s, the raging street game was called Fast Pitchin'. You'd find rectangular boxes drawn on nearly every factory wall facing an open area. With a baseball bat and a rubber ball, you were equipped to start a game.

The pitcher got a strike for firing a ball past the batter and hitting that box drawn on the wall. The batter would "walk" after four pitches outside the box. A batted ball caught on the fly would be an "out." To get an out on a ground ball, the fielder (who may not have a baseball glove) would need to hit that batter's box from his position after catching the ball.

Depending on the size of the field, a batter would score a single, double, triple, or home run, if he could clear a fence or smack a ball off a wall of one of the surrounding houses or factories. I guess you could compare it to New York stick-ball because the balls would ricochet off surrounding buildings.

(left) Gordon Tech's Bobby Merk. Check out my shoes (Davis Shoes, 9109 S. Commerical Ave.), and Otilio "Junior" Arzola.

It was a lot like English cricket, too. Games would last until you ran out of balls or daylight.

Older guys (and screaming wildmen) hanging around Knickerbocker School (Belden and Clifton) or the old car barns would play. I never thought about joining a competitive hardball team, much less starting one. A lot of my future teammates killed a lot of time and beer waving at rubber balls.

Thomas School Phenomenon

The caliber of street ball was a lot higher than I ever anticipated. Remember what I said about Junior Arzola? He was only 15 years old when he started playing center field in a competitive men's league. How did he gain that much experience without any formal training? It came down to one person. This chapter of my book would be vastly different if not for him.

Without this guy, I doubt there would ever have been a Spark Plugs baseball team, Junior and I would likely have never met, and I'd be missing out on a 45-year friendship. I forgot to mention Junior was also the one who set the wheels in motion for getting my book project under way.

At the corner of Belden and Janssen avenues, Thomas Elementary School is now a four-story brick condominium. Back in the '60s and '70s, there was an adjacent schoolyard that served as a regular hangout for one crazy bunch of characters. A few of them would eventually play ball with me and Junior at Humboldt Park.

During the summer of 1969, I was dealing with my own version of the empty-nest syndrome after the Daughters of Eve disbanded. I pointed my Buick Riviera toward Janssen Avenue, just west of my home. Maybe I hoped to find one more garage band (refusing to learn my lesson). Instead, I pulled over to check out the activity and sounds that drowned out my car speakers.

There were maybe six or so guys shooting baskets near the west fence of the Thomas schoolyard. In front of me, on the east side, there was a pickup softball game with maybe a dozen or so players. There also was a fast-pitchin' game going on right in the middle of everything else. Those batted rubber balls could raise a hefty welt if you were hit with one.

The basketball and softball players were forced to duck at various times. The fast-pitchin' players didn't even seem to notice anyone else. It was crazy to see those rubber balls constantly rocketing all over the schoolyard or off the surrounding buildings. At the epicenter, one guy was doing the play-by-play announcing for the fast-pitchin' game. He kept a running line of chatter going with the guys in the other games at the same time.

This unofficial athletic director, coach, and community activist was a guy named Jimmy Scholtes. In Ed Kelly's chapter, I mentioned Chicago Park District programs. Official supervisors would manage sports programs and instruct participants. By 1969, the park district money was siphoned off for other (worthwhile?) enterprises. Neighborhood kids were left to their own devices.

I barely stepped around the iron fence separating the schoolyard from the sidewalk before I got into the fast-pitchin' game. If I wanted to play anywhere else on the field, it wouldn't have mattered. Jimmy's voice projected past all corners of the yard and to the front porches of the buildings across the street. I met my match.

If any game needed another player to even up the sides, he would just call out. Everybody was invited to play, regardless of age or skill level. The first time I played in Thomas schoolyard, Junior Arzola wasn't around. However, there were a few kids his age who were fully involved in the activities.

I think this would be the perfect time for Junior to tell us how he first met Jimmy, his lifelong friend and mentor.

"I was in the schoolyard with another guy throwing darts up in the air, trying to get them to stick in the asphalt. We were just stupid kids. You had to throw them pretty high," he said. He wanted me to know in case I wanted to try, huh?

"My dart sailed through the air, and I watched it arc right toward Jim Scholtes. I was going to get my ass kicked as soon as that dart hit something or someone," Junior continued. I could imagine Junior frozen in horror. He had to be a little curious about how much damage one dart could cause though. Jimmy lived through the experience, and so did Junior. How well they lived is the real story.

"That dart stuck in the bill of Jimmy's baseball cap," he said. No other mortal would have reacted the way this guy Jimmy did.

"I heard him shout 'whoa,' like he still does. Instead of charging at me, he started laughing and showed his hat to everyone in the schoolyard," Junior told me. He surely wanted to know who was responsible. Instead of displaying some kind of macho posturing, Jimmy made Junior the center of attention.

They became fast-pitchin' teammates. Maybe it was the safest way for Jimmy to keep an eye on Junior. Thank goodness he still had two eyes. Nobody played fast pitchin' better or longer than him. You know, if Jimmy is your nickname, you most likely were a ball player, unless you were Sicilian. The Jimmys I knew … well, you didn't want to know. Old school, don't ask—don't tell.

I came back pretty often and got to know Jimmy very well. I don't think we ever sat down to talk. We were often on different teams, but it didn't slow down our dialogue. Here's what else I discovered—that simple game really developed your batting "eye" and timing. You were swinging an official-sized baseball bat at a rubber ball that was maybe one-third official baseball size.

I found out Jimmy also got guys together to play the "big boy" game at the North Avenue diamonds that shared the parking lot of Lincoln Park Zoo (not to be confused with the musical group that I recorded).

Man, once you've played the schoolyard game, that real baseball looked like a grapefruit. You could also put some wicked spin on the rubber ball. The curve balls that I saw on the regulation diamond were nothing in comparison.

Defense was the "equalizer" between the two types of competition. There was really no "glove work" to speak of in fast pitchin'. In the official game, fielding any type of ball could result in grave injury.

Or, maybe we were supposed to forget that. I don't recollect which one. I must have taken a ball or two off my head. We also needed a lot of practice when it came to judging trajectories of batted balls. Maybe they taught that stuff at Cooley Vocational in one of those classes I missed my senior year.

A lot of guys from Thomas School played ball in Lincoln Park. We started to get serious about putting a weekend league team together. I didn't know how well Jimmy could help me assemble a team until I took a good look around. There were two teams (granted there may be only six or so players for each team at the start) in front of me.

They had to drive or walk about a mile and a half to get to the diamonds. He had to be pretty persuasive. You know, a natural promoter who could match me word for word and decibel for decibel. By the time our unofficial game ended, we had a nine-man team on the field and more than that waiting to bat.

Jimmy and I would make another game-within-a-game by luring passersby with a chance to take a few swings at the plate. Some would stick around. Others would just head for the pedestrian bridge to North Avenue Beach and the girls sunning themselves at the shoreline. That's another way Jimmy sold the whole ball playing bit in the first place.

Could we field a team to play games in a weekend league? No doubt in my mind anymore. Nobody said it would be the same team every time. That's where we developed the star-of-the-week strategy. We had a couple of spare uniforms, or we would drive to the house of someone who couldn't play that weekend. On the way to the game, we'd tell the "star" what name to sign on the roster before the game started.

Jimmy (with Junior) also discovered a "hidden" location for practices. Procter and Gamble operated a plant on the near north side of Chicago. It had a padlocked baseball field for employees. It was patrolled by a couple of dobermans trotting outside the main gate. We would slip an entire carload of players through an outfield gap in the chain-link fence surrounding the park.

With the dogs safely outside, we would play within. The company guards were pretty cool about it (as long as there wouldn't be any damage or police reports to explain to their bosses). I think they were a little envious, too.

Scouting for Talent

Here's one of the musical connections I mentioned earlier. Jimmy and Junior invited a character named Bob Raines to our Lincoln Park practices. Years before, I hired him to strum and sing at the Swiss Hall. Now, he was entertaining nightly at Arkie's Corral, a country bar at Southport and Webster.

Bob had a full-size station wagon with "Melody Ranger" painted on the passenger door. Every weekend, he would chauffeur ballplayers to practice. With Raines' honkin' wagon, my Riviera and Jimmy's four-seater, we transported nearly two full teams with their gear to the designated ball field.

We would even call a weekday practice at times. You'd be surprised how many guys would skip work to play ball. I had a nighttime job. Other guys would have to come up with an excuse. There was an unbelievable amount of death and illness during the summer weeks.

I turned to restaurant and service station owner Frank Milito for team sponsorship. Just like in the music business, you want to increase the amount of stakeholders in your project. Sponsors could write off the membership expense. It was easy to recruit players if there was no cash involved. The Humboldt Park leagues were a good choice for us.

There was room for 25 players per roster. Nearly all of the spots were full, though some guys would only play a couple of games each season. This guy Jim Cooper was one of the schoolyard regulars who saw spot duty.

There was another guy who wasn't available nearly as often as I would have liked. Former Schurz High School phenom Hank Zemola (who has his own chapter in my book) should have been a major league ballplayer. Just like in the music business, a number of factors could derail a sports career. The Hank Zemola story is still one of phenomenal success. You'll see. Or, check it out right now. I'll wait for you right here.

Junior reminded me of guys who had a lasting impression on me.

"Do you remember that south side team we played against in Humboldt Park, Carl? The one with Sam Puckett and Quinn Buckner on it?" he asked. Yeah, I do. Everybody knew them by name and basketball reputation. Sam (only 5-foot-9) gained national attention by leading Hales Franciscan High to three Chicago Catholic League titles.

Quinn played at Thornridge High in south suburban Dolton, Illinois, and helped Thornridge win two consecutive state basketball titles. He would later win an Olympic gold medal, NCAA championship (Indiana University, 1976), and NBA championship (Boston Celtics, 1984).

Junior Arzola competed with that caliber of talent and gave them all they could handle on the baseball field. Those guys were rugged. Neither of them, however, was the biggest celebrity we ever met at Humboldt Park.

"Carl, remember when Sergio Oliva showed up at our game that one time when you thought he was going to kick your ass?" Junior asked. Oh, yes. Let me give you a little background. Cuban-born Sergio beat Arnold Schwarzenegger for the Mister Universe title in 1969. He was going to use his 230 or so pounds (on a 5-foot-11 frame) to stomp me into the ground. Or so I thought. Junior was having too good of a time repeating this story.

"Sergio thought we stole some equipment from his sporting goods store, and he came looking for it," Junior started. "That's when Jimmy called out, 'Hey Carl, Sergio is looking for you'" … the clueless driver of the get-away car!

Yeah, I remember. I was looking over my shoulder the whole time while packing up after the game. Jimmy and the team got a big kick out of my terror.

"Yeah, you guys might have taken a couple of softballs," I said. Even now, I was trying to minimize the larceny. By the way, the late Sergio (2012) went on to become a Chicago police officer for some 25 years.

"Oh, yeah, and maybe we took a couple of gloves," Junior admitted (ready to confess a half-century later). At the time, I wasn't going to let anybody on my team get thrown under a bus, even one Sergio could have picked up single-handedly.

"I took a pair of spikes and found out that they didn't fit me. So, I brought them back to the store and exchanged them for the right size," he told me … finally! These guys set me up for a beating with a world-class body builder. Remember what many of those guys did to build muscles (when it was legal)?

"Sergio was a little temperamental," Junior said with a laugh. Sergio was too classy a guy to hold grudges. The whole story was a team prank. Sure, it's funny now.

"If anyone has any old roster information and pictures, it would be Jimmy Scholtes," Junior said. I plan to track him down. I promise you all.

The Entrepreneur

I wanted Otilio Arzola Jr. in my book for three reasons. First, he was one of the Spark Plugs. Next, he is an immensely successful self-made businessman. Finally, I also knew senior (or should I say señor?) Arzola long before I became lifelong friends with his son.

Otilio Arzola Sr. had an appliance store a couple of miles west of the lockshop where I'm taking up space normally reserved for paying clients.

"2701 W. Waveland. That's where he moved his shop. When I was a kid, like five or six, my dad's store was at Madison and Kinzie. One day, I'm sittin' there and my dad calls out, 'Hey, would you like to meet your countryman?' It was like looking at a photograph. I'm staring right at Roberto Clemente!" Junior exclaimed. We had the look of recognition and jealousy when he mentioned his name.

Roberto Clemente was the first Latin-American and Caribbean player enshrined in the Major League Hall of Fame. When Junior met him, he was the All-Star right fielder for the Pittsburgh Pirates (in town to play the Chicago Cubs).

"He would always visit the Puerto Rican stores when he came to town," Junior explained. He was obviously a great asset to his community. His last act on this planet was one of humility and humanity: His plane was lost en route delivering supplies to Nicaraguan earthquake victims (New Year's Eve 1972).

Arzola Sr. was a community advocate as well. It didn't turn out very well for him either.

"During the Chicago riots, my dad's first store burned to the ground," Junior reminded us. Do a Google search for "Chicago Riots." In April 1968, civil unrest after the Dr. Martin Luther King assassination turned into something sinister. That's when Junior's dad was ushered out of the neighborhood.

The Democratic National Convention triggered another riot in August that same year. In between, Robert Kennedy (headed for Chicago) was assassinated on June 5.

Time to lighten the mood, I'd say. I met Junior's dad at his new store. He had three gold stars in his teeth. That doesn't mean much to you all. I just wanted Junior to know how well (and fondly) I remember him. I didn't expect to talk about music at all during this interview, but something I found out about Otilio Senior never surfaced until now.

"Did I ever tell you my dad was a music composer? My dad wrote music and sold it in the Spanish community," Junior said. No, I never knew that.

"It is part of a Stanford University collection," he continued. I found one of the links for you. https://searchworks.stanford.edu/view/7843040 Watching his father in action must have sparked Junior's enterprising drive. He opened Southport Security some 25 years ago. After the Spark Plugs disbanded, Otilio emerged as an accomplished businessman.

"I played baseball for a year at Southern Illinois University. Famous coach Itch Jones told me I had to cut my hair. Instead, I quit the team. I only went to college about a year," Junior said.

"I used to get back to Chicago pretty often. You could take Air Illinois from Carbondale and land at Meigs Field in Chicago," he added. Maybe he was homesick or felt a little displaced after his baseball hopes slipped away.

Junior traveled to a few Spanish-speaking countries, and even spent some time in Canada. He became friends with a guy named Joey Gruber. I was just about to ask him how he became a locksmith, but he beat me to it.

"Joey's dad owned Ashland Lock. He not only gave me a job and taught me the trade, he also let me sleep in his shop. I got free rent and utilities. I got paid fairly and could pick up extra money by answering calls after working hours," he said. That sounded a little bit like me. Junior certainly wasn't afraid of hard work.

"I wasn't good in school. I was approaching 30 and could barely read newspapers. I hired a tutor for reading comprehension," Junior told me. Success and formal education don't necessarily go hand in hand.

"I played tennis to get in shape and remembered my dad told me I'd be successful once I found a way to make money while I slept. Made sense to me. I bought my first building (2035 N. Winchester). I bought more buildings in the Bucktown area," he continued. He did very well in Chicago real estate. His dad also taught him how to tell good advice from bad.

Otilio sold a few of his buildings to Chicago Bear Shaun Gayle. Their first transaction blossomed into a business that lasted 20 years and had 145 apartments at its peak.

"I would be roaming the sidelines during home games while he was playing. A lot changed for him, and us, once his career ended," Junior sadly recalled. When their business relationship dissolved, it seemed as if their personal relationship also took a different direction.

Junior's success has more to do with relationships than enterprise. Our friendship dates back to the late 1960s. Jimmy Scholtes and his family moved west some years ago. He and Junior still catch Arizona Coyotes' or Chicago Cubs' spring games every year. Junior got this book started and deserves the thanks. If you're unhappy, I'll take the heat, like I did for Junior with Sergio, the former Mr. World!

Locksmith and center-fielder "Junior" Arzola

Hank Zemola

It's hard to get an interview with guys like Hank Zemola. Like so many of the other characters in my book, myself included, Hank seldom sits still long. He's the main man at Chicago Events (http://www.chicagoevents.com). I caught up with him for a late supper in one of his favorite Lakeview restaurants near Diversey and Kenmore.

For decades, his company also managed international events, like cycling in Nuremberg, Germany. I would often see him working at the Puerto Rican Festival and Gay Pride and Bud Billiken parades, just as I do.

Hank carries a walkie-talkie to coordinate security and facilities at multiple venues. I man my push cart and sell umbrella hats to party-goers.

As you already read, there are three different phases in my life. First, there was the passionate pursuit of a musical career and the many roles that evolved from those pursuits. Then, I entered into my wild time in competitive sports, particularly bowling and baseball. Now, I am drawing on my organizational experience in both earlier phases.

I'm still promoting on behalf of the groups and folks I introduced in my book. They are all equally dear to me. Folks my age might call this the do-whatever-the-hell-you-want phase. We've earned it.

Triple Success

Just like me, Hank Zemola stayed in the same neighborhood all his life. He loves Chicago like I do, and it loves him back. He grew up alongside a few characters who helped mold his athletic career (without knowing it).

In the Lakeview neighborhood, Draper Street was a dead-end (geographically, of course) where the kids could play every kind of sport imaginable with minimal interference from traffic.

There was even a competitive game in the city called "Ledge." It seemed as if many schools and apartment buildings had decorative stone outside the first floor. The angled stone capped the stonework, and players would stand at the curb and whip a rubber ball toward that angled "ledge" at the top.

You would count a "ledge" if the ball angled up and outward so you could catch it on the fly. If you missed the ledge, you had to catch the ball on a single bounce or you were "out." Any number of players were welcomed, as long as the players promised to be fiercely competitive. You'd be surprised how many neighborhoods adopted that game. Hank used something as simple as this to develop his coordination. The neighborhood kids helped him develop his competitive nature and determination.

"I can still remember playing pickup baseball when I was 12 or 13 years old. I hit the ball and was thrown out at first base from left field. That inspired me to start running, everywhere. I made the Schurz track team my freshman year," Hank said. That would be Carl Schurz High School at Addison and Milwaukee, a little west of Lane Tech. In the late 1960s, Schurz had two distinct advantages over rival Lane. The school had a killer baseball team, and it had girls. Lane was an all-boys school back then.

"I also made the baseball team. My first two official at-bats were home runs. One right-handed and one left-handed," Hank continued. I guess you couldn't be thrown out at first that way either, huh? In 1969, Hank's team won the state baseball championship. I swear, he should have still been playing on Addison Street years later. I'm talking about Wrigley Field, home of the Chicago Cubs.

I just started to get the Spark Plugs off the ground at the height of Hank's high school baseball success. To be competitive in the Humboldt Park Latin Leagues, you needed some "brass" and a willingness to hustle. I had plenty of both.

Local businessman Frank Milito offered to sponsor us. I had to round up the best neighborhood players possible. I didn't have a problem asking local coaches if any players were open to playing summer ball. My most sought-after player was already a Chicago celebrity.

Hank and his coach agreed to play for the Spark Plugs, and it proved to be a good experience. Occasionally, major-league baseball scouts ventured out to Humboldt Park on North Avenue. The first time Hank suited up for our game, I asked him to pitch for us. He would normally be the right-fielder because he had an incredibly strong arm. He pitched a no-hitter that day. Would I be able to one day brag about helping him get national recognition?

His demeanor and talent enabled him to make several friends on the team. Many of them, like sponsor Frank Milito or Armando DeGuzman, would maintain contact with him throughout the decades.

"Frank and I remain good friends. I consider him like a godfather," Hank said. "I remained quite active in Humboldt Park baseball long after I stopped playing. Thousands of people watched the games (then and now). There was community and sunshine. Great memories."

New Phases and New Faces

Hank's family encouraged him to apply for a job at UPS—you know, the kind of talk you hear from family members: need a good job with benefits, need a plan for after a sports career, etc. He started part-time and worked his way into full-time employment. He was promoted to manager and then became a customer service representative. Eventually, he became a corporate lobbyist for the industry. While still working his way up, he was asked to set up a community service project.

"I suggested a Christmas party to benefit an orphanage [when there was still such institutions]. It was a huge success and became an annual event," Hank mentioned. So, that's where he got his first taste of community organizing. As expected, he would take his accomplishments to extraordinary levels.

Hank witnessed (and certainly contributed to) his company's success. When he started, the company was only operating in 21 states. By the time he left in the mid-'80s, the company was in all of the lower 48 states and Canada.

"If I'd known they were planning to go to Europe with next-day air, I might have stayed," he told me. So what would get a guy to walk away from that type of success within an industry-leading corporation? I'm pretty sure I know. Could it be the love of music?

"My manager told me he was going to give me a week to decide if I wanted to be a manager or a musician," he said. Hank's band was very popular with the UPS employees. It sounded like he was leaving something out of the story. Maybe I just wasn't listening.

"Carl, I probably didn't mention this before, but I was a pretty good drummer for a group named Boatload. We were pretty well known on the northwest side of Chicago and recorded a couple of albums at Midwest Sound at 63rd and Cicero near Midway Airport. One of our sessions came right as Styx left the studio while working on Light Up," Hank related. "Our group was getting so many offers for gigs, I had to start referring them to other bands."

That sounded like the beginning of a solid promoting career. Why just go "solid" when you can go "spectacular" instead? Hank had an eye for talent and for business. He kept both eyes open. Instead of waiting for the next big thing, why not take part in creating it?

"John Mellatello from the Jolly Club on Irving Park would always recommend our band," Hank said. I think John must have shown Hank how this "club thing" worked as well.

"My first show was at Stages Music Hall on Clark Street near Wrigley Field," Hank continued. Now he was starting to sound like me. He opened some edgy venues like East End, West End, and the legendary Tut's in the 900 block of West Belmont Avenue.

"We made the front cover of *Billboard Magazine*," Hank told me. "At Tuts, we did a WGCI night. We proved REM was far more than a garage band. At the West End, we used Savoy Brown to open the club. The BoDeans, Violent Femmes, and Cheap Trick were like house bands there. We would book them every few weeks. Ken Adamany asked me if I would book his groups," Hank continued. Ken (who I met while working at CASK Attractions) was also the manager for Cheap Trick.

"We booked the Time. Morris Day was the lead singer, and Prince played guitar. The Spice Girls were the backup singers. Prince's first record release was at Tuts. I did most of the booking," Hank added. He also booked Baby Huey and the Babysitters, among countless others.

Until Next Time

Our interview closed with recollections of classic appearances by John Belushi and Bill Murray at the Earle of Old Town in the 1600 block of North Wells. Then, we circled back to other Hank Zemola athletic feats.

Hank played with the Chicago Stars baseball team near Amundsen High School at Damen and Foster. He hit a ball measured close to 450 feet. He also mentioned he joined the "650 club," meaning he was able to heft a barbell loaded with roughly a third of a ton.

"I have to be careful about getting too bulky, or it will affect my flexibility," he cautioned. Hank, that is one of my concerns as well.

I learned a few new things about my baseball teammates. We talked more about music than I anticipated. I'm certainly not surprised by their success. As long as I keep doing what I'm doing, I like my chances of running into one of them on any given day.

That's a comforting feeling for a guy my age. It's great when they remember who I am. That's nearly as good as *me* remembering who I am. The next dinner is on me, as long as it is not past my bedtime.

There you have it: the Spark Plugs from A to Z. That is, from Arzola to Zemola, with a few others in between.

RIP Prince—
Here are more fond memories and the grief that goes along.
Prince Rogers Nelson passed away on April 21, 2016.

In My Spare Time

I started bowling seriously in 1965. I know, that was probably the busiest time I ever had. Think about it. I would just wrap up a gig, dance, or concert and have nothing but nervous energy coursing through me. What was I going to do? Go home, drink, and smoke cigarettes until I could fall asleep? How about drink, smoke cigarettes, mingle with a different insomniac crowd, compete, and make a little money in the process? Bowling, to the rescue.

My first gig in this newly discovered world was at Lakeview Bowling Lanes on Clark Street. After 34 years (1999), I finally gave up the grind of competition and the hassle of trudging through the snow and cold of winter while hefting 16 pounds or so in each hand. I counted about 65 places where I bowled during those years. I included a list here (to prove I still know how to remember stuff). This also shows what I consider important enough to remember. If I haven't returned your call by now, oh well …

By the way, I didn't just bowl in some of those leagues: For some, I was the secretary-organizer-treasurer—the master of ceremonies, if you will.

You can skip these next few paragraphs if you choose (especially if you are a stickler for spelling). I did my best.

20th Century Bowl (Many Leagues); Grand Bowl (In League); Windy City Bowl (Tournament); Riviera Bowl (In League); Holiday Bowl (In League); Hi Spot Bowl (League); Ago Bowl (In League); Norridge Bowl (In League); Beryn Bowl (Tournament); Monte Cristo (In League); North Center Bowl (In League); Drake Bowl (In League); Bel Bowl (In League);

Willow Brook Bowl (Tournament); Howard Bowl (In League); Sun Set Bowl (League); Sky Bowl (Tournament); Diversey River Bowl (Tournament); River Grove Bowl (In League); Castways Bowl (In League); Habetler Bowl (Tournament); Irving Park Lanes (In League); Wooddale Bowl (Tournament); Town Hall Bowl (Tournament); Classic Bowl (League); Hill Side Bowl (In League); Brunswick River Grove Bowl (In League);

Star Dust Bowl (Tournament); Town & Country Bowl (In League); Mont Clare Lanes (In League); Waveland Bowl (Tournament); Schiller Bowl (Tournament); All Star Lanes (Tournament); Timber Lanes (League); Broadview Bowl (Tournament); Turner Bowl (In League); Marigold Bowl (In League); Lawn Lanes; Arena Bowl (Tournament); Idle Hour Bowl (In League); Fire side Bowl (In League); Bal Mont Bowl (In League);

Ever Green Bowl (In League); Thunder Bird Lanes (Tournament); Mages Bowl (League); Maner Bowl (In League); Nilies Bowl (Tournament); Sim's Bowl (Tournament); Forest Lanes (In League); Super Bowl (Tournament); Lawrence & Western Bowl (In League); Ridge Bowl (In League); Golf Mill Bowl (In League); Ford City Bowl (Tournament); Scottsdale Bowl (Tournament);

Maple Lanes (In League); Downer Grove Bowl (Tournament); Clearing Bowl (In League); Karlov Bowl (Tournament) ; Miami Bowl (In League); Gage Park Bowl (In League); Marzan's Bowl (In League); New Playdium Bowl (In League); and National Lanes (In League).

Long before I actually won the grand prize in Chicago's Beat the Champs tournament (more on that later), I was a big fan. I spent a crazy amount of time listing the past winners in this section. FYI, this was done without a computer. You decide whether I'm bragging or confessing.

Every time I step out of my modest apartment, I consider it a meaningful adventure. The day I laid out this chapter, I walked to the CTA Brown Line Armitage station and cruised to the Harold Washington Library stop.

When I was growing up, the station was just called Van Buren & State. Now it has a much classier name. It should remind us all of our place in Chicago history. We'd be better people if we compared ourselves to a guy who died in office while serving as mayor of the greatest city in the world from 1983-87.

Harold Washington and I were alike in many ways. He was born in Chicago, too. Don't you like the guy already? Neither of us was too "keen" on school. He was a member of the first DuSable High School graduating class. I was part of the first group to get a Cooley High diploma.

He and I were both kind of community organizers. We were both headstrong and passionate. Okay, now I have to stand back in awe from here on. He studied law at Northwestern University after his WWII tour of duty with the Army Corps of Engineers.

He gained prominence in 1980 with his work on the Illinois Human Rights Act while part of the Illinois legislature. I'm not sure who picked up the slack since his departure. I suggest you do your research at the Harold Washington Library. Take the easy way like I did. Harold Washington has a public building named after him—the hard way.

Okay, here's my best presentation of the information I promised. You'll recognize how many houses I also bowled in. See, if you are a bowling insider, you refer to the establishment as a "house" rather than an "alley." That's how you add a touch of class to an activity that combines sweating, aggression, and alcohol.

Man, did I ever feel right at home. I apologize again for any typos, especially if you bought a book. I'll make it up to you with an autograph. Or, you can put your autograph in my book. I have one right here!

I want to recognize teammates who helped me through a lot of this confusion: Kenneth Dower, Randy Holmgren, Darwin Skrzynecki, Mike Paolicchi, and Al Brown.

You'll meet Victor Lobello later in this chapter.

Beat the Champs

Skip to 1993 to see a familiar name: I was among a handful of winners with a pinfall smaller than my female counterpart. I didn't cry about it. That would have ruined the upholstery in my *new car*. Once again, Jamie Tam did typing and formatting.

Year – Women Winners; Men Winners

1962 – Bredand Anderson (887) Cinderella Rec; Nick Levas Jr. (915) Lorraino Bowl
1963 – Joann Brandley (917) Legion Lanes; Lonnie Williams (972) Stevenson Bowl
1964 – Sharon Hanson (894) Meadowdale; George Neesan (953) Riviera Bowl
1965 – Alice Azzarello (900) Bel-Bowl; Jack L. Milller (911) Bel-Bowl
1966 – Patricia Flowers (885) Schneider's Bowl; Perry Grimes (913) 3-D Bowl
1967 – Betty Rhoads (940) Evergreen Bowl; Michael Suslik (944) Andys Rock Bowl
1968 – Fran Metallo (892) Mages River Grove; Russell Zastro (854) Prima Bowl
1969 – Mary Wolhkes (850) Plaza Lanes; Louis Vihnanaek (902) Austin Bowl
1970 – Donna Schumacher (868) 3-D Bowl; Warren Simon (937) Jay Bee Rec
1971 – Lois Freitag (916) Sports Bowl; John Lindmeier (879) Elmurst Rec
1972 – Anne Stair (895) Niles Bowl; Kenneth Dower (918) Calo Bowl
1973 – Kathie Overton (880) Welcome Lanes; Donald Copeland (876) Stiker Lanes
1974 – Sharon Anerson (894) Jeffery Lanes; Nick Mariano (927) Hi Spot Lanes
1975 – Sue Hunter (868) Meadowdale Lanes; Bob Wronski (982) Laredo Lanes
1976 – Natalie Ballack (868) Frontier Lanes; David Macek (916) New Playdium Bowl
1977 – Lyn Gray (890) Glenwood Bowl; Mike O'Gradney (920) Bruswick Bowl
1978 – Shirley Berling (887) El-Mar Bowl; Bob Sckwarz (900) Bruswick Bowl
1979 – Lois Byford (899) Lisie Bowl; Vic Yongberg (887) Bowling Green Sports
1980 – Joan Proper (872) Highway Lanes; Randy Holmgren (925) J&W Playdium
1981 – Kathy Bartley (867) Country Club Hills; Joseph Meyers (948) Bowlers Club
1982 – Arline Curtis (900) Stevenson Bowl; Peter Sobo (963) Riviera Lanes
1983 – Earlene Smith (864) Classic Bowl; Al Ehn (986) Arena Bowl
1984 – Paulett Reed (903) Super Bowl; Ed Konkel (903) Sports Bowl
1985 – Charmatne Metzer (889) Mote Cristo Bowl; Martin Miller (983) Paliside Bowl
1986 – Joyce Cunningham (903) Gala West Bowl; Jim Williams (873) Arena Bowl
1987 – Pam Pobat (860) Stardust Bowl; Harry Brand (941) Classic Bowl
1988 – Ann Rutenbar (916) Fox Bowl; Mike Madle (892) Amf Forest Lanes
1989 – Bev Chistensen (835) Arena Bowl; Darwin Skrzynecki (971) Woodfield Bowl
1990 – Marilyn Daliege (912) Arena Bowl; Carl Edelmen (926) Elk Grove Bowl
1991 – Jackie Katch (859) Beverly Bowl; Dean Thompson (962) Hawthorn Lanes
1992 – Christine Puccinelli (920) Elk Grove Bowl; Mark De Felippis (920) Lawn Lanes
1993 – Jackie Todaro (913) Elk Grove Bowl; Carl Bonafede (897) Mages Bowl
1994 – Dee Marnell (940) Arena Bowl; Mike Paolicchi (937) Thunderbide Lanes
1995 – Roselia Thacker (856) Dolton Bowl; Bob Hjeim (905) Lombard Lanes
1996 – Wada Wells (916) Parkview Bowl; Mike Katula (947) Peotone Bowl
1997 – Sandy Pickham (914) Palos Bowl; Nestor Oga Lesco (935) Hillside Bowl
1998 – Antoinette Hooks (832) Diversey River; Angelo Sutton (888) Globo Bowl
1999 – Cindy O'Keefe (851) Arena Bowl; Steve Salerno (987) Eden Bowl
2000 – Patsy Johnson (915) Hillside Bowl; Jerry Morano (1018) Fox Bowl
2001 – Mary Arsinow (899) Schiller Bowl; Al Brown (965) Mon Clare Lanes
2002 – Kelly Pacewood (934) Centennial Bowl; Kevin Nielfeldt (952) Peotone
2003 – Velmarie Clavell (948) Carpenter Dolton Bowl; Mike Piper (1036) Irving Park Lanes
2004 – Mary Ann Gates (908) Skokie Lanes; George Hardison (1068) Schiller Bowl
2005 – Dolly Honaker (988) Habetler Bowl; Hussein Forouzi (939) Habetler Bowl
2006 – Anne Dancy (945) Skyway Lanes; Nickolas Haase (961) Stardust Bowl
2007 – Beverly Lane (943) Diversey River Bowl; Jason Wojnar (1039) Burr Oak Bowl
2008 – Jan Schmidt (909) Fox Bowl; Mike Nape (967) Fox Bowl
2009 – Lisa Partynski (913) Elk Grove Bowl; Bob Mosher (917) Hoffman Lanes
2010 – Teresa Sowell (938) Bluebird Lanes; Tom Finnen Jr. (1058) Oak Forest Bowl
2011 – Carol Szubart (976) Habartler Bowl; Scott Lengyel (1021) Habatler Bowl
2012 – Yorlaunda Taylor (954) Irving Park Bowl; Robby Spigner (972) Dolton Bowl
2013 – Jen Laskov (966) Timber Lanes; Kyle Lane (1037) Lisie Bowl
2014 – Vicki Guadagno (943) Wood Dale Bowl; Ryan Yanel (1143) Raymonos Lanes
2015 – Danyell Simmons Oak (1010) Castways Bowl; Jason McReady (1060) Sururbanite Bowl
2016 – Wilhelmina Brown (985) Skyway Bowl; Kevin Kullman (1018) Centennial Bowl

The Day I Beat the Champs

Did you notice my "spare time" play on words? I made never having any spare time a priority. I found one passion after another to fill up my days. As I mentioned, I did far more than roll my ball at the pins. I organized a number of leagues at my "house" at Cicero and School: Northwest 20th Century lanes. At age 52, I entered the annual Beat the Champs bowling competition run by the *Chicago Sun-Times* and Metropolitan Bowling Association. In a nutshell, you used your league handicap to square off against many of the area's top bowlers.

Seymour "Sandy" Shub, the reporter who created the charity tournament in 1961, and Jack Whitehead of the MBA supervised. That year, I only bowled in the Monday Night Industrial League at Mages Bowl. In the final match, the dude I bowled against was a heavy-hitter, averaging 215. Obviously, he had no handicap (what they call a "scratch" bowler). My league average hovered just north of 140 pins per game.

I came out "smoking" with 193 and 196 opening games. My opponent opened with 257 and 237. In the world of handicap bowling, I actually had the lead. My nerves overtook me, and I posted a 150 in Game 3. My opponent followed my downward spiral (though not quite as far) with a sub-par 200. Apparently, we were both fixated on the "math" of the handicap, rather than rolling the best ball possible. One of us would be handing over the keys of the first-prize Ford Tempo to our opponent.

In the last game, my slim lead steadily dwindled. Remarkably, my opponent was still unable to return to form. The last frame determined who would dejectedly lug home a 27-inch color Zenith instead of the Holy Grail. My shaky toss left a split on the first ball, and I posted a 170 final score. I told myself to head for the door. With a routine "mark," he would drive away in my car. Maybe he felt I was looking over his shoulder when he left the 2-10 split (then again when the 10-pin held its ground after his second roll).

His 257, 237, 200, and 193 were good for a total of 887, above his average. My 193, 196, 150, and 170 put me above my league average every game. My 188 handicap pins gave me a score of 897: a 10-pin victory! This was after I was only four pins away from being ousted in the semi-final round. Was this better than managing the Buckinghams during their surge to rock-and-roll royalty? Only on this single day, it was.

Since 1961, the tournament raised over $2.5 million for charity. My windfall was born of a noble cause. I feel better about that. I also know it takes a great deal of effort (some say sandbagging) to come into a tournament with a 148 average (after competing for decades in scratch leagues). An average (pun intended) guy or gal wouldn't be able to handle the humiliation. He or she wouldn't be driving away in a new set of wheels, either.

Victor Lobello

I was driving to Habetler Bowl during rush hour. Actually, there's nothing rush about it when you head west down Foster Avenue toward the intersection of Central and Northwest Highway. Obviously, nobody ever thought the Chicago city limits would extend this far. That's why Foster is a single lane in each direction with an agonizing bend just east of Milwaukee Avenue.

Along with Northwest Highway and Foster, they created a Bermuda Triangle for unsuspecting motorists. A Chicago police department building is located right there as well (diabolical). After a couple of questionably legal turns, I was heading northwest on Northwest (go figure).

The only sensible diagonal street in this area is Milwaukee Avenue, originating just west of the Merchandise Mart at the Chicago River. It meanders all the way to the border of Wisconsin and Milwaukee (kind of). I've heard all diagonal streets radiating outward from downtown were originally Native American trails. Urban planning had deep-seated roots.

I was on my way to meet a guy I haven't seen in nearly two decades. Victor Lobello and I bowled in a number of leagues at a shaky time in my music career. I never actually gave up but was searching for distractions. Bowling in a few leagues each week was just the thing I needed.

He and I started hanging out together just as I broke ties with Thee Prophets. Music still defines my timeline. I remember (while sitting in traffic that would drive me crazy other days) bowling in a dozen leagues at one time. You read that right. I was working the graveyard shift at a gas station and needed about sevem hours to kill before clocking in at midnight.

As I recall, Victor was managing the Little Caesars at Howard and Western. Our jobs were a lot more stressful than you might imagine. Even musicians never had it that tough. Bowling was not just a diversion: It was a form of somewhat affordable therapy. I say "somewhat" because bowling could get pretty expensive and time-consuming. For talented people, obsessions could become profitable. Just like in the music world, fate and luck would determine overall bowling fame.

I often bowled in the second or third position on my team. I was valuable for adding handicap pins to the overall pin count. Without getting too technical, you were either someone who could or could not average 200 pins a game. I was not—Victor was.

Victor was our "cleanup" bowler: one of the guys who thumped down enough pins to transform defeat into victory. He's one classy dude and well worth the trip I was enduring at that moment.

He seemed thrilled to meet me, I think. He might have been a little flattered (if not confused) when I asked if he would like to be interviewed for my book.

On the phone, he sounded just like the Victor I knew back a quarter of a century earlier. Then, he was a svelte, athletic specimen. He was an ultra-competitor as well. No wonder I liked him from the start.

He once tried out for the Chicago Cougars hockey team. In those days, budding hockey stars got a chance to meet legendary Chicago Blackhawks like Bobby Hull and Eric Nesterenko. He was too modest to tell anyone, of course. The word just circulated among his many bowling friends.

"I remember meeting you at 20th Century Lanes when I was in my early thirties, Carl. That was my house at the time," Victor said. See what I told you? Wherever someone feels most productive and connected, it becomes their "house." The Holiday Ballroom was my house in another life, I guess.

"I often bowled with a guy named Bob Wallace. We would bowl around a hundred games a week. Carl, you were an inspiration to me," he said. Come again? I already bragged about my athletic prowess. Victor must have noticed I never gave up and would do anything to help my team.

I wasn't shy about assembling the best group I could to compete in the leagues where we appeared several times per week.

"Carl, you were a fierce competitor. Most of all, you had integrity," Victor said. There had to be a reason why a guy of Victor's character and skill could be coaxed into yet another league. Maybe this is also a good time to explain how guys with a day job could afford the time (and cash) to spread themselves as thin as many musicians had to.

I didn't have a wife or steady girlfriend to please, or at least, appease. In my days as a manager, I learned how truly talented musicians were able to pull it off (at least for a while). I did everything I could to support them in their juggling act. Some say this was aiding and abetting a crime.

Victor thinks I have integrity (or at least I did back then). So here's how I helped people every way I could. I wouldn't do this for just anyone. A guy would have to be a talented bowler (and be devoted to his significant other) to make this all work. Check, check!

Here's the most important factor: She would have to be a devoted, though concerned partner. After all, a wife wanted to be supportive of a guy's dream while keeping at least one eye focused on necessary stuff like paying the bills.

See how well I was suited for my role? I was just promoting a dream they both had. Victor Lobello hoped to become a pro bowler without endangering the good things his wife and he already enjoyed. Good bowlers with the support system Victor enjoyed could engage in some serious "pot" bowling—you know, the kind of pot you put money into. Just trying to add a little clarity.

The Mont Clare Lanes and Banquet Hall was on Harlem Avenue near Wellington. It was one of many establishments built on the strength of Chicago's working class (now shuttered after 50-plus years in business). Then, talented bowlers would "clean up" during hours when average people were sleeping.

"My wife would watch me bowl in leagues with earlier start times. After she headed home, the pots would get serious. I could bring home a grand, maybe $1,400 at times. I remember it was $4,200 once," Victor said. Mostly, I would offer moral support during the late hours at the alley (I mean "house").

I could contribute "handicap" pins to Victor's teams, and we could also win "scratch" and "handicap" pools, where you put money into a "kitty" each game and the high-roller would cash in. I could win a few of those myself. Guys like Victor had enough "game" to cash in, pay for bowling, beer, and then some. Once your wife is sure you won't lose the rent, she heads for home before unworldly money rested on nearly every shot.

Victor Lobello currently bowls in (only) three leagues and maintains an average in the 180s. He said that almost apologetically or wistfully. Topping out at a 209 average would be awesome (unless you one day hoped to cash substantial paychecks on the pro tour). My music friends shared the stage with national stars and held their own. Victor did the same.

"I once went head-to-head against [PBA touring pro] Brad Snell. My first eight shots were strikes, and I won the match. I got a chance to bowl in many national tournaments with Hall-of-Famers over the years," he reminded me. It's hard for Victor to talk about himself. I have to coax him to list his 300 games.

"I've got seven total," he said. How about the rings? I'm still prompting him in his own chapter (my attempt to thank him for good times and friendship).

"We used to get a ring for every PBA-sanctioned 300 game," he said. So, he has a collection. Since then, the cash-strapped organization no longer bestows a permanent memento. Twelve straight strikes in a row? Times must be tough.

"I never managed a single 800 series," Victor mentioned. Maybe that's a defining mark (get it?) for bowlers hoping to tour professionally. Then, he "blindsided" me with a compliment that I barely deserve.

"Carl, some of my best times were bowling pot games with you on Saturday morning," Victor said. That would be the Saturday mornings following league games that started sometime late on Fridays. Legendary Chicago news anchor Harry Porterfield once featured Victor Lobello on his "Someone You Should Know" segment, which aired regularly on CBS Channel 2.

I don't need to be the first (or the most famous) to say Victor Lobello is someone you should know. Mutual respect and lasting friendship drew us together for a rewarding and long-remembered afternoon. I brought him a boxed set of my CDs. He asked me to autograph the booklet I included with them.

Maybe this part sounds like idle chatter. It probably would to me, too, if it hadn't been so long between conversations.

"I think my favorite house would be Marzano's," he said. I remember bowling there, of course. Marzano's was a house in every sense. It had a whopping 80 lanes, two restaurants, pool tables, and a banquet hall featuring live entertainment. I'm convinced the sport is just as appealing as ever (but less affordable for the average family).

We concluded with the recent changes Victor noticed in league play. Out of the 60 or so bowling balls that he owns, one of his favorites would be the Teal Rhino (ask him why yourself).

"People no longer use 16-pound balls," he told me. "The trend is to roll a 15-pound ball around 17 miles an hour." Speed is more important than weight. I don't think knowing that will get me out of retirement.

"I taught a lot of people to bowl. Actually, I encouraged them to create their own style," he concluded. Throughout our years of competition, Victor taught me a lot as well. His personal style creates lasting friendships.

I hope he enjoys his chapter as much as I enjoyed our reunion.

The Beat Goes On …

Lifelines

The title of this section just came to me. The people in this chapter had a lasting influence on my life. They may not have known it at the time (or ever), but each was the strongest thread connecting me to the rest of the world for a little bit. That's why it was so important to mention them in the last (and only) genuine book I will write.

That's quite a statement from someone who had no intention of writing a book at all, until the last couple years. Every one of my contributors saw my true self. All entertainers maintain a fiercely guarded private side, often to a greater degree than other folks experience. That doesn't make us better, just different.

My friends in this chapter (I don't know why all of them are female at the start, or do I?) are rockstars in their own right. They just let their fantastically human side show far more often than I would dare. If you are lucky enough to already know them, congratulations. If you meet them sometime in the future, let me be the first to tell you how lucky you are.

The first person in my chapter took time out of her busy days to visit me in the hospital when I needed the company and somehow still craved a little recognition. Why I needed to be poked and probed in a clinical setting is secondary (and part of the private side I mentioned). Anyway, that's the reason I decided she should be first on my list of introductions.

The rest are equally important and also came along at precisely the right time. Our relationships have evolved to the point (I think) that we have just the right amount of concern (and distance, where necessary) to keep it healthy.

Susan Rakis

Susan Rakis was an only child. When she was around 9 years old, the song **Susan** by the Buckinghams was falling just short of No. 1 on the Billboard Hot 100. Her mom took her to one of the band's concerts somewhere on the north side of Chicago. Afterward, the band members came out to sign autographs, and pre-teen Susan was in awe. Every member in the group was in their twenties when they patted her on the head and kissed her mom on the cheek.

They then set about pleasing the more "mature" girls in the audience, who promptly started ripping off the band's jackets and shirts. Susan's mom rescued her from the mayhem. That was the last time the little girl saw them for years.

As I mentioned in the Buckinghams' own chapter, the members disbanded (I love that pun) just as the heroine of this section was forming the Buckinghams fan club. Charismatic Carl Giammarese and Dennis Tufano formed a duo and were entertaining the diehard fans. Around 1971, Susan's mom took her and a friend to see Carl and Dennis perform once again.

This was a "cocktail" performance in a place that had a strict over-21 policy. Her mom's persuasive powers didn't get Susan front and center, but she was at least able to drink in another performance at age 14 or so. A mom's love and a teenage crush fused to create an everlasting (wiser and passionate) fan.

Shortly after the Buckinghams reunited at the Chicago Summerfest in 1980, Carl Giammarese got a first-hand account of this story from Buckinghams Fan Club President Susan Rakis. From that time on, there was growing Chicago interest in all things Buckingham.

By 1988, Buckingham Carl and Susan were talking about rekindling the fan club. However, it would now be in the hands of an energetic community activist, instead of a star-struck teenager. Of course, we're still talking about the same person. Shortly afterward, she took on booking responsibilities, merchandising, correspondence, and publicity for the Buckinghams brand.

Carl and Susan were hitting on all cylinders in the 1990s, and Susan planned a lot of community events where the band would challenge local radio celebrities in bowling tournaments. It was great

Susan Rakis—
I didn't get a chance to meet Carl Bonafede in person until Carl Giammarese started writing his book. Right from the beginning, I fell in love with Carl Bonafede. He was such a nice guy—so giving, with a story behind just about everything he does. He is such a funny guy, and he seems to remember everything. He's a true "fan" of Chicago, aside from still being one of its most engaging and colorful characters. Who else could pull off a "gig" like selling umbrella hats outside Wrigley Field or at the Bud Billiken parade on Chicago's South Side?

publicity. They also had annual picnics for which Susan booked appearances for several personalities from the days when the Buckinghams originally struck gold with **Kind of a Drag**.

That's when I first met Susan Rakis (the original Bucks Girl). I'm sure she heard a lot about me long before then. It took a few tries before we could sync our schedules. At first, I was worried that she already drew her own conclusions from the Buckinghams' stories and I would have to work hard to clear my name (just kidding).

It didn't take long for us to develop a great relationship. Needless to say, I was drawn to a new, younger, accomplished, personable, energetic, and creative version of myself. Opposites may attract, but like-minded people have an admiration and respect that last a lifetime.

She is still hard at work here in 2016, attending most Buckinghams shows and acting as road manager while retaining her role as an avid advocate for the Girl Scouts. That sounds a little like me, except I got more excited (some say unhinged) in my day. I'm thrilled the Buckinghams remain in such capable hands.

Dawn Lee Wakefield

The Jan./Feb. 2010 issue of *Keep Rockin'* magazine includes an article about the Screaming Wildman written by Dawn Lee Wakefield. When I started going through my scrapbook (more like a crate) of remembrances, the printed edition of her article found its way near the very top of the stack.

She called me a "rock impresario" in the article. There's another word I never would have used myself. This is the only place you'll see it. Only someone as talented as she could use it the right way. I'm guessing it means something good because the rest of the article was very flattering.

She's collaborating with Carl Giammarese on *The Buckinghams: My Journey* scheduled to hit the bookshelves in 2016. You can find out far more about her on her website http://www.dawnleewakefield.com. Aside from being a versatile and talented writer, she is also the president of West Communications. Once you see her varied list of accomplishments, you'll understand how honored I feel about her kind words.

I'm pretty sure I was one of the most taxing relationships she ever had as the subject of that article. It wasn't my intent (just the way of the Screaming Wildman). I can only hope it was in some way worth it for her.

Michele Abrams

Our paths would most likely have never crossed if not for the Buckinghams. Or maybe they would have after all, since her fierce independence and talent attracted a lot of attention. I count Michele Abrams as one of my lifelines because she helped keep me from completely slipping into the past. Setting up my website may seem like a small and charitable gesture to her, compared to her jaw-dropping accomplishments. It takes me a while (and a rare quiet moment) to really appreciate how much people do on my behalf.

Even now, this internet thing still baffles me. Michele approached it as a true pioneer and created a website that captured my essence. She used a modern tool to transport my fans back to the time near and dear to us. Most of all, I want to thank her for the patience it takes to deal with the Screamin' Wildman. Maybe I helped her prepare for another facet of her career.

Michele Sweeney Abrams has several credits as an actress and stunt person. The IMDb database http://www.imdb.com/name/nm4636732 (who knew there would be such a thing?) lists the mystery sci-fi *Divergent* among her credits. She's also known for her work on the *Chicago Fire, Chicago Med,* and *Chicago P.D.* television shows. Are you seeing a trend there? Then there's that stunt thing. I stopped far short of setting myself on fire to promote my groups.

 She's also credited as a writer for several songs on Carl Giammarese's **Trying Not to Fade** album. Maybe it takes stunt-person skills to truly keep your life in balance. I guess there are more things I could learn while proudly watching her either take flight or gently touch down (whatever the script calls for). Thanks again.

Isa Giallorenzo

Isadora Giallorenzo is the editor of Chicago Looks http://chicagolooks.blogspot.com and a contributor to the *Chicago Reader* http://www.chicagoreader.com newspaper. I was actually featured in the print edition of *Cracker You R Wardrobe* magazine. I found out that this is a Korean publication that started in late summer 2007. Look out for the July 2014 edition (No. 83), and you will see yours truly in the full-page color gallery a few pages from the back cover.

I was sporting one of my umbrella hats and decked out in full Bonafede splendor, right down to my toes. I managed to capture Isa's attention on Damen Avenue, and it led to her "Selling Shade" article in *The Reader* newspaper. Maybe a week later, she invited me to the photo shoot I just mentioned.

I know I've said it other places in this book. It's important for me to be engaged when I step out my door. The entertainer in me still wants to be noticeable and approachable. Isa reminded me that I was still making an impact at a critical time in my life and career. She knows fashion, so I'll take her word for it.

New Girl Band

The rockin' times of the late '60s always stay with me in some form. During some of my manic moments (you'd be surprised at how many there still are), I dream of once again fronting an all-girl band like the Daughters of Eve. Without the modern contraptions of the 21st century (like email), I did a pretty good job finding a couple of gifted musicians to get things rolling. Of course, I didn't have all of the "things" mapped out yet.

Gina Knight and **Michele Hubbell** made a lasting impression on me in the fleeting time we spent together (so far). See, my book contains a lot of looking back to the past. Some glimmer of hope keeps me grounded in the present and looking forward to another day. When you can associate names and faces to these fantasies, they sometimes become melodies, lyrics, or even bands.

Gina http://drumlessonsgirl.com is a versatile entertainer who just happens to "kill" on drums. When she (not often enough) steps to the microphone, she captivates jazz, blues, pop, and rock audiences with some charismatic vocals. Check out the best rendition of **I Want Candy** https://youtu.be/bXhaXNf7xHI I've ever heard or seen. I'm not just waving Chicago colors here. She could hold her own on a national stage.

Take North Avenue west from Chicago and stay on the road until they don't call it North Avenue anymore. Somewhere short of the Fox River, you are in Michele Hubbell territory. When musicians hear about dreams like mine, they do everything they can to take them to the next level. That's what happened in the case of building my Daughters of Eve tribute band.

Some might say a group that only existed a few (too short) years doesn't deserve that kind of attention. They were no ordinary band. They flat-out captivated the nation and the Midwest in particular.

Michele (sound engineer, musician, and owner of Stagedoor5 Musical Arts) must have seen promise in my vision.

Our new enterprise was put on hold after a few sessions, as you may have guessed by now. I'm grateful for the time we spent wishing on the same star and jammin' on the same stage.

Bernadette Vanno

I include Bernadette in my Lifelines chapter, but what I really mean for her is "bloodline." My dear niece and I shared far too few conversations over the decades, especially when compared to the fond remembrances we have of my "sis," Nancy.

It was an emotional time for me when I started pulling family photos together—so emotional that I got up the nerve (something I usually have in abundance) to phone Bernadette. Even though I'm getting used to (shame on me) calling people "out of the blue" after long periods without contact, this conversation was different in a few ways.

I could sense she recognized my voice right away, and later on said so herself. Of course, my call was a surprise (if not a shock to her). You know maybe the timing was a surprise, but deep down I think she knew I'd be calling her. I finally determined it really was my job, as her somewhat eccentric elder.

Bernadette knew me better than anyone else thanks to her mom's stories. We have a bond we could only feel and not explain. I'm guessing (before I quickly move on) conversations might have seemed too painful. That's my reason, which I know is no excuse.

Bernadette and I were also that awkward half-generation apart. Nancy and her young family were still only minutes away (at Oak Park and North). For a time, everybody would come over on Sunday for family-style pasta fagioli. I was already developing my teenage independence (and secretly fearing my parents' failing health), so Bernadette and I never really hung out.

She still remembers trips to the Lincoln Park Zoo, which was walking distance from the future home of Chi-Town Records (AKA Grandma's house). Bernadette was in 4th or 5th grade when her family headed for Columbus, Ohio. Both she and her brother went to Bishop Hartley High before Bernadette majored in English and comparative literature at Ohio State University.

She worked on an international studies quarterly for the political science department and with international students there. Bernadette thought about coming back to Chicago at times. I say it's never too late. It would be great to have family close to me again (especially this part of the family). She still remembers the way to the house. It pretty much looks the same (like me).

Bernadette got a chance to see some of Bill Moore's YouTube videos of yours truly. She mentioned hearing Paul Shaffer's shout-out, though she was not a regular Letterman watcher. I can only attribute it to a force that holds our worlds together. Perhaps, it was the intervention of a saint.

Lifelines Part 2

This is the testosterone-infused version of the previous section. You know, guys provide moral support in a macho kind of way. They are a group that doesn't expect, or won't tolerate, Screaming Wildman behavior very long. That was also true about the ladies who adorned this chapter, now that I think about it.

Some of them had more subtle ways of telling me my crap was wearing thin. Others didn't. A select few got a chance to see me without a jacket or tie. That's how you really know when you are in my inner circle (like it or not).

All the while I've been churning out these pages, I'm still struggling with the best way to introduce them all. I'm just going to "wing it" from this point onward.

Joe Pytel

If you liked any part of this book so far, you are already familiar with Joe Pytel's contribution. This is as close as you will get to a song collaboration. I did my best to cobble the words together. The melodies (and pictures) are mostly his doing.

This book is every bit as much his as it is mine. I thank him for the growing internet presence I now have. When it comes down to electronics and computers, the Screaming Wildman is painfully timid. I know this angers and confounds my friends. It would be disrespectful to say something like he works behind the scenes. It's all him.

I'm inviting you to read his book. I've stolen enough thunder up until now. You've most likely seen a ton of links to his YouTube clips on these pages. If you haven't already, I suggest that you subscribe to his channel (https://www. youtube.com/user/jayjay331). Come back in a few days and start reading again if you still feel a need.

I'm beginning to appreciate the amount of work it takes to put one of these productions together. He often meets the performers personally, gathers photos and histories, then lays the track down and infuses it with picture transitions. It's a mini theatrical production (and a labor of love) in my eyes.

He is much more of a music historian than I am, and he has the electronic savvy to go along with it. The Screaming Wildman YouTube channel, my website, my blog, the production of covers, and labels for my CDs are primarily the work of Joe Pytel. His playlists encapsulate the golden age of Chicago rock.

Joe has an exhausting full-time job and a family, aside from his passion for vintage Chicago rock-and-roll. I know it's unfair to expect anyone with those responsibilities to acknowledge those whims I generate on an hourly basis. I must be just lovable enough for everyone in this chapter to stop short of "decking" me at times.

As if that weren't enough, Joe did a lot of the electronic legwork to establish contact with many contributors to my (his) book. His knowledge and passion are the main reasons it may have entertainment value. Like I said earlier, it couldn't be anywhere near as good if we started five years ago. In all of that time, Joe's been entertaining and promoting us all.

As many of you know, I'm a very hands-on type of guy (except for computers). I hand-craft my own artwork. The very first time I met Joe was during his shift at the FedEx Office Print & Ship Center on Southport Avenue. Sounds like a commercial, huh? I was having an issue with one of my photos and Joe offered to help me. I thanked him and mentioned there were so few people willing to work with guys my age.

We talked a bunch (or more like he listened a bunch) while I wove together a few rock-and-roll tales. Over those few years, he's gone from attentive bystander to aficionado. He accompanied me to many interviews when putting this book together. I just flat-out enjoy his company. We attended a bunch of concerts during the year.

He and I posed for a picture at Mariano's (my favorite hangout and makeshift interview room) during one of our jaunts. He's too humble to accept any praise or thanks for everything he's done for me. I know there's a way to comment on YouTube. Let him (and the groups we all love) know you are still listening and reminiscing.

Joe Pytel and I hang out at Mariano's

Dave Hoekstra

From 1985 through 2014, Dave was a columnist and critic at the *Chicago Sun-Times*. He's also known for contributing to *Playboy* and *Chicago* magazines as well as the *Chicago Reader* newspaper. We were introduced a few years ago by Joel Bierig, another *Sun-Times* columnist, who you are about to meet.

Sorry if I sound like I'm bragging here, but Dave seemed to take an interest in my career and the groups I've worked with over the years. Of course, the Buckinghams have been my musical calling card for a half-century now. It will always be my conversation starter. This book is a prime example of what happens when you get me started.

If you put the Screaming Wildman in a room with a 2013 Studs Terkel Community Media Award winner, the resulting book would make both his fans and mine extremely happy. Unfortunately, it just wasn't in either of our cards. Maybe the room would have been too small to hold me. By now, you know how restless I can get.

So, a Bonafede-Hoekstra book collaboration didn't happen. Sometimes even two stars (modestly speaking) can't align. You've seen a form of that story repeated with many of the other groups I've featured—one big break away from the recognition they've earned. Anyway, by the time that book idea percolated, Dave was involved in a multitude of projects.

That's not to say we didn't collaborate in a very meaningful way. I'm grateful to list him as one of my lifelines and friends. In the *Chicago Sun-Times* Sunday Show magazine section published on October 10, 2010, Dave Hoekstra presented the Screaming Wildman, Carl Bonafede.

It included flattering photos and insights from Debi Pomeroy (Daughters of Eve) and Carl Giammarese (Buckinghams). Dave also did a shallow dive into the groups (unreservedly) less known: Lori Lee Williams, the Rail City Five, Baby Huey and the Babysitters, and my earliest group, the Gem-Tones.

By shallow dive, I mean there is a lot of information within the borders of a single article. I'm having second (maybe twelfth) thoughts about venturing out on my own in these pages.

If you enter Giammarese-Bonafede-Hoekstra into your search engine, a link to that entire show is one single click away. This is great. Why didn't anyone tell me about this new technology earlier? I'm getting carried away with my new discovery (at least to me).

Hoekstra-Nocturnal-Journal takes you right where I want you to go next. On the Dave Hoekstra website, you'll see travel, music, sports, and food among his passions. Dave-Hoekstra-Books (I'm getting carried away, Screaming Wildman style) will bring you to *The People's Place: Soul Food Restaurants and Reminiscences from the Civil Rights Era to Today.* You'll also notice awesome collaboration with two other Chicago legends: The foreword was written by Chaka Khan, and the photographs are from the legendary Paul Natkin.

The foreword of *The Supper Club Book: A Celebration of a Midwest Tradition* was written by none other than worldwide literary and broadcast icon Garrison Keillor. Man, this Hoekstra guy knows how to put a pitch out of the park. To think what he might have done with … you know.

Joel Bierig

During the 42nd and final season of Ray Meyer's illustrious career as the DePaul Blue Demon head basketball coach, a young sports writer from the *Chicago Sun-Times* got his first major assignment. Joel Bierig and I didn't meet until several years after the 1983-84 season, when they posted a 27-3 record and reached the Sweet Sixteen round of the NCAA national tournament. Joel went on to cover both the Cubs and White Sox from 1983-90.

The saddest part of the final run for the Blue Demons under Ray Meyer was the team was no longer playing at Alumni Hall. This was literally a stone's throw from my home and the equally legendary Roma Pizzeria, where I once worked and hung out, as you probably read earlier. I worked with Joel during the production of my short series of memories called The Screaming Wild Man – Carl Bonafede, a Man of Many Faces.

We also spent countless hours sharing our recollection of sports, music, and our love for all things Chicago. I consider him an enthusiastic friend, confidant, and collaborator. I know I can count on him to support me in new endeavors and share my fond recollections of days long gone.

Joel Bierig—
Carl possesses the drive and determination to succeed at whatever he undertakes, at any age. He says he sleeps, but I can't picture it. Blessed with boundless energy, he may be the best salesman, marketer, and innovator I've met. Simply put, he taught me a little about a lot of things, and it adds up to a wealth of knowledge that can't be found in textbooks.

Without Joel Bierig's perspective and sense of real English (not to mention his patience), this book would have never found its way into your hands. He's far more than my editor: He's a trusted friend and overall great guy. Thanks, man.

Rob Matijević

Conventional wisdom would say don't do business with friends. Maybe that is your fault. If you read any part of this book up to now, you've seen none of my friendships are conventional. Let me give you a crash course. First, seek out the best providers of a service. Next, take the time to visit their place of business. If you are an observant guy like me, you will see how they treat everybody. I have a talent for explaining what it takes to please me. So, what if someone thinks that I have certain "brass" parts? The most reliable and virtually indestructible connectors are made of brass.

Finally, once the individual matches your integrity, generosity, and professionalism as a business person, you'll have the makings of a lasting friend. Every meaningful conversation reinforces your judgment. I can appear as a "tough customer" to some; however, real professionals, actually real people, always rise to the occasion and deliver more than you expected. This is certainly the case with Rob, whose family business welcomes new members daily. Follow this link and decide for yourself: http://www.dnainfo. com/chicago/20140910/edgebrook/glad-cleaners-celebrates-75-years-on-northwest-side

I didn't read about him first. I could tell what he was "made of" from the very beginning. That also means that I told others about him. For instance, I told him that I have a pretty good "eye" for watches, which he enjoys collecting. He already knew how I like my clothes cleaned and tailored. I drive miles to benefit from his exceptional work. He drives miles every day for the pleasure of serving his customers. Maybe you wouldn't mention your background, or the fact that you are writing a book about it, to your dry cleaner. But if he was a friend …

"One of the guys who set me on the right path was a guy named Eddie Thomas," I remembered saying.

"Eddie Thomas?" Rob asked. You could see the wheels turning (if you get off your behind and talk face to face with your friends). Could it be that classy dude (who might have been of that era)? The one who also expects perfection but doesn't demand it? The one who will modestly admit that he was a record promoter? The one who lives down the street? The one who just might give me a call if I leave my number with Rob? Yeah, that one.

Rob Matijević—
I have known Carl for 10 to 15 years. He is one of the nicest, funny, story-telling guys who I ever had the pleasure of encountering. It's a pleasure every time he walks in. He says that *no one* can clean or alter his custom clothes like Glad Cleaners. Carl has taken me to numerous concerts and introduces me as *"Rob the cleaner"* – makes me laugh every time. Carl is so generous he refuses to let me, or the other people he brings, pay – a class act. He is an original – always on the move, thinking of his next gig. A promoter like no other. It's a blessing to have someone like that in your life. I am proud to call Carl my friend!

What do you want me to call Rob from Glad Cleaners (http://www.gladcleaners.com/)? Eddie and I, among many I am sure, call him a friend.

 "I keep hoping I don't see Rob until I'm on my way out. If he is at the counter, he won't take my money!" Eddie said. Good business creates lasting relationships.

Now Rob gives me a reason to stop in and say hello to Eddie. Eddie gives me a reason to drop off an armload of clothes at Rob's shop. Any time I drop in, he pulls a chair into his office and invites me to sit. I should mention the chairs already in his office are almost always occupied by other "customers" like me. Think of his business as a cross between the old-fashioned barber shop and VFW hall (without the booze). One of the best, and most welcome, social hubs that I can think of is near the corner of Central and Devon avenues. Bring your laundry. Drop in and pull up a chair. Just save one for me!

Chuck Mosier

Chuck is one of my oldest and dearest friends. We met at the Maxwell Street Market (obviously a man of my own heart), and I was just blown away by his record collection. He does some recording work for me. Occasionally, I'll come across some Super 8 film (because I never throw anything away). I'm still hoping there are snippets of live performances from my groups, and Chuck would show me what I saved. Sometimes, we have a laugh over why this stuff ever existed.

We've logged dozens of road trips through the years, including a couple of pilgrimages to the Surf Ballroom in early February to annually commemorate the last concert of Buddy Holly, Ritchie Valens, and the Big Bopper. This is a frigid seven-hour trek starting out on westbound I-90 from Chicago and heading nearly due north from Waterloo, Iowa. We've encountered swirling snow and menacing darkness many times, making it a truly authentic experience. It didn't keep us from trying again. We won't rule out a future trip, either!

We'd often meet the crew from Beverly Records, and we'd pay once "native son"-turned-radio-station-owner Jim Bernard a visit. I'm glad Chuck is there to enjoy the company of his new "old friends." Even at my age, I look forward to a road trip or two each year. Good friends make time stand still while the miles go by. Thanks, my good friend!

Oh, Man!
I could kick myself (if I wasn't afraid of breaking something). There are more people keeping me grounded and whose company I love. Ed Ogonowski is a 90-year-old fan of great music. From "day one," I promised myself to thank him in my book. Pete Weber, from Weber Press on north Western, worked with me on numerous projects throughout our decades. Thanks to you both!

CASK Attractions

As I mentioned, The Call-Allen-Stuart-Kalb booking and management company was known as CASK Attractions. I just remembered Ted Allen played piano, and I sang with him at some college gigs. I often would catch a group's first set while the club management would do some last-minute accounting. I would steer clear of wrangling with union officials.

I stumbled across some CASK keepsakes after my Dwight Kalb interview. I'm still amazed at how many acts I booked or recorded (actually booked *and* recorded). The CASK promotion method was much like it was at Willard Alexander. The best way to get clubs interested in various groups was to get their "vinyl" circulated. A disc jockey might get a program director to put it on the air. Of course, it was a long shot. It was often the best (or only) shot for many groups.

I already introduced you to many talented and charismatic bands that were just one performance, song, year, singer, arrangement (or manager) away from national (at least local) celebrity. There were other groups that deserved the chance to stay together and provide solid entertainment (in other words, earn a living) for years, even decades to come. The "only" obstacle would be finding a manager, a studio, and willing bandmates (and supportive parents or spouses) who allowed you to be there on the "one" day in your life the planets aligned. Here are a few you may recall. If so, you're welcome.

I also found some promotional photos for the following groups. Some developed a history and a following of their own. They all deserve mention, in my opinion.
The Impressions – Okay, the planets did align for them, though a record producer (whom I don't need to mention) was able to lure Jerry Butler away from his original group.
Gilbect Ross (I think) – I think these guys came from Poland. As I remember (and am not sure why), their leader spoke broken English.
Original Fenders – I remembered booking them and they were a popular night club act.
Vince Garrett Revue – They were a CASK Attractions act managed by Allen or Call.
Love Between Us – I remember them because of their strange publicity pictures.

Freddy Jones Band – The Freddy Jones band was formed in 1988 by college friends Wayne Healy and Marty Lloyd in South Bend, Indiana. In Chicago, they began playing with Jim Bonaccorsi. I don't know how the name came about.

Freddy and the Freeloaders – They were another Mickey Call group.

Sheri and the Right Brothers – The were promoted by Ken Adamany in Wisconsin, if I remember correctly.

Bob Kuban and the In-Men – Best known for The Cheater, which nearly made it to the Top 10 nationally, are part of the Rock & Roll Hall of Fame's one-hit wonders exhibit. Mickey was booking them in a number of locations. Walter Scott, frontman for the group, eventually struck out on his own after a while, and sadly, was a homicide victim in 1983.

Baby Huey and the Babysitters – They were managed by Eddie Thomas and often booked by CASK. I included a link to an entire album. YouTube® https://youtu.be/8g3yocin8DA Marsha Tomal from the Daughters of Eve played with them for a while as did Nick Fortuna from the Buckinghams.

Ravelles – I found the YouTube song called **Psychedelic Movement** from 1968 https://youtu.be/hfhzsftHtnc for you. The group played throughout the Midwest and was at a few venues with the Buckinghams. I recorded them, but we never brought a record out. Leo Johnson from the Barn in Sterling, Illinois, sent me their tape. The Buckinghams and DoE played there, too. I can still remember how hard it was to get there and back. They named the place well—there were horses all over the place.

I found my CASK lists from back in the day. I thought you would be impressed with the number of acts we hooked up and the places we booked them. You might still find some of your favorites on Facebook.

Groups – I apologize for any misspellings. This is an extremely old list that was mimeographed decades ago. Google that, you youngsters! Groups mentioned somewhere else in this book are *emphasized in boldface*.

Appleton Century, Acropolis, Ayes of Aquarius, Ask Rufus, Aorta, Apollos, ***American Breed***, *Brotherhood, Brass Taxi, Black Veil, Big Happy Family,* ***Baby Huey***, *Buddy & the Citations*

Cars, Catakon, Checkmates, Crystal Ship, Cleveland Wreckin Co., Choo Xpress, Corp. Limited, ***Chips***, *Come Vega, Congregation, Cheaters, Country (Brass Triangle), Chicago's Own, Centrifugal Force, Democratic Convention, Don Drum & the Ascension*

Elgin Watch Band, Epic's, Fadeaways, Fourth Chapter, Family, ***Facts of Life***, *Five Blind Mice, Feminine Gender, Fushia, Gerald Sims Trio, Genesis, Gin Mill, Humphrey & the Palookas* (**Careless Love**: https://youtu.be/HMnDmgi540Q), *Hard Rock Candy, His & Her, Hi Guys*

Invaders, Ivory Tower, In the Beginning, James St. Overpass, Jimmy Vee & the Scamps, Journey, Jet Set, Jimmy Head & the Headlyters, Johnny Ross, John Basil, Jory Ray Group, Johnny Lee & the Brotherhood, Kasinos, King Sopl & Heart of Soul

***Lincoln Park Zoo**, Loves Children, Life, Lettuce Prey, Lonely with Tear Drops, Lavender Pond, Mod Squad, Maxima Show Band, Merry Widow, My Brothers Keeper, Madison Avenue, Magnificent Seven, My Friend, Morning After, Nick Rogers Trio, New York Centenniel, North Side*

*Organization, Outside Chance, Outfit, Outrage, Original Fenders, Opp's, Power & Glory, Pot Luck, **P.C. Limited**, Peanuts Popcorn & Cracker Jack, Pleasure Seekers, Percy Cat & the Knight Watchers, Plastic People, Quiet Tear, Quiet World, Ron Knight & the Daze, Rage, Rotary Connections, Ralph, Rest, Rock Collection*

Sidney, Soul Set, Soul Sensation, Soul System, Soul Breed, Salt and Pepper, Sound of Music Revue, Soul Machine, State & Madison, Second Hand Store, Something New, Side Show, Soul Enterprise, Soft Bread, Sheri & the Right Bros., Sunny Januare & the Suede Reign, Sas Shades, Sebastian Shane & the Sinns, Sheffields, Sunday Funnies

#3330 Lake Shore Drive, the Day & Night Soul, 26th & Main, Toy Factory, the Truth, Third Generation, Vanishing Americans, With Love, Why Knots, West Side Story, West Wind, Work Shop, Young System

List 2 - Clubs Venues without a city or state designation were in Chicago.

*Associated, Annex, After Hours, Aragon, **Attic** – Milwaukee WI, Atlantic, Alley, **Apollo Theatre** – New York NY, **Barn**, Brown Jug, Bullets Lounge, Bowery & Speak Easy, Bay Lanes, Black Eye, Bitter End, Bambies, Bang Bang, Bull & Bear, Beverly Lounge, Blackhawk Pump – Jacksonville IL, Beneath the Street – Milwaukee WI, Burtons, Benny's, Beavers, **Black Knight** – Lake Geneva WI, Basin Street West – San Francisco CA*

*College Inn, Cheraid, Crystal Lounge – St. Petersburg FL, Cape Cod – Burnham IL, Club Cornelia, Club Bonanea, Club Aladdin, Club Motown, **Castaway Lounge** – Calumet City IL, Club Peorian – Peoria IL, Club 67 – Muncie IN, Crystal Ship Ballroom – Pocatello ID, Crystal Ship Ballroom – Lincoln NE, Carousel Club –Toledo OH, Cat's Meow – Ft. Wayne IN, Chez-Mousetrap, Cherry Lounge, Club House – Long Beach CA, Caldwell – Houston TX, Club Continental – Ft. Walton Beach FL, Club Hello, **Cord & Blue***

Dry Martini, Decatur Cocktail Lounge – Decatur IL, Don Davidson, Draught House – Davenport IA, Dick Kaplan, Diamonds, Den Downstairs, Driftwood, Dino Enterprises, Doll's, DJ's, Diamond Club – Dayton OH, Exchange Lounge, Ebbtide, Edispisrecs, Exit, Fred Petty, Flame – Minneapolis

MN, Frontier Lanes, Fox Valley, Frontier Club – Minneapolis MN, Frontier Club, Flo's, Fab – Toledo OH, Factory – St. Paul MN, Fairways – Kalamazoo MI, Factory – Calumet City IL, Four Horsemen, Filling Station

Green Onion, Greek Letter Four – Ft. Worth TX, Gigi, Grotto, Georges Show Lounge, Gomeries, Galaxie Attractions, Gigolo, Golden Key Club – Norfolk, VA, Gables Club, Golden Gauntlet, Garage, Hello, Hilltop, Hue Rodgers, Harold and Sid Kudlets, Holiday Club, Hollyoke Club – Indianapolis, IN, Hour Glass, Hi Ho – Wichita KS, **Holiday Ballroom**, Hungrey Eye Agency, Inner Circle, Image, Indiana Acres, Idle Hour, Jeff Franklin, Jockey, Jim Murray, John Emerson, JD's – Phoenix AZ

Kapson, Mike, Kittens Corner – Atlanta GA, Kings Castle – Macomb IL, Lucas, Lally's, Limit – Long Beach CA, Losers – Dallas TX, Long Horn – Portland OR, Lord Jims, L-NYOPIA, London House – Grand Rapids MI, Last Resort, Last Chance, Marty Saxon, Mint Julep, Mist, Magoons, **Moulin Rouge**, Mr. Mikes, Mas Lounge, Mothers, Mr. Edwards – Elk Grove Village IL, Millers Lounge, Misty Lounge, Melody Lounge, Murphys Station – Sunnyvale CA, Mousetrap – Park City IL, Mission – Northbrook IL, Music Box – Waterloo IA, Midnight Hour – Cicero IL

Nino Bari – Philadelphia PA, Nickel Bag, Nightingale Inn, Occasion, Office – St. Petersburg FL, Oriental Club – Lawton OK, Office Lounge – Louisville KY, Office, Chicago, Office – St. Petersburg FL, Psychiatrist, Place, Pudges – St. Paul MN, Purple Twig, Percussion, Pepe's, PJ's, Poinsettia, Phelps Lounge – Detroit MI, Peppermint Lounge – New York NY, Peanut Pub, Profile, Palace, Pacific Playhouse – Stockton CA, Platwood

Quiet Village, Quartertime, Rich Bernoski, Riverside Lounge, Rush Up, Rush Over, Rush North, Rob Roy, Red Rooster, Rectory – Albuquerque NM, Rock – Albuquerque NM, Richardos – Redding CA, Red Dog, Sound Show Case – Knoxville TN, Stardust, Stan Bulleu, Safari – Muskegon MI, Side Winder, Store, Snoopy's – Madison WI, Star Lounge, Shor E Club, Show Bix, Starlite A Go Go, Sweeter Than Honey, Shullas – Niles MI, San Fan Club – Muskegon MI, Store North, Some Place Else, Star Treck – Dallas TX

Twist of Lemon, Tantrum, That's Life, Taste of Honey, Tree House, the Way In, Troch Club, 3200 Club – Richmond VA, Trail Lounge – York PA, Town & Country, Teen Club, Tracer Club – Ft. Worth TX, Tropicana – Sacramento CA, Trophy Room, Twins Club, Velvet Lounge, Valley View, Walter Daisey, Wells Fargo, William Morris Agency, Wonder Gardens – Atlantic City NJ, Willard Alexander, Yoois Den, Yankee Clipper, Your Uncle's Place – La Crosse WI,

Special thanks – Ms. Jamie Tam for compiling and typing these lists.

My original copies listed the names and contact phone numbers. It's amazing how much we got done without the luxury of email or voicemail. I scanned some posters I found. I hope this section jogs some happy memories.

Lunatic Fringe

HER

Sheri and the Right Brothers

The Children Between Us

Love Between Us

Filet of Soul

The Original Fenders

Gilbect Ross

Freddy and the
Freeloaders

The Freddy Jones
Band

The Vince Garrett Revue

Bob Kuban and the
In-Men

Katch

The Ravelles

Out Rage

The Witching Hour

It took me awhile to name this chapter. I hope you find it mysterious enough to check out. In my *Cemetery Dance* story, you got an early glimpse of Screaming Wildman thoughts and methods.

As you remember, the dance was held on Halloween. My editor and advisors suggested I choose a significant date to toss my (wizard's) hat into the publishing ring. Tell me how you think I handled it.

This is a five-year project, stuffed into a two-year time frame. Yeah, I'm working harder than I thought I would need to. Think about the folks who gave me so much time and support. Dragging this process on any longer would unfairly extend the publication date.

My earliest contributors (who deserve tons of praise for their own bodies of work) are looking forward to being acknowledged. This chapter could have been called *People I Wish I Could Have Included, But I Ran Out of Time* (or some such).

Honorable Mention sounds too trite and a little judgmental for my final words. If you got this far, you deserve my thanks and compliments. Artists and groups in this section deserve all the respect and praise I tried to pack into these chapters. I guess *Deadline* would have worked for a chapter heading, but it seemed overused and not quite wicked enough for my purpose.

Maybe you know someone willing to pick up where I'm leaving off. I know some people who will teach you things about getting your story out there. It's never too late to learn, and it's never too late for me to make another introduction. The Screaming Wildman never rests.

All right, here are seven more "encore" pages for you (and that's it!). I tried to portray you accurately, humorously, and most of all, lovingly (just not the mushy kind—I have an image to maintain). I apologize ahead of time for any omissions. If you check my index (another monumental task), you'll know how hard I tried.

Rich Histories

Maybe you don't realize how hard this chapter was to write. Yeah, I didn't devote many words to each of my subjects. I spent a lot of time tossing in my (three hours at a time) sleep. You know how worry can put you in a zombie-like state? I thought I would outgrow or outlive that stuff. Anyway, each paragraph I wrote was followed by hours of worry and regret.

I sincerely hope nobody feels slighted in any way because I care so much about you all. I only have a few words left to convey my utmost respect. The following are in no apparent order. Don't get me started again!

Shameless Name Dropping

There are hundreds of "snippets" I couldn't weave into earlier pages. Here, I do my best to highlight each new name in my ramblings.

From 1963 through 1970, I produced somewhere between 200 to 225 single records from all sorts of different groups. I was fortunate to have done so many different things—all at one time. At night, I'd be recording in the studio. During the day, Herb Gronauer and I were booking these bands for the Willard Alexander Agency.

Okay, here's what I'm talking about. I used to talk with Herb a few times a year. By the time I could schedule an interview, he was no longer able to take calls. That kind of news forces a guy to take a moment. You know what I'm sayin'?

I wish I had time for a group we called the Illinois Tollway. The band recorded **Another Summer to Remember** and **Candy and Me**, written by James Holvay and Gary Beisbier, produced by Carl Bonafede, Dan Belloc, and Lew Douglas on the SpectraSound Records label. (See how this is going to work?)

As you remember, Dan and Lew were instrumental (pun intended) in the success of many groups. If I went into detail, I'd have something more like an old-fashioned telephone book.

I mentioned my love for "personality radio." Promoters, DJs, recording studios, and labels responded to opportunities in record time (get it?). For instance, I hired WCFL disc jockey Joel Sebastian at record hops the same time I managed the Buckinghams.

When **I Call Your Name** by the Mamas & the Papas was playing constantly, then suddenly stopped, I asked Joel why.

"They're not bringing it out as a single," he explained. "We were just playing it off the album."

The Buckinghams went right to the studio and recorded **I Call Your Name**, written by John Lennon and Paul McCartney and recorded by the Beatles. Our up-tempo version https://youtu.be/-oMMI-TDB28 was nearly as popular as the Buckinghams' hit **I'll Go Crazy** on U.S.A.

We had a virtual "engine" for turning out records on demand when DJs and promoters found a need. Speaking of DJs …

Ron Riley grew up in the Northeast corner of Illinois and idolized the disc jockeys at WOKY in Milwaukee, Wisconsin, where he landed his first Top 40 station gig. His first, but certainly not last, job in Chicago was at WJJD. When they changed to a country format, he was forced to seek his fortune elsewhere, at least for the time being. Some time before, Ron befriended **Gene Taylor** at WLS.

In 1963, after Dick Biondi left the station, **Clark Weber** urged Ron to call Gene, and he eventually landed a job. DJs were touring the various dances and concerts much like the musicians. They built energy off of one another and drove crowds crazy while being broadcast live, at times.

There was so much competition for listeners and advertisers between megastations WCFL and WLS in Chicago. Listeners felt the electricity. In 1966, the somewhat campy Batman TV series became the rage. As I recall, it aired during Ron's time slot. He would give live updates of the TV episode on his radio show. This was an enormous hit with the listeners.

This "morphed" into the Ron Riley Batman Club, complete with membership cards. Ron started to do personal appearances in a Batman costume and got a cameo appearance in one 1967 Batman TV episode.

WLS radio early morning DJ **Clark Weber** and early evening DJ Ron Riley started verbally jousting on the air. Advertisers were loving a 50,000-watt feud beaming countrywide. I narrated a spoof of the Riley/Weber conflict, injecting lyrics from popular tunes to tie the whole thing together. WLS feared copyright lawsuits, so my masterpiece never hit the air. I found my original 8-track and got it reengineered for my compilation CD.

WLS DJ **Don Phillips** hosted the East of Midnight show from (you guessed it) 12am to 5am during our golden age of celebrity radio. At first, you might think the majority of loyal listeners would be Screaming Wildman types. However, there is a lot of vital labor going on during the graveyard shift.

Firefighters, police officers, nurses (a few doctors), and those responsible for getting out early edition newspapers needed energy during "their" morning. His show was fast-paced because he handled the "scripts" himself. Along with Top

40 tunes, Don would engage in lively discussions of current topics and his other passions (like his pilot's license and single-engine four-seat plane).

Why go to one concert or record hop when I could tag along with "Dimple Donnie" to several on a single night? He balanced family and work responsibilities. His wife and kids could count on him to be home before school started, then once again at dinnertime toward evening (after his mid-day nap).

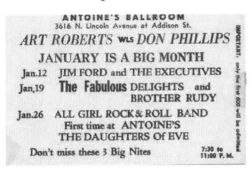

I often hooked a (scary) ride to his personal appearances. Afterward, he would head to his WLS midnight show. I had no solid schedule or plan of my own most nights.

Art Roberts started at WLS in 1961 after successful runs in Dallas and Buffalo, New York. He first had the noon to 3pm slot and eventually replaced Dick Biondi from 9pm to midnight before he headed to San Francisco 10 years later. He was known for his quick wit and storytelling. Hooty Saperticker, one of his fictional characters (who wanted to do nothing), inspired unofficial holidays and a novelty song.

Needless to say, Art was a fan favorite at our dances. Joe Pytel found a ticket for Antoine's Ballroom (Lincoln and Addison) for the Daughters of Eve debut in January 1966. The ticket stated "only the first 600 will be admitted." Those dances were unbelievably popular. Art Roberts and Don Phillips were generous personalities and regulars at our events.

Joel Sebastian came to WLS early in what I call the "second wave" of radio personalities. AM radio (particularly WLS) was still "smokin' hot" thanks to the jocks I mentioned here and guys who have their own chapter in my book. I recall Gary Gears, John Records Landecker, and Yvonne Daniels. I know, there are many more you'll remind me of later.

Native Chicagoan of Polish ancestry (two well-known facts to her devoted fan base) Connie Szerszen started her broadcasting career at WSDM-FM. She was an awesome and quite marketable on-air talent. ABC-TV (Chicago Channel 7) was looking for a hostess, as they were called back then, for a daytime talk show to compete with some guy named Phil Donahue. She was among two finalists and ultimately lost the gig to none other than Oprah Winfrey.

There are many facets to a jewel like Connie. Crain's Chicago Business did a feature story on her portraiture in its February 2006 issue. What if she just tells you herself? Her memoir, *Top Rock Girly Jock*, is available on Amazon.

Floyd Brown was at WYNR when Lucky Cordell and I ran a successful string of dances at Luigi's starting in 1963. I hired Floyd several times as well. He had a long and industrious career at WGN Radio and TV. He preferred jazz and hosted a Sunday night jazz music program. The *Floyd Brown Show* on WGN Radio was an entertaining mix of music and interviews.

His wife, Betty Brown, is a nurse, newspaper columnist, and civic leader who was interviewed by the HistoryMakers in 2006. http://www. thehistorymakers.com/biography/mary-betty-brown-41

By the way, I recommend the Chicago Radio Spotlight blog by Rick Kaempfer http://chicagoradiospotlight.blogspot.com to research your favorite radio personalities.

Thee Prophets

In 1962, rock-and-roll groups were forming all across the country. Thirteen-year-old Brian Lake, from Milwaukee, Wisconsin, longed for action. Friend and guitar player Dave Leslie persuaded Chris Michaels to buy drums to accompany them.

They built a modest following, playing parties and school dances. When I met Thee Prophets in 1968, Brian Lake on lead vocals and organ, Jim Anderson on lead guitar, David Leslie on bass and vocals, and Chris Michaels on drums were locally popular. They hoped I could get them to the next level.

I saw big things in their future as did many great names in the business, like Herb Gronauer (Chartwell Artists, Ltd.) and composer, arranger, and conductor Lew Douglas. Well-known orchestra leader Dan Belloc and I had created SpectraSound, Inc., and the three of us produced **Playgirl**, released by Kapp Records (New York).

Tex Meyer from WRIT/Milwaukee, Wisconsin, was the first DJ in the country to air **Playgirl** by Thee Prophets, and Bob Barry from radio station WOKY also promoted airplay. Despite the slick vocal blends that characterized our Midwestern groups (like the Buckinghams, Cryan' Shames, or Lincoln Park Zoo), **Playgirl** peaked on Billboard's Hot 100 at only #49. Despite a well-crafted album, Thee Prophets never attracted national attention.

KAPP Records
PLAYGIRL (Linda & Keith Colley) 2:06.
THE PROPHETS
    Produced by Carl Bonafede-Dan Belloc-Lew Douglas
    Engineer on Records: Bill Bradley-Ed Cody
    KAPP RECORDS, a division of Universal City Records

I always wanted a closer relationship with Keith Colley. He authored songs released by country singer Bobby Bare, among others. **Father Sebastian** was recorded by the Ramblers and got Chicago airplay. Along the way (as far as the Screaming Wildman goes), we lost touch after he sent me some of his new material. My self-imposed exile cost me (and some folks I could have helped) a bunch.

We first met after he sent me a demo tape while I was working for Willard Alexander. I thought he had a couple of big hits in the making. Lew Douglas put his own arrangement with them. Keith came to see me at the Holiday Ballroom, and we spent some time together. He sent me a whole bunch of other songs. I was interested in **Magic Island**, **Man Enough**, and **Rag Doll Boy**.

Tom Thumb

My mind goes back to a guy named Alan Campbell (part of Tom Thumb and the Four Fingers). Let me backtrack a little. I knew this group from my days at the Swiss Hall. Let's say Campbell could just flat-out sing.

Kapp Records (based in the Big Apple, where "sure things" migrate after being developed in Chicago) was committed to producing Thee Prophets recordings. Alan Campbell had the voice and got credit on later Prophets songs under the Kapp label. I guarantee you are going to marvel (or shake your head in disbelief) at this set of circumstances.

To provide a little more background for this segment, I suggest you check out the YouTube clip for **Come To Me Girl** https://youtu.be/CwEkDIK90o0 by Thee Prophets

(sort of). This was posted by another aficionado of eclectic music, who certainly deserves some recognition as well. Don't you love this? Check out the label shown in the video, and I'll do my best to fill in the blanks.

Let's start at the top. Songwriter and lead vocalist Alan Campbell has two well-deserved credits. Brian Christian was a celebrated producer and engineer in Chicago and Los Angeles (I could have said legendary in many places, but I'm trying to not repeat words too often). He worked with the Guess Who, Alice Cooper, Pink Floyd, and the Tufano / Giammarese (former Buckinghams) band. Check out his other musical credits at your leisure.

Back then, even demo records were pretty awesome musical pieces, with professional instrumentation. Legendary (I had to use the word here) composer and arranger Lew Douglas had dual credit on this record. Dan Belloc of the Billy May Orchestra and owner of the Holiday Ballroom along with yours truly are also listed as producers. StereoSonic (Ed Cody) ties a neat bow around this single offering to the music public.

A Little Bit of Love (Never Hurt Anyone) https://youtu.be/WqGvqr2xBG0 went pretty much the same way, with the exception of the songwriters. Credit goes to Sandy Salisbury and Jill Jones. We owe all the kind folks who make these songs electronically available a hearty "thank you." Subscribe to their YouTube channels and post positive comments, if you would.

But Wait, There's Always More

I could fill another volume (and more – but I won't) with all the fascinating people, groups, and talented individuals I've met. There are names and places I'm trying to mash in someplace. I often remember the first/last time we met and where. I just don't have time (and I never had the patience) to fill in all of the details. Here are more jumping-off points for your own research.

WGN-TV Channel 9 hosted Ron Terry's Polka Party in the 1950–60s. Chances are, you would have seen performances by Lee and the Dynatones. I toyed with thoughts of forming my own band with performers who impressed me over the years.

Dwight Kalb would be our drummer and Larry Nestor would play keyboards (and most likely write a new song or two for us). You already know where we would record and who would produce our CDs (if you've been reading). Now to the belated point.

Russ Vestuto and the Downbeats backed a ton of recordings in the early '60s. Russ would be the "primo" guitar player in my dream band. Larry was part of the Downbeats along with Harry Manfredini (you met much earlier) on saxophone. Carmine Menna (bass) and Eddie Hough (drums) rounded out the group backing me on the **Good Old Days** and others.

Enough about me already…

Liverpool group Billy Pepper and the Pepperpots caused quite a stir (get it?) with their own Beatle-esque musical stylings around 1964. There's speculation about connections between the two bands. You take it from here.

That same year Phil DeMarco and the Valiants released **Lonely Guy** https://youtu. be/fpAj9p09I0w. I included a link for you here. The late Gary Loizzo (featured earlier) played saxophone. I first saw Phil's band around 1957 at Tuscany Hall (with DJ Dennis DeVito) on Grand Avenue. The band was the first to incorporate choreography into its act. Nick Fortuna of the Buckinghams told me the Valiants were the best he ever saw.

Though they were around a lot earlier, I often associate the Masqueraders http://www.soulexpress.net/masqueraders_story.htm with Vee-Jay Records. The band covered a lot of songs as well (or better) than the original artists.

The Masqueraders have been called one of the longest-lived, yet little-known soul groups in music history. "Google" **Average Guy**-Masqueraders to start. I'll meet you back here later.

Some entertaining groups took their music more seriously than they took themselves. My dances attracted a lot of fans and the groups that sought to "rock" them. One was **Spot and the Blotters**. The band wanted the audience to picture the members' racial makeup before their funky tunes washed over them. Google them to hear **Soul Circle**, released by Equal Records. Check out their label graphic while you're at it.

Jimmy Peterson also had label credits as **James Butler** and **James Dawg**. He released records on the **Limelight** and Chess labels. He also had Mob ties. Got your attention, didn't I? I'm talking about Jim Holvay's band. **Kathy My Darling**, released on Limelight Records, https://youtu.be/eNdoAP5KXug lists him as the singer and co-author, along with **Joe DeFrancesco**. There are valid reasons for having an alias or two (says the Screaming Wildman)!

Google Happy-Day-Band and you can link to the **P.C. Limited's** Facebook page. The band was one sought-after group and a Dick Biondi favorite. The band was originally called Purple Cucumber (PC, get it?). The band had a **Smash Records** connection (among others, of course) to the Hudsen Bay Company (formerly the Delights). Oh, wow … somebody take it from here!

Okay, this is probably the most random recollection in the entire book. Most of us know **Fred Gwynne** as affable and imposing Herman Munster from *The Munsters* TV series or the judge in the *My Cousin Vinny* movie. I met him in New York during my Kapp Records days. He was going to do voice-overs or something. If I only had more time, who knows what we might have done!

Remind Me to Tell You …

You gotta leave 'em wanting more: I'm doing some jewelry repair (a while after my musical success in the '60s) and this dude pulls a gun on me …

The Making of . . .

When I envisioned my project, I saw myself pounding away at a keyboard for weeks on end. I'm not talking about a computer keyboard, either. Put yourself in my position. Imagine the dread. After completing my manuscript, I saw boxing it up and shipping it off to a list of publishers, hoping one might take an interest, or hearing nothing for months, if ever.

What if someone was interested? In my imagination, the possibility seemed more awful. I would be at the mercy of an editor I just met, telling me I had to do almost everything over again. In the few moments we weren't at each other's throats, we'd eventually turn in another draft to the publisher and wait. This just isn't my nature.

What if this goes pretty well and we reach the next step: the one where they really let me know how much (or how little) profit each book will generate? When I compared publishing to the music business, I saw a lot of similarities. It didn't look good. As a producer and promoter, I went without (nearly everything, including sleep) to get my people paid. I didn't see any difference here.

All of the generous people who poured their feelings and efforts into my chapters were going to have to wait indefinitely. There would be far too much out of my control. It was going to take something more to move forward.

People told me there was an alternative and asked if I was willing to check it out. My imagination went into overdrive. I would still have to interview my subjects. I could sit at the keyboard or use a tape recorder to capture my thoughts and those of my friends. I could then get someone to transcribe them into electronic format. I could embrace the recording technology, but word processing somehow made me fearful.

At least it was doable. It was something I could control. It would cost me, of course. All the time I logged at Chicago's Maxwell Street would guarantee I would negotiate a good deal. A couple of my well-established author friends would encourage and guide me. I promised myself I wouldn't be a burden to them. These guys already had a full plate, and deservedly so.

I still worried about the pitfalls of self-publishing. I would have to pay a typesetter to get my words into genuine book format, with pages, a cover, a spine (really the only thing visible on a bookshelf), plus pictures inside and out.

I would have to find a printer who would create a carload of them (to maybe deliver to my house), or more likely stack them in my garage. That's where I found a lot of the photos that would appear in my book. The pictures would have come full circle. The rest of the book hasn't gone anywhere yet.

I got confused and concerned. Even big-name publishers were in a bind with conventional bookstores going the way of the dinosaur. This was a lot like the music publishers on Record Row, many of whom you met on earlier pages. You may have noticed I used the word "whom" (correctly). I do have accomplished editors helping me.

How would I distribute a few hundred books (if I was lucky)? I pictured myself loading a case into my hatchback and driving around until they were gone. Don't get me wrong: I love the bantering and bartering of a flea-market environment. At least, I could control the price of the book and easily calculate my profit, which wouldn't come until the bills were paid.

This still seemed like a nightmare. This marketing part might be the very worst of all. The labor and humiliation of (literally) a ton of books hanging over me was a deal breaker. In a few of my chapters, I blame technology for the unsteady state of the music business. Book publication looked just as sorry to me. Case closed, except …

I was never a guy who took "no" for an answer (at least not a final answer). In the past, I embraced new technology. Recording engineers like Ed Cody knew how to incorporate and innovate as 8- and 12-track recording revolutionized the business. Technology is a bigger part of this book than I ever imagined. The science and strategy involved in the production and marketing of my book is also greater than I could ever have known.

You have no idea how hard this is for me to say. Even as I'm watching this happen around me (and even to me), I'm glad the technology has caught up with the vision of the Screaming Wildman.

There's one more piece to this fascinating puzzle. Once again (since you have this book in front of you), I allowed technology to work for me. I'm not sure how I felt about Amazon® until now. I relied on what others told me about this mysterious company that had infiltrated the marketplace with practically everything. Let's talk about books (especially mine) for the time being.

Was Amazon responsible for the fold of many conventional bookstores? I just knew fewer were still around. Say what you want about Amazon, they took care of a major concern for me. How was I going to distribute my book? Remember, the very last thing I wanted to do was cart a trunk full of books across town or spend my hard-earned cash on postage and handling (by me). I have my hands full with my CD collections, for which I prefer my proven "hands on" sales and distribution method—so far.

Once I heard Amazon could do the heavy lifting, I started gradually moving in their direction. Will they take their cut? Of course. Would I get a greater percentage of the purchase price of each book? You bet. Another cautious step forward. The technology was developing on my behalf, whether I was aware of it or not. What if my potential readers could enter Screaming-Wildman-Amazon into their browser window and buy my book?

I was finally sold. Apparently, so were you. While my good friends and I were kicking around publishing possibilities, I visualized getting invited to my next Buckinghams concert. They've been doing that regularly, as well as shouting out that I'm "in the house" each time. They'd probably acknowledge that I have a book out on Amazon and the audience could order one before they'd be asked to turn off their phones or tablets. Ain't technology wonderful?

The only thing left to do was get the manuscript together.

I Had No Idea

Actually, I had dozens of ideas circling around me. The challenge was getting them into some kind of order. This was going to be hard, and all I could see were long periods of time spent in total isolation. That just wasn't me. I got some good advice about getting started: Get a tape recorder and just describe the things you see displayed on your wall.

Before long, I was also digging through the photos I ended up storing in my garage. As you read in the beginning, some of my treasured acetates met that terrible and permanent fate. That's no way to treat heirlooms, to be sure. I should have learned my lesson. I confess, I wasn't really as enthused as I hoped to be at this point. Then it dawned on me: Why write chapters *about* the folks who are important to me when I could write their chapters *with* them?

I invited a bunch of great folks to meet me at one of my favorite hangouts for interviews (or I went to them). They presented pictures and posters, ideas and memories. As you now know, I even played private detective for a while and landed much unexpected interviews with true media giants.

Once I committed to getting this thing done, I started to obsess about doing it right and learning as I went along. I don't think anyone I asked for an interview turned me down. Of course, some folks were not as available as others, but everyone was generous with their time.

I'm impressed with how many folks did live interviews and let me snap a picture with them. Once again, we took advantage of the kindness of strangers when necessary. Many of these exclusive pictures found their way into the book, allowing me to show that it was always about them.

By far, this was the very best way to go about it, though certainly not the easiest. It was emotional and exhausting for me and my guests, but there was no shortage of enthusiasm. This is all I could have hoped for. I was able to push forward when things got difficult.

I broke one of the main rules for creating a book. A real writer would not (maybe never) show a draft of chapters in development. After I completed an interview, I often sent it to my "subject." Conventional wisdom (at least in the publishing world) cautions some folks may want to change their quotes once they see them in "print" or want to make other alterations.

I'm not an ordinary guy, and the friends I introduce in my book are spectacular. I tried to pay them fitting tribute, and they reciprocated in classy ways. They made suggestions and corrected my inaccuracies. Some were embarrassing (like putting Branson in Montana instead of Missouri). Once I found an editor I could trust (who also was already a dear friend), I was rolling.

I was looking for the best way and time to say this. Out of deep respect for the folks who contributed to my book, I had to create a firm deadline for its release. I could have gone on for years and hundreds of pages more. At some point, it would become a disservice to everyone's patience and kindness.

Eventually, we chose a Halloween 2016 deadline. The year signified (roughly) 50 years since both the Daughters of Eve and Buckinghams were poised to take the rock-and-roll world by storm. The ghostly holiday pertains to my famous Cemetery Dance, at a time when I was too young to know any better. There are dozens of people and groups I wish I had time to mention.

I apologize in advance for any oversights or omissions. I hope you will attribute this to a timing issue, rather than any form of disrespect. This book should inspire other hesitant authors of my era. Now that I have a better idea about how all of this is possible, I would be happy to offer a little guidance.

For instance, I learned that a good editor is much like a recording engineer when it came to putting together a final product. Once you find one you can trust, you're free to focus on the mechanics and strategy in front of you.

Behind the Scenes

Maybe this is the subtitle, but YouTube® is really not behind the scenes. It's a 24-7 in-your-face phenomenon. It's one of the ways my fans know I'm still alive. As you know, I don't have the patience to learn this new technology, but I'm starting to understand how it can be used. You read about Joe Pytel in the preceding chapters, and deservedly so. He's the main reason the Screaming Wildman is out there (even though I'm a little unsure about where "there" is).

Joe and dozens like him work tirelessly to upload videos to enhance the marketability of vintage groups. Enter a couple of terms into your browser search window (I've been coached on this, if you couldn't tell), and you can hear a recording and often view several photos associated with the clip.

You'll see background information and be invited to add your own comments. I'm not the one to tell you how YouTube works. I'm just suggesting technology saved me a ton of time and paper. Are there any advantages for the original artists? Aside from being remembered fondly, any vintage vinyl still out there may start to circulate. Each artist can decide for him or herself.

As a performer, I want to be noticeable and approachable. Those two traits helped me cut deals. YouTube (and this book) give me a chance to continue.

Facebook® also helps me keep in touch with my friends and fans. By now you may have seen dozens of pictures in my gallery. I'm grateful to the folks (particularly Joe and Michele Abrams) who upload fresh stuff on my behalf. I'm reminded how much I'm still missing with my old-school approach to the internet. Only a couple of my book contributors are in the same boat (in shallow water).

I'm anticipating there are a few of my readers (thanks again) who think the same way. I suggest asking (or forcing) a kid or grandkid to enter in three "key" words to see what they are missing. I suggest *Screaming-Wildman-Facebook* or *Screaming-Wildman-YouTube* to start. You may not be hooked, but you will certainly be intrigued and entertained.

Maybe I just needed to see it enough times myself. I don't have to collect those images to put in my book. I only have to give you the right combination of words that will guide you to your own threshold of adventure. It took me a long time (and the persuasion of well-meaning friends) to come around. Five years ago, we couldn't have this conversation.

You Won't See This Anywhere Else (Yet)

As I mentioned, a lot more technology and research is at work in this book than I ever anticipated. I hope it will make for an interesting read for all generations. I included a number of relevant hyperlink references to websites and YouTube clips.

In the print edition, a few hard-working folks embedded QR (Quick Response) codes near the page margins. Anyone with a "reader" app (somebody can probably describe this better) can wave it over the printed page to access the featured video.

Once again, I can see how involving more people (of all generations) made the book a far better product. This is more than a book: It is a social experiment with improvisational theater elements. I just laid out my wildest dreams while somebody found a way to take me seriously and literally.

I hope my book will be referenced in other books about our era and out hometown somewhere down the line. To make that easier, I will make my book available to people who prefer to read books on a Kindle, iPad, or other mobile device sometime soon. I don't know who comes up with this stuff, but I like it.

As you probably guessed, I found some young people who have the patience to work with guys like me. They even understood my concern about that huge inventory of books I envisioned. Apparently, Amazon understood that, too, and created a print-on-demand option. My book very likely shipped directly to you like conventional Amazon orders.

I wasn't worried about selling books, necessarily. But, if nobody ever wanted one, I would have zero print costs or inventory. Yeah, I still needed to find someone to "compose" the book and send it to Amazon, but that's all.

There's more, if you can believe it. Let's say there is an awkward error or two, because stuff happens. I can ask my trusted new friends to make these changes and send a new file to the Amazon people. The very next (you are reading that right), person to order the book will have the revised version. There is no inventory to get rid of first. This is too good to be true!

Next Steps

I have a plan for us all. Mostly you. If you like any parts of my book, I hope you will mention me favorably in the social medium of your choice. I would also encourage you to review my book on the Amazon website. Favorable reviews attract Amazon's attention. My book will likely be recommended when folks search for rock-and-roll or Chicago books.

I encourage you to follow the links and view the videos I selected for you. Once again, leave encouraging comments, subscribe to the YouTube channel, and encourage others to visit (to bump up the number of views).

Like I said, we have some power to increase the demand for vinyl editions from artists I hold dear. Wouldn't it be cool if we could spark just a single re-press of a record? Why couldn't this happen?

I hope my words will rekindle the demand for your artistry. So many folks in my book still want to rock. The majority still do in fascinating ways, much like they did back then. Younger generations want to hear it. Really, they need to hear it. Folks of our generation can reach them using the latest innovations.

For us, it was television, radio, and vinyl (digitally recorded and mastered by innovative sound engineers). Today, artists reach their devoted fans digitally. They download individual songs if they choose. Is the system better now than before? Do vintage artists profit from decades-old work? Did they ever? These are things I want all generations talking about. I'm doing my part to bridge that gap (or show that none really exists). My book gets the conversation started.

OK, that sounded like a blatant plug, because it is.

Deliberate Omission

You may notice I don't have a Foreword in my book. There are a few reasons. First, there are so many gifted folks who already contributed so much time during the interviews and follow-up, I didn't want to burden them any further. Heck, by the time I got to the final stages, I didn't want to read all of these chapters anymore, either.

Anyway, some forewords look a lot like an endorsement, and I'm not one to solicit praise for myself. (For my groups and associates, that's another story.) As I mentioned earlier, anyone inclined to recommend my book can do so on the Amazon site. I also mentioned how easy it is to update an edition (within reason). If there is popular demand, my editor may persuade me to put a little more time in (or not).

My Apologies

I violated a few style rules preparing the manuscript for the book. The "T" in a group name is not capitalized. I would have needed both hands to type a single character. Same thing goes for quote marks around song titles. There are so many in this book, I didn't see how extra "two-handed" characters helped you or me. I did use a different typeface for song titles, though. You'll notice I use italics when referring to *TV shows* or *album* names and *book* titles.

Sometimes I call myself the Screamin' Wildman or the Screaming Wildman, as the mood strikes me. Both uses are intentional – or not.

Index

A

ABC Records...136
Abrams, Michele.......................................294
Ace Kluver...204
Acuff, Roy... 87
Adamany, Ken..................... 134, 143, 282
Adler, Lou..238
Ahert, Bob..216
Alan Campbell..............................153, 314
Al Brown..284
Albums
    1935-1977: I've Been Away For Awhile
        Now 122
    Aware of Love................................181
    Christmas in Chicago......................183
    57-Years and Still Going..................240
    Five Decades Of Musical Memories from
        the Windy City Chicago 223
    FlashBack 241
    Lazaretto.......................................181
    Mercy, Mercy, Mercy......................237
    Playgirl, Thee Prophets...................196
    Play Piano Play...............................183
    Precious Memories 88
    Saturday Night Fever............43, 45, 49
    Serenade...............................123, 126
    Sharing Christmas 207
    The Cowsills Plus The Lincoln Park Zoo.....196
    Thriller.. 46
    Time and Charges, then Portraits.................221
    Together Again........................86, 87
    Trying Not to Fade.........................294
    Worried Life Blues 52
    Wreckless Heart 124
Al Cory 49
Aleat Maciejewski...................................135
Alice Cooper...................................155, 314
Ali, Muhammad.. 77
Allen, Bernie..178
Allen, Ted..133, 303
Alley Cat Records....................................223
Alligator Records...................................... 47
Allstate Record Distributors 94
All Time Hits (Show) 221
Alltop, Larry.. 89
Alvin Cash & the Crawlers.......................187
American Bandstand 118, 234, 236
American Breed, The 155, 178, 240, 304
A&M Records 171
Andee Levin 248, 249, 251
Anderson, Jim..313
Anderson, Woodtake.................................. 44
Angela Davis...264
Angus MacBump.......................................186
Animals, The.....................................256, 265
Anka, Paul...185
Anthony Quinn 236
Antoine's Ballroom 13

Apollo Theater 116
Aragon Ballroom...............................209, 226
Arcada Theater...240
Arie Crown Theater.................................109
Arkie's Corral 275
Arlo Guthrie...121
Armando DeGuzman 270, 280
Arnold Schwarzenegger.............................276
Arthur, Brooks 43, 47
Arthur Stallard 82
Art Roberts......................................161, 312
Arvy Tumosa 189
Arzola, Otilio, Jr......................................269
Arzola, Otilio, Sr.....................................276
Auditorium Theater, the 170
Avalon, Frankie.......................................178

B

Baby Huey and the Babysitters 45, 53, 263,
    282, 299, 304
Bachman, Curt...................222, 225, 226, 227
Balkan Recordings...................................153
Ballard, Florence......................................131
Banks, Ernie......................................46, 71
Barbara Lawless 191
Barbra Streisand.......................................150
Bare, Bobby..314
Barn, The...304
Barry, Bob..313
Barry Gordy 131
Barry Plost 209
Barry White.......................................45, 46
Basie, Count 68
Bass, Fontella.. 48
Beach Boys, The...............................107, 237
Beatles, The.............85, 119, 157, 174, 230, 244, 252
Bebanko, Bob....................................257, 259
Bedno, Howard 140, 153, 229, 230, 233, 235
Bee Gees, The 45
Beisbier, Gary...................................154, 310
Belloc, Dan 86, 101, 126, 174, 191, 210, 221,
    229, 230, 241, 242, 266, 310, 313, 314
Bell Sound Studios 120
Belushi, John 3, 282
Ben Cowall 83
Ben E. King..265
Benton, Brook... 47
Bernadette Vanno 296
Bernard, Jim 101, 173, 226, 302
Bernie Allen 178
Berry, Chuck 174
Berry, Richard 263
Berwyn, IL...205
Betty Brown...313
Beverley Shaffer 187
Beverly Records 51, 110, 160, 176, 179
Bierig, Joel 223, 299, 300
Big Bopper, The.......................................302

Big John Evans 165
Big Thing, The 231, 241
Bill Bradley 313
Bill Hall 49, 59, 153
Bill Jackson and Dirty Dragon.......................... 69
Bill Moore............................ 120, 156, 296
Bill Murray 282
Bill Putnam 155
Bill Tavern and the Drunkin' Four 6
Billy May Orchestra............................ 193, 242, 314
Billy Pepper and the Pepperpots 315
Billy Williams 67
Biondi, Dick 117, 157, 194, 233, 241,
    243, 311, 312, 316
Bishop, Joey.. 236
Bitter End, The 134
Black Knight.. 305
Black, Stu.............................49, 59, 153
Blood, Sweat and Tears 220, 237
Blue Moon Ballroom................................. 216
Blues Brothers (Movie) 91
Blues Hall of Fame................................... 52
Boatload.. 281
Bob Ahert 216
Bob Barry... 313
Bob Bebanko 257, 259
Bob Buff.. 214
Bobby Bare 314
Bobby Darin 243
Bobby Hull... 288
Bobby Merk 270
Bobby Vinton 120
Bob Campbell 153
Bob Carroll 67
Bob Cotrell 95, 104
Bob Dearborn 175
Bob Hale 161, 178
Bob Kuban and the In-Men 304
Bob Newkirk 67
Bob Raines 275
Bob Seger 155
Bob Trendlers Band................................... 67
Bob Walicki 189, 192, 194
Bob Wallace.. 288
Bob Walsh.. 77
Bob Weiner 63, 154
BoDeans, The 282
Bonnie MacBump.................................... 186
Bouchelle, Jack 26
Boulevard Recording Studios 153
Bradley, Bill 313
Bradley, Harold 86
Brad Snell.. 289
Brenda Lee & the Casuals............................. 131
Brian Christian 155, 194, 314
Brian Epstein 85
Brian Highland 47, 130, 178
Brian Lake.., 192
Brian Wilson 107, 215
Brickhouse, Jack...................................... 71
Broad Daylight....................................... 263
Brokop, Herb 195

Brook Benton 47
Brooklyn Bridge, The 123
Brooks, Arthur.......................................43, 47
Brooks, Richard 43
Brown, Al 284
Brown, Betty... 313
Brown, Floyd.......................................165, 313
Brown, James..129, 230
Bruce Otto 195
Bruce Springsteen.................................... 198
Bryant, Jimmy 194
Buccaneers, The 84
Buckinghams, The 46, 98, 103, 124, 132, 151,
    153, 161, 162, 174, 179, 191, 203, 221, 247,
    254, 256, 292, 294, 299, 304, 311, 313, 315
    Carl Giammarese 179, 182
    Curt Bachman 222
    Dennis Miccolis 222
    Dennis Tufano 222
    George LeGros 222
    John Poulos 222
    Marty Grebb 222
    Nick Fortuna 222
    Susan Rakis 179, 182
Buckner, Quinn 275
Buckner, Ray 47
Buddy Good.. 146
Buddy Holly 176
Buffalo Springfield................................... 213
Buff, Bob 214
Buff, Robert 209
Bunky Sheppard...................................... 217
Burdon, Eric 98, 265
Butler, James........................... 254, 265, 316
Butler, Jerry 43, 51, 53, 116, 181, 303
Byrne, Jane..200, 238

C

Cab Calloway 67
Cadet Records 203, 258, 266
Caesar & Comari Pepe.................................. 10
Cal Clemons 110
Call, Mickey... 133
Calloway, Cab.. 67
Cal Starr (Calvin Stallard) 81
Cambridge Five, The 95
Campbell, Alan 153, 314
Campbell, Bob 153
Candy Johnson and Her Exciters 90
Canned Heat 170
Cannon, Freddie.....................................119, 120
Capitol Records...................................... 107
Captain Stubby 84
Caravan, The 131
Caray, Harry 71
Card, Dex 101, 167, 178
Carioscia, Mike...................................... 221
Carl Giammarese....46, 124, 126, 155, 179, 182,
    201, 222, 224, 238, 243, 292, 299, 314
Carl Greyson 73, 74
Carmie Zack... 198
Carmine Menna...................................... 315

Carole King 238
Carone, Don 120
Carroll, Bob... 67
Casey, Warren 242
CASK Attractions 127, 221
Castaway Lounge 305
Casteel, Jim.. 204
Celeste Bedford Walker 48
Centinaro, John. 146
Centuries, The..................................154, 225
Cerretti, Ken... 26
Cetera, Peter.. 235
Chad and Jeremy 220
Chaka Khan... 300
Chandler, Gene.................................53, 217
Charles Fuller Studios............................ 147
Charles, Ray......................................45, 53
Charles, Sue 67
Charlotte O'Neill 135
Chartwell Artists, Ltd............................. 313
Cheap Trick 160, 198, 282
Cheech and Chong................................ 238
Cherokee Cowboys, The......................... 84
Chess Records ...48, 59, 108, 151, 155, 174, 187,
    203, 210, 211, 221, 231, 246, 253, 316
Chez Paree (Nightclub)......................... 116
Chiappe, Steve....................................... 198
Chicagoans, The...............................216, 265
Chicago (Band)...............160, 235, 237, 241, 242
Chicago Beat the Champs 284, 285
Chicago Catholic League........................ 275
Chicago Cubs 277
Chicago DJs
    Art Roberts 312
    Clark Weber........................... 229, 233, 311
    Connie Szerszen 312
    Dan Belloc.................................... 314
    Dennis DeVito............................... 315
    Dex Card 167
    Dick Biondi.....117, 157, 233, 241, 243, 311,
        312, 316
    Don Phillips................................. 311
    Floyd Brown 313
    Gary Gears 312
    Gene Taylor................................... 311
    Jim Bernard...............................226, 302
    Jim Lounsbury............................. 115
    Joel Sebastian.........................310, 312
    John Records Landecker................... 312
    Larry Lujack 53
    Lucky Cordell 163, 313
    Ron Riley...................................... 311
    Yvonne Daniels.............................. 312
"Chicago" Eddie Schwartz....................172
Chicago Fire Records 121
Chicago (Group)...................................129
Chicago Olympics 79
Chicago Riots 277
Chicago Sun-Times...........................119, 179
Chips, The..135, 304
Chisholm, Malcolm 155
Chi-Town Records.............................154, 231

Chris Michaels 313
Chris Sands..100, 103
Christian, Brian 155, 194, 314
Christie, Lou. 130, 178, 226
Christine Dreznes................................... 179
Chubby Checker 118
Chuck Berry 174
Chuck Francour....................................95, 103
Chuck Mosier... 302
Chuck Panozzo 170
Civic Opera House 122
Clapton, Eric 53, 109, 213
Clark, Dick 129, 216, 234
Clark Dufay 109
Clark Weber 161, 217, 229, 233, 311
Clay, Otis 188
Clayton Fillyau 129
Clemente, Roberto 277
Clemons, Cal.. 110
Clifford, Linda 53
Cline, Patsy 123
Clive Davis...234, 237
Coasters 130
Cobra Records 142, 153
Cody, Ed 48, 55, 110, 112, 121, 151,
    154, 155, 184, 266, 192, 313
Cole, Nat King....................................... 230
Cole Porter 70
Colley, Keith 192, 314
Colley, Linda 192, 313
Columbia Records 83, 221, 234, 236
Connery, Sean 186
Connie Szerszen 312
Constellation Records............................. 218
Cook, Don 95, 99, 104
Cooke, Sam.. 52
Cool Jazz Festival................................... 264
Cooper, Alice...155, 314
Cooper, Jim 270
Cooper, Sheldon ...., 80, 65
Cordell, Lucky 163, 313
Corky Siegel... 99
Cornelius, Don....................................... 46
Cory, Al.. 49
Cotrell, Bob 95, 104
Count Basie 135, 68
Country Cavaleers, the 148
Cowall, Ben 83
Cowsills, The 195
Coy Lowehorne 110
Craig McDowell 204
Creations, The 30
Creighton, Harry 72
Crews, Doree 67
Crossover Records 53
Crowley, Mort 161
Cryan' Shames, The 98, 107, 160, 170, 240, 313
Crystal Ballroom 111
Crystals, The... 130
Cufferin, Matt.. 195
Curt Bachman.............................222, 225, 226, 227
Curtis Mayfield 43, 134

Curtom Records 43, 44, 53
Custom Audio Studios...154
Czyż, Leonard & Phil (Chess Brothers).............151

D

Daley, Joe 194
Daley, Richard J. 96
Damascus, John 249
Dan Belloc 86, 101, 126, 174, 191, 210, 221,
    229, 230, 241, 242, 266, 310, 313, 314
Dan Belloc Orchestra, The 191
Daniel Murphy 225
Daniels, Yvonne 163, 312
Danny Seraphine 129
Daren Pasterik...135
Darin, Bobby 243
Darwin Skrzynecki..284
Daughters of Eve, The 35, 55, 58, 124,
    151, 161, 174, 177, 179, 203, 235, 236, 247,
    272, 295, 299, 304, 312
Dave Clark Five..109
Dave Hoekstra....................46, 124, 179, 240, 200
Dave Leslie...313
David Letterman..233
Davidson, Marilou...255
Davis, Angela 264
Davis, Clive..234, 237
Davis, Sammy, Jr. 116
Dawg, James 316
Dawn Lee Wakefield...293
Day, Morris 282
Dearborn, Bob 175
Debbie Dovale..265
Debi and the LA Classmen......................................249
Debi Pomeroy 179, 248, 249, 299
DeFrancesco, Joe 217, 316
DeGuzman, Armando 270, 280
Delaware Records 214
Delights, The 209, 256, 316
De Luca, Pat...223
Del Vikings, The 8
DeMarco, Phil 315
Democratic National Convention 62, 96, 192
Dennis DeVito 315
Dennis DeYoung..170
Dennis Miccolis 222, 227, 235, 244
Dennis Sierens 103
Dennis Tufano 155, 222, 227, 238, 239, 241,
    292, 314
Denny Doyle and the Irish Gravediggers............... 6
Denny Grounds 95
Denny Murray...62, 189
Derringer, Rick 226
Destination Records..102
DeVito, Dennis 315
Dex Card 101, 167, 178
DeYoung, Dennis..170
Diamond, Neil... 98
Diana Ross 131
Dick Biondi ...117, 157, 194, 233, 241, 243, 311,
    312, 316
Dick Clark 129, 216, 234

Dick Justin 154
Dick Kemp..163
Dick Kluver 204
Dick Schaeffer 195
Dick Shannon...175
DiMaggio, Vince... 99
Dirty Wurds, The...249
Dixie Cups 130
Dixon, Willie 178
Dogs of War...45, 50
Donahue, Phil 68
Don Carone 120
Don Cook 95, 99, 104
Don Cornelius.. 46
Don McLean...176
Donna Summer 45
Donner, Ral 115, 135, 242, 266
Donny Hathaway..139
Don Phillips 209, 311
Doree Crews 67
Dorsey, Jimmy 67
Doug Gast 95, 96
Douglas, Lew................... 85, 124, 125, 154, 193,
    230, 266, 310, 313, 314
Dovale, Debbie...265
Dower, Kenneth 284
Downbeats, The 315
Draper, Ken 158
Drawing Room, The
    Dwight Kalb..134
Dreznes, Christine..179
Dreznes, Jack............................. 51, 110, 160, 179
Drifters, The 130
Drury, John... 66
Dufay, Clark 109
Duke Ellington..67, 68
Dunbar, Jim 161
Dunhill Records..238
Duprees, The 123, 126
Dwight Kalb ...., 127, 120

E

Earl Scruggs.. 84
East of Midnight Show..311
Ebbins, Gary...235
Ebert, Roger 68
Ed Cody 48, 55, 110, 112, 121, 151, 154, 155,
    184, 266, 192, 313
Eddie Hough 315
Eddie Mascari 190
Eddie Schwartz 177
Eddie Silvers 63
Eddie Thomas 43, 116, 134, 160, 179,
    181, 301, 304
Ed Kelly 70, 74
Ed Ogonowski...302
Ed Redmond 101, 173, 174, 176, 226
Ed Sullivan Show 218, 236
Ellarde, Gerald 226
Elligton, Duke 68
Elliman, Yvonne... 45
Ellington, Duke.. 67

Elvis Presley................83, 86, 115, 158, 242
Ely, Jack...13
Embassy Ballroom............101, 173, 226, 238
Emil Rotondo...26
Epstein, Brian...85
Equal Records..316
Eric Burdon......................................98, 265
Eric Clapton.............................53, 109, 213
Eric Nesterenko.....................................288
Ernest Tubb...84
Ernie Banks..46, 71
Ernie Leaner...187
Esposito, Mickey.....................................89
Etta James..264
Everingham, Phil...............................95, 100
Everly Brothers.....................................253
Exceptions, The.....................................235
Executives, The.....................................216

F

Fabulous Centuries, The........................221
Facts of Life, The............................221, 304
Fats Domino...161
Feldman, Marty.....................................155
Ferlin Husky...88
Ferrara Manor Ballroom...........................13
Fifth Dimension, The.............58, 147, 194
Fillyau, Clayton....................................129
Five Emprees, The...................................99
Five Satins, The....................................117
5 Stairsteps, The.....................................45
Flack, Roberta.....................................139
Flamingos, The.....................................217
Flatt, Lester..84
Floaters, The...45
Florence Ballard...................................131
Floyd Brown....................................165, 313
Foggy Mountain Boys, The........................84
FONA Records................................194, 196
Fontana Records...................................121
Fontella Bass..48
Ford, Jimmy..129
Ford, Whitey...160
Fortuna, Nick.............222, 226, 243, 304, 315
Four Seasons, The.................89, 117, 189
Foyer, Tom...195
Frances Patry.......................................187
Francour, Chuck................................95, 103
Frankie Avalon.....................................178
Frank Mantooth....................................187
Frank Milito...................................275, 280
Frank Pisani....................................154, 242
Frank Tesinsky.....................................231
Frazier Thomas.....................................230
Freddie Cannon................................119, 120
Freddy and the Freeloaders.....................304
Freddy Jones Band.................................304
Fred Gwynne..316
Friends of Distinction, The.....................147

G

Garrett, Sue.....................................63, 154
Garrison Keillor...................................300
Gary and the Nightlights.......................155
Gary Beisbier...................................154, 310
Gary Ebbins...235
Gary Gears...312
Gary Knipper...................................61, 266
Gary Lewis and the Playboys.....................68
Gary Loizzo....................114, 155, 178, 315
Gary Peterson..................................183, 187
Gast, Doug.......................................95, 96
Gayle, Shaun..278
Gears, Gary...312
Gehron, John..239
Gem-Tones, The...................26, 153, 299
Gene Chandler...................................53, 217
Gene Pitney....................................13, 130
Gene Siskel.., 68
Gene Taylor....................................167, 311
Gents, The...115
George Foster Peabody (Broadcasting Award)
    Eddie Thomas................................46
George Gershwin.....................................67
George Leaner......................................187
George LeGros..................................222, 227
Gerald Ellarde......................................226
Geraldo Rivera..72
Germansen, Jerry..............................169, 209
Gerry & The Pacemakers...........................85
Gershwin, George....................................67
Giallorenzo, Isadora...............................294
Giammarese, Carl........46, 124, 126, 155, 179,
    182, 201, 222, 224, 238, 243, 292, 299, 314
Gilbect Ross...303
Gina Knight...295
Glad Cleaners.......................................302
Glass, Paul...229
Glenn Miller Orchestra.............................67
God..41
Golden, Jim.................32, 102, 145, 178, 233
Gone Records...................115, 117, 121
Good, Buddy..146
Gooden, Sam..43
Good Old Days, The...............................315
Gordon Lightfoot..................................194
Gordon McLendon.................................163
Gordy, Barry...131
Grand Ole Opry...............................84, 86, 87
Grass Roots, The....................................190
Grease (Musical)....................................243
Grebb, Marty................139, 222, 235, 243
Greg Grimes.....................................209, 214
Greg Waldron.......................................198
Greyson, Carl....................................73, 74
Grimes, Greg.....................................209, 214
Gronauer, Herb...............228, 310, 313
Groucho Marx.......................................240
Grounds, Denny......................................95
Gruber, Joey..278
Guercio, James..................................132, 234

Guess Who, The 155, 314
Gus Mossler 197
Guthrie, Arlo 121
Gwynne, Fred 316

H

Hale, Bob 161, 178
Hall, Bill 49, 59, 153
Hall Recording Studios 49, 59, 153
Hamilton, Steve 108
Hank Jones Trio 263
Hank Snow 84
Hank Zemola 275, 279
Happiness Is (group) 109
Hardy Boys 214
Harmonicats, The (group) 59
Harold Bradley 86
Harold Ramis 76
Harold Washington 284
Harry Caray 71
Harry Creighton 71
Harry Manfredini 26, 315
Harry Porterfield 289
Harry Volkman 66
Hartmann, Klayre 135
Hartman, Sheri 135
Hathaway, Donny 139
Heartsfield 177
Hebel, Jim Bernard 173
Hendrix, Jimi 237
Herb Brokop 195
Herb Gronauer 228, 310, 313
Herman, Woody 232
Hey Look – I'm on TV (Book) 32
Highland, Brian 47, 130, 178
HistoryMakers, The 53, 166
Hoekstra, Dave 46, 124, 179, 240, 200
Hoffmen, Ken 110
Holiday Ballroom 96, 101, 106, 161, 191,
    210, 226, 230, 238, 242, 288, 306, 314
Holiday Star Theater 86
Hollies, The 230
Holly, Buddy 176
Holman, Sam 161
Holmgren, Randy 284
Holvay, James 132, 154, 215, 231, 236, 246,
    265, 310, 316
Hooker Lake Inn 199
Hooty Saperticker 312
Horton, Mike 95, 103
Hough, Eddie 315
Hour Glass, The
    Chips, The 135
Howard Bedno 140, 153, 229, 230, 233, 235
Hubbell, Michele 295
Hudsen Bay Company, The 214
"Huggy Boy" Hugg 141
Hull, Bobby 288
Humboldt Park 3, 13, 79, 91, 209, 229, 275, 280
Husky, Ferlin 88

I

Ides of March, The 155, 160, 161, 178, 199,
    205, 223
Illinois Tollway, The 310
Impala Records 30, 183
Impressions, The 43, 45, 53, 116, 303
Independents, The 45, 46
Independent Superstars Recording Artists Hall
    of Fame 146
Ink Spots, The 117
International Amphitheater 217
Isaac Newton 155
Isadora Giallorenzo 294

J

Jack Bouchelle 26
Jack Brickhouse 71
Jack Dreznes 51, 110, 160, 179
Jack Ely 13
Jackie Gleason 93
Jack Mulqueen 69
Jack Sigler, Jr. 147
Jackson, Bill 69
Jackson Five, The 91
Jackson, John 108
Jackson, Tom 99
Jack Weiner 63, 154
Jack White 181
Jack Whitehead 286
Jacobs, Jim 115, 242
Jagger, Mick 231
James Brown 129, 230
James Butler 254, 265, 316
James Dawg 316
James, Etta 264
James Guercio 132
James Holvay .... 132, 154, 215, 236, 246, , 265,
    310, 316
James L. Jones 188
James Marvell 145
James Peterson 190
James Ramey 45
James William Guercio 234
Jane Byrne 161, 200, 238
Janis Joplin 237
Jay and the Americans 13, 266
Jay Rock 168
Jennings, Maurice 134
Jerry Butler 43, 51, 53, 116, 181, 303
Jerry Germansen 169, 209
Jerry Kowalczyk 194
Jerry Leiber 265
Jerry Lewis 236
J.F.K. Assassination 164
Jill Jones 315
Jim Anderson 313
Jim Bernard 101, 173, 226, 302
Jim Casteel 204
Jim Cooper 275
Jim Dunbar 161
Jim Golden 32, 102, 145, 178, 233

Jimi Hendrix...237
Jim Jacobs 115, 242
Jim Lounsbury 31, 115, 174, 216
Jimmy Bryant 194
Jimmy Dorsey Orchestra 67
Jimmy Ford..129
Jimmy Ford and the Executives...................242
Jimmy Peterson...................61, 153, 216, 265, 316
Jimmy Scholtes........................272, 273, 278
Jim Peterik 161, 199, 205, 241
Jim Vareneski 154
Joan Rivers..68
Joe Daley...194
Joe DeFrancesco..............................217, 316
Joe Eich Singers..67
Joel Bierig.........................223, 299, 300
Joel Sebastian 249, 310, 312
Joe Pytel 46, 56, 77, 96, 103, 125, 154, 176,
     204, 240, 297, 312
Joey Bishop...236
Joey Gruber 278
John Belushi.......................................3, 282
John Centinaro 146
John Damascus 249
John Dillinger Jr. and the Gas Station Gang 4
John Drury 66
John Gehron..239
John Jackson...108
John Lennon...108
John McGuire..195
John Mellatello 281
Johnny and the Hurricanes 26
Johnny Casino & the Gamblers 115
Johnny Tillotson 130
Johnny Watson..236
John Opager ....,74
John Panozzo 170
John Poulos 169, 222, 227, 238
John "Radio" Russell 123
John Records Landecker............................312
John Russo...110
John Serafini..266
John Sills and his Rhythm Jets 29
Johnson, Candy..90
Johnson, Judy 248
Johnson, Leo..304
John Turner 237
Jolly Club 281
Jones, James L..188
Jones, Jill 315
Jones, Quincy 45, 46
Jones, Tom 130
Joplin, Janis...237
Jordanaires, The 83, 116
Joseph "Lucky" Scott 134
J.P. "The Big Bopper" Richardson................176
Judy Johnson..................................246, 248
Julius LaRosa...185
Junior Arzola 269
Justin, Dick 154

K

Kaempfer, Rick.......................................313
Kalb, Dwight ...., 127, 120
Kallos, Nick...204,
Kapp Records 47, 196, 313, 314, 316
Kasuals, The..................................129, 216
Kath, Terry...242
Kathy Young and the Innocents 266
KC and the Sunshine Band 45
KCZQ-FM 102.3 Radio 177
Keen Records 52
Keillor, Garrison 300
Keith Colley...................................192, 314
Kelly, Ed ...., 70, 74
Kemp, Dick..163
Ken Adamany.......................... 134, 143, 282
Ken Cerretti 26
Ken Draper..158
Ken Hoffmen 110
Kenneth Dower.......................................284
Kenny Miller 189
Khan, Chaka..300
King, Ben E..265
King, Carole 238
Kingsmen, The................................13, 211
Kinks, The...109
Klayre Hartmann.....................................135
Kluver, Ace..204
Kluver, Dick...204
Knight, Gina..295
Knipper, Gary.................................61, 266
Kool & The Gang 45
Kowalczyk, Jerry.....................................194
KQV 119
Kracker (Band) 103, 177
Kraus, Norm.......................... 223, 229, 259
KRLA 157
KUSF..263

L

Lake, Brian...................................., 192
LA (Loyola Academy) Classmen, The 249
Lance, Major..53
Landecker, John Records...........................312
Lane Tech....................................., 69, 73
LaRosa, Julius...185
Larry Alltop 89
Larry Lujack 53, 175
Larry Nestor 30, 56, 112, 153, 183, 222, 235,
     241, 315
Latin Leagues...................................270, 280
Lawless, Barbara 191
Leaner, Ernie 187
Leaner, George 187
Led Zeppelin 115
Lee and the Dynatones 315
Lee, Brenda..131
LeGros, George.................................222, 227
Leiber, Jerry...265
Lemon Pipers, The....................................190
Lennon, John..108

Leo Johnson... 304
Leonard Czyz 151
Leslie, Dave... 313
Lester Flatt... 84
Letterman, David.................................... 233
Lettermen, The.. 189
Levin, Andee 248, 249, 251
Levy, Morris 191
Lew Douglas............85, 124, 125, 154, 193, 230,
     266, 310, 313, 314
Lewis, Gary... 68
Lewis, Jerry... 236
Lewis, Ramsey.. 155
Liberace.. 46
Limelight Records 316
Lincoln Park Zoo, The 34, 62, 189, 240, 305, 313
Linda Clifford.. 53
Linda Colley.................................... 192, 313
Little Kings, The 107
Livers, The 218
Lobello, Victor 287
Locke, Ned.. 230
Loizzo, Gary 114, 155, 178, 315
London House 168
London, Lori 85, 123, 299
Loretta Lynn 84, 123
Lori Lee Williams/Lori London
     (Lori Stallard) 85, 123, 299
Lori Wax 258
Los Bravos 253
Lot, The 203
Lou Adler 238
Lou Christie.............................. 130, 178, 226
Lounsbury, Jim................. 31, 115, 174, 216
Lou Rawls 220
Love Between Us..................................... 303
Lowehorne, Coy...................................... 110
Lucky Cordell................................... 163, 313
Ludwig van Beethoven............................ 200
Luigi's Banquet Hall 13, 164
Luis Sanjurio 209, 214
Lujack, Larry 53
Lynn, Loretta.................................... 84, 123

M

Maceo Merriweather................................. 52
Maciejewski, Aleat.................................. 135
Madison McQuade.......................85, 125, 299
Magic Lantern, The 192
Major Lance.. 53
Malcolm Chisholm................................... 155
Mally, Paul J... 197
Malo, Ron 61, 151, 155, 174, 211, 213, 231,
     232, 246, , 265, 266
Mamas & the Papas, The 310
Manfredini, Harry.............................26, 315
Manhattans, The 45
Mantooth, Frank..................................... 187
Marilou Davison 255
Markon, Mel.. 128
Marshall, Randy..................................... 204
Marsha Tomal 248, 304

Marty Feldman 155
Marty Grebb..................139, 222, 235, 239, 243
Marty Robbins 83, 84, 85
Marvell, James.. 145
Marv Stuart (Hyman) 133
Marx, Groucho 240
Mary Thompson and the Guardian Angels 7
Mary Wilson 131
Mascari, Eddie 190
Mason Dixon Line, The 194
Masqueraders, The 315
Matijević, Rob 301
Matt Cufferin 195
Matthews, Ron 198
Maurice Jennings.................................... 134
MayBees, The 216
Mayfield, Curtis 43, 44, 134
Mayfield, Todd 52
McCartney, Paul 108
McCormick Place 109
McCoys, The............................... 226, 240
McCoy, Van 45
McDowell, Craig..................................... 204
McGuire, John.. 195
McLean, Don.. 176
McLendon, Gordon................................. 163
McQuade, Madison...................85, 125, 299
Medallionaires, The 44, 116
Mellatello, John 281
Mel Markon 128
Mel Tillis 84
Menna, Carmine..................................... 315
Mercury Records 190, 196
Mercy (group) 147
Merk, Bobby... 270
Merriweather, Maceo 52
Meyer, Ray... 300
Meyer, Tex.. 313
Miccolis, Dennis 222, 227, 235, 244
Michaels, Chris...................................... 313
Michele Abrams..................................... 294
Michele Hubbell 295
Mickey Call 133
Mickey Esposito..................................... 89
Mickey, Larry & the Exciters...................... 89
Mick Jagger... 231
Mike Carioscia 221
Mike Horton 95, 103
Mike Paolicchi 284
Mike Sistak 219
Mike Smith 204
Mike Stoller 265
Milito, Frank....................................275, 280
Miller, Glenn 67
Miller, Kenny.. 189
Mindy Sterling 243
Minor, Raynard....................................... 48
Missing Links, The 133, 246,
Mob, The (group) 219, 316
Monkees, The 221
Monsma, Ron 95, 104
Monterey Pop Festival....................170, 237

Moonglows, The 217
Moore, Bill 120, 156, 296
Morgan, Rick 95, 104
Morris Day 282
Morris Levy 191
Mort Crowley 161
Moses "Lucky" Cordell 163
Mosier, Chuck 302
Mossler, Gus 197
Motown Records 131
Moulin Rouge 306
Muddy Waters 108
Muhammad Ali 77
Mulqueen, Jack 69
Murphy, Daniel 225
Murray, Bill 282
Murray, Denny 62, 189
Murray, Tommy 62, 189, 192

N

National Puerto Rican Congress 271
Nationwide Recording Studios 154
Nat King Cole 230
Natkin, Paul 200, 300
Natural Four, The 53
NBC- TV 79
Ned Locke 230
Neighborhood, The 194
Neil Diamond 98
Nelson, Rick 222
Nesterenko, Eric 288
Nestor, Larry 30, 56, 112, 153, 183, 222, 235,
    241, 315
Nestor, Tom 186
New Colony Six, The ... 153, 160, 170, 212, 223, 240
Newkirk, Bob 67
Newton-John, Olivia 243
New York Yankees 160
Nick Fortuna 222, 226, 239, 243, 304, 315
Nick Kallos 204,
Nikola Tesla 200
Nocturnal Journal 240
Norbert Soltysiak 209, 214
Norm Kraus 223, 229, 259
Nykodem, Wayne 189

O

Ode Records 238
Officer Vic Petrulis 159
Ogonowski, Ed 302
Okuda, Ted 69
Oliva, Sergio 276
Olivia Newton-John 243
One-derful! Records 62, 183, 187
O'Neill, Charlotte 135
Opager, John 74, 222
Oprah Winfrey 312
Original Fenders, The 303
Orlando, Tony 120
Orsi, Phil 63, 107, 120, 155
Orsi & Sons 108
Otilio Arzola Jr. ("Junior") 269

Otilio Arzola Sr. 276
Otis Clay 188
Otis Redding 90
Otis Rush 142
Otto, Bruce 195
Outsiders, The 253

P

Page, Patti 193
Panozzo, Chuck and Don 170
Paolicchi, Mike 284
Paragon Recording Studios 155
Pasterik, Daren 135
Pat De Luca 223
Patry, Frances 187
Patsy Cline 123
Patti Page 193
Paul Anka 185
Paul Glass 229
Paul J. Mally 197
Paul McCartney 108
Paul Natkin 200, 300
Paul Revere and the Raiders 267
Paul Shaffer 233, 296
P.C. Limited 221, 305, 316
Peg Richards 96
Pepper, Billy 315
Peter Cetera 235
Peterik, Jim 161, 199, 205, 241
Peterson, Gary 183, 187
Peterson, Jimmy 61, 153, 190, 216, 265, 316
Pete Walsh 26
Pete Weber 302
Petrulis, Officer Vic 159
Phil Czyz 151
Phil DeMarco and the Valiants 315
Phil Donahue 68
Phil Everingham 95, 100
Philips Records 136
Phillips, Don 209, 311
Phil Orsi 63, 107, 120, 155
Pierce Arrow Recorders 197
Pink Floyd 314
Pisani, Frank 154, 242
Pitney, Gene 13, 119, 130
Plant, Robert 115
Platters, The 92, 117
Plost, Barry 209
Pomeroy, Debi 179, 248, 249, 299
Pomeroy, Ralph J., Rev. 250
Porter, Cole 70
Porterfield, Harry 289
Porter Wagoner 84
Poulos, John 169, 222, 227, 238
Powers, Stephanie 46
Presley, Elvis 83, 86, 115, 242
Price, Ray 84
Prince Rogers Nelson 282
Prophets, Thee 62, 192
Puckett, Sam 275
Pulsations, The .... , 66, 67
Pumpkin Studios 155

Putnam, Bill 155
Pytel, Joe 46, 56, 77, 96, 103, 125,
154, 176, 204, 240, 297, 312

Q

Quill Records 212
Quincy Jones 45, 46
Quinn, Anthony 236
Quinn Buckner 275

R

Radio Hall of Fame................................. 157
Rail City Five, The ...., 240, 197
Rainbow Ranch Boys, The....................... 84
Raines, Bob 275
Rakis, Susan.......................... 179, 182, 292
Ral Donner 115, 135, 242, 266
Ralph J. Pomeroy, Rev. 250
Ramblers, The 314
Ramey, James 45
Ramis, Harold 76
Ramsey Lewis.. 155
Randy Holmgren 284
Randy Marshall....................................... 204
Rasputin's Stash...................................... 53
Ravelles, The.. 304
Rawls, Lou 220
Ray Buckner 47
Ray Charles.......................................45, 53
Ray Meyer 300
Raynard Minor 48
Rayner, Ray......................................., 65
Ray Price 84
Ray Rayner 230
Ray Stevens 120
RCA Recording Studios...............155, 194
Record Row 45, 50, 55, 155, 173
Red Bird Records 121
Redding, Otis 90
Redmond, Ed 101, 173, 174, 176, 226
Reflections, The...................................... 130
REM (Band) 282
Rev. Jesse Jackson 60
Rhythm Jets, The 29
Rice, Ronnie 212, 223
Richard Berry 263
Richard Brooks 43
Richard J. Daley 96
Richardson, J.P. "The Big Bopper"...............176
Richards, Peg 96
Rick Derringer 226
Rick Kaempfer 313
Rick Morgan..95, 104
Rick Nelson 222
Righteous Brothers, The 91
Riley, Ron............................... 167, 249, 311
Rising Sun Records.................................. 121
Ritchie Valens.............................141, 176
Rivera, Geraldo 72
Rivers, Joan 68
Rivieras, The... 99
Rivileers, The.. 266

Robbins, Marty 83, 84, 85
Roberta Flack 139
Robert Buff... 209
Roberto Clemente 277
Robert Plant 115
Roberts, Art.....................................161, 312
Robert Stigwood 49, 50
Rob Matijević 301
Rochkus, Vic 195
Rock & Roll Hall of Fame............. 43, 139, 143, 304
Curtis Mayfield.................................. 134
Dick Biondi...................................... 157
Ral Donner 115
Rocky III (movie) 207
Roger Ebert 68
Rolling Stones, The....................174, 177, 221, 231
Ron Malo 61, 151, 155, 174, 211, 213, 231,
232, 246, 265, 266
Ron Matthews 198
Ron Monsma 95, 104
Ronnie Rice 212, 223
Ron Riley 167, 249, 311
Ron Riley Batman Club 311
Ron Santo 71
Ron Terry 315
Roosters, The... 43
Ross, Diana 131
Rotary Connection, The 178
Rotondo, Emil... 26
Roulette Records.....................................191
Roy Acuff 87
Royal Recorders 199
Roy Stingley...84
RSO Records 49
Rudy Salas 209
Rush, Otis 142
Russell, John "Radio" 123
Russell Thompkins Jr 49
Russo, John 110
Russ Vestuto and the Downbeats 187, 315

S

SAR Records... 53
Sabre Room, The..................................... 84
Salas, Rudy...209
Salisbury, Sandy 315
Sam Cooke... 52
Sam Gooden 43
Sam Holman..161
Sammy Davis, Jr......................................116
Sam Puckett 275
Sands, Chris....................................100, 103
Sandy Salisbury.......................................315
Sanjurio, Luis....................................209, 214
Santo, Ron 71
Satan and the Nail-Drivin' Four 5
Savoy Brown 282
Schaeffer, Dick 195
Scholtes, Jimmy...................... 272, 273, 278
Schraub, Vince 209, 214
Schwartz, Eddie 172, 177
Schwarzenegger, Arnold................................276

Scott, Joseph "Lucky" 134
Scruggs, Earl.................................... 84
Sean Connery................................... 186
Sebastian, Joel 249, 310, 312
Seger, Bob..................................... 155
Serafini, John.................................. 266
Seraphine, Danny 129
Sergio Oliva................................... 276
Seymour "Sandy" Shub 286
Shadows of Knight.........................170, 240
Shaffer, Beverley............................... 187
Shaffer, Paul..............................233, 296
Sha-Na-Na.................................... 115
Shannon, Dick................................. 175
Sharpees, The.................................. 188
Shaun Gayle................................... 278
Sheldon Cooper .... , 80, 65
Sheldon Recording Studios 63, 154
Sheppard, Bunky............................... 217
Sheri and the Right Brothers................... 304
Sheri Hartman................................. 135
Shirelles, The.................................. 130
Shub, Seymour "Sandy" 286
Shure Microphone Company................... 92
Siegel, Corky.................................. 99
Sierens, Dennis................................ 103
Sigler, Jack Jr................................. 147
Sills, John.................................... 29
Silvers, Eddie................................. 63
Siskel, Gene .... , 68
Sistak, Mike................................... 219
Skopes, the (group) 145
Skrzynecki, Darwin............................ 284
Sly and the Family Stone....................... 92
Smash Records..........................139, 316
Smith, Mike................................... 204
Smith, Wendell................................ 66
Smokey Joe's...........................91, 230
Smothers Brothers, The........................ 236
Snell, Brad.................................... 289
Snow, Hank................................... 84
Soldier Field 200
Soltysiak, Norbert......................209, 214
Songs
   Alice in Wonderland 196,
   A Little Bit of Love (Never Hurt Anyone) ...315
   Ann 203
   A Story That's True........................ 153
   A Thousand Stars....................258, 266
   A Whole Week of Mondays................. 125
   Baby Sittin' Blues.............. 30, 153, 183, 185
   Beatle Time................................ 218
   Bend Me, Shape Me...................112, 155
   Black is Black.............................. 253
   Break It Gently............................. 136
   California Sun..........................99, 253
   Call Me Your Baby.......................... 203
   Candy and Me.............................. 154
   Careless Love.............................. 304
   Cinderella Twist............................ 115
   Come To Me Girl........................... 314
   Comin' In and Out of Your Life 149

Countin' My Money...........................183, 241
Cowboy Joe................................... 86
Diesel Cowboys................. 85, 124, 125, 126
Dirty Down to the Bone........................ 47
Don't Leave Me Now 121
Don't Let It Slip Away......................... 266
Don't Waste My Time.......................... 253
Don't You Care 221, 236, 240
Don't You Just Know It........................ 113
Dream With Your Eyes Wide Open 136
Drivin'....................................... 198
Every Minute, Every Hour, Every Moment. 212
Eye of the Tiger.............................. 207
Floatin'...................................... 102
For Your Precious Love........................ 117
Get Ready.................................... 204
Girl of My Best Friend........................ 117
Go Now...................................... 154
Gypsy Woman................................ 47
Hang on Sloopy.............................. 226
Happy Ending................................ 154
Heads I Win Tails You Lose 95
Heartbreak Hotel 242
Help Me Boy................................. 256
Hey Baby.................................... 99
Hey Baby, They're Playing Our Song.... 132,
   221, 236
Hey Lover.................................... 254
I Call Your Name 230, 311
I Can't Quit You - Baby 142
If You Gotta Go (Go Now) 190, 196
I Got Burned................................. 120
I Hate To Laugh Alone....................... 102
I'll Go Crazy..............................230, 311
I'll Know Then..........................30, 185
I'm a Believer............................... 221
Im Gonna Sit Right Down and Write
   Myself a Letter 67
I'm Ready 102
I'm So Tired of Being Lonely................. 188
I See Her Face................................ 214
I Still Want You..........................193, 196
It All Adds Up to Nothing 193, 196
It's a Beautiful Day........................... 237
I've Been Wrong............................. 230
I've Got Money.............................. 129
I Want Candy................................ 295
Jailhouse Rock.............................. 116
Johnny Shiloh............................83, 87
Just Like Me................................. 267
(Just Like) Romeo and Juliet 130
Just Out of Reach 139, 212
Kathy My Darling............................ 316
Kind of a Drag......... 85, 124, 132, 230, 231,
   241, 243, 246, , 256, 293
Kissy Face................................193, 196
La Bamba 141
Lady 170
Lawdy Miss Clawdy.....................221, 223
Leaving Me.................................. 46
Life's a Catastrophe 198
Little Miss Sad 99

Little Serenade 154
Lonely Guy 315
Long Green 210
Long Long Time 214
Louie Louie 225, 264
Love Is Slipping Away 109
Love Theme From Haight Street 190
Loving on Borrowed Time 113
Loving You Is All I Do 203, 204
Lydia the Tattooed Lady 240
Made in the USA 198, 240
Magic Moonlight 44
Margie Cha-Cha 29
Maria (Forever) 122
Mercy, Mercy, Mercy 221, 236
Mixed-Up, Shook-Up Girl 136
Mr. Clean 63
My Baby Can Do It 193, 196
My Old Kentucky Home 86
Only in America 13
O-O-Oh Child 45
Oop-Oop-A-Do 102
Palisades Park 120
Peg O My Heart 59
Playgirl 192, 196
Please Don't Go 118
Pretend 230
Psychedelic Movement 304
Rainy Night in Georgia 47
Ready For Your Love 100
Rescue Me 48
Ruby Tuesday 221
Sambanette 193, 196
San Francisco Waits 149
Santa Doesn't Smoke Anymore 183
Sara Lee 240
Save the Last Dance for Me 92
Shame Shame 192
She Cried 258, 266
She's Got Bad Breath 145
Shy Guy 185
Sittin' on the Dock of the Bay 90
Social Tragedy 258
Someone New 113
Sorry (I Ran All the Way Home) 113
Soul Circle 316
Stand By Me 254
Stay 113
St. Louie Here I Come 154
Story That's True 30
Stranded in the Middle of No Place 89
Superfly 44, 52
Susan 236, 292
Sweet Home Chicago 52
Symphony of My Soul 34, 191, 196, 254, 256
Tapestry 238
Tears in Your Eyes 145
Tell Me Why 117
The Ballad of the Mad Streaker 53
The Battle of New Orleans 86
The Greatest Moments in My Life 191, 196
These Boots Are Made for Walking 191

The Worst That Could Happen 123
Things 240
Time Won't Let Me 253
Town Without Pity 13
Transistor Sister 120
Twine Time 187
Two Months out of School 29
Vehicle 205, 241
Virginia Wolf 223
Were Wolf 153
(What a Sad Way) to Love Someone 121
When I Think About You 187
When You Hold Me Baby 136
Where Will You Be Boy? 187
Whoever He May Be 107
Why Don't You Believe Me 126
Woman Don't Let Me Down 194, 196
Write A Letter 203
You 214
You Are My Sunshine 86
You Belong to Me 123
You Don't Know What You've Got 118
You're My Inspiration 193, 196
You're the One That I Want 243
You Send Me 52
Zoo's Blues 196,
Soul Train 46
Spark Plugs, The 280
    Al DePisa 271
    Armando DeGuzman 270
    Bill Mazurek 271
    Bobby Woods 271
    Carl Bonafede 269
    George Garland 271
    Greg Mazurek 271
    Jim Cooper 275
    Jimmy Scholtes 273
    Johnny Mazurek 271
    Otilio Arzola Jr. ("Junior") 270
Spector, Abner 203
SpectraSound Records 152, 258, 266, 310, 313
Spectropop 250
Spencer Davis Group, The 190
Spice Girls, The 282
Spot and the Blotters 316
Springsteen 198
Stallard, Arthur 82
Stallard, Calvin (Cal Starr) 81
Stallard, Lori
    (Lori Lee Williams/Lori London) 84, 123
Stammich, Tom 95, 100, 104
Staple Singers, The 53
Star Fire Records 121
Starr (Stallard), Cal 81, 124
Statesiders, The 84
Stax Records 60
Stephanie Powers 46
StereoSonic Recording Studios 49, 55, 151, 154, 203, 204, 192
Sterling, Mindy 243
Steve Chiappe 198
Steve Hamilton 108

Stevens, Ray 120
Steve Yates Recording 155
Stigwood, Robert 49, 50
Stingley, Roy 84
Stoller, Mike 265
Streisand, Barbra 150
Stuart (Hyman), Marv 133
Stu Black 49, 59, 153
Stylistics, The 45, 49
Styx 170, 178, 281
Sue Charles Dancers 67
Sue Garrett 63, 154
Sullivan, Ed 218
Summer, Donna 45
Sundi Records 147
Sunlight Records 121
Supremes, The 131
Surf Ballroom 176, 258, 302
Surprize, The 147
Survivor (band) 207
Susan Rakis 179, 182, 292
Szerszen, Connie 312

T

Taft High School 115, 241, 248
Tampa Theatre 123
Tangerine Records 53
Tavares 45
Taylor, Gene 167, 311
Tear Drops, The 85
Ted Allen 133, 303
Ted Okuda 69
TEK Records 30
Temptations, The 102, 204
Terry Kath 242
Terry, Ron 315
Terry Wilson 116
Tesinsky, Frank 231
Tesla, Nikola 200
Texas Troubadours, The 84
Tex Meyer 313
That Odor and the Highway Skunks 5
Thee Prophets 313
Thomas, Eddie 43, 116, 134, 160, 179, 181, 301, 304
Thomas, Frazier 230
Thomas, Verlene 44
Thompkins, Russell, Jr. 49
Three Dog Night 171
Three Stooges 85
Thunderbirds, The (group) 109
Thunder Records 121, 122
Tillis, Mel 84
Tillotson, Johnny 130
Time, The 282
Todd Mayfield 52
Tomal, Marsha 248, 304
Tom Foyer 195
Tom Jackson 99
Tom Jones 130
Tommy and Jimmy Dorsey Orchestras 193
Tommy James and the Shondells 99

Tommy Murray 62, 189, 192
Tom Nestor 186
Tom Stammich 95, 100, 104
Tom Thumb and the Four Fingers 153, 314
Tony Orlando 120
Tony Zale 78
Top Dog Disc 197
Trammps, The 45
Trendler, Bob 67
Tribune Entertainment 72
Tubb, Ernest 84
Tufano, Dennis 155, 222, 227, 238, 241, 292, 314
Tumosa, Arvy 189
Turner, John 237
Turtles, The 200, 237
Twinight Records 94, 139, 192, 196
Twin Lakes Ballroom 199

U

Uni-Beats, The 109
Universal Recording Studios 49, 121, 155
U.S.A. Records ...... 102, 107, 113, 152, 154, 178, 196, , 221, 232, 233, 246, 254, 256
      Jim Golden 178

V

Valens, Ritchie (Valenzuela) 141, 176
Van McCoy 45
Vanno, Bernadette 296
Vareneski, Jim 154
Vee-Jay Records 140, 187, 218, 315
Ventures, The 189
Verlene Thomas 44
Vestuto, Russ 187, 315
Vic Petrulis 159
Vic Rochkus 195
Victor Lobello 287
Vietnam 237, 259
Vince DiMaggio 99
Vince Garrett Revue 303
Vincent Schraub 209
Vince Schraub 214
Vinton, Bobby 119, 120
Violent Femmes 282
Virginia News Crew 159
Vogue Ballroom 13, 108, 111, 225, 238
Volkman, Harry 66

W

Wagoner, Porter 84
Wakefield, Dawn Lee 293
Waldron, Greg 198
Walicki, Bob 189, 192, 194
Walker, Celeste Bedford 48
Wallace, Bob 288
Walsh, Bob 77
Walsh, Pete 26
Warner Brothers Records 206
Warren Casey 242
Washington, (Mayor) Harold 284
Watson, Johnny 236
Wax, Lori 258

Wayne Cochran and the CC Riders 90
Wayne Nykodem 189
Wayne Worley and the Worleybirds 60
WCBA
    Dick Biondi 157
WCFL. , 157, 173, 191, 175, 178, 152, 192, 194, 192
    Bob Dearborn 175
    Dick Biondi 157, 194
    Dick Shannon 175
    Jim Bernard 173
    Ken Draper 158
    Larry Lujack 175
WDCB
    John Russell 123
Weber, Clark 161, 217, 229, 233, 311
Weber, Pete 302
Weiner, Bob 63, 154
Weiner, Jack 63, 154
Wendell Smith 66
WGES 163
WGN .... , 209, 124, 210, 65, 66
WGN-TV 221, 315
WGRY
    Lucky Cordell 163
White, Barry 45, 46
Whitehead, Jack 286
White, Jack 181
White Stripes, The 181
Whitey Ford 160
Who's Who in Americas
    Eddie Thomas 54
Wild Goose Clubs 169, 178
Willard Alexander Agency .. 133, 153, 176, 203,
    210, 212, 224, 226, 230, 234, 247, 310, 314
William Morris Agency 235
Williams, Billy 67
Williams, Lori Lee 85, 123, 299

Willie Dixon 178
Willie Mays 28
Willowbrook Ballroom 216
Wilson, Brian 107, 215
Wilson, Mary 131
Wilson, Terry 116
Winfrey, Oprah 312
WJJD 311
WLS 119, 191, 159, 192, 194, 152, 233, 192
    Dick Biondi 117
WLS Silver Dollar Survey 139
WMAQ-TV
    Bob Walsh 77
WOKY 313
Wooden Nickel Records 170, 171
Woodtake Anderson 44
Woody Herman 232
Worley, Wayne 60
Wrigley Field 71
WSDM-FM 312
WVON 166
WYNR 163, 313

Y
Yates, Steve 155
Young Rascals, The 213
Yvonne Daniels 163, 312
Yvonne Elliman 45

Z
Zack, Carmie 198
Zale, Tony 78
Zemola, Hank 275, 279
Zombies, The 212

Made in the USA
Columbia, SC
29 June 2018